A LITERARY HISTORY OF THE FOURTEENTH CENTURY

Currents in Comparative Romance Languages and Literatures

Tamara Alvarez-Detrell and Michael G. Paulson
General Editors

Vol. 242

This book is a volume in a Peter Lang monograph series.
Every volume is peer reviewed and meets
the highest quality standards for content and production.

PETER LANG
New York • Bern • Frankfurt • Berlin
Brussels • Vienna • Oxford • Warsaw

Natalino Sapegno

A LITERARY HISTORY OF THE FOURTEENTH CENTURY

Dante, Petrarch, Boccaccio
A Study of Their Times and Works

(Storia Letteraria del Trecento)

TRANSLATED WITH A FOREWORD BY
Vincenzo Traversa

PETER LANG
New York • Bern • Frankfurt • Berlin
Brussels • Vienna • Oxford • Warsaw

Library of Congress Cataloging-in-Publication Data

Names: Sapegno, Natalino, 1901–1990, author. | Traversa, Vincenzo, translator.
Title: A literary history of the fourteenth century: Dante, Petrarch, Boccaccio:
a study of their times and works / Natalino Sapegno;
foreword and translation by Vincenzo Traversa.
Other titles: Storia letteraria del Trecento. English
Description: New York: Peter Lang, [2015] | Series: Currents in
comparative Romance languages and literatures, ISSN 0893-5963;
Vol. 242 | Includes bibliographical references.
Identifiers: LCCN 2015010728 | ISBN 9781433131158 (hardcover: alk. paper)
| ISBN 9781453916070 (e-book)
Subjects: LCSH: Italian literature—To 1400—History and criticism. | Literature and
society—Italy—History—To 1500. | Dante Alighieri, 1265–1321. | Petrarca, Francesco,
1304–1374. | Boccaccio, Giovanni, 1313–1375. | Italy—Civilization—1268–1559.
Classification: LCC PQ4071 .S313 2015 | DDC 850.9/001—dc23
LC record available at http://lccn.loc.gov/2015010728

Bibliographic information published by **Die Deutsche Nationalbibliothek**.
Die Deutsche Nationalbibliothek lists this publication in the "Deutsche
Nationalbibliografie"; detailed bibliographic data are available
on the Internet at http://dnb.d-nb.de/.

Natalino Sapegno, *Storia Letteraria del Trecento*—per gentile concessione dell'Istituto della
Enciclopedia Italiana Treccani, collana Riccardo Ricciardi Editore 1963

© 2016 Peter Lang Publishing, Inc., New York
29 Broadway, 18th floor, New York, NY 10006
www.peterlang.com

To Professor Cesare Foligno, fervent Italian patriot, distinguished scholar, and educator.

Acknowledgments

Thanks are especially due to Ms. Ruthy Stephan of California State University, East Bay, for her technical suggestions, the kind staff of Peter Lang Publishing and of the Istituto della Enciclopedia Italiana S.p.A. for their interest and assistance. But most of all I wish to thank my wife Gina for her valuable opinions and generosity.

Table of Contents

Foreword

Anyone wishing to investigate into the literary development of the golden century of early Italian literature, the *Trecento*, must read Natalino Sapegno's extensive writings on the subject and, among them in particular, his *Storia letteraria del Trecento* (Literary History of the Fourteenth Century), that appeared in April 1963 as part of the vast collection, *La Letteratura Italiana—Storia e Testi* (Italian Literature—History and Texts), directed by Raffaele Mattioli, Pietro Pancrazi and Alfredo Schiaffini for the Riccardo Ricciardi publishing house. At its introduction, this work was announced as *un 'opera diversissima*, a most different work in the purpose that it pursued and, consequently, in the general plan that characterized it, as well as in its choice and distribution of the material. Furthermore, rather than an independent study, it was meant to become a part and a complement of a "system" so as to offer a panoramic synthesis and the essential characteristics of a very important moment in the development of the Italian and European culture.

The volume that Sapegno wrote dedicates, in its original Italian version, about one third of its pages to Dante (excluding its bibliography), an almost equal number of pages is dedicated to Petrarch and Boccaccio, while the minor writers are introduced more summarily, in proportion to their importance and position, in the cultural, historical and social events of the time.

When Sapegno completed this study, he had already been conducting an active research and written numerous documents on the subject (as well as several others on different authors and periods) for approximately three decades. The *Storia* in question, therefore, constituted the crowning moment of an investigative labor matured through a long period of evaluation by means of a well developed critical methodology, and it was immediately recognized and favorably received.

At the outset, the author introduces the crisis of the medieval civilization at the point when its century old ideological underpinnings were starting to give in, when the very order of Christianity, the prestige of its universal institutions were in crisis and the moral and civic unity of Europe began to fragment. Dante (1265–1321), Petrarch (1304–1374), and Boccaccio (1313–1375), living through this tumultuous period of time, represent, then, three moments of cultural history and aesthetic progress and contribute to "establish and characterize" a new civilization by reaching the apex of European literature and culture and by taking the lead in the unfolding of a new development.

The importance of the *Trecento* in Italy derives from these premises, hence the necessity to comprehend the nature of the impending crisis and the efforts that were made with the purpose of establishing the basis of a new vision of life.

The key to a more persuasive interpretation of humanism that may go beyond the issues mentioned, says Sapegno, lies perhaps in a deeper and more careful study of the Italian *Trecento* that needs to shed light on the internal contradictions that existed on a cultural and civic basis and grasp all active and passive aspects, namely, the novelties and the remnants of the past, the intellectual span and weakness of its social and political foundations. Consequently, for the author, it was certain that the aspects of modern civilization took shape in fourteenth century Italy and that civilization then matured in the wake of Italian art and thought in the three following centuries until it revealed itself in the "manifest rationality of the European Enlightenment." And if it was true that the humanistic movement could be viewed as the symptom of a deep crisis in the history of European civilization, and if it was conceivable that it was time for Italy "to bear its burden" and be the first to evaluate its importance and magnitude, it appeared certain that in that century, in Italy, one could notice "the initial moment" of that crisis, its emergence from the recesses of history to the light of awareness as well as its becoming conscious of itself while attempting to transform the new concept of life into suitable cultural moulds.

How can one understand the influence that Dante, Petrarch and Boccaccio were to have on European society as well as the later influence on the same exercised by future figures like Ariosto, Tasso, Machiavelli and Galileo? Sapegno responds by becoming aware of the novelty and the creative ability of the Italian cultural effort that came to life in a "scornful and proud isolation," to the point of opening a chasm among the freedom, lack of prejudice and refinement of its cultural achievements and the real conditions of civilized society to the point of being under the illusion of leading and directing without participating, humbly in its labor, and by assuming some of its misery and contradictions.

From this epochal background there emerge gradually the figures of the major protagonists, persons and currents of the century, while philosophy, faithful to scholastic forms, and theology accept rational and worldly elements; historiography, without renouncing its providential, transcendent interpretation of human events, opens to the circumstances, passions and struggles of everyday existence. Political doctrines are still circumscribed within the framework of a twofold universal authority and deal with the relationship between the Church and the Empire but this pattern becomes more flexible with specific and concrete issues, while political life witnesses the rise and consolidation of the *comuni* and the *signorie.* Even religious concepts, still very strong and deeply rooted in people's minds, show tendencies to become less anonymous and collective and appear embodied in strong, free and combative personalities.

At the same time, Sapegno indicates that above the doctrinal and creative literature there rise the early figures of the new poets. Along the learned language of the scholastic writers intervenes the new linguistic style of the vernacular, the *volgare.* Dante himself, in fact, participates and is one of the most authoritative creators of this period that concludes the Middle Ages and heralds in the Renaissance. In him, medieval religiosity and theology come together with the curiosity of human contrast and natural things, the longing for transcendence does not eliminate the concern for political events while the study of the scholastic philosophers does not clash with his great love of literature and, quite importantly, the new language and his didactical and allegorical preferences do not weaken his firm faith in art as a formal instrument of beauty.

As for the material that constitutes his works, he is linked with the entire medieval culture. He elaborates, as it were, all its aspects and renews them in his own manner while, concerning their forms, he is connected with the learned trends of courtly poetry, of the vast and refined rhetoric and moral culture that, in the Florence of his time, had its most notable representatives in Brunetto Latini and the poets of the "sweet new style."

Such are, in Sapegno's presentation, the starting points of Dante's human experience and intellectual preparation, if not of his powerful sense of synthesis and classic stylistic balance, and it was only from that tumult of imagination and intentions, artistic vision and doctrinal aspirations that "a flower of eternal, divine poetry" could be born. He also affirms, on one occasion, that Italy recognized in the Florentine its "national poet" par excellence and in its hours of difficulty and in those of the Risorgimento it proclaimed him the father of its civilization, the symbol of its suffering and of its mission. The cult and study of Dante's personality and work went along, step by step, with the evolutions of Italian history, it assumed in the nineteenth century a highly ideal value and continues in the present through a wealth of definitions, enlightening of doctrines and institutions of historic and linguistic ideas from which the understanding of poetry gains fullness and depth.

In the case of Petrarch, Sapegno prefers to follow an analytical process that differs from the one adopted for the presentation of Dante particularly because Petrarch's works do not lend themselves to be classified in a precise and well defined chronological framework "as the modern philologists' investigations have amply demonstrated, namely how those works came into being and developed in a process of composition organized in successive layers that, at times, span an ample period that goes from his youth to old age. And while the constantly increasing uncommon wealth of archival documents and, above all, the abundant information provided by the writer and his contemporaries allow us to follow the progress of his life in every phase, ... it increases, nevertheless the difference between personal history and general anecdotes that seem to be interconnected only by rare and intermittent links."

Born in Arezzo on July 20, 1304, he was the son of a Florentine notary, ser Petracco, and Eletta Canigiani. Because of political reasons, ser Petracco decided to move his entire family, including another son, Gherardo, who was born in 1307, first to Pisa and then, in 1312, to Avignon, in Provence, where the pope had transferred the Curia. But due to a scarcity of houses caused by the sudden arrival of a large number of new inhabitants, Eletta and the children were lodged in the nearby town of Carpentras where Francesco began to study grammar, rhetoric and dialectic under the guidance of Convenevole da Prato.

At the early age of twelve, he was sent by his father to study law at Montpellier and then, from 1320 to 1326, to the University of Bologna. But he was ill disposed toward the legal studies and already strongly attracted to the classics and the Provençal and Italian poetry of love.

While he was still in Bologna, he was attracted to the happy, carefree life of the students of his age and when he returned to Avignon, after his father's death in 1326, he began to join, with Gherardo, the elegant, pleasure loving society of that city where he was sought-after because of his wit and sharp intelligence, as well as his attention for fashionable clothing, apparel, pleasant conversation and superficial love affairs. Many years later, in a letter to Gherardo, he evoked this time of youthful distraction with words of repentance and irony about his behavior.

Without doubt, the episode of this period of his life that was to be more significant in his spiritual experience and was destined to influence deeply his poetical work was his love for Laura that he met for the first time in the church of St. Claire, on April 6, 1327.

It is by now commonly believed that Laura's identity escapes most attempts of historical definition. Even Petrarch's poems do not give a precise "image" of her but see her as a literary figure related to the various spiritual states of mind of the writer. Sapegno suggests that it will suffice to believe that Laura's love was a real episode in the poet's life, although it raised some doubts even among his contemporaries.

Love and vanity did not mould his entire life, however, if it is true that since that time he made careful plans in order to secure for himself an honorable and tranquil life style by assuming limited ecclesiastical duties. At the same time, he was expanding his knowledge through a sedulous study of the classics, particularly Cicero, Virgil, Livy and the Fathers of the Church, predominantly Saint Augustine, while avoiding the Scholastic writers that had played such a major role in Dante's intellectual background.

Petrarch's connection with the church grew in importance from 1330, when he established very friendly ties with the powerful Colonna, Giacomo, in particular, who was the bishop of Lombez and with whom he spent the summer of that year on a vacation journey near the Pyrenees, and then with cardinal Giovanni, Giacomo's brother, in whose household he resided as a family chaplain.

In 1333 he traveled extensively through northern France, Flanders and southern Germany, driven by a natural desire to know new things and his innate restlessness that wearied him of every land or event that occurred in his existence, unable to find peace, thirsting for novelty and perhaps hopeful to divert his mind from his passion for Laura.

Finally, in 1336, he could return to Italy and visit Rome, in the early part of the following year, where he was able to admire the sacred vestiges of the ancient monuments and the symbols of the Christian faith.

When he was back in Avignon in 1337, after a protracted journey where it seems he visited Spain and England, he secluded himself in a small house not too far from Avignon, at Vaucluse, a lovely, shady place bathed by the river Sorgue. A desire of solitude drove him away from the life of ease and corruption of Avignon and the burden of his passion, while a strong drive to cultivate his cherished studies, the planning of original works of a vast scope and an anxious urge to remove himself from worldly matters seemed to him to be the best way to seek his spiritual salvation. As his writings show, a serious moral and religious crisis had begun for the Aretine and created a conflict between the eternal and the transient, the world and God that affected so deeply his literary works and lasted nearly all his life without ever reaching a final stage of conversion.

In 1336, he climbed Mt. Ventoux in the company of his brother Gherardo. At a certain point, he opened at random St. Augustine's *Confessions*, a book that he frequently carried with himself, and found words that seemed to refer to his spiritual condition, "... men go and admire the heights of the mountains, the large waves of the sea, the vast, flowing rivers, the immensity of the ocean and the movements of the stars, yet they neglect themselves," He then had become indignant at himself for indulging in an excessive admiration of earthly things whereas he should have learned even from the pagan philosophers that nothing is marvelous except the soul.

He found it arduous, however, to subdue his ambition for honors, desire of glory and carnal passions and even more difficult it was to set aside his cultural and literary dreams. From this condition stemmed the constant swaying of his thoughts and the moral uneasiness that are at once the signs of his weakness but also the marks of human dignity as they appear in his abundant confessions.

In 1337, he became the father of a child who originated from a superficial affair. He named him Giovanni and six years later, in similar circumstances, he had a daughter, Francesca.

In September 1340, he received the offers to be crowned poet from both Paris and Rome. He opted for Rome and after being examined for three days by King Robert in Naples, he was solemnly crowned with laurel in Rome's Capitol by senator Orso dell'Anguillara.

The conversion of his brother Gherardo who became a monk in the Charterhouse of Montrieux in April 1343, acted powerfully on Petrarch's conscience. As in the case of Gherardo, also in his mind there came a deep crisis, more complicated, however, and devoid of a practical solution. Evidence of it remains in the invocations to God in his *Psalmi penitentiales* (that Sapegno defines as true passionate and anguished prayers to God for help with his tumultuous feelings) and in his *Secretum*.

From 1343 a series of frequent journeys saw the poet in Naples, Parma, Modena, Bologna and Verona; then in Vaucluse, Parma, Verona, Ferrara, Padua and Mantua. In 1348 he learned of Laura's death that occurred on April 6 during the great plague that swept through Europe. He suffered also other personal losses such as the death of his influential protector, Cardinal Colonna and several friends, among whom the poet Sennuccio del Bene. These events could only increase his sadness and world-weariness and burdened his mind with the inanity of material things and the disastrous consequences of sinning. After another stay in Avignon, he returned to Italy in 1353, where he remained, except for a few brief periods, till the end of his life.

The twenty-one years spent in Italy constituted a period of intense study, writing and important official responsibilities as an ambassador or speaker that did not preclude long periods of leisure in Milan with the Visconti or in the elegant *ville* of wealthy families in Lombardy. From there he took frequent trips to Padua and Pavia, the guest of Galeazzo Visconti. In Venice, Giovanni Boccaccio, his close friend, came to visit him in the summer of 1363, and later he was joined by his daughter Francesca and her husband Franceschino da Brossano. He finally moved to the Euganean Hills, at Arquà, and resided in a little, graceful *villa* that was surrounded by an olive grove and a vineyard, where he lived "fully at peace in his soul, in spite of his illnesses, far from the turmoil, gossip and cares, reading constantly, writing and praising God." He died in Arquà on July 19, 1374, and was buried there according to his wishes. He was given solemn funeral honors at the presence of the Lord of Padua.

Sapegno's portrayal presents the poet's character and ideals by drawing information from various sources, essentially his epistolary writings, where those aspects that better represent his humanistic personality take shape through self analysis contained in the *Rerum familiarum, Seniles* and *Variae*. They reveal the poet's vast range of acquaintances and friendships, personal interests, concern for his ceremonial duties, love for the classics and political beliefs. They represent the effort of a man who wants to leave behind as thorough an image of himself as it is allowed by his doctrine and discretion. Thus we learn about his humanistic concerns that contribute to make him a precursor of a new age, and, besides that, his thoughts concerning the faith that undergoes profound alternations through the mutable episodes of his experience.

When compared with Dante's, Petrarch's political ideas appear to Sapegno less passionate and fervid but more free and modern. While Dante cherishes the institution of the empire, for example, Petrarch notices its decadence and considers it a foreign form of monarchy, detached from, if not indifferent about, the destiny and interests of Italy. More modern that Dante's, the critic thinks, is Petrarch's love for Italy that he does not view as the garden of the empire but as an historically and culturally living entity. In the absence of a city to love and venerate, as in the case of Dante's Florence, that could be the object of his political passion, Petrarch goes beyond the local and partisan discords that beset the peninsula and brings forth the concept of the superior unity of a nation. And in his love for Italy, the humanist who evoked ardently from the ancient books its glorious memories, and the man who traveled through it admiring its beauty shared one and the same sentiment and brought a new era to life.

At the beginning of the chapter dedicated to Boccaccio, Sapegno directs the reader's attention to the relationship, that constituted a deep spiritual communion, between the author of the *Decameron* and Petrarch. He indicates how Boccaccio kept during his entire life a secondary position not differently from the other followers and disciples who were invited to collaborate with the poet, each one within the limits of his ability, in an operation of profound cultural transformation. Boccaccio was, then, a follower among the many, although much more gifted with intelligence and enthusiasm. But this did not happen only in the years of Boccaccio's early youth, when his admiration for Petrarch began and drove him to transcribe and imitate the Aretine's Latin writings, and, later, to write a biography and a praise in *De vita et moribus domini Francisci Petracchi*, but also when he could make his personal acquaintance in Florence in the autumn of 1350, and establish that friendship and mutual trust that was to end only with their death.

Compared with Petrarch's, Boccaccio's personality appears less rich and not as complicated by political, moral or philosophical questions. In essence, it is the personality of a poet and artist. Even his minor works do not correspond, as in the case of Petrarch's, to ideological issues; they are purely narrative, namely, pleased with their own form.

Among the great writers of the fourteenth century, Boccaccio is the one that best suits the modern aspect of a poetry that is satisfied with its achievements. And in Boccaccio's minor works, furthermore, that preceded the *Decameron*, one finds a rich and vivid, albeit unilateral, experience, the love experience that had filled the writer's youth with its impulses, hopes and disappointments. It is a form of love that does not harbor anything purely ideal or *stilnovo*-like inspiration but is based essentially on the carnal reality of instincts, the impetuosity of passion, a love that is entirely human as Francesca's in Dante's *Inferno*, similar to a flame that envelops the whole individual, body and soul, and drives to the achievement of the desired object, in an atmosphere of drama or tragedy.

These characteristics, for the critic, existed because of a close connection between literary creations and Boccaccio's own life, they were autobiographical, in a word, and tended to enter into his writings as a confession of his emotions and desires. Yet, in the presence of those characteristics, there arose the vigilant artistic and rhetorical conscience of the writer stemming from his study of the classics and the courtly love poetical tradition, his need to conform to admired examples and his determination to inject into his works the dignity and perfection of creativity, language and style.

The history of Boccaccio's minor works, in a certain sense, constitutes a struggle between the urging of the autobiographical substance and the restraint imposed by Boccaccio's literary and technical studies; a struggle that ends rarely in the supreme peace of poetry.

In Sapegno's study, however, the *Decameron* opens a different phase in the narrative style of Boccaccio. Composed between 1348 and 1353, it is a fruit of the writer's maturity. In it converge rich and varied experiences of ancient and recent art and it contains, elaborated and structured, Boccaccio's ideal and cultural world. It marks a moment, as it were, when the early influence of impetuous passions and personal experiences are sublimated in an ideal world of art. The writer's endeavor to observe human feelings not from a personal, painful point of view but purely as one of a keen observer reaches its goal in the *Decameron*. The author, at this point, has reached that conclusive moment of his life set between the troubling experiences of his youth and the gravity of an incipient senescence when, free from passion, he may indulge in contemplating them occurring in other individuals with the empathy of the man who has experienced them but is now in a condition of detachment, when they no longer represent a source of distress but the pleasure and final comfort of a mind ready for peace.

This way of thinking helps the reader to understand first the structure of the book, the *cornice*. Seven young women and three young men meet in the church of Santa Maria Novella, in Florence, at the height of the plague of 1348, and decide to escape for some days from the dreadful, oppressive atmosphere of the city, ravaged by death, its citizens incapable of staving off mortality, beset by fear and the disintegration of social structures and mores.

The ten young people decide to go and stay in a villa, far from the city, where they will spend part of their leisure telling stories, dancing, singing and resting, isolated in an idyllic setting, enlivened by their cheerful moods and enchanting natural surroundings. The *cornice*, that reminds the reader of a magical, colorful and serene image enveloped by the gloom of death, had also the purpose of offering a backdrop to the events of the stories that are being told. And it is plausible to believe also that behind the names of the young ladies, Pampinea, Filomena, Elissa, Neifile, Emilia, Lauretta and Fiammetta, live aspects of women known by the author and personified in a joyously creative moment, while their male companions, Dioneo, Panfilo and Filostrato may represent aspects of Boccaccio's character itself, the daring, the fortunate and the betrayed lover, respectively. These characters, writes the critic, "are like as many exemplary and typical projections of that world of loves and passions that had interwoven the frame of Boccaccio's work until then. The narrator's ideal lives are embodied in their attitudes, actions and words and, above all, in their ballads that each one of them sings at the end of each day. And although they rarely achieve a high poetic value, built as they are with a technical style that rests between the ideals of the 'sweet new style' and the refinement of musical lyrics, serve to bring forth a narrator's image that is, at once, symbolic and allegorical."

To add balance to this impression, however, Boccaccio introduces frequent elements of a realistic nature. One learns, for example, about the social level of the *brigata*. The ladies belong to rich families who own a large quantity of landed estates. Also Filostrato, Dioneo and Panfilo must enjoy a similar financial status since each one of them has a personal servant, Tindaro, Parmeno and Sirioco respectively. These and the maidservants of Pampinea, Lauretta, Filomena and Fiammetta, namely Misia, Chimera, Licisca and Stratilia, provide assistance to the group, each one with specific tasks. An elegant *villa* that is as aesthetically charming as are the lands and gardens that surround it, the abundance of choice food and the impeccable refinement and tastes of the *brigata* suggest that one witnesses events that might have occurred in the lives of members of a wealthy bourgeoisie as was the Florentine class that wielded power in the city.

The critic suggests also that Boccaccio's major work is not, as some think and have thought in the past, a form of *divertimento* containing cynical and bawdy overtones but a true poetic creation, conceived seriously, rich in varied elements, tragic, pathetic, elegiacal, composed in every part with a meditated, serious intention.

Boccaccio, however, does not assume the position of a reformer in an attempt to guide or correct human behavior in the light of personal convictions but with the mind of a viewer who is pleased to observe and inquire into human behavior and the relationship that connects the individual persons with the ethical and social ambiance that surrounds them, disposed to extol sublime virtues or describe with good-natured indulgence the narrow-mindedness and egoism of many.

Thus, through the critic's analysis, we envision an attitude that remains unchanged in that balance that is constant in Boccaccio's art, as he portrays the highest and the basest feelings of humanity as one would expect to see in a man of deep knowledge and experience who remains detached from the material that he employs to represent the agreeable or disconcerting aspects of life.

Biographical Note

Natalino Sapegno was born in Aosta, November 10, 1901. His early life saw him in Turin, where he attended elementary and secondary schools and where he met Carlo Levi with whom he was connected by a friendship that lasted his entire life.

The outbreak of WWI and the untimely death of his father caused the family to move to his maternal house in Aosta in 1916. While there, he attended the first two years of *liceo* and, in the autumn of 1918 he was enrolled in the *Facoltà di Lettere* at the University of Turin. In that city, he became a friend of Piero Gobetti with whom he collaborated extensively in cultural activities by contributing articles to his publications. (Piero Gobetti, 1901–1926, was an intellectual, radical liberal and journalist. He founded his own review, *Energie Nove*. He promoted the cause of radical, political and educational reforms, as well as the right to vote for women. Having taken an anti-fascist stance, he was forced to close his review, was assaulted by *squadristi,* and compelled to emigrate to France where he died.) When fascism came to power in 1922, the year of Sapegno's graduation, his activities took a different direction. He won a position as an instructor in the secondary schools and moved to Ferrara where he taught and had the opportunity to expand his literary learning from the early Italian writers to the contemporary, while pursuing an intense series of readings of both Italian and foreign literatures. The result of his studies were essays, book reviews and articles published by various journals and magazines and, in 1930, he received an academic teaching position at the University of Padua. His imposing book on the *Trecento*, part of the Literary History of Italy, published by Vallardi in 1933, brought him into a position of prominence in the academic world and in 1936 he was invited to teach at the University of Palermo.

After only a year, however, he was offered the professorship of the prestigious (and unique, at that time) center of Italian literature at the University of Rome. Meanwhile, in 1936, he published for *La Nuova Italia* the first volume of the series on the history of Italian literature, that was followed by the second in 1941 and the third in 1947.

The years between 1938 and 1950 mark the period when the already established scholar entered in contact with the young left-wing members of the Roman *Facoltà di lettere*, several of whom were going to participate in the resistance and the political straggles that took place before and after the end of WWII. In conjunction with these events, Sapegno joined the Italian Communist Party that he left, however, in 1956, after the Soviet repression of the Hungarian rising. That was also the time when the writer reached the full development of his critical interests that produced a vast amount of essays and articles to be collected later, together with other works that he authored in the successive decade, in two important volumes, *Pagine di storia letteraria* (Pages of Literary History), and *Ritratto di Manzoni* (A Portrait of Manzoni), published, respectively, by Sansoni in 1960, and by Laterza, in 1961.

His commentary of the *Divine Comedy* was prepared in large part in the 50's and, in many scholars' opinion, it remains a major example of critical method and philosophical rigor. In 1954, he was inducted into the premier Italian cultural institution, the *Accademia dei Lincei*.

Other major works appeared in the 60's: the *Storia letteraria del Trecento* (Literary History of the Fourteenth Century), published by Ricciardi in 1963, the nine volume *Storia della letteratura italiana* (History of Italian Literature), that he directed with Emilio Cecchi and that was published by Garzanti between 1965 and 1969 (where he contributed the sections on Dante, Petrarch, and the literary criticism of the twentieth century), as well as the *Storia letteraria delle regioni d'Italia* (Literary History of the Regions of Italy), in collaboration with Walter Binni, published by Sansoni in 1968.

Sapegno stopped his university teaching in 1976 but continued tirelessly his work as a critic with articles and essays published in different sources, and through revisions and new editions of some of his preceding publications. In 1980, Bulzoni published the last of five books written in his honor. It contained his uncollected writings.

Natalino Sapegno died in Rome, April 11, 1990, and was buried in the cemetery of his native city.

Introduction

The literary historian who proceeds from the study and the description of the documents concerning the literary civilization of the thirteenth century to the study of the age immediately following, has the impression of witnessing a sudden broadening and complication in the object of his research. That object that, at first, tended to be grouped into fundamental themes in their development and relationships, now seems to branch out in a variety of diverging and contradictory directions, a variety that represents both wealth and confusion as well as discordant attitudes and requirements. As much as such distinctive and temporal patterns may be valid (where one may clearly find a considerable latitude of arbitrariness, empiricism and didactic convenience), it does not seem possible to withhold from that confused yet vivid and preconceived view a certain essence of validity and truth. Furthermore, considering it in the course of a study will not lead to damage or impediment but rather to an advantage and an incentive since it will be useful at least in eliminating the never sufficiently lamented danger of a hurried synthesis. It will lead constantly, rather, to a greater emphasis of the variety and differences of its contents and forms, the unforeseeable and irrepressible richness of a cultural situation rather than to the ideas that even this one, as all others, may confront the person who intends to frame it in a total picture even at the risk of sacrificing and distorting too many factual elements that might be secondary yet not less real and vital, that go against the researcher's attempts to systematize them.

It is quite certain, however, that when compared with the preceding century, the Trecento's rhythm of activity and internal modifications and settlement quicken and seem to replace a slow, organic, coherent process of acquiring and refining its sentimental themes and forms of expression by imparting a quick and uneven motion through abrupt transitions and changes of direction.

The very presence of some great personalities that emphasize considerably, in the span of a few generations, the contrast, violent at times, of the intellectual positions, doctrinal interests, poetic forms, tastes and sensitivity and while it seems to embody almost symbolically the changed rhythm of cultural life, it reveals the broadness and the importance of the minor and vast ramifications of its collateral experiences that said presence can hardly exhaust and synthesize in itself even though it draws its substance and the reason for its contrasts from them and reacts in turn upon them by constantly enriching and changing them.

Dante, Boccaccio and Petrarch are three poetical worlds, three epochs of cultural history and aesthetic progress, so profoundly different from each other and, in certain aspects, even antithetical, who succeed and overlap each other in such a brief span of years within the frame of the same civilization that they helped to establish and characterize with their ingeniousness, suddenly placing it at the apex of all European culture and literature by imposing upon it the role of director and guide. And around these prominent figures there is a rich flowering of minds and works variously distributed at all levels of knowledge and technical awareness, from the highest to the lowest. It was a sign of an extraordinary, general vividness and restlessness and also (a new phenomenon that does not occur in equal measure in any other time of our history) a broad, divulging tendency that comes to life in countless documents of popular and other forms of literature.

It is not possible to grasp and fully evaluate such a series of events if one does not realize that the crisis of medieval civilization is that it ages, reflects and finds its conclusion at a time when the powerful ideological structures that had supported it for centuries collapse. At the same time, the prestige of the universal institutions on which Christianity's order had rested grows weaker, Europe's moral and civil unity begins to fragment itself into a multitude of particular regulations, of multiple experiences that do not collaborate but diverge from each other. It is not by chance that it is precisely in Italy that the crisis of medieval thinking is felt earlier and more consciously than elsewhere and the early foundations of the cultural renewal are established. It was in Italy, in fact, that there came from several directions those forces aiming at the disintegration of that tight structure of ideas and customs, as well as social and political orders, that had converged and risen to the most explicit and modern forms. And if the scholastic and hierarchical concept of life had reached its highest and most comprehensive expression in the work of an Italian, it was equally from there that, through the success of the Franciscan

movement, the drive toward the subversion of that concept, along mystic and fideistic lines, had originated. Hence the importance of the Italian Trecento, and the
cluster of historical and cultural problems that centers in it. Its full understanding
implies on the one hand the awareness of the meaning and magnitude of the mentioned crisis, on the other the effort to establish the terms of a new vision of reality
and the struggle between the old and the new, between a compact and experimental ideology and another one barely beginning and still unshaped that is realized in
every aspect and is reflected by each one of the protagonists, as well as the minor
and minimal characters of this age of transition. It implies, in short, the need to
confront and evaluate that complex, twofold phenomenon that is identified with
the transition from the Middle Ages to humanism with which it is connected, not
by chance, in the century old historiographical tradition, but, for what concerns
Italy, with alternations of contrasting definitions.

Such definitions now tend to find in early humanism the premises and foundations of the great Renaissance message and its European function to recognize
its essential duty but then, especially in the nineteenth century and romantic criticism, they tend to define in it the outset and the feeling of a profound regression
of Italian society and the expression, if not actually the cause, of the missing development of an autonomous national culture.

The key for a more persuasive interpretation of humanism that may go beyond
this dichotomy of definitions, that are both arbitrary and unilateral, and may solve in
a dialectic link this contrast of polemic evaluations, lies perhaps in a deeper and more
careful study of the Italian Trecento. It should shed light on the internal contradictions that exist on the cultural and civil basis, it should be capable to grasp all active
and passive aspects, the novelties and the remnants of the past, the intellectual span
and the weakness of its social and political foundations. For it is quite certain that
the features of modern civilization take shape at first precisely in 14th Century Italy
and said civilization will then mature first in the wake of Italian art and thought,
then, in different and autonomous ways, in the three centuries that followed until
it discloses itself in the manifest rationality of European Enlightenment. But it is
equally certain that the discovery of a new cultural and human perspective coincides,
among us, with the weakening of a promising bloom of civic life and carries within
itself the seed of that painful division that will become apparent, within and after the
Renaissance splendor, as a characteristic of our history, between political conscience
and the intellectual and moral life, between the citizen and the writer.

If it is true that the entire humanistic and Renaissance movement, when considered in its entirety, may be interpreted as the movement of a deep crisis in
the history of European civilization, the laborious gestation of a new economical
and political order and a new ideological conscience that grew upon the ruins of
the universal institutions and the hierarchical order of the Christian and feudal

Middle Ages as well as on the slow and inevitable erosion of the scholastic synthesis unable to accept and systematize in its solid conceptual framework a wider and complex view of intellectual interests and vital experiences and, if it is equally true that it was Italy's turn to bear its burden and to be the first to evaluate its importance and magnitude and draw the main lines of the developing process until she became exhausted in the concluding phase of its fulfillment, it is indubitable then that in the Trecento, in Italy, one may perceive the initial moment of that crisis, its emergence from the dark recesses of history to the light of awareness and its becoming conscious of itself while attempting to transform the new concept of life into suitable cultural moulds.

No less certain is the fact that the transition of the crisis to an intellectual basis, whence it is received and raised in a cycle of brilliant, mainly poetic and literary solutions, goes along with an excessively and abnormal view of the independent function of culture that, having the tendency to be superimposed over common experience outclasses it into a condition of inferiority rather than merge with it and permeate it in all its elements and stratifications, separating, that is, from social reality, and it foreshadows, in short, what will constitute the pride and the limits of our Renaissance civilization in the fifteenth and sixteenth centuries, the conviction and the illusion, "perhaps never as acute as at that time ... that a cultural element, the *studia humanitatis*, the *humanae literae*, could transform, reshape and dominate by itself all human life." (Garin)

Only by becoming aware of the novelty and the immense creative ability of this cultural effort and, at the same time, of its tendency to set itself up as an independent value and of separating itself from the customary experience in a scornful and proud isolation, till the point of opening a chasm among the freedom, lack of prejudice and refinement of its cultural achievements and the real conditions of civilized society, to the point of being under the illusion of leading and directing without participating humbly in its labor and assuming upon itself some of its misery and contradictions, are we able to understand, on one hand the enormous influence that the powerful personalities of Dante, Petrarch and Boccaccio, as well as the influence, later on, of the great Quattrocento's philologists, from Ariosto, Machiavelli and Galileo, were to have on European civilization intent upon freeing itself of medieval forms and shaping its modern aspect. But we may become aware also of how the novelty of those achievements had to await the full ripening of those fruits only when and where they could take root in a different ground, and increase their effectiveness by enhancing their value and becoming involved in the demands of a concrete, historical process.

To those who refuse to consider it within this broad historical view, in time and space, the aspect of the Trecento culture appears particularly chaotic and the contrast becomes more marked to the point of being incomprehensible, between the great doctrinal and poetic syntheses of universal importance and European interest and the contradictory, manifold action of the minor influences that are dominated by a sense of restlessness and anguish that reflects the deep anxiety of a social reality in crisis. This occurred precisely because in those years the historic process of western society reaches a crucial moment of its evolution, whereby the relatively united and unanimous course of *civitas christiana*, far from renouncing to develop a traditional patrimony of common culture, tends to break up in a variety of political orders and distinct national cultures. Furthermore, if one observes it against general European civilization or in the specific perspective of Italian history, the fourteenth century appears, in turn, either as the crucible where the humanistic ideas and the premises of the modern world come to maturity, or as the focus where the brilliant but equally ephemeral experience that precedes the communal bourgeoisie converges and becomes blocked while the decadence and regression of our political orders and, ultimately, of our very cultural function are set in motion.

The fact remains that, as a typical aspect of the century, there is the interweaving and mingling in every field of experience of ancient and new elements, of medieval and humanistic attitudes, while new elements surface in indefinite and partial concepts as the old ones still stand owing to the strength of a century-old tradition. The rapid rising of the civic, bourgeois social ranks, the developing and prospering of the new particular state organizations, such as communes and *signorie*, give life to the conditions of a different concept of political life. They transform in a modern and secular sense the very instrument of action, they undo the rigid economical and juridical structures of the feudal system, they wear away the strict relationships of distinction and subordination among the social classes and between clergy and laity, they emphasize the real values that, within the individual communities, act outside, and often against, the theoretically accepted hierarchies, the ceaseless, even intensifying change of hegemonic relationships, intelligence, shrewdness, initiative, power of sudden, large earnings, unscrupulousness in choosing ways of fighting and winning that become more and more frequently arbitrary and violent. A fight without quarter goes on within the states, where, while the great ideal principles grow weak and feeble, the concrete motivations of economic predominance and real political forces establish themselves. Outwardly, there grows a desire of expansion and power that has similarly its root in mere motivations of vitality, exuberance and prestige along with the territorial expansion that may reach the ambition of building large regional and multiregional states and accompanies the attempt to bring about a political and fiscal leveling of the conquered cities, of the various civic social classes and the population of the countryside. But the deep rending that breaks up the communes' vitality, the severity of class, party and family conflicts, the persecutions, massacres, and exiles, create a feeling of weariness, a desire of order and peace that promotes and quickens the evolution of juridical rules toward forms of a centralized, potentially egalitarian control and opens the way to the *signorie* and principalities.

On the other hand, the experience under authoritarian regimes arouses in new and more serious forms the terror of oppression and despotism and a polemic, so lively and widespread in the entire century, against the danger of tyranny. The picture of political life in its entirety shows aspects of extreme anarchy, restrained but not overcome by methods of merciless repression. Both communes and *signorie* lack a common base of legitimacy and the sentiment of justice, order, and a stable and harmonious civil coexistence melts away, hence the appeal that arises from every direction and becomes a sorrowful and anxious voice in the words of exiled, oppressed and persecuted people, for the ancient ideals and the universal institutions that seem to constitute a superior concept of authority capable of prevailing over the unleashed contrasting forces and of checking the rampant anarchy. These universal institutions, the Church and the Empire, that are partly deprived of power, obliterated and not seldom scorned in the harshness of political strife, remain the only powers where an ideal principle survives, as the continuing symbols of a necessity of justice and peace, of the Christian order that is threatened and almost destroyed by arising desires and particular corruption.

The contrast between an entirely new and modern yet chaotic experience of social and political reasons and the survival of the patterns and leading ideas of a traditional order, is mirrored also in the rich and contradictory signs of the juridical and institutional thinking of the time, where the ideas of a doctrine that strives to accept and settle the elements of a new experience are framed and emerge laboriously through the forms and procedures of antiquated themes where the concepts of Church and Empire still stand out in their mutual relationship of coordination and subordination. In the intense polemics that occurred during the conflict between Boniface VIII and the King of France, and then in those, not less acrimonious, of the time of Ludwig the Bavarian, in a context of medieval argumentation, there comes forward the antithetic problem between Church and State, which is expressed in embryonic and unwitting forms and concerns the limits of the state's autonomy and sovereignty as well as the relationship between politics and morals. While for Dante and the other Ghibelline theoretitians the concept of sovereignty is enriched by an ideal significance, the totality of an entirely valid authority in its secular and temporal sphere asserts itself, albeit somewhat hesitatingly, in the books of the supporters of the Church and is effectively expressed in the need to resort to a superior basis of morality that may rule, contain and solve the clash of the mere relationship between force and power and solve the game of human passions and social reality within the sphere of a transcending concept of the mission assigned to the individual man.

Even the formula that is progressively elaborated in the law schools by Cino da Pistoia, Oldrado da Ponte and Bartolo da Sassoferrato, the modern concept of state is expressed as independent and sovereign in its own sphere in that it actually exercises its full authority over its subjects ("*civitas superiorem de facto non recognoscens habet in se ipsa imperium*"), and is much less revolutionary of what it might seem at first sight because it does not explicitly invalidate the superior power of the universal institutions and it does not affect the philosophical and religious principle of the "*ordinatio ad unum.*" Thus the other order that finds in Dante its most decided expression, of the distinction, that is, of mutual authority of the two spheres of the temporal and the spiritual, of Empire and Church, of secular happiness and heavenly beatitude, of the philosophical and theological sphere, remains uncertain and hindered, entirely enveloped in an intricacy of cautious distinctions and finally ends up in the limitation of a relative subordination of the secular authority and philosophy to spiritual power and theology.

On the other hand, while on the basis of Aristotelic naturalism and the *Corpus iuris* gloss some strength is acquired by the absolutistic theses that were to prevail in the practical context and to influence the structure of the states and the ecclesiastical order, the Agostinian concept remains alive, as it was never explicitly rejected by the scholastics, concerning the conventional origin of the state, that was ordained to function as a remedy to the malady of human nature that had become corrupt after the original sin. Such a concept performs the opposing function against the threat of despotism and the excess of individual power, the ideal of Christian justice and the limitations set upon political authority by the instrumental nature of its function.

Within this doctrine we notice the activity of the abundant literature against the evil craft of the tyrants from *De Regimine Principum* by Egidio Colonna to *De Tyranno* by the humanist Coluccio Salutati. To this is connected also that work that is the richest in new creativity and the most indicative of the Trecento's political thought, the *Defensor Pacis* by Marsilio da Padova, born around 1326 in the Averroist atmosphere, not without the influence, and perhaps the direct collaboration, of Giovanni Jandun. It is stated in the work that the legislative power resides in the "*universitas civium*" and it is expressed according to the principle of numerical majority, so therefore it is the people that must lead, restrain and, when necessary, remove the ruler to whom the government had been entrusted by way of a contract. Similarly, in the Church, sovereignty is based on the "*universitas fidelium,*" that is represented by the ecumenical council and the pope but only in an indirect and controlled fashion. Without doubt, these are doctrines imbued with premonitions and future perceptions but that, for the time being, do not abandon the framework of traditional universalism and, in reality, they find their place precisely in the fiery air of the Ghibelline polemics at the time of Ludwig the Bavarian.

If we then go back from the particular ground of juridical doctrines to the general concept of life, it is quite certain that the mighty structure of scholastic thought that had just reached the full of its elaboration in the great *summae*, begins to deteriorate precisely in the Trecento under the thrust of the critical reasons that rise to attack it in its particular aspects and in its entirety, from the outside to the innermost parts. Averroism, that sharpens the rigidity and immobility of Aristotelic naturalism, aims at destroying the individual's autonomy and it nullifies the dialectical balance established by Christian philosophy between man with his personality and his moral freedom, the world and the divine. William of Ockham's and his numerous followers' nominalism breaks the foundations of the system, shatters the hierarchy of essences and spreads the unit in an infinite multiplicity of autonomous and distinct elements and ends up by separating faith from reason and by setting them one against the other. The rising humanism, at last, working no longer from inside in order to uproot the foundations of systematic thinking but going against it from outside and opposing it radically, proclaims the uselessness of laborious dialectical analysis, replaces abstract speculation with conscience's reality, philosophy with psychology and philology, the unity of the system with multiplicity and the variety of concrete research and historical experiences. The first two currents mark the decadence of scholasticism and prepare somehow, but negatively above all, the development of naturalism and Renaissance empiricism. Humanism is essentially the voice of a new philosophy that is centered on the concept of man and of the rules of concrete action. However, all these three tendencies are too weak to give a decisive blow to the structure of traditional philosophy. Averroists and nominalists operate still within the framework of the Aristotelic Christian concepts and express themselves in the jargon of the elaborate syllogistic procedures while the humanists carry out their protest on a sentimental rather than a logical ground, by way of poetic myths and eloquent statements rather than elaborating a new philosophical language and a coherent system of ideas. So that, even in this field, the new cannot win the upperhand on the old, and together with the ideas and the foreboding it resists and carries out its unaccomplished function, the traditional concept.

Only in literature, for some time, can the contradictions and intrinsic perplexities of the culture of the Trecento find an expression of their own, totally valid in its sphere and more intense as it breaks out into uneven, contrasting and multiform ways, in the literature that elaborates the myths and the synthetic forms of a civilization that is pervaded by deep movements of renewal. It expresses through Dante the conscience of its moral crisis; in Petrarch it declares the need of a more flexible and humane culture, in Boccaccio it pauses to observe the teeming and picturesque substance of the new secular reality, and also in the literature of the minor writers that offers to us in several ways the partial and fragmentary documents of the crisis that works in this "sunset of the Middle Ages," while the early blossoms of a new civilization begin to germinate.

CHAPTER ONE

The Literary Civilization of the Age of Dante

The picture of Italian culture between the end of the Duecento and the early decades of the Trecento is doubtlessly much more varied and distinguished than it seems to the person that is satisfied to notice its essential lines and prominent contours and is too easily led to forget, for instance, that they develop almost simultaneously or with minor chronological differences, in widely different experiences unsusceptible to form an orderly and homogeneous view, such as those of Dante and Jacopone, Cino da Pistoia and Bonvesin da la Riva, Francesco da Barberino, Mussato, Cavalca and Simintendi, Folgore da San Gimignano, Giovanni Quirini, Cecco d'Ascoli and Bartolomeo da San Concordio, Bindo Bonichi, the author of the *Entrée d'Espagne* and so on. But beyond the contrasts of a literary and even linguistic image that lets us identify centers of sharply distinct traditions and preferences, such as religious poetry in Umbria, the experience of high lyrical works of Provençal origin, the allegories of French inspiration concentrated in Tuscany, and the predominantly didactic literature of Northern Italy, there is a clearly evident tendency (or at least an aspiring) toward the settling of the scattered and contradictory elements in a united framework, a hierarchical organization of the various cultural bases whereby some experiences tend to prevail over the others and assert themselves through an expanding, exemplary energy that forces upon the entire cultural life a hegemonic direction. This tendency appears equally beyond the stratification of the cultural centers that arranges and distinguishes the types and forms of expression from the quasi-vernacular Latin of some monastic chronicles and hagiographers to the technical one proper of the philosophical and theological schools, the chancery style of the rhetoricians and jurists up to the deliberate attempts of classical restoration of certain coteries in Emilia and Veneto. And the same is also valid in the case of the vernacular tradition, along the verses that go from an extra-aesthetic purpose of popular education and information, the minstrels' poems and the poetry clearly directed toward the goal of a deliberate form of art, not to mention the prose work of mere diffusion and simple entertainment and those that are characterized by precise stylistic ambitions and in the very sphere of pure literature, the contrast of the "learned" and abstract styles of high lyric and the "humble" and realistic form of the confession, polemic or narrative verses.

In the meantime, the laborious process of acquisition and assimilation with which Italian civilization is ripening its natural characteristics during the thirteen century, even in the area of linguistic institutions and formal traditions, is taking place, or better, has been already accomplished. It is carried out, however, with the overpowering drive that it draws from its most original and laborious historical experience: the establishment of the new communal bourgeois classes and the flourishing of the great religious movement of popular inspiration and diffusion, from the mendicant orders to the laic confraternities. Almost in every sector there had happened, or was already at an advanced stage of development, the transition from an attitude of passive acquisition that accepts en masse the patrimony of the already established forms and contents, conceptual and imaginary material and stylistic inventions (together with them also the language, as a means of expression indissolubly connected with that essence of thoughts and imagination) to a different and quite mature attitude of an active imitation, at first, and then of original reelaboration where the adaptation of the acquired forms to the needs of a changed civilization proceeds along with the establishment of a new instrument of expression, the maturation and the refinement of the new vernacular. And this progress, and action of emancipation that occurs in the span of a few generations, coincides with the simultaneous occurrences of special concentration, with the slow but constant convergence of the various experiences deriving at first from peripheral areas, from the north to the south of the peninsula, toward those central areas, mainly Tuscan, where the elaborative effort of new civic patterns and therefore of a similar culture, reaches deeper roots and progresses at a much faster pace.

The early signs of this process appear, in a clearer fashion, obviously, at the level of the superior poetical culture, in the manner in which Italy gets hold of the Provençal experience and, on the basis of that experience, it assimilates in depth and builds progressively the forms of its new poetry.

After an early phase of immediate and almost complete transplant of the old Provençal literary culture that had reached by then its deepest maturity and decline, in a mainly similar and well disposed environment ready to receive it, the late troubadours, Pietro Vidal, Rambaldo di Vaqueiras, Ugo di Saint-Circ, visit the northern Italian courts where feudal customs and rules of chivalric life continue to remain unchanged in Monferrato, Lunigiana, and the Marca di Treviso, and impose their style and language in a way that will generate in a favorable ground the numerous anthological transcriptions of the main poetical texts and the late grammatical, rhetorical, exegetical arrangements of an illustrious tradition that is nearing extinction in its country of origin. But then, what follows quite early is a second phase of congenial imitation and emulation, when the voices of troubadours born in Italy begin to emerge. And they are deep participants in that cultural ambiance, such as Sordello from Mantua, who moves from the court of Este and the Ezzelini to those beyond the Alps, and competing in ability with the Provençal poets of his generation, creates in their language love songs as well as political and moral sirventes.

Early enough, also the taste for troubadour poetry enters from the courts into the commune especially where the relationships of vicinity or contrast are more intense and frequent between the commune and the still powerful feudal lord (between Genoa and the Marquis of Lunigiana, Bologna, and the Este house). The growing prime of the town culture expresses its need of cultural refinement and it grafts in the body of the established literary tradition its polemic passions and municipal pride through the voice of its troubadours, from the Genoese Lanfranco Cigala and Bonifacio Calvo, to the Venetian Bartolomeo Zorzi and the Bolognese Rambertino Buvalelli. It is the expression of sentiments that are still connected with a kind of ideal expression, where the literary genre merges with a consecrated heritage of language and style.

Only when the Provençal style descends toward the south and finds its center in a court decidedly large and powerful, with an ample cultural magnitude and political drive already oriented in the modern sense, the Swabian court of Palermo, there occurs in a contemporary and parallel fashion the split between the refinement of the courtly tradition and the institutions of the feudal life and between the lyrical material and the language where it had found its expression and form whose potential for expansion saw a barrier in the new ambiance owing to the distance and the dissolution of direct connections and the stronger difference vis-à-vis the local dialects.

Thus the poetry of the "Sicilian" school is born, still entirely Provençal in discoveries and forms of expression but written in the new vernacular that established itself from the south toward the center and the north, wherever the influence of Frederick's power arrives, directly or indirectly, even when it accepted in its expansion movement and desire for prestige that is not bound by regional limits, a noticeable variety of idiomatic shading and acquiring, in its ambition of courtly elegance, in its lexicon and structure, a tint of latinizing and Provençal forms. Ornamental rather than a substance of life, a pattern of refined courtly patterns rather than the expression of civil reality, the "Sicilians'" poetry surrounds its patterns of affected and evasive images within conventional limits and the exhausted subject of erotic homage and it does not consider it, rather it excludes the theme of the rising popular sensitivity and, least than ever, of morality and political strife or, if it sporadically accepts the former and refers to the others with detachment and discretion, it is only a way of varying and innovating on the surface its action by remaining true in its substance to the rules of its aristocratic taste.

A most clear and rigorously observed separation remains between literary pastime, the real spirit of things and practical action. Pier della Vigna does not allow any contaminations between the two well separated parts of his personality: the poet of love and the minister and adviser of Emperor Frederick, the stylized invention of the vernacular verses and the concrete involvement of political formulations and diplomatic refinement that leavens the most elaborate Latin of the chancery letters.

The Genoese Percivalle Doria, a magistrate, governor and commander in the service of Manfred, composes in "Sicilian" the songs of love homage, but he adopts Provençal in his sirventes on war and on the passionate praises of his sovereign. The rigorously circumscribed themes of the Sicilian school determine the characteristics of the dawning literary language that is a truly poetic language, raised in an ambient of high culture, and is built in its syntax, basic lexical elements and even sporadically in some phonetic preferences, on the comparison of the two major linguistic traditions—Latin and Provençal. That will help from the beginning, and even more later, to facilitate its adoption and expansion, beyond its natural borders, in areas of similar cultural tradition. However, when the center of poetic activity moves from the south toward Tuscany and Aemilia, the school's poetic horizon broadens and the fragile balance of an exclusive taste brakes up first in the effort to proclaim a richer and more complex matter. The great Guittone and, with him, Bonaggiunta da Lucca, the Florentine Monte Andrea and Chiaro Davanzati, while they take after the Sicilians and directly from the old Provençal models, they sharpen the technical experiences and bend toward the cultural requirements of the new bourgeois aristocracy, they interpret their ethical and religious contents and the civic passions, formulate a broader dialog and a more articulate syntax, they combine and alternate the high and the humble style, the courtly, meditative, polemical and autobiographical aspiration, and create the pattern of the new oratory *canzone* of moral and political nature that will be inherited by Dante and the Trecento authors. Then Guinizelli introduces in those ampler structures, enlivened by the ferment of a new sensibility, the pride of the Bolognese philosophical and rhetorical culture and with him there arises the sense of an aristocratic distinction where the learned coterie replaces the court and the traditional concept of refinement is defined by a concept of intellectual superiority of feelings and conventions. After him the various mental and stylistic tendencies, that in Guittone's experience were established and progressed in an alternate and confused way (such versatility will constitute the sharp reproach of Dante to the municipality people), are defined again. In fact, they are defined for the first time by developing and perfecting independently their possibilities of expression.

There are two cultural bases, two varying, almost contrasting mental attitudes, and consequently two fashions and solutions equally different on stylistic and linguistic grounds. On one hand the learned form of the *dolce stil nuovo* poets, from Cavalcanti to Cino, and, on the other, the humbler, more current language of the religious, satirical, polemic and hortatory verses from Rustico to Bonichi, from Angiolieri to Folgore, Tedaldi and Faitinelli. Both styles grow out of the foundation of a long literary tradition that grew in the heart of the Latin and romance Middle Ages. Both assert themselves, although on different levels, as models of a literary tradition that is solid and rich in expansive potentials. What matters even more is that both develop in the spirit of a modern sensibility, directly or indirectly connected with the tastes and feelings of the new communal and popular civilization and affirm concretely the supremacy of Tuscan culture and of its language as the substance and form of the budding national literature.

In the early Trecento this ideal primacy is near its realization beyond its regional borders. In Ravenna, Guido Novello da Polenta, and in Veneto, Giovanni and Niccolò Quirini adopt entirely the forms and the language of the sweet new style poets. Niccolò del Russo, the jurist from Treviso, orders the collecting into a codex in sequential order, of the examples of the *stil nuovo* and realist poets and alternates in his verses the imitation of both styles, while the Paduan Antonio da Tempo, quickly imitated by Gidino da Sommaruga from Verona, working on the rhetorical norms of the new poetry, asserts on the theoretical ground the already established common and prominent poetic forms and recognizes the primacy of the Tuscan language *"magis apta ... ad literam, vel literaturam."*

Not as clear and linear, yet not substantially different, is the process that takes shape in the other areas of the fertile literature between the thirteenth and the fourteenth centuries. Such is due to a development at the level of a not so distinguished and specific culture that is instinctive and therefore more ready to comply with the stimulations and ephemeral inducements of a public that is humble and seldom prepared to reflect critically on its own experiences.

The taste for chansons de geste, romances, sermons and moral parables, legends and short stories that came from France is, at first, an immediate assimilation of a particularly rich and interesting material and also a passive acceptance of a technique and language, especially in northern Italy, where it soon has the tendency to change into autonomous forms and formulate more expressive and original patterns that are more original and of a higher level.

Although they stand on a more accessible and popular ground, Giacomino da Verona and Bonvesin da la Riva are proof of an artistic necessity, an aim at stylistic elaboration not dissimilar from the one of the Tuscan poets; and within the limits of narrative and adventure poems, the author of the *Entrée d'Espagne* and Niccolò da Verona express in the late Trecento a capacity of personal inventiveness and a wealth of technical discoveries suitable to the Aemilian and Lombard aristocratic environment.

But also the French material enters earnestly in the course of national literature only where it penetrates in Tuscany, through humble channels, owing to the work of anonymous translators and lesser writers, where it encounters the critical expectations of a more mature and refined civilization and is confined immediately to an inferior ground of entertainment and vernacular prose. From it will start the development, toward the end of the Duecento and then for the entire successive century, not only of the early narrative attempts to reflect concretely the bourgeois customs and sensibility, as well as the *Novellino*, but also the varied and rich literature of the romances and the ballads.

Yet precisely in Tuscany, that deliberately aims at establishing a more rigorous and aristocratic civilization, there arises another more difficult and refined aspect of that imported culture—the taste for the ample and scholarly allegories. Brunetto Latini, the author of the *Fiore*, the *Detto d'Amore* and *Intelligenza*, and Francesco da Barberino resume and renew the model of the *Roman de la Rose* and open the way that the poet of the *Comedy* will not disdain.

Also the immense production of the vernacular writers goes back to the Tuscan tradition. It goes progressively back from the Roman texts to those of the Latin Middle Ages and the classical prose and poetry writers. In a steady and productive exchange between the Tuscan centers and the University of Bologna is developed the parallel activity of rhetoricians and grammarians, from Guido Faba to Buoncompagno and Guittone who compile in the vernacular the rules of the chancery style and the *ars dictandi*. They set up the patterns and pave the way to the incipient aesthetic prose.

With Tuscany is also connected, finally, the most original experience of our literature, the religious *laude* and the sacred representation that had been developing from a basis of a native and popular spontaneity to the isolated, most elaborate mystical language of Jacopone. The prose of the chronicles achieves its more mature and complex results in Tuscany. They flourish simultaneously in the various dialects or in Latin everywhere in the peninsula. And it will be a great Tuscan poet, Petrarch, to give a final form and full critical awareness to the necessities that, even within the Latin writings, begin to assert themselves over the medieval distortions in favor of a return to the simplicity and greatness of the classics and initiate a literary practice and a pre-humanistic manner of perception, in the circles of the Aemilian and Venetian grammarians and men of letters, such as Lovato, Mussato, Giovanni del Virgilio and Ferreti.

Certainly, near the beginning of the Trecento, the concept of a uniform civilization of the nation is quite far from being accomplished. An Italian culture will come to life only toward the end of the fifteenth and the early sixteenth centuries. Meanwhile, around the culture that was built in different and vigorous forms on the fertile ground of the communal world of Tuscany, from the south and the north, experiences of taste and language deeply different and of an enduring vitality exert their pressure.

Contemporary and almost without contacts with the very intense and exemplary flourishing of the great Florentine Dante, Petrarch and Boccaccio, northern Italian literature in vernacular or in Latin and the one that from the south draws inspiration from the Adriatic regions, resist persistently and produce works of a unique flavor, such as the prose work of Anonimo Romano and the rhymed chronicle of Buccio di Ranallo. Yet it is very clear where resides the vital center of a civilization that from several points of view is still confused, uneven and fragmented. As from the Tuscan center a fruitful experience of cultural exchanges branches out and concentrates in an atmosphere of highly refined sensitivity and susceptibility, the sequence of political conflicts and ideologies, it is equally to Tuscany that go back in different fashions and in a more or less direct form all the most varied experiences in literature during the years that witness Petrarch collect the lines of the high lyrical tradition of Provence and Italy and establish the foundations of humanism, while Boccaccio, as he collaborates in this foundation, elaborates in a style of supreme decorum but with a warm participation the themes of the narrative production of France.

At the beginning of the century Dante is at the center of this rich and varied cultural experience and undertakes the task of interpreting and placing it in the framework of his powerful personality and poetry. None of its contrasting aspects may be considered totally foreign to him and the awareness of the tendential unity of its historical process is equally very strong in him. At the top of *De vulgari eloquentia*, there is, quite correctly, the linear and coherent process of the noble lyric, from the Provençal to the French, Sicilian and *stil nuovo* troubadours. And the concept of learned, supra-regional language is not only an ideal necessity, an abstract proposition, but rather the awareness of a present reality, of a style that is realized in the refined research of a group of poets endowed with critical perception, that has already achieved expansive potentials to the point of establishing itself as a model for the most refined style of the literary civilization in the entire country.

But that very treatise, the rhymes and the *Commedia,* reveal Dante's ability to approach all the most different aspects of this civilization: the French narrative and didactic prose, the realistic chronicles and poems, the short stories and moral parables, religious lyrics, and, on the horizon, the pre-humanistic tendencies (with which he meets, among others, Giovanni del Virgilio in his correspondence) and the vast heritage of moral and philosophical literature, of the encyclopaedias and the medieval *summae.* In any case, it is important that all this material is always acquired by him on the basis of a superior intellectual decorum, contained in a framework where every experience finds its place and its validity, perceived in the light of that united concept of language, doctrine, sentiment, and political structures toward which he attempts to bend a still shapeless and reluctant material. For this reason Italy was able to identify in him, not by chance or wrongfully, the father of her history.

CHAPTER TWO

Dante

From the heart of that Tuscan civilization where the dispersed elements of the complex cultural experience converge and integrate, the personality of Dante emerges in the last decades of the Duecento. Little by little it becomes one of the richest and strongest voices, more dynamic and restless, albeit isolated and conflicting, but in full harmony and agreement with the requirements and the ambitions of that bourgeois world that is just reaching the apex of its political and intellectual prestige. Only later, when exile will have caused a sharp brake between him and that world, the poet's voice will become isolated, almost detached, no longer a Tuscan or Florentine but an Italian cosmopolitan voice.

Yet not even then, the thread that connects him with his original roots, the nature and history of his people will ever break completely in spite of its painful and polemic nature. For some time, however, in the years of his adolescence and youth, the events of his life, his interests, works, customs and sensitivity coincide entirely with the spirit of the new bourgeois society, and reflect through a vibrant participation the blossoming and restlessness of a governing class that is proud of its growing power, eager to achieve political and economical primacy and anxious to become distinguished by adopting and modernizing in new ways the courtly style and refined culture of the feudal society.

And in the thirteenth century, Florence is not only the richest and strongest of the Tuscan communes, driven in its effort to win and consolidate its supremacy that is prospering through industries and trades that foster the development of a wide network of banking connections, but, starting from 1266, it is equally the center and the mainstay of the Guelph forces who hold sway in the peninsula; it is the center of political connections and diplomatic intrigues as well as of brisk and lively cultural exchanges with the major Italian and transalpine cities.

Scanty information, limited in number, unsatisfactory and superficial, can be obtained about the events of Dante's life, his origins and family, his formation as a citizen and man of letters from documents and the oldest biographies. Other data, more vivid and numerous, may be drawn from his writings, but they are often altered by his idealizations and his proud and polemic resentment. If it is not possible, however, to reconstruct the particular events of his life, one may envision the main ground of his education, his direction and cultural sources, the seriousness of his affections as well as his moral and civil ideals.

If we assuredly conclude (and there should not be any doubts), that his birth occurred in Florence in 1265, between the last ten days of May and the first twenty days of June in the sign of Gemini that predisposes the mind to letters and study, it will not be too difficult to reconcile the few real facts with the information that the author of the *Comedy* offers about his ancestors as his son Pietro does, after him, in his commentary. He comes from an ancient family of pure urban blood, where the seed of the Romans who had founded Florence continued, untainted by the "new" people originating from the *contado*. A non-feudal aristocracy, therefore, that grew in time through the exercise of authority and constant allegiance, within living memory, to the Guelph tradition of the commune.

The most glorious ancestor, perhaps the first in the memory of the family, was his great-great-grandfather Cacciaguida, who was knighted by Emperor Conrad III, and who died fighting in the Second Crusade. Related perhaps to the illustrious Elisei family, Cacciaguida had married a woman from the Po valley who gave her name to one of her children, Alaghiero, who is mentioned in a document of 1189. The latter, according to a not altogether unreliable statement by Pietro, presumably took as a wife one of the daughters of Bellincione Berti, a very distinguished citizen, hence the two sons Bellincione, the father of that Geri that Dante puts in the *Inferno* among the sowers of discord and scandals, and Bello, father of a Brunetto who fought at Montaperti and of Alighiero II, from whom Dante was born. The Alighieri's name never emerges with particular renown from documents and archival papers and it is certain that the poet's father stood away from public life and lived tending the administration of his modest estate, exercising, perhaps occasionally, the activity of money lending.

That his family's social condition was a precarious one appears from the fact that one of Dante's sisters or step-sisters was given in marriage to a town-crier of the commune. That this situation had also episodes of difficulties, if not actual penury, can be inferred from the loans that he and his step-brother Francesco, orphaned at an early age, had to obtain repeatedly. Yet that condition was wide-spread in all their social class, the lower aristocracy, that in the rapid transformation of the rest of society due to the growing of the "arts" and trades and the new pace of the economy that favored the most hard-working, enterprising and unscrupulous individuals, saw its margin of credit and the real value of its income grow thin and struggled to keep even the appearance of an ancient decorum.

At any rate, Dante lived the life of an upper class gentleman. In 1289 he participated in the war between Florence and the Guelph league against the Tuscan Ghibellines and was present, in June, at the battle of Campaldino and in August at the siege and conquest of the Caprona castle, as a fighter in the ranks of the light cavalry.

At a rather early age he must have married Gemma, daughter of Manetto Donati (the wedding had been settled with a notary act by the two families since 1277), and he had from her three children, Jacopo, Pietro and Antonia (probably the same person that later became a nun with the name of Beatrice in a convent in Ravenna) and perhaps a Giovanni who is mentioned as *filius Dantis Alagherii de Florentia* in a document from Lucca in 1308. In 1294 he was almost certainly among the knights assigned by the commune to Charles Martel who had gone to Florence to meet his father who was returning from France, and received from the young Angevin prince words of sympathy and gratifying promises.

More significant are the indications that remain about his early intellectual development and his previous participation in the intense cultural life of Florence. Particularly noteworthy is the tie of reverent friendship that he established with Brunetto Latini. From that elderly, influential literary man in whose broad and varied work converge an ambitious encyclopedic doctrine, the taste for allegories, the cult of the rhetorical discipline already directed to a pre-humanist thinking as well as a strong practical, pedagogical and political interest, the young poet drew an ample amount of knowledge, his initiation to *ars dictandi* and, as he himself attests, the ardent desire for that glory through which man becomes immortal. The study of rhetoric and eloquence was, among other things, the promise for the exercising of the citizen's activity in councils and offices and it might even be possible that Dante studied those disciplines in a more regular fashion at the university of Bologna, if he really lived, as one might surmise, in that city during his early youth.

Evidence of the interests and various concerns of the young poet's culture are his connections that certainly go back to those years with artists, such as Giotto and Oderisi da Gubbio, the musician Casella and the lute-maker Belacqua, and perhaps with minstrels and courtiers, such as Ciacco and Capocchio. Nor should one ignore his participation in the custom and practices of courtly life, hunts and dances.

But even more important are his connections with the culture, imitation and sentimental and stylistic affinity with the poets of the time, because the vocation for writing had to become prevalent in him, if not altogether exclusive, at a very early age. In the *Vita nuova* he states that he had learned on his own, when still an adolescent, the art of "saying words in rhyme," but it is quite certain that he matured in a climate of particularly lively and refined literary experiences, absorbing rapidly and following closely the evolution and progress of preferences and tastes. It is also difficult to say what role was played in this process respectively by the enthusiasm of a self-taught person, the maturation and development of his feelings and the authority and influence of masters and friends.

It is also not easy to define exactly the picture of this literary culture that is characterized at first by an attitude of versatile openness and restless acceptance on the part of the poet, since, in many cases, direct evidences from the writer are not available. All one can do is refer to what is known from different sources concerning the lively and varied cultural activity of bourgeois Florence of the thirteenth century and try to capture some reflections of it in his pages for, where evidence abounds, it reflects a much later phase of critical awareness in detached or indifferent judgements or negative and polemic aspects and directions of that culture that at first had consisted of phases and components more or less important in Dante's youthful experiences.

But the *corpus* of his rhymes and prose of the *Vita nuova* demonstrate how the attention of the young man was bent with curiosity and benevolence to accept the most varied voices of the sentiment around him and acquire directly or indirectly the Provençal and French contributions both in prose and in verse, courtly material as well as stylistic and metrical exercises, in an atmosphere where converged and stratified, according to different degrees of culture and taste, all the patterns and inspiration of European artistic civilization and, with them, the attempts and the canons of a new literature that was eagerly created.

One may rightfully conjecture that no aspect of this confused but intense and vital fervor remained essentially alien to the young man's curiosity as he was starting out in an environment that was still dominated by the strong personality of Guittone and where Monte Andrea and Chiaro Davanzati were still alive and producing while, on the Guittonian branch, were ripening the experiments of a deliberately anti-literary poetry, of popular inspiration, satyrical and polemic in the works of Rustico di Filippi and from neighboring Siena the influence of Angiolieri and Folgore.

Meanwhile, early steps were taken in the gender of allegorical and didactical poetry by adapting the French models to the demands of the new communal civilization in the works of Brunetto and the authors of *Fiore* and *Intelligenza,* and following the steps of the Bolognese Guinizelli, there arose and became established the taste of a Provençal-like art, no longer formal and technical but intimate and substantial with Cavalcanti and his imitators, while in the domain of prose, along with the intense activity of the vernacular writers came the compositions, on a level of spontaneity and elegant directness, of the chroniclers and the author of *Novellino*. At the level of learned art there appeared oratorical and epistolary models, governed by the *cursus*, ruled by the rhythms and internal rhymes, embellished by the clever use of rhetorical patterns and expanded at time by a naïve ambition of classical eloquence.

On the other hand, those texts of Dante's early activity indicate immediately a tendency, still unconscious perhaps but already quite strong, to differentiate among the variety of experiences without excluding any one of them, however, but including them under the symbol of a nobility of sentiments and stylistic solution, by moving naturally toward the most difficult and refined currents in high prose and poetry. Dante always marks it with a reflected literary sense, a noble and elaborate style and language without any easy and improvised forms.

But it is even more significant to recognize that such literary sense never becomes a mere technical exercise but is always or almost always connected with a visible affective life and that the earnestness of Dante's artistic commitment tends to coincide in every case with the earnestness of his moral dedication. The formal and rhetorical discipline and the simultaneous enfolding of feeling and meditations meet in the common goal of a constant growing of his sensibility and the artistic means that are engaged to express it so that at no time the technical exercise is an end to itself and it is used everywhere in a human conquest. Conversely, every modification and acquisition of intellectual and practical experience comes about in an increased potential for instrumental resources. There is never any trace of skepticism or superficial mental exercise but always an ardent and pure soul and a most serious mind for which the valiant quest for perfection and perhaps stylistic abstruseness represents the indication and the sign of the validity and depth of his emotion and is integrally combined with it. And even where it rarely prevails and stands alone, it draws its significance from the demand of nobility and expressive richness that transcends it, and becomes an exercise and a means for a successive, richer and deeper experience.

It is certainly not easy to render in term of empyric biography the personal events of the passions that underlie the *Vita nuova* within the framework of a culture, such as that of the late Middle Ages, that was so uninclined to solve in direct and straightforward forms the elements of a real experience, that appeared quite ready to transform and reconstruct them in an exemplary structure.

The masters of historical and positivistic criticism, with their bold confidence directed to the identification and classification of the external signs that often drove them to confuse the two distinct and opposing fields of life and poetry, have tried in different ways to reconstruct the history of the occasions of the individual compositions and, for example, of the many loves or of the unique love of Dante. No lasting and reliable result came from this patient labor but for the conviction of its uselessness and the belief that the only valid criterion to establish a chronology of the texts and a number of internal distinctions is the meticulous and minute analysis of the stylistic changes and progress.

But even if we renounce the idea of building fragile castles of hypotheses by combining and forcing into an agreement his own confessions, most vague and occasionally contradictory, against the tendency that is emerging at present of evaluating those texts on a strictly technical basis, as an evidence of a long and laborious formal education, it may be useful to reaffirm that they certainly reflect no less the line of a spiritual education, and that the intensity and complexity of the technical effort cannot be explained without the thrust of an activity that was ardently and candidly experienced.

This is, obviously, even more valid as regards the most important biographical elements that come to the surface in Dante's literary production: his love for a woman named Beatrice, that the reciprocally independent and reliable indications of Graziolo dei Bambagliuoli, Pietro Alighieri and Boccaccio identify as a Bice, daughter of Folco Portinari, wife of Simone di Geri of the Bardi family. To confirm the authenticity of the fact we not only have the statements of the earliest biographers and the considerable number of concrete and realistic traces that remain through the poetic transfiguration of the episode created by the writer on several occasions, but also the complete view of Dante's life and works where that love that assumes idealized forms from the beginning, holds a prominent place and its unexhausted power of transfiguration in symbolic terms becomes primary always within the warmth of a sentiment that is perpetually renewed and that, in its absence, would appear absolutely arbitrary and inexplicable.

*

In the *De vulgari eloquentia* and then in the *Commedia,* Dante will judge severely the art of Guittone and the other Tuscan writers because it appears to him limited and not elevated. Yet the first phase of his poetic activity had come about within the Guittonian influence that is in the atmosphere of an entirely formalistic and scholastic environment, where weak structures and conventions corresponded to the rigidity and vapid abstruseness of the linguistic modes, the uncertain rhymes, the ethimological figures, and the puns. The sonnets exchanged with Dante da Maiano, the other one addressed to "the faithful of love" that opens the *Vita nuova* that the author says he composed at the age of eighteen, as well as a few other things not always easily attributable to him, belong certainly to this initial phase, where one rarely perceives the signs of an autonomous personality or any sign however slim of the future poet. We shall barely point out the lighthearted tone that we sense in the Bolognese sonnet for the Garisenda (that certainly predates 1287 because it was transcribed with that date in a notary record), and in another epistolary sonnet, *Com più vi fere Amor co' suoi vincastri* (that on account of its conventional theme and development, fits appropriately in that poetic time). They indicate an early robust future of the incisive technique that will bear fruit much later. But the evidence of a stronger commitment of that time is the canzone *La dispietata mente,* that although not quite close to the level of poetry, represents the crowning of a stylistic and metric experience, proves its knowledge of it and forebodes its mastery. Its psychological motive is tenuous: the distance from the loved woman and the tormenting nostalgia that only her greeting will assuage. The development of the theme is more conceptual than imaginative, dialectical and oratorical but the syntactical structure is vigorous and solid in the terse yet complex sentence structure and in the amplitude of its metric form. It indicates the most vivid and positive essence of Guittone's teaching, transposed into an atmosphere of emotional lyricism where the epistolary and personal pattern, whose origins go back to the old Provençal literature, allows occasionally expressions of tender immediacy.

> *E voi pur sete quella ch'io più amo,*
> *e che far mi potete maggior dono,*
> *e'n cui la mia speranza più riposa;*
> *ché sol per voi servir la vita bramo,*
> *e quelle cose che a voi onor sono*
> *dimando e voglio; ogni altra m'è noiosa.*

Very early Dante began to conform to the style of the new school that was developing in Florence in opposition to the declining Guittonian method. It was natural that the developing personality of the budding poet should lean willingly toward the appeal of the new style. And equally natural is for his move to take place on the occasion of his friendship with Cavalcanti, if it is true that friendship, understood as an ideal collaboration and harmony in an aristocratic refinement of sentiments and conventions to the point of resembling manner and hermetic language, constitutes the background and almost the living space where that group of poets was flourishing. Very little is known, in a strictly biographical sense, about the friendship between Dante and Guido (and even less about the ties that Alighieri must have had more or less at the same time with Lapo, Alfani and Dino Frescobaldi, and later on, with Cino da Pistoia). The famous sonnet *Guido i' vorrei,* offers a glance at that climate of literary evasion, where there germinates and attains vigor a rare communion of sentiments, removed from all vulgar contacts, pursued and perfected in the observance of a privileged detachment. The other sonnet, addressed by Cavalcanti to Dante, *I' vegno il giorno a te infinite volte*, that marks the zenith of a relationship nearing its end, stresses equally the value of an intense sentimental rapport that arises from a common ideal of refinement and disdainful contempt for the "bothersome herd."

It is certain, at any rate, that the powerful influence of Guido's fully developed and mature personality affected Dante at an early stage and, if that influence was helpful in directing him toward a more refined poetic culture yet not so dry and scholastic, it is equally true that it drove him to forsake the most genuine character of his inspiration so that, far from representing a conclusion, it was the way that led to the encounter with the art of the other Guido, the Bolognese Guinizelli, from which Dante's truest and most congenial poetry of his youthful years was to begin. But the objective character of the psychological analysis that Cavalcanti brought to the limits with an almost scientific rigor was ill-suited to accept and reveal the reluctant feelings that lived in the uncertain and dreamy ideas of an adolescent's sensibility. Also, the dramatic style of the second Guido, the secret and painful fervor that is manifested in a series of learned and elaborate verses, dwelt uneasily in Alighieri's mind that, in its optimistic candor, could accept it only as a cultural contribution but not as a vibrant and personal experience. Therefore, the poems that may be attributed to this time, the canzoni *E' m'incresce di me sì duramente* and *Lo doloroso amor che mi conduce* (the former written most probably for Beatrice, the latter certainly for her because her name recurs in it), the sonnets of *gabbo* (joke), considered in one with the scattered rhymes, namely those that were gathered later in the *Vita nuova*, reveal a formal rather than a lyrical progress. The vigor and stylistic efforts, the true skill used by Dante in his invented dramas, the way he elaborates the patterns of the psychological symbols over Cavalcanti's models, are not sufficient to conceal a considerable dryness of feelings. The style of Cavalcanti's minor works, his joyful lines and lyrics for music as well as the *stilnuovo*'s easy, mannered compositions were suited better to the world of the adolescent poet, immersed in delicate and sensitive affections and gifted with a new, progressively acquired expertise.

To this genre belong some of Dante's ballads written probably for the screen-ladies that are mentioned in *Vita nuova*, such as *Per una ghirlandetta* and *Deh, Violetta, che in ombra d'Amore*, harmonized in a tenuous elegance that brings to mind the minor *dolce stil nuovo* poets, Lapo, Gianni Alfani, as well as the mentioned sonnet written to Guido and the most graceful one on the hunt, *Sonar bracchetti, e cacciatori aizzare*, that is inspired by Cavalcanti's *Beltà di donna* and proposes anew in a *stil nuovo* fashion the bourgeois poetry of Folgore da San Gimignano.

In these alternating "anguished" and musical expressions and musical *scherzi* and *fantasie* (where an ideal chronology essentially based on stylistic motives corresponds to a real chronology of psychological motives), vague feelings seem to appear, open to all possibilities, mutable, light but not consolidated in a single sentiment. The anguish and agitation, the woman's cruelty and Love's attacks, the frequent defeats of the "frightened spirits" give certainly the impression of being cherished and exaggerated in jest while the "sighs" and "great desire" in the ballads or the reverie of an amorous evasion in the sonnet *Guido, i' vorrei*, seem to arise and grow from an entirely literary plot, in a series of desires and surprises that appear idealized rather than experienced. Yet, there are already concepts in it that lead to a tenuous narrative plot, names and *senhals* of women around whom converges that scattered body of emotions that is found in the lines of the other *stil nuovo* poets. In the canzone *E' mi incresce di me*, a love story, a "new passion" begins to take shape whose following stages are indicated "in the record of the mind," by the miraculous amazement and anxiety that come to life in the poet's heart at the time the lady was born, the foreboding of his total dedication when he first meets her and the future realization of her fateful domination.

At a later time, in a retrospective view, those motives that had been at once established and modified, will give Dante the opportunity to draw from them the invention of a parallel development of love for Beatrice that is uniquely true and constant since his childhood and a number of fictitious loves for the screen-ladies (Fioretta and Violetta of the ballads) to avoid curiosity and indiscretions. Also, as far as Beatrice is concerned, he will trace the developing progress from tormenting passion to pure exaltation, from desire to gratified contemplation, and will find his conclusion in placing all his "happiness" in those words that praise the noblest woman, after he renounces any "reward" from her and [he seeks] that greeting that is the good, consolation and cause of the soul's bliss.

> *Sì lungiamente m'ha tenuto Amore*
> *e costumato a la sua segnoria,*
> *che sì com'elli m'era forte in pria,*
> *così mi sta soave ora nel core ...*

In the meantime, and most importantly, the young poet has been restricting progressively the atmosphere and the ambiance of his "literature" as well as the circle of friends united by an exceptional sensibility that isolates and unites them "in one desire"; the general group of the "gentle ladies"

> *(Io ho parlato a voi, giovani donne,*
> *che avete li occhi di bellezze ornati*
> *e la mente d'amor vinta e pensosa);*

and in that scene there is a flowering of literary variations and delicate imagery where there emerges the gift of an adolescent grace and solitary fervor despite its circumscribed scholastic and restricted atmosphere: Love assuages the weariness of the journey and dissolves the sorrow of the heart by talking with the poet about his woman (*Deh ragioniamo insieme un poco, Amore*). And again there is Love who, tearfully, in mourning attire, returns, preceded by a procession of minor person-ifications to announce the death of his beloved (*Un dì si venne a me Malinconia*), as well as the plaintive attempts of the lover that are expressed in a literary form influenced by a biblical and liturgical language

> (*Ne le man vostre, gentil donna mia,*
> *raccomando lo spirito che more:*
> *e'se ne va sì dolente ch'Amore*
> *lo mira con pietà, ch'l manda via.*
> *Voi lo legaste a la sua signoria,*
> *sì che non ebbe poi alcun valore*
> *di poter lui chiamar se non:-Signore,*
> *qualunque vuoi di me, quel vo' che sia—*);

and the solemn tone of his early references to the exalted "praise":

> *De gli occhi de la mia donna si move*
> *un lume sì gentil che, dove appare,*
> *si veggion cose ch'uom non pò ritrare*
> *per loro altezza e per lor esser nove ...*

The positive merit, the stimulating force of Cavalcanti's influence, resides in having introduced Dante into this climate of aristocratic feelings and refined literature, not in having given him at first a model of psychological patterns and dramatic solutions that represent, rather, a negative poetically stagnant aspect. Thus a way may be found to explain, at least in part, the rather enigmatic devel-opment of this friendship that Alighieri honors in secret and allusive ways in Canto X of the *Inferno*: an intimate and intense confidential relationship that comes to life on the common ground of intelligence, "nobility of mind," followed by a separation that, for the younger of the two, represents the rejection of a closed intellectual experience, of a doctrinal "Epicurean" and materialistic atti-tude and finally by silence.

It is certain that the start toward a more personal poetry occurs in the spirit of discovery that represents a return to the origin of *stilnovismo*, of the early Guido, the "father" and master who had shown the way to the new "sweet, fair verses of love." It was precisely Dante who marked the beginning of the "new rhymes" in his canzone *Donne ch'avete intelletto d'amore*, that initiates the group of the laudatory poems, from which it is impossible to separate the sonnet *Amore e il cor gentil sono una cosa*, an explicit tribute to Guinizelli's doctrine.

The importance of the two compositions is measured not only by the progress in the artistic forms but rather in the novelty of a poetic style, a mental attitude that includes virtually the gift of a new poetry. Dante acknowledges implicitly the two fundamental elements of the latter one in the famous canzone of early Guido, the equating of love's virtue with nobility, understood as a moral condition rather than as a blood inheritance, and thus love itself as a foundation of all the virtues and ways of acting of a naturally and really noble heart.

Secondly comes the exaltation of woman as an instrument of ethic perfection that is the first sign of a mystic transfiguration and liturgy of loving sentiment that Alighieri will later develop and bring to its highest level. In this case one cannot correctly speak of imitation but of a kind of congenial "mannerism", not only because Dante goes beyond the ideas brought about by the Guinizelli's canzone, that he groups and coordinates in a coherent system but also because those ideas find a close response in his sensibility and in the nature of his imagination. In this case the literary style, that is a constant element of the Dantean lyrics, is no longer an external and voluntary notion but becomes the tone and form of a delicate world of images and affection, of that fantastic and dreamy imagination that is peculiar of a novel intellectualism and the vague fervor of a youthful mind. By refusing to complicate the aspects of his psychological situation through the creation of fictitious conflicts and abstract symbols, the poet reduces his target to the praise of the angelic woman who descended miraculously from heaven to purify his heart and make it happy, reduces the structural elements of his poetry, describes his "idol" with vague lines, and portrays delicately his precious icons with soft hues against a golden background by using, as an instrument, the refined substance of the inventions and terms which constitutes the treasure of that group of poets.

And if the above quoted texts already constitute a poetic plan imbued with personal feelings, and other compositions, such as the two on a grieving Beatrice, *Voi che portate la sembianza umile* and *Se' tu colui ch'ai trattato sovente*, seem to indicate a passage from the conventional sadness of the preceding period and the full charm of the new style, other sonnets reflect, in their tenuousness, a full lyric character whereby they are justly counted in the memory of the following [generation] among the most perfect creations of the *stilnuovo* and the young Dante.

It is a minor poetry, without a doubt, that originates from an almost absurd amplification of a rarefied spiritual substance. But it would be wrong to find in it, as Croce did, an imbalance between the sentimental content and the language acquired from the school, while it is true that it is impossible to imagine its delicate and tenuous content expressed in another, less refined and elegant style as in the lines *Tanto gentile e tanto onesta pare, Ne li occhi porta la mia donna Amore, Vede perfettamente onne salute* where the structures and styles of Dante's school coincide so easily with the feelings of a poet for whom that candor, elegance and beauty were not artificial and "precious" but a spontaneous outpouring of an exalted youthful condition. By common consent, the canzone composed on the foreboding of Beatrice's death excels among the laudatory compositions, *Donna pietosa e di novella etate.* Because of the complexities of its structural elements, and its sorrowful and dramatic tone, it seems to drift away from the ecstatic atmosphere of the other compositions and indicate a return to the form of Guido's rhymes. In fact, it is true that in it Dante uses some of the forms of Cavalcanti's language. And in the dramatization of a psychological event, he surpasses Cavalcanti for his inspiration and reflects the disturbing scenes of despair of the "distressed women", the representation of the cosmic commotion and the imagery of the exalting angels that accompany the little cloud to heaven that derive directly from the contemporary painting and iconography before and during Giotto's time of the representation of the Passion, Deposition and the Ascension. Yet the canzone fits appropriately among the other laudatory compositions because it lives in the same climate of mystic exaltation and delicate affection that are so essentially remote from Cavalcanti's terse, intellectual structures. While the latter's dramatic style turns toward an abstract rigor, Dante's directs his attention to a figurative and unforeseeable form, it replaces the scientific and analytical representation with the intensity of the vision, it does not lead to a definition but to an ecstasy (*Beato, anima bella, chi te vede*), up to the reversal of the traditional idea of '*morte villana*' to that of '*morte dolce*' that has become '*cosa gentile*' as it meets with the most gentle lady. Also from a conceptual view, the theme of death, as Dante affirms repeatedly, originates naturally and spontaneously from the theme of praise. The idea of transition is implicit in the miracle of a superhuman nobility. Just because the Lady '*è disiata in sommo cielo*' her sojourn on earth must necessarily be brief and fleeting in the course of her mortal life.

Such a concept is expressly developed in the canzone written in 1290, on the occasion of Beatrice's untimely death:

> *Ita n'è Beatrice in l'alto cielo,*
> *nel reame ove li angeli hanno pace,*
> *e sta con loro e, voi, donne, ha lassate:*
> *no la ci tolse qualità di gelo*
> *nè di calore, come l'altre face,*
> *ma solo fue sua gran benignitate;*
> *chè luce de la sua umilitate*
> *passò li cieli con tanta vertute,*
> *che fè maravigliar l'etterno sire,*
> *sì che dolce disire*
> *lo giunse di chiamar tanta salute ...*

After the phase of the praises, a new one begins in Dante's poetry to which converge all the poems that were collected in the last paragraphs of *Vita nuova*, whether they describe the poet's dejection and dismay caused by the loss of Beatrice or the others that represent the brief deviations of his heart and imagination that are divided between Beatrice's image and another woman's who attracts them because of her empathy, as well as those that represent the spiritual return to the memory of the deceased Beatrice and transform that memory into a cult by preparing the hagiographic themes of *Vita nuova* and, further on, the symbolic themes developed in the *Commedia*. Also in this case, it would be difficult to say if and how far the new themes of his poetry correspond to a real change of life, to a series of precise anecdotal facts. For example, the degree of historically verifiable reality concerning the "merciful lady" that in the *Convivio* is identified with philosophy, while the spirit of the lines referring to her as well as others, including the "stony rhymes", and the late references in *Purgatorio*, lead one to imagine a moment of real sentimental deviation, such as *pargoletta o altra vanità* and false *immagini di bene*. It is certain, however, that the poems of this period indicate a more complex and less schematic psychology, a tendency to confess and unburden himself where feelings become less harsh while, on the other hand, they show evidence of an already worn literary ability, an uncertainty of formal solutions, lying in the exhausted repertory of schemes originated by the poetic school.

We are already on the way to a *stilnovismo* reduced to the role of autobiographical anecdotes that will characterize Cino's compositions. And not by chance the poet from Pistoia responds with a consoling song to Dante's canzone '*Li occhi dolenti*' that develops in a style of grave eloquence the theme of the dirge.

Undoubtedly, it will be interesting to see how sorrow, partially free from the precious character of learned poetry, regains the motives of a moved spirit, a plaintive softness that reminds one of Petrarch, yet free from the rigorous style and intense remembrance that reaches its maturity through practice, as it can be observed in the best lines of Petrarch:

> *(E quando 'l maginar mi ven ben fiso,*
> *giugnemi tanta pena d'ogne parte,*
> *ch'io mi riscuoto per dolor ch'i' sento;*
> *e sì fatto divento,*
> *che da le genti vergogna mi parte.*
> *Poscia piangendo, sol nel mio lamento*
> *chiamo Beatrice, e dico:-Or se'tu morta?-;*
> *e mentre ch'io la chiamo, me conforta);*

or, finally, in some cases, here and there, especially in the sonnet '*Oltre la spera*', where they stress new celestial visions, the elevation of the "pilgrim" soul that gazes at Beatrice's transcending beauty within the resplendent background of the Empyrean,

> *spirital bellezza grande*
> *che per lo cielo spande*
> *luce d'amor, che li angeli saluta.*

It is a fact, however, that no one of these motives reaches its full expression in the lines written between 1290 and 1292. They remain simply hints, without continuity or a broad development. Only in the most analytical and ample prose style this new material, based on psychological situations observed in their development, and in an initial narrative process, will be allowed to reach the level of a limited poetic order.

*

The *Vita nuova* was composed most likely between the end of 1292 and the early months of 1293, shortly after the events that the book describes took place. Philological topics and stylistic reasons go against any attempt to attribute it to a later date and even more so against the hypothesis that the text in our hands is a late reelaboration that might have been done at the same time of the conception and the beginning of the *Commedia*. The book contains a large amount of the earlier poems; it arranges them according to a particular chronological order, and connects them with a prose narration that clarifies their events, intentions and verses. Besides the examples that are not rare in medieval literature from Boethius on, of composite works in prose and poetry, the *vidas* and *razos*, composed along the poetical Provençal texts, represent the closest and most relevant model of the Dantean narration but for the fact that for Dante the material is autobiographical, conceived lyrically, not anecdotically, and the structure of the narration is far more organic and arranged according to a personal concept. Furthermore, every poem is followed or preceded by a "division", developed according to the rules of medieval exegesis, particularly those applied to the Holy Scriptures.

The plots of the events, on the other hand, are weak and flimsy. Dante meets Beatrice for the first time at the age of nine and, from that moment on, Love rules over his soul. He sees her again nine years later, and she greets him. (The reappearance of number nine, that will reoccur later, is explained by Dante according to his mystic interpretation of numbers, in that Beatrice is a "miracle whose roots … is only the wondrous Trinity.") Immediately after receiving her greeting, the poet has a dream that is a presage of his immutable love and of Beatrice's approaching death. One day, while he is in church looking intently at her, his attention is mistakenly considered as addressed to another woman who sits between Beatrice and the poet. He then decides "to make that gentle woman a screen of the truth", and when she leaves Florence, he composes for her and for another woman poems of courting, to increase the curious people's difficulty in guessing his secret. But this courteous device arouses people's gossip that defame him maliciously to the point that Beatrice denies him her greeting, and it will not avail him to write a ballad of apology where he declares his total dedication to her since his childhood. When Beatrice meets him at a wedding reception and notices that he is lost and shaking in her presence, she makes fun of him with the other women. He then writes two sonnets where he, addressing directly Beatrice, describes his "battle of Love", the tumult of the overbearing imagination that forcibly pulls him to the place where he can see the object of his passion as well as the confusion and bewilderment of all his senses at her sight.

Later on, when the secret of his heart is disclosed, he is questioned by some ladies about the aim, certainly "most novel," of his hopeless love for a person whose presence he cannot endure. He answers: "The aim of my love was once the greeting of this woman … and in that rests my bliss … But when she deemed to deny it, my lord Love, out of his grace, placed all my bliss in that which cannot fail me," that is, "in those words that praise my lady." He, therefore, makes the resolution to neglect from then on any other less noble topic and to "take as a topic of his poetry that which was in praise of his most gentle lady."

After he had had "for several days the desire to write and the fear to begin," one day it happened that "walking on a path along which ran a very bright rivulet," he is suddenly assailed by the desire "to speak" and his tongue moves "almost as if speaking by itself." When that early inspiration was followed by the meditation and work "of several days," he writes the canzone *Donne ch'avete intelletto d'amore*, that is followed, in a rush of great fervor, by the other parts of the praise. In the meantime, Beatrice's father dies and shortly afterwards also the poet is affected by an illness that causes him "most harsh suffering" for nine days.

While he is in this condition, and meditates on the transience of human life, he begins to think that also his lady will not be able to avoid an inexorable death. In his raving imagination he has the vision of a dead Beatrice taken to heaven by a host of hailing angels while the earth, covered in darkness, shakes frightfully, birds fall unconscious and specters of weeping and disheveled women grope in the dark. The foreboding of his vision comes true, and the gentle lady dies. By combining the elements of the Arabic calendar (ninth decade of the century), Dante sets the date of her passing on the evening of June 8, 1290. His sorrow inspires his lament *Li occhi dolenti* and other poems, where he continues on the theme of praise and on the different state of his lady that worked miracles on earth and now is blessed in heaven. Thus his grief and the eagerness to see her again in the light of paradise prompt him with equal force to call upon death also for himself "as a gentle, sweet rest." A fair amount of time after the first anniversary of Beatrice's departure, being in a place where he is bitterly stung by the recollection of the past that throws him in a "state of utter dismay," he becomes aware that a "young and beautiful gentle woman" looks at "him" from a window "so compassionately, at the sight, that it seemed all compassion had gathered in her." The paleness of her face brings to mind "the pearly complexion" of Beatrice while her sympathetic expression stirs memories of tears, it moves and comforts him at the same time.

This is the place of major novelty in the entire book, where the psychological analysis becomes subtler and soft. The ambiguity that resides in the sentimental disposition of the gentle lady, that is compassion but also love, in the poet's intention, is echoed by the ambiguity and remains cloudy in the poet's feelings. It does not constitute a new passion but the growing need of a friendly presence, a desire of consolation where the heart is progressively and unconsciously overcome while reason remains alone to resist and fight.

But one day Beatrice's image, emerging much more vividly in his imagination with the appearance he had witnessed the first time, returns to put to rout the "evil desire" and stirs up remorse in his "ashamed heart," bringing him back to his loss and his sighs. His mind, completely rapt in her thought, raises to contemplate the image of the saintly woman in her celestial glory. Then he receives the comfort of a "stupendous vision," where he perceives things that prompt him to decide "not to write any longer about the blessed one until … he could speak more suitably about her."

Contemporary criticism considers entirely useless the question that was discussed at length by the positivistic historian if *Vita nuova* should be seen as an autobiographical document, a narration of experienced events, or as an allegory, the transcription in a narrative system of the conflict between personified ideas and sentiments. Both hypotheses originated from a naïve and unprepared reading of the work where some were searching for facts, historical information, anecdotal details of a close significance while others, disappointed, rejected those data owing to the impossibility of extracting from those indefinite or imaginary elements the heart of the positive and credible reality.

While it is absurd to deny the book the basis of a real experience without which even those aspects that become disagreeable to our lives would have the appearance of mere arbitrary inventions, unjustifiable even in an allegorical plan, equally absurd would seem the attempt to find in the writer a disposition toward reality along the line of a modern autobiographical novel. The basis on which Dante operates is, in this case, as it will be later in the *Commedia*, the transformation of the biographical element in the light of a universally valid concept that is carried out with an intense trust in the conceptual values that derive from a real experience expressed through a refined and elegant literary form. The mystic, liturgical atmosphere of the narration, the intentional vagueness of places, persons and events, the hermetic language, the symbolic meanings of numbers and colors, even the doctrinal digressions on the validity of poetic personifications and the limits and objectives of the vulgar poetry, have their raison d'être in the framework of a composition that aims at depersonalizing the biographical elements by attributing to them a significance that transcends any personal interest while it ennobles, in an intrinsic and formal totality, the individual situation.

The fact that the work turns out to be "fervent and passionate," that the feeling of a restless youth does not grow weaker in the tangle of intellectual intentions and stylistic "preciosity," while the mannerism and scholasticism of the analyses reflect meekly the sentimental exaltation of the heart, all of this may appear miraculous but, instead, it is the sign of a poetic rather than of an intellectualistic nature that presides over inspiration. Intellectualism and literature are, perhaps, at the root of the life experience that feeds his poetry, a dreamed of life rather than suffering, an inner experience that resolves into a rapt reverie. More than in his lyrics, the poetic school's atmosphere is noticeable in the *Vita nuova*. This is the reason why the book represents one of the pinnacles of the *stilnovista* taste, both for maximizing the mystic exaltation of the sentiments and for developing with total coherence the foundations of a doctrine and a number of technical schemes. Affections, doctrine and literature coincide; they reinforce and foster each other in the lively experiment of the adolescent mind. Certainly, such poetry cannot be understood if one cannot enter and go beyond the cultural structure that envelops it.

Let us read one of the best episodes of the book, namely, the episode of Beatrice's greeting:

> Dico che quando ella apparia da parte alcuna, per la speranza de la mirabile salute nullo nemico mi rimanea, anzi mi giugnea una fiamma di caritate, la quale mi facea perdonare a chiunque m'avesse offeso; e chi allora m'avesse domandato di cosa alcuna, la mia risponsione sarebbe stata solamente "Amore", con viso vestito d'umilitade.
>
> E quando ella fosse alquanto propinqua al salutare, uno spirito d'amore, distruggendo tutti li altri spiriti sensitivi, pingea fuori li deboletti spiriti del viso, e dicea loro:- Andate a onorare lo donna vostra-; ed elli si rimaneva nel luogo loro. E chi avesse voluto conoscere Amore, fare lo potea mirando lo tremare de li occhi miei. E quando questa gentilissima salute salutava, non che Amore fosse tal mezzo che potesse obumbrare a me la intollerabile beatitudine, ma elli quasi per soverchio di dolcezza divenia tale, che lo mio corpo, lo quale era tutto allora sotto lo suo reggimento, molte volte si movea come cosa grave inanimata. Si che appare manifestamente che ne le sue salute abitava la mia beatitudine, la quale molte volte passava e redundava la mia capacitade.

Even by a casual analysis of this passage, there stands out in this place as well as in the most moving passages of the book the tendency of the language to turn into metric forms that are more or less identifiable. Here is a sequence that, although unchanged, may be reduced to a series of hendecasyllables: "*e chi allora m'avesse domandato/di cosa alcuna, la mia risponsione/sarebbe stata solamente "Amore,/"con viso vestito d'umiltate.*" Other hendecasyllables appear here and there in the story (*li deboletti spiriti del viso," "andate a onorar(e) la donna vostra," Far(e) lo potea mirando lo tremare," "redundava la mia capacitade,*" etc. mostrly coinciding with the syntactical rules. The rhetorical education appears through its refined language, more poetic than prosaic, rich in classical and scriptural Latin forms (*risponsione, propinqua, obumbrare, redundare, abitare, far stare*) embellished by images drawn from a lyrical tradition, particularly Cavalcanti's (*fiamma di caritade, viso vestito d'umilitade, spirito d'amore,* that *distruggendo tutti li altri spiriti sensitivi, pingea fuori li debiletti spiriti del viso ... ed elli si rimanea nel luogo loro,* and similar forms of psychological representation portrayed by images and personifications.) One should add that the entire passage rests on a real pun (the double meaning of the word *salute,* commonly found in the Latin and Provençal literature that was favored by the Florentine language of the time) ending in the pattern that is a sort of etymological figure: "*Questa gentilissima salute salutava. N*or are images left out of the usage of the time, such as that of the body that "*molte volte si movea come cosa grave inanimata,*" a simile used by the first and later Guido.

Passing from the analysis of the form to that of the structure, one should point out a sentimental experience by an objective representation, "scientific" as it were from which arise the rigor of the internal distinctions and parallellisms: three situations (*quando ella appariva da parte alcuna; quando ella fosse alquanto propinqua al salutare; quando questa gentilissima salute salutava*) that correspond to three degrees or shades of the feeling (*fiamma di caritade, trepida aspettazione, soverchia di dolcezza*) *and three suitable physical expressions (viso vestito d'umilitade, tremare de li occhi*) and the body that becomes (*come cosa grave inanimata.*)

Better than in a lyrical "movement," the narration ends in a clarifying demonstration framed between the preceding description (*voglio dare a intendere quello che lo suo salutare in me vertuosamente operava*) in the last sentence of the preceding paragraph and that sort of "*quod erat demonstrandum*" that ends the entire passage: "*Sì che appare manifestamente che ne le sue salute abitava la mia beatitudine.*" Far from being unusual, this analytical process could be easily repeated for all the most beautiful pages of the book: the joke (XIV), the illness (XXIII), the episode of the compassionate lady (XXXV–XXXVIII) and so on. It destroys only apparently the poetry of *Vita Nuova*; at the most it shows its limitations within the picture of a culture determined historically in its rhetoric and style.

Within the limits of an historically determined culture, the allusive strength of the book and its historical/literary importance remain intact. With respect to the earlier prose attempts in the vulgar language, wanting and awkward as they were, the poetic prose of *Vita nuova* constitutes an absolute innovation, a stroke of genius. And not less notable is the fact that that model of literary idealization and stylization of an autobiographical work will inspire, more or less directly, many writers of the centuries to follow. It will be sufficient to mention, among those where the influence is more evident and close, Boccaccio in *Filocolo* and *Ameto* and Sannazzaro in *Arcadia*.

*

The *Vita nuova* is the conclusion of a period of Dante's biography, a human and literary biography, the experience of a love that is exalted to the limits of hagiography as well as of a technique, the *stilnuovo*, that was accepted and experienced with zeal and determination, quite free from self-indulgence but inspired by the desire to experiment and try innovative forms that, in turn, offer the writer a model and bestow upon him the function and dignity of a leader. Such had this work to appear in Dante's eyes when, as he reconsidered and judged it later in *Convivio*, he contrasted it as a "fervent and passionate" work written "at the outset of his youth" with the "tempered and manly" style that was his in the age of maturity and reflection. It was to remain in his memory forever, united with the human experience that it embodied, almost as a mirror and symbol of a spiritual condition that is originally pure and virtuous, of which one may lose sight for a while, but that remains alive in the depth of the soul, to re-emerge in our conscience at the time of repentance and conversion.

There is no point in dwelling excessively on the well known places in *Purgatorio*, C. XXX and XXXI, where Beatrice reproaches Dante the character for having strayed from her soon after her death in order to pursue false images of young maidens and other "vain things," thus going little by little down toward sin, reaching almost the edge of damnation, from which he would be saved only in 1300 by the last-minute intervention of Grace. Ten years of obliteration of Good, therefore, that is the real truth, and the abandonment of the right way in behalf of the ephemeral worldly pleasures. Moral corruption, namely dissipation of affection and senses in favor of frivolous loves and worldly pleasures? Intellectual corruption or pride of intelligence that penetrates the maze of speculating and dialectical games on the verge of religious indifference, doubt or heresy? We only know for certain that just in those years Dante's personality and culture are maturing through an unusually close interaction with the life of the contemporary society. On one hand, it becomes associated, through deep and intransigent commitment, with the *comune*'s political problems and the government itself; on the other, it applies itself seriously to reading and meditating over the works of philosophers and theologians while consolidating his experience of poetic technique through the discovery of the classical authors and the major Provençal writers.

There is no doubt that these larger mental and practical interests that were maturing in the young man's mind involved renouncing the strict rigor and the abstract purity of adolescence and shifting from introversion to a condition of lively and varied curiosity for the external world, different incentives and contrasting inducements. It is also quite likely that Dante experienced moments of laxity, or mental and spiritual wavering. Yet, from a biographical viewpoint, it is not correct to read beyond the limits of confirmed data, nor to consider his poetry as a document and even less to superimpose the real Dante over the protagonist of the *Commedia*, or build up events on the themes developed in the verses. Or better, one might say, at the most, that the poems of these ten years indicate a remarkable expansion, an extraordinary mutability of attitudes along with a lesser sentimental engagement, an experimental disposition that is typical of all of Dante's poetry and are emphasized in this case. Attempts and experiments follow one another and overlap in rapid sequence. However, he who sets about establishing a thematic order, a classification and chronicle of these lyrics, will have to refrain from making hypotheses of a biographical nature that are frequently extravagant, and adopt as an exclusive principle, the intimate reasons concerning their content and style. On a stylistic ground, some groups are self-defined, with obvious characteristics, such as the sonnets to Forese and the "stony" rhymes.

In other cases it is the author's explicit statements that lead us to establish relationships and connections, as in the case of the cycle that begins with *Voi che 'ntendendo*, written in praise of a gentle lady who represents allegorically Philosophy. A separate group is represented by the doctrinal canzoni on nobility and loveliness, even though one leaves out of consideration the subject matter and includes just the forms of expression.

Finally, it may occur that an apparent affinity and correspondence of themes considered in abstract, may induce the historian to gather in the same group compositions that are not altogether uniform, such as the lyrics on the "young lady," and in this conclusion arbitrariness already would play a large role.

In the latter group it is usual to include, after Barbi's direction, two ballads, a sonnet and the two canzoni *Amor, che movi* and *Io sento sì d'amor la gran possanza*. Of the last two, one is typically didactic, "a subtle and philosophical comparison of the sun's and Love's effects," as Leonardo Bruni already indicated in the fifteenth century; the other, that celebrates through reasoning rather than representation, a most noble and difficult love, leaves in the reader a strong allegorical impression and might very well go together with the other allegorical canzoni on Philosophy.

As for the ballads, they revisit the linguistic and metaphorical material of the *stilnuovo* composers on the basis of an abstract, cold exaltation to end in an image that gradually turns into a symbol. This figure of the "beautiful and young woman," whose youth makes her reluctant and untamed, proud and cruel, constitutes the relative unity of the group. It is entirely arbitrary to identify her with the Stone that is central in another group of stylistically different compositions. At most, its way of employing and exhausting the *stilnovista* formal instruments in an entirely intellectual and logical condition suggests a matching with the allegorical lyrics, yet the uncertainty always remains about the appropriateness to classify in the same section a series of poems that show among them somewhat different characteristics.

It is important to remark, however, that both the lyrics for the "beautiful and new young woman" and those for the gentle lady Philosophy, allegorical by the author's explicit admission, reflect the transition undergone by Dante in those years from courtly love poetry to that based on moral themes that is, in a cultural and historical sense, an amplification and enrichment of intellectual interests and the conquest of a new dimension that had remained precluded in the young poet's experience. Such a transition, at first, seems to be the application of an acquired technique to the new subject matter and is developed in the great allegorical canzoni, and, along with them, through the myth of a powerful woman of a superhuman virtue, who forebodes salvation of the heart provided that it submit to her stern rule and agree to proceed along the way of a devotion harsh, difficult, excluding and persevering.

Such a myth implies also a kind of abstract conflict between the real and symbolic lady, between Beatrice and the gentle lady (that Dante will identify in the *Convivio* with the compassionate lady of the *Vita nuova*), a conflict that is variously portrayed in the canzone *Voi che 'ntendendo* and in a few sonnets that should be considered with the other, most elegant sonnet, about Lisetta's amorous temptations.

But the personal struggle and the hesitation that in the episode of the *Vita nuova* was a human and painful sentimental experience, is renewed in this composition in the form of intellectual abstraction and the conflict is resolved in the conscience of the adult poet who has renounced the dogmatic rigor of the school and is now open to a variety of interests and research. "Two women" may share a primary place in the mind: one with her loveliness and kindness opens the way to pleasure and courteousness, the other with her prudence and rectitude shows him the path to virtue and rules its practical performance; "perfect love" becomes both [for]

> *ch'amar si può bellezza per diletto*
> *e puossi amar virtù per operare.*

Also the cult of Philosophy is Love: from the very seed of love poetry, in unchanged forms and language, blossoms the ideal that Dante will define in the *De vulgari eloquentia* as "cantor rectitudinis."

As a matter of fact, that direction allowed Alighieri only a partial and indirect treatment of the subject that interested him. At most, it allowed him to express his new enthusiasm for Philosophy and the anguish of his heart for the difficulties and the dangers of the way he had just taken up but it did not permit him to introduce in his poetry the substance of his meditations that his mind had favored when, after Beatrice's death, he had buried himself for relief in the reading of Boethius and Cicero and had started to attend "the schools of the clericals" and the "disputations of the philosophers" so ardently and tenaciously that "in a short time, thirty months perhaps," he had become capable of understanding the entire charm of that study. But, because of the intense reading and the long waking, he had caught a bad illness of the eyes. Even his enthusiasm and novice's fears, converted into the schemes of the language of love, still contained abstract and oratorical elements.

Thus one should consider as progress, even poetically, the shift to the doctrinal canzoni, where Dante confronts deliberately the topics of his meditations and the elements of his altered culture. Renouncing the allegorical disguise, the writer declares that he wants to abandon also his "gentle style" and the "sweet verses" in order to adopt, instead, "a harsh and subtle poetry." Having set aside his repertory of images and eloquence of sentiments, he will develop a stark web of ideas, through a process of discussions and distinctions in accord with the texts of contemporary philosophers and theologians.

The canzone *Le dolci rime* considers the Aristotelic definition of "nobility," conceived as "virtus et divitiae antiquae," an ornament of fair customs and a quality of acquired wealth (a definition that, at that time, Dante attributed erroneously to Emperor Frederick of Swabia). He maintains that the element of wealth and inheritance is entirely extraneous to the concept of nobility, that it cannot originate with its presence nor remove it from those who have it, if it disappears. Nobility, therefore, is an individual gift, an immense source of virtue placed in the soul by God, aside from any issue of race or family.

The other canzone, *Poscia ch'Amor,* considers loveliness, arguing against the common belief that identifies it with mad prodigality, vain personal ornaments and even the frivolous and dishonest behavior of the worldly individual and defines it in scholastic terms as a manifold concept where virtue or perfect behavior, happiness and love converge in the person of the excellent knight. In both compositions the attitude, above all, or rather the highly polemical idea is notable; it is the sign, in turn, of an aristocratic and disdainful sense of philosophical truth. The very choice of themes shows how Dante approached speculative practice, not to use it as idle dialectical digression but to use it in order to solve the difficulties of real problems and interpret the norms of the civic and social conditions of his time. Thus, the theoretical discussion concludes in the final strophe of every canzone in a type-portrait, the noble and the handsome men, described in the moods of their daily behavior. "Poetic prose," admittedly, "where the rhyme functions as ornamental and mnemonic instrument," according to Croce's fitting definition. But just in that prose, and in the effort to bend the poetic language and the metre according to the requirements of rationalization, one should notice, beyond the intensity of the contents, also the precise search for a lexical and syntactical enrichment. It was the first but awkward step toward the acquisition of a terse and rich expository and didactical language of certain places in the *Commedia*.

The dispute with Forese and the stony rhymes gave rise to hypothetical reconstructions of a biographical and anecdotal nature, the former and the latter ones considered as documents of a moral laxity for reasons of content where the first shows a vulgar topic and the lowly tone of mockery and the others a violent and fierce sensual passion. Yet, the characteristic that is prominent in both groups is the novelty and the zeal of the technical experimentation, the more or less clear intention to enrich the number of the means of expression, an eminently literary attitude that in one case starts from the style of the farcical poets, in the footsteps of Rustico [di Filippo] and Cecco [Angiolieri] and in the other from the familiarity with the superior and more authentic Provençal poets of the golden age, particularly Arnaut Daniel. This does not mean that those Dantean rhymes may be reduced, as it is customary at present, to mere stylistic exercises. Denying a priori the presence of concrete inspiration is, at least, an arbitrary concept and the value of the results that were achieved, also in a stylistic sense, validates its necessity.

It is precisely the degree of maturity and formal skill that appears clearly in them that convinces us about the validity of the chronological hypothesis that sets the composition of the sonnets to Forese between '93 and '96. Certainly there is only the *ad quem* term concerning the friend's date of death in '96, but the relationship between the two poets might have begun much earlier, a few years before '90, when Dante, by marrying Gemma, established some family ties with the main branch of the Donati family.

It is not the case of considering too seriously the insults the two relatives exchange with each other (Dante blames Forese for marital impotency, gluttony, debts and his and his relatives' violent and thieving habits while he expresses doubts on the legitimacy of his origin; Forese turns against Dante the accusations of being needy and a beggar and adds also cowardice, with an unclear reference to a revenge that Alighieri should have carried out but did not because of a certain wrong that was done to his father). Even if the tone of derision and the malice of the allusions seem to become serious to the point of libel, they still remain within the limits of a genre where it was naturally appropriate to have an exaggerated, ludicrous tone and the overstatements of the low-class speech.

It is unfortunate that another sonnet written by Dante to Cecco Angiolieri was lost, because it might have offered us a similar example of Dante's use of the bourgeois poets' style. But the response of the Sienese, who rebuts by accusing Dante of a quackish attitude and bragging, sponging and effrontery helps us, at least in part, to reconstruct its contents and tone.

Comparing Forese's heedless and awkward, chatty and poor creativity with Dante's, the art of the latter emerges in the dispute with quick and clever retorts, the hidden fierceness of the insulting allusions that appears within the most elaborate technique of the obscure and arcane language: it is a coarse jargon held in place by a most skilled *ars dictandi*. We are already on the way that ends with certain representations in the lower hell, in the pits of the seducers and flatterers, barrators and, above all, the falsifiers, in the lewd quarrel between Synon and Master Adam.

The experience of the stony poems, however, occurs at an even higher level, about the lyrics composed for a young woman named Pietra (In Italian *pietra* means stone, tr.), whether this is her true name or a *senhal*, consistent, in any case, with the cold, insensitive and unmerciful disposition of the character. The interpretation of the astral figure, at the beginning of one of them, refers us to December 1296. Such date, that can be extended to the composition of the other poems of that group, given the extreme coherence of this technical episode, corresponds generally to the most plausible demands of an ideal chronology and to what Dante will state in the *De vulgari eloquentia*, where the stony lyrics hinted at as a bold test, *novum aliquid atque intentatum artis*, of a young knight on the day of his investiture; therefore it will not be appropriate to put its date of composition after the poet's exile.

Also in the *De vulgari eloquentia*, Dante stresses the technical and metric aspects of these verses: the *nimia eiusdem rithimi repercussio*, namely the obsessive repetition of the rhyme-word, the *stantia sine rithimo* and *sine iteratione modulationis cuiusquam*, namely the unrhymed strophes without internal symmetry or distinction of melodic phrases; in short, the six-line stanza for which the poet follows Arnaud and declares himself his disciple and imitator, *et nos eum secuti sumus*. The point of departure resides in the taste of a laborious and valiant exercise. In this case it could be said that the stony rhymes end an episode of marked technicality with the canzone patterned on a double six-line stanza, *Amor, tu vedi ben*, that is actually a play along the lines of Arnaud's model, and beyond, a play on metrics, language, and an intellect that invents poetic patterns. It brings about a flowing and merging of the various elements whereby the difficulty of the metric system (sixty lines based only on five rhyme-words) generates the idea of the ambiguous rhymes. Furthermore, the search for harmony and linguistic continuity leads to the preciosity of the rhymes and the abstrusity of concepts. The intellectual taste, finally, dominates everything and is its primary reason for including both metric and verbal technicalities. In the sextet *Al poco giorno* and in the canzone *Io son venuto al punto de la rota*, however, technicality becomes functional vis-à-vis creative imagination and the rhyme-word becomes image-word both in the former where it leads in an analogous process the alteration of the visual and sentimental situation, and in the latter where it reflects the constant presence of a state of mind, the tyranny of love inspiration.

Finally, in the other canzone, *Così nel mio parlar*, although Dante does not reject the difficult subject matter, he deviates from Arnaud's model and follows his own way where the accentuation of his style blends with that of sensitivity. The attractiveness of these poems cannot be explained only by their refined and elaborate elegance. They will influence poetry amply and deeply up to Petrarch and his followers. Their poetic and historical importance consists of the discovery of a broader area of sensitivity and an incipient dramatic character of his poetic invention. Initially there appear natural views, places and seasons—skies saddened by rain, hills withered by winter or in bloom in spring, expanses of water looking like glass because of the cold, valleys ensconced in the impending shadow of the mountains—portrayed with that terse, limpid clearness that concentrates on the sharpness of the individual word and reappears in the places of the *Commedia* where Dante's imagination becomes more elegant and metaphysical in its descriptions, at once rich and fantastic. And particularly in the canzone *Così nel mio parlar*, there surfaces the evidence of a psychology that is tormented, upset, a metaphorical transcription, bold and violently sensual. In the awareness of a fully acquired formal ability, his poetry finds verbal impulses, drives and violent terms and rhymes that reappear in some situations of the *Inferno*:

> *Così vedess'io lui fender per mezzo*
> *lo core a la crudele che 'l mio squatra ...*
> *Omè, perchè non latra*
> *per me, com'io per lei, nel caldo borro?*

In one with the maturing and enrichment of the stylistic and rhetorical devices that already appear in the poet's work of the years preceding his exile, others are developed such as doctrinal and philosophical learning, moral and political experience that will act in Dante's mind more slowly but deeply, whose fruits will become fully apparent only in his later literary works, from the *Convivio* to the *Monarchia* and the *Commedia*.

It is hard to give an exact picture of Dante's culture outside his literary knowledge, its development and limits, because the latter ones always assist us in finding the sources of his knowledge and ideas but only generically and without precision. As for chronology, it is evident that we are confronted by a process that finds its sources in early youth, if not in infancy, of the writer and continues to the very end of his life in the process of new readings and the reconsideration of solutions that he had accepted temporarily.

A comparative study, however summary, of a few main points considered in several works through time, could give us an idea of this cultural evolution considered both in its informative foundation and in its speculative substance. The definition of nobility against which Dante argues in the canzone *Le dolci rime*, was attributed by him, at that time, to Frederick II, and such attribution continued to be accepted by Dante also in the years when he wrote the *Convivio*. Only while he was writing the *Monarchia* did he appear to be aware that the definition went back to Aristotle's *Politics*. The way in which he dealt with the issue of the Empire in the *Monarchia* itself, compared with the one similar in many ways to that of the fourth book of the *Convivio*, reveals not only an evident change of perspective on practical and polemical grounds, but a theoretical deepening and considerable broadening of its cultural background.

Even certain secondary topics that are discussed in the early theoretical writings, such as the doctrine about the moon spots and that of the angelic orders in the *Convivio*, as well as the one concerning Adam's language in the *De vulgari eloquentia*, are given a different explanation in the *Commedia* and the poet himself stresses the resumption of the topic and the reconsideration of the concepts that he had adopted earlier. In a general sense, there is a clear development not only of his intellectual and sentimental attitudes but also in the amount of knowledge and thought, from one book to the other, up to the supreme synthesis of the *Commedia*, and in the time of its composition that covered an intricate and long period of years. It is quite dangerous, therefore, to try to indicate precisely the chronologic order and the origin of the individual facts that contribute to the formation of his cultural richness.

What Dante conforms, however, is beyond doubt and is confirmed completely in an unbiased review of his writings, namely, that the most important and meaningful change of this cultural process occurred during the years that followed immediately Beatrice's death, with Alighieri's fervent and enthusiastic approach to the sources of philosophical and theological thinking.

The cultural basis that we can infer from a careful reading of the *Vita nuova*, is essentially poetic and rhetorical. It is based on the knowledge of the Sicilian and Tuscan lyrical tradition viewed as an element connected with topics of love on a somewhat vague and indirect knowledge of Provençal literature (for the troubadours of the golden time were read and understood completely only at the time of the stony rhymes), and based as well on an elementary reading of the most popular Latin poets, from Ovid and Virgil to Horace and Lucan, still considered on totally external and anecdotal grounds rather than within the organic framework of an historical and cultural interpretation. One should consider also the experience of the *ars dictandi* and art prose in one with an intense and deliberate return to the Holy Scripture. It is a cultural view that, apart from its uncommon intensity of sentimental participation, it reflects the eclecticism and the slightly thin and widespread curiosity of a certain literary environment. Equal contributors were Brunetto, with his pre-humanistic inclinations and encyclopedic knowledge as well as the Guittonian and the *stil nuovo* poets, while the doctrine of the "religious" and the "philosophizing" group remains excluded. In the "libel," Aristotle is mentioned only once, and probably not directly, concerning one of his most obvious and repeated propositions. The doctrinal digressions appear "attached" to the context externally, in a naïve display of knowledge and are developed in an elementary fashion lacking solid and concrete information and keen and original reflection. Only after committing the *Vita nuova* to paper, the fundamental change in Dante's knowledge that was mentioned previously came about. We shall not be far from the truth if we accept plainly the author's assertion where he informs us that after Beatrice's death "the star of Venus had turned twice in its orbit, that shows it in the evening and the morning, at different times," when that gentle woman appeared to him who in the *Convivio* is revealed as Philosophy, and he began to find some consolation in reading Boethius and Cicero's *De amicitia*. Then, when he joined the schools of the philosophers and theologians, "in a short time, perhaps thirty months," he became immersed in that field of study and became familiar with them, in other words between the summer of 1293 and the early months of 1296. It was exactly at that time that he added [the study] of the prose, moral and history writers of the classic time, from Cicero to Seneca, from Horosius to Boethius, to the knowledge of the vulgar poets and the major Latin writers. And, at the same time, Aristotelic commentaries, treatises, issues, summae, a number of new problems and, more importantly, a governing sense of order, distinction, internal organization and hierarchical arrangement of knowledge entered and occupied a prominent place in his education.

Even in this case it will not be easy to specify the content and the sources of his philosophical investigation. [Studies] have been dwelling even too much, or better, too exclusively, on the influence of Thomas Aquinas of whom Dante mentions only the commentary of the *Ethics* and the *Summa contra gentiles*. Yet he must have known also the major *summa* and the other commentaries, as well as some of his pamphlets and *"quaestiones."* Together with Thomist learning, other no less important factors should be considered, above all Albertus Magnus who was thoroughly known owing to his treatises on physics and natural science, Averroës and Avicenna, the surviving texts of neoplatonism, from the anonymous *De causis* to the pseudo-Dionysus the Areopagite. Furthermore, from the conclusion reached by the scholastics, it is certain that he may have considered the works of early medieval philosophy, Anselm from Aosta, Richard from San Vittore, Peter Lombard and patristic philosophy, especially Augustine. He may have been attracted also to the direct study of Aristotle's works. Nor could he have been unaware of the other, contemporary trend of thought, quite distinct from Thomism, of the Franciscan doctors, such as Bonaventura and Matthew from Acquasparta.

The development of Dante's philosophical knowledge was certainly more varied and richer, even more eclectic, than it was, and is often, indicated by insufficient or biased information. At any rate, what should be stressed mostly is the directness with which Alighieri, in his initiation in philosophy, tends immediately toward the most modern and keen theories of the time. It ought to be noted that the renewal of speculative concepts and theology based on the Aristotelic foundation and the Arabian exegesis, was a recent phenomenon that was barely starting to make headway in the schools and met with difficulty and opposition. Aquinas and Albert had died not long before as had that Peter of Spain who contrasted said renewal in each one of his writings while the doctrines of the new school, far from being systematized in an official, commonly accepted view, were the subjects of controversies, acrimonious debates and even ecclesiastical penalties. We should also consider that the formulation of the system and the method had really to be, as Dante says, quite rapid for in his canzoni on gentleness and beauty he shows how easily he can use scholastic terminology.

From the same canzoni there appears also the attitude toward his interest in science, that did not constitute a haven of abstract contemplation but a way to apply it to problems of moral behavior and social life and derive a logical norm for concrete activity as well as the typology of a virtuous man and true knight, while he considers polemically the difference between ideal and real, theory and practice. Speculative interest, ethical and political experience are, from the beginning, closely connected and mutually involved.

*

The period of Dante's active political involvement, the only one that shows his commitment in a concrete action within the framework of a society and public organization having internal clashes and well defined and circumscribed problems, is entirely limited to a few years, from 1295 to 1304. From the defeat that concluded that activity and from the final disappointment that affects, without repudiating it, the whole development of that experience, the opposing factions, the friends and foes, and the very principle of communal autonomy, a new man will emerge who directs his ethical and political passion toward a universal message, above any contingent issue. Yet, without that ten-year long experience, it would be difficult to understand also the prophet, the utopian and the poet of exile.

It is true that in the exiled poet whose country is the whole world, "*velut piscibus equor,*" the Florentine remains tied to his land to the end by an intimate nostalgia and a grudging and cruel affection, and [it is equally a fact] that the new ideals reach far wider horizons than the theories of the *Monarchia* to make him the stern judge of the *Commedia*, penetrating into the pain of his defeat and the bitterness of that disappointment in order to raise them as images and symbols of universal decadence and corruption.

It is likely that since his young age Dante harbored in his mind the essence of that citizen pride that was fueled by the legends of the "Trojans, of Fiesole and of Rome," and by the Guelph tradition that, emerging victorious just then from a harsh struggle, seemed to embody the growing prosperity and the proud liberty of the commune. The lower aristocracy, to which he belonged, free from a feudal past and rising ambitiously, was likely to identify its origin and the source of its distinction in that pride and tradition, as they had evolved in the practice of war and government, even though the recent corporative laws, instituted by Giano della Bella, by concentrating within the arts the wielding of power, allowed a limited segment of the commune administration to these impoverished aristocrats who drew their unsteady means of subsistence from land revenues rather than from trade and industry. For this reason came their nostalgic dreams of the order and customs of the past generation, when their authority was still strong and recognized, when class conflicts were not so harsh, life was "reposeful" and "fair," the community "trusty" and "pure" to the humblest artisan. This nostalgic emotion must have been felt by Dante at an early age and it was to reappear in Cacciaguida's sad remembrance.

Soon after Giano's expulsion, when a law that was passed in July 1295 opened the door to councils and public positions for those nobles who were not prominent and who became members of one of the guilds (arts) even without practicing it, Dante enrolled in the guild of the Apothecaries probably as a practitioner of philosophical studies and thus became able to participate actively in political life. In the semester running from November 1295 to April 1296, he was a member of the special council of the People's Captain (the city's military authority) in December 1295, as one of the district representatives and was asked to be a member of a council charged to establish the procedures to elect the Priors. Between May and September 1296 he was a member of the Council of the Hundred that established the funding and the fundamental policies of the commune's politics. Nor did his activity slow down in the following years but, on the contrary, his authority increased and gained considerable importance for in May 1300 he was sent as an ambassador to San Gimignano at a time when Florence was anxious to strengthen the league with the minor Guelph communes in Tuscany for the defense of their autonomy. In the same year he was elected prior for two months, from June 15 to August 15.

It is not possible to attribute to Dante the common characteristics of a professional politician: ability to maneuver successfully among the factional intrigues and covert plots and shrewdness and quickness in sudden and timely decisions according to the convenience of the moment. Perhaps he lacked also a realistic view of the situation: his controversy, indignation, predictions and reproaches always went beyond the limits of factual reality, they were out of touch with the real historical flow, they did not concern the present time even though they revealed a keen farsightedness and a broad analytical power. The fact is that, in his mind, there arose the awareness of a crisis in the communal circles, unnoticed and hidden for the time being, but destined to come to a head rapidly. Perhaps nobody more than this Florentine, imprudent manager of his future and reckless judge of the nearing destiny of his city as he was, had such a clear and visionary intuition, albeit distorted and apocalyptic, of the profound inadequacy and weakness of the commune's institutions and of its incapacity to insure permanent order and justice in both internal and external relations.

In those years the issue still appeared in his mind within the narrow limits of the city scope, as a necessity to insure, by strengthening cohesion within single interests and desires, the state's autonomy especially toward the growing threat of preponderant external forces that appeared to be invested within the prestige of a universal supremacy: the Empire and the Papacy. In this contingency, his attitude coincided with that sentiment of jealous freedom that at that time was extremely keen in his fellow Florentines, in that Florence that since 1281, in response to the emissary of Rudolph of Hapsburg, had proudly affirmed its sovereignty before the jurists' formulae that later were to set the theory of *civitas sibi princeps* "*Nunquam comune Florentie fidelitatem fecit aliqui imperatori, ... quia semper vixit et fuit liberum,*" and that in 1313 had fiercely opposed the demands and siege of Harry VII. As the imperial throne was vacant (by right, owing to the missed crowning of *German* Albert, and de facto, because of his lack of interest in Italian events), the menace against the commune's liberty took shape in the action of Pope Boniface VIII who, relying on the *plenitudo potestatis* doctrine and claiming, on account of the imperial vacancy, the function of emperor's vicar, openly aimed at securing in behalf of the Church her hegemony over the communes of central Italy and Tuscany in particular. His shrewd and compliant politics benefited from the internal clashes of the cities maneuvering in a smart play among opposing factions. But it also confirmed, in the irreducibility of those conflicts and impending threat of anarchy, the principles of a superior justice and the idea of a universal authority entrusted with the protection of everybody's rights against the arbitrary demands of national or city states: "*Quis errata corriget per civitates et loca provincie Tuscie, et relevabit oppressos, si ad nos non possit recursus haberi?*"

They are principles and concepts that Dante resumed later, albeit within a more appropriate sphere, when, in the name of the empire he reconsidered the demands of its particular power with absolute liberty but on the ground of a complete objectivity, above the factions and biased decisions of the individual states, *civitates et regna*.

In the meantime, the Pope's clever reference to dissent and injustices relating to the struggle among the largest and smaller communes and within each commune between parties and families and even more, the awareness of the opportunity that such circumstances offered to the intrigues and intrusions of an outside authority, had to promote a political approach that supported peace and order among factions and brought about the defense of autonomy. From the scarce data that may be obtained from archival sources, all of Dante's political activity seemed to be based on these essential principles. During his term as a prior, continuing along the signiory's preceding direction, he and his colleagues endeavored to break down the intrigues of Matteo d'Acquasparta, the papal legate, thus facing the risk of excommunication and interdict (that were actually decided shortly after the end of his term in office) and took steps to soothe the minds by banishing the most turbulent leaders of the opposing factions among whom was also his friend Guido. At a later time, as a member of the Council of the Hundred, from April to September 1301, he opposed the decision to continue the military assistance granted to the pope two months earlier for his intervention against the Aldobrandeschi, in Maremma, as well as when he spoke in September of the same year in a meeting of all councils, that had been called for the purpose of establishing the necessary means to safeguard the judicial norms and the people's statute.

As usual, the political strife within the commune assumed the nature of a conflict between two powerful families or political cliques by using as an excuse hatred and private revenge, the Cerchi and Donati (White and Black, as they were named later by borrowing the names from the parties neighboring Pistoia). However, as Compagni suggests, many citizens sided with the Cerchi because of agreement or dependence, as well as "all those who shared Giano della Bella's position," and "regretted his expulsion" and "all Ghibellines, because they hoped they would be hurt less by them." The Donati, more daring and violent and openly prepared to subvert the established order, were supported by several among the great [families] and many people of the middle classes.

Although Dante intended to keep above party lines, he had to side with the more moderate one that appeared less dangerous for the order of the state, even more so when it became clear that the Neri, to secure their triumph, were ready to become tools of the papal goals and accept the help and the suggestions of Boniface VIII. It is probable, however, that from that time he judged severely the uncertain and fearful action of the Cerchi, because of their ineptitude in putting deliberately an end to their opponents' schemes, in taking a deliberate stand against the papal claims and in securing in case of need the concrete support of their friends in Pistoia, Pisa and Arezzo and the Ghibellines' alliance.

As Charles of Valois was moving toward Florence in October 1301, called to Italy by Boniface VIII after the Angevins' conquest of Sicily and appointed papal legate with the apparent charge of bringing peace among the Florentine factions but in reality, to effect the Neri's victory and open the gates to the Church's hegemony in Tuscany, Dante was one of the three ambassadors selected by the seigniory to go to Rome in order to placate the pope's wrath. And, once in Rome, he was kept back by the Curia even after his two colleagues, more compliant and involved in secret schemes with the Donati's side, were permitted to return to Florence.

In the meantime, Charles of Valois did not find it difficult to overcome the weak opposition of the seigniory and the Whites, who constituted its main support. Once in Florence, he recalled Corso Donati with the other previously banished Black leaders, and entrusted to them the government of the commune.

Straight after there began the plundering of houses and property, fires and thefts, persecutions and summary trials of the opposing party for which the Blacks found an obedient tool in the *podestà*, Cante dei Gabrielli from Gubbio.

It seems that Dante never returned to Florence and was probably in Siena when he learned of the verdict of January 27, 1302, according to which he was sentenced in his absence, together with other persons, to a fine, a two-year exile and perpetual barring from [public] offices, under the common charge of corruption in public office, actions against the pope and the peacemaker and schemes with the intent to disturb the city's peace. As he did not appear to pay his fine and free himself from blame, a second sentence on March 10 condemned him to be burned alive if he had fallen in the hands of the commune.

It was obvious that at first he accepted the consequences of a sentence that involved him in the destiny of a faction whose intentions he was far from sharing in full. One can see him take part in the early attempts to return to Florence by force. He is, in fact, one of the more authoritative figures of that *Universitas partis Alborum*, that consists of the Cerchi's supporters in an alliance with the Ghibellines. As such, in June 1302, he participated in the convention of San Godenzio in Mugello in order to promise the Ubaldini a guarantee on the possible damage they might incur in the war against Florence. In 1303 he is in Forlì as a secretary of Scarpetta Ordelaffi, leader of the exiles. In the early months of 1304, he formulates in behalf of all the letter to Cardinal Niccolò da Prato, entrusted by the new pope Benedict XI to lead the agreement negotiations between the commune and the exiles. Since the peacemaker's mission failed, the war was rapidly nearing its end and on July 20, 1304, the Whites suffered the final defeat at Lastra. Dante had already parted from the "wicked and senseless company," and his tepid liking for the Cerchi had already turned into harsh disapproval. As some ancient commentaries indicate, his reservations and objections concerning the military and political actions of the exiles had been interpreted by the latter ones as signs of defection and treason, to the point of causing them to persecute him and wish for his death. From 1304 on, Dante is alone, and he begins his painful peregrination that was to take him "through almost all the lands reached by this language," wandering, almost like "a beggar," as "a ship without sails or direction, driven to different ports, lands and shores by the dry wind blown by grievous poverty."

*

The canzone of the *Three Ladies,* the most famous among those composed by Dante, aptly portrays his bitter and dignified loneliness, and the pain of an endured injustice and the ever open wound of his nostalgia for everything he cherished. [He missed] the objects and the persons he had to leave behind and he felt above all the pride of keeping apart and was aware of being among the very few who, in a world where vice and injustice triumph, always fought for justice and honesty. The urging in the second envoy (whether it is or not a later addition) addressed to the Florentines in order to receive a pardon and the gift of peace, should not be considered as signs of weakness for they would clash with the tone of the composition. They confirm, in fact, his new condition of a lone judge and his position outside and above the factions ("the white feathers" and the "black hounds"), whereby he may rightfully be called a loyal citizen, worthy of being readmitted in his fatherland.

In the myth of the three immortal ladies, God's Justice, Human Justice, the Law, and the Virtues, exclusively moral and intellectual but banished by human society, dispersed and beggarly, is reflected and exalted the destiny of the innocent exile for whom the suffering that had been inflicted upon him, in a world where all values are subverted, becomes an image of dignity, privilege and banishment while all the humiliation that it involves becomes a badge of honor.

Through its language and allegorical structure, the canzone is connected with the style of the poetic culture of Dante's youth. But, between the poems written before the exile and this one, there is a fundamental difference of style, quality and spiritual maturity. In this composition the poet decidedly stresses its ethical contents rather than its formal details. The expedient of the symbolic plot becomes a means to raise the personal and biographical event to a universal level. The very language gains importance from the occasion and reaches a level of incisive strength that foreshadows the sententious moralizing eloquence of certain passages of the *Commedia:*

> *E io, che ascolto nel parlar divino*
> *consolarsi e dolersi*
> *così alti dispersi,*
> *l'essilio che m'è dato, onor mi tegno:*

> *chè, se giudizio o forza di destino*
> *vuol pur che il mondo versi*
> *i bianchi fiori in persi,*
> *cader co'buoni è pur di lode degno.*

Few other poems follow the course of this transition whereby Dante rises progressively to the task of acknowledging the reasons behind his destiny and the universal decadence and sets up the foundations of his poem's conception. A doctrinal canzone, for instance, that begins from the general concepts of virtue and vice and then defines them in the symbols of liberality and greed, assumes the forms of a sharp and violent satire, of an already apocalyptic grand scorn for the widespread corruption of the world, where a prominent position is occupied by obtuse greed, the dull and sterile cult of wealth, while he underscores the contrast between the few virtuous individuals and the multitude of vice's slaves who are surrounded by pomp and arrogance:

> *qui si raddoppia l'onta, …*
> *falsi animali, a voi ed altrui crudi,*
> *che vedete gir nudi*
> *per colli e per paludi*
> *omini innanzi cui vizio è fuggito,*
> *e voi tenete vil fango vestito.*

The sonnet that probably refers to the intrigue between pope Clement V, who "murders justice," and Philip the Fair, the "great tyrant," expresses an even more disheartened and gloomy feeling of decadence that pervades all Christendom. And while it hints at a theme that will be amply developed in the *Commedia*, it portends some traits of sorrowful and anxious eloquence in the final prayer to God that he may bring back to life humiliated Justice:

> *Ma tu, foco d'amor, lume del cielo,*
> *questa vertù che nuda e fredda giace*
> *levala su vestita del tuo velo,*
> *chè sanza lei non è in terra pace.*

All these compositions may be attributed within a fairly good approximation to the years 1304 to 1307, and mark the more intense, lyrical and polemic moments, the heights of a spiritual process that is maturing slowly and organically through various phases of intellectual reflection and theoretical elaboration carried so deeply in its context to resemble abstractness in the two major works that go back to that period: the *Convivio* and the *De vulgari eloquentia*.

As we can derive with sufficient approximation from internal data, Dante set about the two treatises almost simultaneously in 1304, in the time of meditation that followed closely the failure of the political attempts and the writer's separation from the "wicked and senseless company." He had stopped writing them toward the end of 1307 at the latest, when the plan of a great poetic work took shape in his mind and involved and transcended even the intellectual fervor that had inspired the planning and realization of those attempts of doctrinal systematization.

The two works originate from Alighieri's necessity to sum up his human and cultural experience, synthesized and laid out in clear theoretical schemes. They express the confidence in the philosophical orders to clarify and rationalize the data of empyric reality by classifying and arranging them in a systematic organism. They indicate also the man's intention to elevate his humiliated destiny by winning in the eyes of all Italians, and the Florentines in particular, the fame of philosopher and learned man, thus escaping his condition of bitter solitude and establishing a rapport with the real world, from which he felt he was excluded with the ensuing loss of opportunities for a noble and decorous dialogue.

The intention of redeeming through the evidence of a rare knowledge and speculative learning the "scourge of fortune" and his condition of wondering, almost indigent, exile, is explicitly stated in the first book of the *Convivio*, as is his hope to see the gates of Florence reopened to him, the city where he had received life and nourishment and where he longed with all his heart to rest his wearied soul and reach the destined end of his earthly existence.

The image of the adverse and longed for homeland reappears unchanged also in the heartfelt Latin of the other treatises: "Nos autem, cui mundus est patria ..., quanquam Sarnum biberimus aune dentes et Florentiam adeo diligamus ut quia dileximus exilium patiamur iniuste ...;" "et quamvis ad voluptatem nostram, sive nostre sensualitatis quietem, in terris amenior locus quam Florentia non existat ..." If we accept Leonardo Bruni's statement, it was in the years when Dante assumed a most humble attitude, trying, with noble deeds and good behavior, to regain favor and return to Florence through a spontaneous annulment on the part of those who ruled the land. He labored intensely on this issue and wrote frequently, not only to individual citizens in authority, but also to the people. Among others, he sent a very long letter that begins: "*Popule mee, quid fecit tibi?*" These letters, where the poet gave vent to his bitterness for an undeserved exile that had been extended by a decree of 1303 also to his adolescent children, and the lingering illusion of obtaining from his persecutors the recognition of that injustice, have been lost. But the signs of that bitterness and illusion are clearly apparent in the afore mentioned pages of the treatises and in the envoy of the canzone *Three Ladies*.

At the source of his illusion is the trust that characterizes briefly Dante's mind in the clarifying and persuasive virtue of reason and human intelligence, even on a practical ground. The *Convivio* is sustained and enlightened by this trust and it derives from it, besides the enthusiasm of its best pages, also the boldness and originality of its premises and direction. Conceived as a medieval encyclopedia, the treatise soon moves away from this owing to the novelty of its structure and purpose, its freedom in the choice of orders and topics, and the unusual adoption of its mode of expression. As for its structure, it was to consist of fifteen treatises of which one was to be the introduction and the other fourteen would supply a literary and, when necessary, an allegorical comment of as many canzoni based both on love and virtue. The author left it unfinished after the first treatise although, as it appears in several parts, he had already set its organic and complete plan in his mind. And, in this very plan, it is remarkable to find the close connection with the poet's personal life, whereby the book, as in the case of the *Vita nuova*, appears as a systematic and authentic interpretation of a certain phase of the poet's experience, of the bard of righteousness. From this derives the freedom that we mentioned earlier in the choice of subjects that reacts only at the occasional inducements of the text to be commented upon and shuns from any pre-established scheme or formal and external order that is commonly found in similar expressions of medieval encyclopedism.

As for its goal, it is remarkable how, in the *Convivio*, the intention sets itself up, not altogether unusually, to disclose among the uninformed a wealth of knowledge for, on one side, one discovers in the author the humility and the pride of the self-taught person who approached science not through normal studies or for official needs, but slowly and laboriously out of love and consequently knows the limits of his knowledge and the integrity of his enthusiasm when compared with those individuals who acquire knowledge in order to obtain *"money or fame."* [The poet] does not withdraw in an aristocratic scorn for the ignorant crowds, on the contrary, from the joy of his achievement he feels arise in his heart pity for the common people's *"feed,"* for the *"miserable life"* of those that he left behind and, consequently, the desire to raise them, at least in small measure, to the *"blissful table"* of the scholars. On the other hand, also the public that he addressed does not remain an amorphous and generic mass, but constitutes a group of persons endowed with inborn gentleness, naturally inclined toward virtue, inspired to perform within the civic and domestic ambiance, to whom knowledge will confer the means for a more responsible and perfect behavior: *"princes, barons, knights and many other noble people, not only men but women, who are numerous … commoners and unschooled."*

Precisely for the purpose of being helpful to so many gentle people not schooled in Latin, the author adopted the mother tongue for his treatise. He extols it in some eloquent chapters of the first book, against some *"abominable, evil Italians who despise this precious vulgar language, that, if it is lowly in something, it is because it is uttered by the meretricious lips of these adulterers."* It is, in fact, *"the new light,"* *"the new sun that will rise where the usual one sets down and will enlighten those who are in darkness and gloom.*" It will open, in other words, also for the layman the unexplored world of knowledge. The poet loves it for its strength and expressive capacity, because he employed it to progress along the way of knowledge and because he is united with it by the *"benevolence that comes from custom."* Thus, he exalts deservedly its future development and glory.

Any attempt to explain systematically the scientific and philosophical disciplines considered incidentally or amply developed in the various parts of the *Convivio* would be difficult and not helpful in this context. It will suffice, therefore, to stress its main themes and ideas. Thus, in the second book that includes the canzone *Voi che 'ntendendo,* the digressions on the four meanings (literal, allegorical, moral and anagogical) that are used in textual interpretations, on the number and order of the heavens and the intelligences that move them, on the two beatitudes (active and contemplative life) given to man, as well as the immortality of the soul, are problems to be resumed and, at times, solved differently, in the poet's later writings.

More concentrated appears the content of the third treatise, where the commentary of the canzone *Amor che ne la mente mi ragiona* takes the form of an eloquent praise of knowledge so that, better than elsewhere, he shows that condition of philosophical enthusiasm whence the fundamental inspiration of his work started out. Knowledge, that is entirely and mainly in God, and resides in a lesser degree in angelic intelligence, shines also "like a strait beam" and "directly" in man's mind, in that "extreme power" and "most precious place" of the soul that is reason. The latter one, owing to its virtue of being "liberated from matter" is the divine reflection in the created being, it is, somehow, itself "divine," since "it partakes of the divine nature as an eternal intelligence." Consequently, in the act of meditating philosophically, which is "a more than human deed," man attains his perfection and satisfies his thirst both by receiving in his mind the light of truth that is reachable by his understanding, and, by fitting himself in the awareness of his limitations, to accept obediently the principles revealed by truth about those things "that our intelligence cannot speculate, namely God, eternity and the original matter that are clearly seen and believed to exist even though their essence eludes our understanding.

An element of rational trust merges into the foundation of a mystic, neoplatonic concept, because it is quite true that some principles remain hidden for our mind, but, since "the natural desire in every element is measured by the possibility of the desiring element itself," and, consequently, "human desire in this life is measured by the knowledge that can be attained on earth," reason cannot aspire to understand an object that transcends it and, in acquiring a knowledge proportionate to his capacity, "man, as such, experiences the end of every desire and thus becomes blissful."

Lastly, in the fourth treatise, the doctrine of nobility is expounded as a commentary of the canzone *Le dolci rime,* by discussing the Aristotelic definition that was attributed, as it has been indicated, to Emperor Frederick. In an absolute sense, nobility is "perfection of nature in every thing." In man it is "the seed of happiness," the foundation of moral and intellectual virtues that lead the soul toward perfection in active and contemplative life respectively in which consists temporal happiness, a gift instilled by God into the souls that are perfectly disposed through generative virtue and astral influence rather than in the lineage through hereditary privilege. It resides in the individual souls because "the family does not make individual persons noble, but the individual persons make the family noble."

The need to find a justification for daring to rebut "the authority of the Emperor's definition," introduces an ample digression on the Empire, its origin, its necessity, its functions and limits that constitutes the first document, around the year 1307, of the evolution of Dante's political principles and that will be better clarified and discussed later in the *Monarchia* and in the *Commedia.* The foundation of every state organization is "the necessity of human civilization, that is constituted for a goal, namely, happy life." Man's social nature, owing to the insufficiency that is inherent in the individual as well as a partially autarchic group, requires the building up of the families, the links among several families of a territory as well as in the towns, and also the relationship and the "brotherhood" of several towns in a kingdom in order to meet their need of economic development and military defense.

But the natural process toward a united order of society does not stop here since human mind, not satisfied with "a limited possession of land," owing to an unrestrainable greed that is peculiar of a corrupt human nature, causes the arising of "discord and wars ... among the kingdoms that cause suffering in the towns and from them in the territories, in the houses and from the houses among the people. Thus happiness is barred." Therefore, to remove the reasons of such strife and to eliminate the nefarious consequences in every order of political structure, "it is necessary for the whole earth ... to be a monarchy, namely a single realm and have a single ruler who, possessing everything and desiring nothing, is able to keep the monarchs within the borders of their realms so that there may be peace among them. [And in that peace] cities may be settled and in that order neighborhoods may be friendly and in this friendship families may satisfy their needs so that, when the latter are satisfied, men may live happily, which is the reason why they were born." The imperial authority, therefore, finds its justification in the need of justice and universal peace and it is identified with the law or "written reason," that transforms in coercive formulae, protected by strict sanctions the principles of natural fairness.

The emperor is entrusted with the duty of wording, promulgating and applying the law on all people, hence he may be called the "rider of human will." Such horse "is now running without a rider in the field, as it is quite evident, especially in unlucky Italy, that has been abandoned to her own governing without any means." From an historical standpoint, the task of bringing about the principle of universal authority and electing its representative was assigned by God to the "holy people" of Rome. All her history, the extraordinary virtues of her rulers, the peace that was brought by her to the farthest reaches of the world at Augustus' time so that the whole earth could be perfectly prepared for the coming of the Son of God, bear witness to this privilege granted to the "holy city" and to the existence of a providential mission.

Dante's passionate eloquence that enlightens and, at times, arouses the clear expression of these chapters on the empire, is of an entirely intellectual nature, quite detached both from the anxious and passionate spirit of the epistles and from the intense and sharp rigor of the *Monarchia*.

The issue of the political order is still viewed in a rather abstract manner, yet it is connected with the writer's philosophical experience, although not prominently. But it is not so pressing as to create in his mind those violent alternations of hope and dejection that will soon guide all his activity in a prophetic and messianic attitude. It will suffice to mention the absence, in said papers, of any reference to the Church, her corruption and the usurping of the civil power carried out and theorized by the popes. But some of the essential elements of the themes of discussion that will occur in the immediately following years already begin to surface, such as the denial of the self-sufficiency of the individual states, the anarchy of Italy that resembles an untamed and wild horse let loose without bridle by her natural rider, the necessity of a universal arbitration, the written principles and the ruler that embodies them—[the ruler] who, by settling conflicts and abuses of minor entities and restraining their desires, assures the happiness of man on earth with justice and peace.

All this material, where we see an enormously amplified culture, permeated by an ardent systematic intention—the cosmic order that affects every aspect of creation and is reflected in the structure and concordant harmony of knowledge, brought in itself necessarily also the necessity of an equally ample broadening of rhetorical and linguistic devices.

The comparison between the prose of the *Vita nuova* and that of the *Convivio* shows a difference of maturity and boldness revealing the degree of historical progress and the intense and fast rhythm that leads the vernacular tongue to the conquest of a fully expressive possibility. Undoubtedly, other elements of the contemporary literary tradition contribute to this progress, from the attempts of assimilation of the doctrine applied in other Romance areas and resumed even in Florence by Brunetto, to the intense alacrity of the translators from French and Latin. But certainly they would not be sufficient to explain it without the presence of Dante's genius. The simple rhetoric of the *Vita nuova,* directed toward suggestive results, yet substantially easier, of a poetic dialog, woven into slight and quite schematic conceptual notions, is not rejected in the *Convivio* but recycled in a vaster expression, controlled by necessities of order, clarity and terse writing. It ceases, therefore, to be an external element and it becomes functional in each of its aspects. The internal structures, parallelisms, and recurring rhymes accompany and reveal the inherent connections, the circular movement that becomes professionally ampler and more specific in the logical argument. The etymological figures underline their natural origin and the interdependence of ideas. The images have a tendency to increase the reality and the power of discussion rather than to create reactions in the realm of sentiments. The entire syntactical structure, therefore, grows stronger, it broadens its scope and becomes richer with subordinate sentences, interpolated clauses, parentheses, and it unfolds in a constant movement that affects not just the individual sentences but the entire process of expression and leads it toward its conclusive formulation.

The scholastic annotators, the methods and expository instruments of the *quaestiones disputatae,* the reasoning and linguistic technique of the Latin moralists and philosophers, from Cicero to Seneca and Boethius, are now the examples after whom Dante builds and follows in part the course of his new "tempered and virile manner," the forms of that "noble" style that is true to the strictest content and that implies even "a little solemnity through which it appears more authoritative." The author shows a full and proud awareness concerning this development and enrichment as well as the progress of his verbal devices that keep up with the expansion of his cultural knowledge and the training of his speculative power. In his book one will be able to assess that "great quality of the vernacular," that had remained only potential and implicit, its capacity to reveal "appropriately, sufficiently and orderly most high and noble ideas, almost as if it were Latin," the effectiveness of its bare structures deprived by the accidental embellishment" of the poetic language (rhyme, rhythm, metric value), and also "the smoothness of its syllables, the qualities of its constructions and the delicate expressions that it allows which, if one considers them properly, will appear full of a most sweet and lovable beauty."

*

The awareness of the broadened possibilities of expression of the vernacular in the artistic field and of its ability to express suitably all thoughts and feelings constitutes the basis of the other treatise that is written in Latin, because he addresses scholars and not persons who are naturally noble but unschooled in the art of speech in the mother tongue: the *Doctrina de vulgari eloquentia.* Such is the title derived from the text while, of the three manuscripts that contain the composition, two show a clearly erroneous epigraph, *De vulgari eloquio sive ydiomate,* and the third a more correct yet summary title attributed to a later compiler: *Rectorica Dantis.* Such awareness would appear more fully and patently if Dante had succeeded in developing the entire project and in dealing, together with the theory of the learned and tragic style in verse, also with the theory concerning lower styles and prose in its various levels. However, even from this, it is not hard to understand the scope of his doctrine and the writer's attitude toward the object of his research as it appears from the unfinished composition. From the first lines of the treatise he states that his intention is to *"prodesse locutioni vulgarium gentium"* and *"discretionem aliqualiter lucidare illorum qui tanquam ceci ambulant per plateas,"* to teach, for the benefit and use of the many, a doctrine of a precise spoken language that would be discreet and proper and supply a technique for the means of expression similar to the existing one that was minutely developed for the functional languages of the scholars, within the vernacular that is proper of all people as such, independently from their level of preparation, and even, within their possibilities, of women and children.

The procedure used by the author to prove his proposition is that of medieval science: to connect the historical and practical data with the logical principles offered by deductive analysis by drawing from all doctrinal sources (traditional biblical exegesis as far as the concept of language is concerned, its origins and the causes of its expansion and, as far as the technique of its articulation is concerned, Latin grammar and rhetoric, the medieval *artes dictaminis* and the *poetriae,* the treatises on style and versification of the late Provençal culture) and finally, by reconsidering this entire body of concepts and molding it in the light of an organic and personal vision.

Speech is a primary and personal human faculty. Useless both for pure intellects between whom communication occurs directly without words and for the brutes for whose relationships instinct is sufficient, language is a necessary means and a peculiar characteristic of humans in whose minds the exchange of ideas that is possible, since all share a common reason, can occur owing to the duplicity of their spiritual and physical nature only through sensory signs. The first language, Hebrew, simultaneously created with mankind, survives in the speech of the chosen people. But the propagation of the tongues originated as a divine punishment of human pride, through the confusion of Babel and the scattering of nations. The populations that came then to inhabit Europe brought along an *"ydioma tripharium,"* characterized by common elements but distinguished into three different types: the first, widespread in northern, Germanic-Slavic Europe, the second, peculiar to the Greeks that populated south-eastern Europe and part of Asia, and the third that is spoken in the southern and western European lands. The latter one then, became divided into three groups: Hispanic, French and Latin people who use, respectively, the affirmative particles *oc, oïl* and *sì*. Even in the uncertain knowledge that Dante draws from the culture of his time, which contains large lacunae and considerable errors, it is noticeable that the amount of truth to his doctrine grows progressively as he enters the sphere of his personal experience. From what appears as a confused glimmer of the modern concept of the unity of the European languages to the more distinct concept of the common source of the Romance languages that he limits to those directly known to him (Italian, French and Provençal), he expounds the initial moment of the process of differentiation that occurred in a remote, mythical time and he indicates its affinities, not through phonetic and formal elements, but by noticing the evident similarities and even the lexical identities (terms such as God, love, sea, lives, loves and so on). Evidently, the degree of solid research increases even further when Dante ventures into an attempt to classify and describe the Italic languages, divided into fourteen main varieties along the two sides of the Apennine divide, where each one of them is subdivided in turn into a very large number of secondary and tertiary specifications. In this case, his experience concerning French and Provençal that was indirect and literary is joined by the direct experience of the spoken usage that in several cases was acquired by the poet during his wandering as an exile. Furthermore, the intrinsic historical importance of his attempt is determined by the fact that even in its rudimentary form and in its rather schematic and partially arbitrary solutions, it is entirely devoid of appreciable precedents. But even more important is the general principle that Dante advances in order to explain the constant linguistic modification of its subdivision into countless varieties, a principle that he draws from an Aristotelic idea but that he, for the first time, introduces in the realm of experience and enriches with concrete and fitting examples. Being man a most unstable and mutable creature, it follows that all the elements of human reason, including language, are not lasting but they change "*per locorum temporumque distantias*" whereby speech not only changes in the various countries, regions, individual cities and from district to district within the same ring of walls (as it happens in the Bolognese districts San Felice and Strada Maggiore), but it evolves with the passing of time so that if the ancient inhabitants of Pavia came back to life, they could not understand its contemporary citizens.

This doctrine appears also in the *Convivio* and, later, in Canto XXVI of *Paradiso*, without the reservation concerning the *ydioma sacrum* of the Hebrews. Vis-á-vis the *locutio vulgaris*, that is natural and common among all people, although divided into numerous details, there arose later the *gramatica*, a *locutio secondaria* and *artificialis* that for us is written in Latin and in Eastern Europe Greek, and it is, in general, the tool that is used in the educated countries by learned and literary persons to communicate with one another.

A rigid grammatical structure, a system of rules and technical processes ensure the *gramatica* of relative stability and continuity through space and time but its unnatural origin, the learning difficulties and its very purpose limit its range to a limited category of people and a quite circumscribed circle of social functions.

With the quick and growing development of a rich literary tradition in the area of Romance languages, experience showed that the *artificium*, that used to be a distinctive and exclusive aspect of the *gramatica*, is also applicable in a certain measure to the mother tongue, which is confirmed in the early indefinite attempts of grammar and rhetoric books on the use of the vernacular. Even here it is possible to introduce rules and stable art forms and define a series of *gradus construc-tionum*, namely expressions ranging from the simplest to the sublime that imply the skillful use of rhythmic patterns, parallel constructions and rhetorical figures.

The literatures that were divulged in the three main Romance languages show in different measure this process in its artistic evolution aimed at giving a shape and stable structure to the spoken languages. While French, owing to its facility and charm that favored its diffusion, won supremacy in the area of prose with its historical, didactical and romantic narrative, and lyric poetry flourished in Provençal "*tanquam in perfectiori dulciorique loquela,*" Italian, owing to its closer affinity with Latin, is the most suited language to be patterned upon the *gramatica,* and it is natural that within it arose those poets "*qui dulcius subtiliusque poetati vulgariter sunt,*" composers that are distinguished by an exquisite perfection and a broader and deeper cultural preparation.

The concept of a learned vernacular language is an *a priori* conclusion, it is the ideal language of the *aula* and the *curia* and "although in Italy there is not a court constituting a single center, such as that of the king of Germany where all parts are centered around a single prince, the components of the former are united by the power of reason that God gave us by grace. Therefore it would be untrue to say that we Italians lack a court, in spite of things being physically scattered." Clearly, the dispersed elements of this ideal court consist of the excellent poets and scientists that would assemble in it, if it should permanently come owing to the presence of a ruler. Ultimately, it is the duty of those men to establish the legal and learned language.

Such language, therefore, is not a fictitious logic construction but a fact that Dante encountered in his experience. It is not worthwhile to rebut the error of those who interpreted it as a mere dialectic hypothesis or as the result of an arbitrary mix of elements drawn from different dialects and then refined and polished. It is an error that resembles the other made by those who persist in emphasizing the conventional and artificial aspects of the *gramatica.* The latter is merely literary Latin as it was brought about by the superimposition of the individual and conscious activity of the writers and of the learned class over the collective and unwitting activity of the common people. And if the author considers it somewhat unchangeable, one should consider that it was, in fact, a dead language for the majority of people and an exclusive instrument of intellectual relations among clerics, practically unchangeable and enclosed in a limited vocabulary and strict stylistic norms. The learned vernacular is, in itself, the new *gramatica*, the literary language that lives in the works of the most cultured and refined writers and is already influencing actively the municipal vernaculars by eradicating "from the Italian forest the thorny shrubs" and by replacing them constantly with "new plants and seedbeds." It is, in sum, the language of poetry, used originally at the Sicilian court, adopted by the able bards of other regions, especially by Guinizelli, that reaches its peak with the compositions of the Tuscan "stil nuovo" writers. It is the noble language that "among many coarse terms used by the Italians, among uncertain constructions, defective pronunciations and rough inflections, represents such a distinguished, terse, accomplished and urbane choice as it appears in the canzoni of Cino da Pistoia and his friend," namely Dante himself.

The theory of the *De vulgari eloquentia* originates from the concrete experience of the lyric poet. And although it is a theory in more than a few particular aspects, it transcends it and marks the beginning of a definitive progression.

The explicit statement, at the beginning of the second book, that the use of the learned vernacular is appropriate also in prose, reflects naturally the contemporary preparation of the *Convivio*. The broadening of the scope granted to poetry that is no longer limited, as it is in the *Vita nuova,* to topics of love but considers also virtue, arms, epics and morals, reflects the increased knowledge of the Provençal tradition and more specifically the effort made by Dante to bring about in his allegorical, doctrinal and political poetry the new character that he is inclined to personify, of the "*cantor rectitudinis.*" But, on the whole, the *De vulgari eloquentia* remains an affirmation on a theoretical basis, of the new Italian poetry, the lyrical works of the "stilnovo" manner, to the point of marginalizing, in a sort of lesser perspective, even some of the poet's experiences that appear newer to us but that move away from the rigor of that taste, such as the Provençal manner of the stony rhymes.

Here lies the historical importance of the treatise and here perhaps lies the reason that persuaded the writer to leave his work unfinished when there appeared clearly to him the partial inadequacy of those patterns when compared with the concept of poetry, much broader and complex as it was, that his widely increased experience as a man, philosopher and prophet brought to him when, in other words, from the still unripe seed of the *cantor rectitudinis,* there blossomed the mature poet of the *Commedia* in full awareness of his potential.

*

The stages of Dante's peregrination after he separated from the "evil and senseless company," cannot be safely determined, except for a few cases. His statement of having gone "to almost all the places where this language has expanded" is an expression that one cannot accept literally. It is true, however, that several passages of the poem reveal a knowledge of landscapes and natural aspects, of customs and even anecdotes of local events, that is quite ample, nor is it easy to discern from case to case what is, in these references, the consequence of a direct experience or of things that were heard or written.

It is Dante himself who says that he found his "first shelter" at the Scaligeri family in Verona. But it is possible that he went there in the early months of 1304, under the rule of Bartolomeo, in order to ask for the help "of soldiers and cavalry" in behalf of the exiles, according to relatively reliable information kept by Flavio Biondo. It is not as probable that he returned there a short time afterwards, under the ruling of Alboino of whom the poet expressed a scornful or not so favorable appraisal in the *Convivio*.

Some of his observations in the *Convivio* and the *Commedia* lead us to conjecture that he stayed in Treviso, at the court of the good Gherardo da Camino while the *De vulgari eloquentia* offers plausible support to the hypothesis of a prolonged stay in Bologna where, better than elsewhere in Italy, he could easily find and gather the appropriate material for his grammatical and rhetorical studies. In 1306 he was certainly in Lunigiana, the guest of Moroello Malaspina. In fact, in a document, he is mentioned as a proxy charged with the task of negotiating a peace between those marquis and Antonio, Bishop of Luni, while one of his sonnets directed to Cino da Pistoia is still in existence. At that time, from Casentino, he addressed to Moroello IV the epistle that accompanied the canzone *Amor, da che convien*, and in *Purgatorio* he will dedicate to that family's fame of liberality and virtue some of his spontaneous and heartfelt complimentary lines.

It is probable that to this period of Dante's life one may refer also to his stay in Lucca, that was comforted by the kindly hospitality and protection of a young lady, a Gentucca, about whom nothing is known. Finally, it is quite likely that from Lunigiana Dante traveled along the Ligurian coast to France, as Boccaccio and the chronicler Villani indicate, in order to attend the most distinguished schools of theology and philosophy in Paris. Yet one cannot confirm this fact by considering the so called letter to Brother Ilario, which is a forgery, or better, a pastiche composed at a much later date perhaps as a rhetorical exercise.

The year 1310 is a fundamental date in the poet's biography. From an external point of view it offers the exiled poet the chance, or the illusion, of reestablishing ties with the historical situation from which he had been forcibly ousted and from a more personal consideration it encouraged him to resume and deepen a number of doctrinal issues and to assess in a definite way his understanding of the recent historical events and of a poetic and prophetic mission.

The descent to Italy of the new ruler, Harry VII of Luxemburg, that had been announced by the imperial legates and sanctioned by Pope Clement V, who defined him in an epistle as a just and peaceful sovereign called by the necessity of calming disagreements and reestablishing order with the impartiality and authority of a supreme judge, had to rekindle in Dante's mind and in the other exiles as well, the hope of a reversal of the situation and a nearing return to Florence.

But the poet may have been more impressed, as in the case of a large portion of contemporary opinion, by the sudden news concerning the end of the imperial vacancy, the reasserted intention of Harry to resume the control of Italian affairs and in particular the agreement of the two universal powers, with the clear distinction that it implied between the temporal and the spiritual, and the pope's renunciation of the usurpation of the ruler's powers and duties that had already been theorized and widely put into practice by Boniface VIII. By returning to Italy and adopting the idea of a coronation in Rome as the foundation of the legitimacy of a power that reached the entire Christian world, Harry seemed to realize the doctrines that the writer had just developed and discussed in the fourth book of the *Convivio*. These doctrines, in fact, are resumed, but in a totally new order of concreteness, in the three epistles that he wrote at that time.

The poet was hurt even more severally by the almost incredible and strong resistence opposed everywhere against the practical realization of his theories or utopian ideas. On the other hand, as during his exile, the scope of his views had broadened, the scene of the political struggle had become uncertain, complicated and full of contradictions while, at the time he was observing it from Florence, it still appeared distinct, clear and coherent. Even more narrow-minded, easily lured into a deceitful diplomatic game, and willing to compromise were the protagonists of the quarrel and the lesser participants in their unpredictable actions. On the one hand, there was the firm stance of the national monarchies that considered universal (Philip the Fair and the house of France "that overshadows all the Christian land") the prompt and vigorous defense of the Guelph communes, first of all Florence, and the shrewd and meddling diplomacy of Robert of Anjou, the originally hesitant and then openly hostile attitude of the pope who was ready to take advantage of a favorable situation in order to lighten the burden of the French yoke but not to the point of eliminating the system of powers that kept the Church in a precarious balance.

On the other hand, he saw the increasingly evident weakness of the emperor's politics, the serious compromises, the accepted limitations and the hesitations in waging a vigorous and speedy war while, among the emperor's supporters, there appeared the lack of an ideal and firm vision and the arising of peculiar and mediocre interests.

Finally, there were rulers and tyrants aiming only at assuring by force or by legal means the power they had already seized through violence or fraud, while the Ghibelline exiles and other refugees, inspired by revenge and consumed by their ill-feelings, were trying exclusively to assure the triumph of their factions.

When Dante, with the detached mind of a judge and the soul of a poet, will be reconsidering the course of the historical events in Italy, he will still be able to see the protagonists of the old generation, both friends and enemies, still immersed in the light of greatness: the leading aristocracy of the early Guelph commune and their tenacious enemy Farinata, the sovereigns of the Swabian court, and even Boniface VIII and Charles of Anjou, but he will unite in a single contemptuous condemnation all or almost all the people of the current generation, Philip of France and Robert of Naples, the little and fierce tyrants of the Po Valley, the Gascon pope, the Guelphs rebelling against justice and the Ghibellines not opposed to dishonor it by turning it into a party symbol and a tool of personal power.

In the meantime, one should consider his anxious and religious attitude as demonstrated in his participation in the events that occur during a short sequence of years. It was as if the entire world had reached a final stage, an irrevocable choice that he unhesitatingly compares with that which confronted humankind at the time of Redemption. Harry is the "novel Moses who will drive his people away from the Egyptians' tyranny to lead it to the land of milk and honey." In him, as it was in Christ, Isaiah's prophecy will be fulfilled when he said "in truth he strengthened us in our weariness and took upon himself the burden of our sorrows." In order to exalt him, the most solemn statements of the biblical scriptures and liturgy are mentioned in the fourth eclogue and in Virgil's *Aeneid* and in seeing him, the cry that greeted the coming of the Redeemer comes spontaneously to his lips: *"anch'io, che ti scrivo in mio nome e di altri, ti vidi benignissimo e clementissimo come si conviene all'imperiale maestà, quando le mie mani toccarono i tuoi piedi e le mie labbra pagarono il debito tributo: allora il mio spirito esultò, mentre tacito esclamavo dentro di me:-Ecco l'Agnello di Dio, ecco colui che toglie i peccati del mondo."*

We do not know where and when he met the emperor. In Asti, perhaps, in the fall of 1310, or in Milan, in the early days of the following year. In both places, among the many noblemen that had gathered to pay homage to the sovereign, there was also Moroello, the poet's friend and protector. Even in this case, documents and chronicles do not mention Dante's name while they mention several other minor individuals in Harry's fleeting Italian entourage and even men of letters, such as Albertino Mussato. It is quite probable, however, that he soon left northern Italy to go to Tuscany where he accepted the hospitality of the Guidi counts. From the Poppi castle he dictated three letters in behalf of countess Battifolle addressed to Empress Margaret of Brabant and from the springs of the Arno he wrote at least two of the three great political epistles that constitute the sole evidence of his state of mind in that crucial moment, the voice of his impassioned enthusiasm and hopes that later turned into anger and despair.

The first letter, that was addressed in the autumn of 1310 to the Italian kings, the Roman senators, the sovereigns of the estates and the communal regents, is a declaration of faith and exaltation. The poet, "*humilis ytalus ... et exul inmeritus,*" points out the sacred nature of the undertaking, that is willed by God, so that justice could be restored and the destiny of the oppressed people be raised again. The refined stylistic development, the thoroughly medieval elegance of the rhetorical touches, the constant and yet subtly varied adherence to the *cursus* even in minor clauses do not hinder but rather support and elevate the fervor of his eloquent emotions: "*Ecco che un nuovo giorno comincia a risplendere, preannunziando dal suo sorgere l'aurora, che già dirada le tenebre della grande sventura; le aure orientali si fanno più intense, rosseggia il cielo ai suoi orli estremi e con il suo carezzevole sereno conforta gli auspici dei popoli. Anche noi vedremo la gioia intensa, noi che così lungamente pernottammo nel deserto. Perchè sorgerà Titano apportatore di pace, e la giustizia, che era stremata come eliotropio privo di sole, non appena quello avrà vibrato il suo primo chiarore, riprenderà forza. Si sazieranno nella luce dei suoi raggi coloro che hanno fame e sete di giustizia e saranno confusi dal suo volto corruscante quelli che amano l'iniquità ... Rallegrati dunque, o Italia, che eri caduta in così basso stato da meritare la compassione perfino dei Saraceni, e tosto sarai oggetto d'invidia in ogni parte, perchè il tuo sposo, consolazione del mondo e gloria del tuo popolo, il clementissimo Arrigo, divo e Augusto e Cesare, già s'affretta alle nozze. Tergi le lacrime e cancella i segni dell'angoscia, o bellissima, perchè è vicino chi ti libererà dal carcere degli empi ... Svegliatevi tutti e levatevi incontro al nostro sovrano, cittadini d'Italia, riserbati non al suo impero soltanto, ma direttamente, come liberi, al suo regno.'*

The second letter of March 31, 1311, addressed to the "most iniquitous Florentines within the city walls," while the rulers of the commune were quickening their diplomatic game and were making pacts with the Angevin monarch and the governments of Bologna, Lucca, Siena and Perugia for a fight to the bitter end, reveals the Poet's tormented heart for his city. Pity and resentment alternate; the intention of reasoning and persuading is overcome by rebukes and threats and the tension of these feelings reaches its height with the vision of a dreadful punishment: "*Vedrete le vostre case, innalzate non con prudenza a norma delle vostre necessità, bensì trasformate stoltamente in luoghi di delizie, precipitare sotto i colpi dell'ariete ovvero ardere nell'incendio. Vedrete la plebe sollevarsi d'ogni parte furente, dapprima incerta e divisa, ma poi tutta paurosamente minacciosa contro di voi, perchè non sa essere nello stesso tempo digiuna e intimorita. Con strazio vedrete spogliare le chiese, dove ogni giorno concorrono in folla le vostre donne, e i vostri bambini attoniti ed ignari chiamati ad espiare le colpe dei padri. E se non erra il presagio della mente, fondato su segni certi e infallibili argomenti, voi, quei pochi che sopravviverete a patire l'esilio, quando i più saranno dispersi dalla strage o nella prigionia, assisterete piangendo alla resa a discrezione in mano altrui nella città stremata dalla lunga sofferenza.*

In the third epistle, compiled soon afterwards, on April 16, Dante addresses Harry directly and speaks not only for himself but in the name of all "Tuscans who want peace." The more the solemn and official nature of the document and the importance of the addressee exact from its style a supreme effort of rhetorical knowledge, the more the writer's anxiety becomes evident as does his fear of being disappointed once again in his hopes and of missing the last, and perhaps unique, opportunity. The intense expectation, the "long thirst" of the followers of justice burst furiously, on the brink of doubt, ready to "cry with the words of a precursor: Are you the man who is to come or is the one that we await someone else?" Why doesn't Harry rush into Tuscany, after pacifying the Po Valley? Does he believe that "the imperial rights to be safeguarded are limited within the borders of Liguria?" Isn't he aware that "hesitation is encouraging the Tuscan tyranny that grows stronger every day and stimulates the pride of the wicked people?" While he lingers in the siege of Cremona, doesn't he see where is the vital part of the hydra of the thousand heads, root of the tree of rebellion? The fox that gives off such stench is lurking along the Arno and its name is Florence: "*Essa è la vipera che si rivolta contro le viscere materne; essa la pecora infetta che corrompe col contagio tutto il gregge del suo signore; la Mirra scellerata ed empia che arde negli amplessi del padre Ciniro; l'Amata furiosa che, respinte le nozze stabilite dal fato, non temette di scegliere per genero quella che i fati le vietavano, e anzi follemente lo provocò a far guerra, e infine pagando il fio della sua pazzesca audacia, s'impiccò:*"

Let the emperor cut short all delays and show his anger and strength to the rebels by scattering and destroying their most dangerous nest: "*Allora il nostro retaggio, che senza posa piangiamo a noi tolto, o ci sarà restituito intero; e come ora, memori della santa Gerusalemme, lacrimiamo esuli in Babilonia, così alfine, rifatti cittadini e respirando nella pace, rievocheremo nel giubilo i tempi della miseria e della confusione.*"

Apart from the style that in these cases is essentially oratorical or polemical, the three epistles add little to the doctrinal considerations that Dante introduces in the fourth book of the *Convivio*. The emperor's authority coincides with the juridical rules; it is, in fact, the presupposition behind every accomplishment of the public and private right. In it resides the basis of order and peace as well as of true freedom that consists in the observance of the law. "What is this, in fact, but the free exercise of the will in action that the laws guarantee in behalf of those who comply with them?" Whatever the limits of the monarch's power may be, it extends *de iure inviolabili* to the whole world; "what the sky surrounds is its land and lake," "it spreads in every direction as far as Amphitrite's waves and can hardly be circumscribed by the Ocean's waters." It does not tolerate limits of any other kind because "it is not subject to rule and it will end only with the end of the world."

The origin and divine nature of the monarch's duty are insured by the wondrous history of Rome, by the explicit recognition of Christ and by the consent and blessing of the Pontiff. By the supreme goodness of the Lord *"velut a puncto biffurcatur Petri Cesarisque potesta,"* both supreme authorities within their spheres, according to the task and end assigned to each one of them, so that, in their concomitant and uniform work, in the emperor's respect for the Vicar of God and in the independence recognized by the latter in behalf of the former, on the basis of the temporal rule, the peaceful and rightful governing of the Christian community is realized.

Opposing or resisting the will of the sovereign is a sinful act, for it is written that "who resists legitimate authority resists the order established by God; [it is] almost as sinful as to refuse to obey the Church." You, Florentines, who abandon the holy empire to find new kingdoms, as if the foundation of the civilized society of Florence was different from that of Rome, why don't you try to replace the apostolic monarchy so that, since the moon doubles in the sky, also the sun will be double?" Indeed, with their eloquent proof, facts prove the necessity of a united government. "Since Augustus' throne is empty, the whole world goes astray, in the bark of Peter the pilot and the oarsmen are dozing off; wretched Italy, widowed, at the mercy of private interests and deprived of moderating laws is indescribably tossed around by winds and waves while her unfortunate inhabitants can barely express their sorrow with their tears."

A radical change of feelings and perspective through which the writer observes and judges the events can be noticed in the other epistle, the most beautiful, that he addresses to the Italian cardinals in 1314.

In the period of time that separates it from the three epistles that concern Harry's undertaking, the great dream of the poet has dissolved. Clement V's about-face, the broken alliance between the Church and the Empire, the failed siege of Florence, the long desired but vain campaign against Robert of Anjou and finally the emperor's death in August 1313 had sealed the destiny of Christendom and Italy, perhaps for a long time, in a totally different manner from what he had hoped. Even the man's destiny had been concluded when, in September 1311, the rulers of Florence, in retaliation, had officially excluded him from the broad amnesty granted the Guelph exiles, that went under the name of Baldo d'Aguglione. The possibility of his honorable return to his fatherland was ruled out forever. In May, 1315, he refused to take advantage of another amnesty that required his admitting an undeserved guilt: *"Se in Firenze non mi è dato entrare per nessun'altra via, ed io in Firenze non entrerò giammai. E che per questo? Le sfere del sole e degli astri, non potrò forse contemplarle dovunque? Non potrò in ogni luogo sotto la volta del cielo meditare i dolcissimi veri, se io prima non mi renda spregevole, anzi abietto al popolo e alla città tutta? E neppure un pane mi mancherà.* In the month of November of the same year, the signiory confirmed with a new sentence the death penalty against him and his children. In the brief life span that God gave him after Harry's death, Dante appeared isolated, overwhelmed and left behind by the new events that he, not understood by them, could not understand even though the renown of the *Commedia*, already known in some measure, and the expectations for the last canticle whose completion he was assiduously pursuing, crowned the sullen and tired image of the courtier, in the halo of an almost posthumous glory.

Living in a world that "rids itself day by day of all good," his will is already longing for the other life. He did not renounce his ideals, but his mind, averted from the present, turned toward an idyllic commemoration of the past, to the triumph of justice that by then rested entirely not in mankind's vain plans but in the patient and unforeseeable will of the Almighty whose intervention, sooner or later, will not fail to occur.

At times, his secret anger appears, inflicting harsh punishments on the wicked: The death of Clement V and Philip the Fair in 1314, as well as the defeat of Florence and the Guelph league at Montecatini in 1315 at the hand of Uguccione della Faggiola. And since the main root of the world's corruption resides in the ambition of the Church for political and economic power, the premise of salvation will consist of a radical reform within the ecclesiastical institutions that will lead them back to their original purity, poverty and spirituality through God's direct intervention.

The political issue assumes more and more a religious character and is defined in a concept of history that concerns a grand temporal and special design in which the ideas of the present become irrelevant and vain.

All the words of his later life generate from a condition of noble detachment from worldly affairs. They have the sound of authority and abstractness of the person who observes from a remote vantage point, sublime and beyond his time. This refers both to his magnanimous attitude in the mentioned letter to his Florentine friend, where he refused a dishonorable amnesty, and to his calm and solid reasoning of the *Monarchia*, so detached in every part from the style of occasional writings, and also to the canti of the *Paradiso* where both passion and polemic spirit show no evidence of the immediate and contingent, while anger and anxiety are replaced by an implacable condemnation and the firm certainty of truth.

These are the years when the mind of the writer devotes ample time to the fathers of early Christianity, the medieval mystics from St. Bernard to Richard from San Vittore, the monks and ascetics scourging the corrupt Church, such as St. Peter Damian and the prophecies of Joachim widely discussed among the spiritual Franciscans.

In this atmosphere of ideas and inclinations he wrote his epistle to the Italian cardinals. On April 20, 1314, Clement V "the lawless shepherd" had died. He had moved the papal residence to Avignon and submitted the pontiff's spiritual mission to the ambitious politics, the insatiable greed and violent injustice of the French king, Philip the Fair. Twenty-four cardinals had assembled in conclave at Carpentras for the election of the new Vicar of Christ. Among them were only six Italians while all the others were either French or connected with the French side. One could not reasonably expect that the Italians' intentions should prevail in the assembly.

As they had become familiar with the dire consequences of the preceding election that had humiliated the Church and afflicted Rome and Italy, in the hope of bringing the apostolic seat back to Rome, they attempted as much as possible to secure the majority of the votes for William, Bishop of Palestrina. But the activities of the conclave were carried out in an atmosphere of intrigues, corruption and violence that culminated with an invasion of the building by the Gascons' armed bands lead by Bertrand de Got, a nephew of the deceased pope, who forced the Italian cardinals to flee and caused the temporary suspension of the assembly's work.

When the cardinals resumed their work two years later, the man elected was that John XXII who, in the *Paradiso*, is branded as the ruin of the Church's vineyard. Therefore, when Dante was compiling his letter to the Italian cardinals, the actual situation was such that it did not allow him to believe in the prompt effectiveness of his intervention.

The author is aware that he is the only seer in a world entirely engulfed in darkness taking long strides toward a catastrophe. He has no illusions of being able to help with his weak forces, he does not assume upon himself the task of preventing the Holy Ark from falling. He speaks only for the sake of that truth that is always "*amicis omnibus preferenda,*" as Aristotle teaches.

"*Tra le pecorelle del gregge di Gesù Cristo io sono una delle minime; come colui che non posso abusare di dignità alcuna pastorale, perchè non son meco ricchezze. Non infatti per forza di ricchezze, ma per la grazia di Dio io son ciò che sono e lo zelo della casa di Lui mi consuma. E così già pur nella lingua dei lattanti e dei bimbi risuonò la verità che piace a Dio, e il cieco nato confessò quel vero che i Farisei non solamente tacevano, bensì anche si sforzavano di torcere a male.* And precisely not without God's will and inspiration it happened that:"

Fra tanti che usurpano l'ufficio di pastore, fra tante pecore, se non proprio distolte, certo neglette e incustodite nei pascoli, una sola voce, la sola pia (e d'un privato), si oda, in questo quasi funerale di Madre Chiesa. Una sola vox, sola pia, et hec privata, in matris Ecclesie quasi funere ..." And the sound of that voice has already the stress and intensity of the most distressed and proud, most fiercely apocalyptic tone of the

Commedia. In no other epistle do the thoughts and images present such a frequent possibility of comparison with the *Commedia.* As in Canto XVI of the *Purgatorio,* he affirms here the principle that the ills of Christianity originate from the ill will of humankind not from the influences of the stars. As in Canto XIX of the *Inferno,* the connivance between the Papacy and the House of France are compared with the shameful pact of alliance between the Syrian kings and the false priests of Israel and as in Cantos XVII and IX of the *Paradiso,* the Curia is the place where "things that cannot be valued by money are rendered venal." It is the nest of the false shepherds, immersed in the arid and mundane studying of the pettifoggers, forgetful of the Gospels and the "great doctors" [of the Church.] *Gregory lies among the spider webs; so does Ambrose and the clerics' neglected closets. Augustine lies in contempt, like Dionysus, Damascene and Bede. But they exalt I do not know what Speculum, Innocence and the man from Ostia. Why not? The former were searching for God as a supreme and a maximum good, the latter look for gains and favors."*

Finally, also in this case, Dante's pleading concentrates on the image of Rome, "widowed and lonely" (*solam sedentem et viduam*), bereaved of her "two suns … who showed one and the other way, the world's and God's (*utroque lumine destitutam*). What is more relevant is that he now stresses decidedly the religious rather than the political aspect of the crisis, on the "bad example" of the Curia whence the infection spreads and infects the body of the militant Church. Because of the fault of those whose duty it was to "lead the chariot of Christ's Bride on the clearly assigned path" and who have "gone astray, not differently from Phaethon, the inept charioteer," the entire flock has lost its way and has been led "to the edge of the abyss" (*ad precipitium*). The lamentation takes a universal scope, similar to the immensity of the impeding catastrophe. And like a final, desperate appeal it sounds the exhortation "to fight bravely for Christ's Bride, for the seat of the Bride that is Rome, for our Italy, in fact, for the whole community of human beings who are pilgrims on this earth," *"pro tota civitate peregrinante in terris."*

*

The issue concerning the date of the composition of the *Monarchia* is very far from being agreed upon by scholars, nor does it offer an easy solution owing to the almost complete absence of internal and external evidence. The only important fact is a passage in the twelfth chapter of the first book, where there is a specific reference to the famous lines in the fifth canto of *Paradiso* concerning free will, "the greatest gift which God in his bounty bestowed in creating."

The critics who place the writing of the treatise at the time of Harry VII's enterprise, or even before it, consider that phrase a late interpolation of an educated scribe. But it is a rather bold hypothesis contrary to the unanimous evidence of the manuscript tradition.

The other topics that some propose in order to support the assumption the *Monarchia* was written between the end of 1312 and August 1313, such as the fact that, at the beginning of the second book, Dante refers to the Emperor with the title of "anointed" and mentions the conspiracy against him as a current event, and also the fact that, at the outset of the third book, the writer minimizes the Pope's and the Curia's opposition against the monarchy attributing it to an excess of zeal rather than wickedness and bad faith, are not elements of a determining value. The reason for this is that, in the first case, the title pertains by right to the ideal kind of a monarch, without referring necessarily to Harry VII's crowning, and in the second case it concerns a very understandable prudence in accordance with the nature of the treatise as a polemic discussion which is rigorously carried out on ideal and theoretical grounds. It is true, however, that if the mentioned quotation is considered authentic, we would face another uncertainty concerning the available elements at our disposal, which could be used to establish the beginning of the composition of *Paradiso*. But, without going deeply into the intricate question of the poem's chronology, that piece of information helps in considering a relatively late dating of the *Monarchia*, following, but not by much, Harry's death and the fading of the writer's hopes.

It is certain, however, that it would be useless to search in this work even a minimal indication of the anxious eloquence and the close interest that characterize the political epistles. Enthusiasm, hope, exhortation or scorn are absent and so are reprimands and invectives. One notices only a valiant and detached intellectual tension and, in the rare moments where the discussion becomes heated, an infinite and painful compassion for the world's disorder: "*O umanità, fra quante tempeste e iatture e naufragi ti conviene andar travolta, mentre, mutata in belva dalle molte teste, ti dibatti in tentativi stolti! Sei inferma nell'uno e nell'altro intelletto e nel sentimento: nè curi l'intelletto superiore con la medicina di ragionamenti inoppugnabili, nè l'inferiore con la considerazione dell'esperienza, e neppure il sentimento molcendolo con la suasiva dolcezza del monito divino, che per bocca dello Spirito Santo ti richiama:-Oh come è bello e dolce, quando i fratelli vivono tutti uniti*"

Among Dante's minor doctrinal writings, the *Monarchia* is not the only one to be completed (together with the *Questio*, of lesser size and importance), but also the most uniform, having a more united and organic structure.

From the very beginning the subject matter is orderly, divided into three main problems, each of which will constitute a book: is universal monarchy necessary for the world's welfare, have the Romans claimed their right, and does it emanate directly from God or is it under the influence of his minister or vicar? No less orderly and clear than the general one is the internal organization of each book in the distribution and development of the topics until the final conclusion that summarizes the entire contents of the treatise in the same way that the initial demonstration of the purpose destined to humanity had set its speculative foundation.

In the introduction the author states that, by obeying the duty that every person has not to use idly but to cultivate the wealth of knowledge inherited from tradition, he intends to explain to the readers "*intemptatas ab aliis ... veritates.*" This novelty consists mainly with the intention to order a systematic exposition where even the scattered elements of political doctrine deduced from Aristotle, the Church Fathers, the medieval treatise writers, and the Scholastics, take on a value and often a new significance. But, and more specifically, such novelty becomes evident in the perspective in which the problem is introduced and discussed and it gains emphasis especially in the first and last chapters of the book where the modern scholar, not differently from the poet's contemporaries, deliberately perceives the most daring and personal peaks of Dante's philosophy.

Dante says that in the sciences pertaining to operable issues, the principle that constitutes the basis of deductive research is identified with the aim of the study. If the discussion concerns monarchy, namely a universal political power, one should find out if a purpose imposed on the whole of human society exists and what it is, apart from the individual purpose of the single individual, the family, the city and the kingdom. Such an end could be found by considering the "ultimate power of entire humankind, the "*vis ultima in homine*" is the "*virtus intellectiva,*" the attitude to learn through the intellect that distinguishes man and "belongs only to him and no other creation, above or beneath him." The realization of the whole power of the intellect cannot occur "either by the action of a single man or by that of a particular community" from the family to the kingdom. The possibility of a man's knowledge at a particular time is realized only in part in single individuals or human associations. Only mankind in its totality can exhaust it from time to time.

The goal, therefore, the "*proprium opus humani generis totaliter accepti,*" consists in "realizing always all the possible intellectual power, first in speculation and secondly, by extention, in action." Here the concept already expressed in the *Convivio* reappears, namely that man's happiness and perfection on earth consists in the realization of all possible human knowledge. The source of this doctrine is now explicitly pointed out in Averroës' commentary to the *De anima*. Furthermore, in order for mankind to be "in a position to carry out its proper function more freely and easily," it must "exist in the calm and tranquility of peace," hence the need for "a single person to command and to rule," so that the world's order can be assured by discipline and justice, above individual interests through their balance and mitigating effect.

The reasons that Dante cites afterwards in order to confirm the hypothesis that "temporal monarchy is necessary for the world's well-being," can all be related to the common doctrines of the late Middle Ages, although he avails himself of them for a different purpose and perhaps even contrary to that of the doctrine he adopts. For example, the Aristotelic principle of unity, that for Egidio Colonna and the French treatise writers is necessary to establish the needs of a kingdom within a nation, is extended by Dante to the idea of a supra-national authority and progressively coordinated with the other concept of hierarchical order that becomes consolidated from the basis of the social pyramid to the top.

Thus, the other topic concerning justice, "wherever there might be reason for a dispute, there should be a judge "and the need of an authority that may solve through a sentence with no appeal the conflicts among states," was adopted by Boniface VIII to support the *plenitudo potestatis* of the pope while Dante applies it to the monarch and strengthens it with a subtle line of reasoning: only the emperor, whose jurisdiction extends by right to the borders of the inhabited land and owns everything, has nothing else to desire; his will is completely free from greed, that often corrupts and clouds human reason, and his love for all human beings is pure and unselfish, "*ergo eo existente iustitia potissima est vel esse potest.*"

Also more novel and closely connected with the writer's feelings is the importance that the idea of freedom takes as regards the monarch. Free will is defined as the unrestricted judgment that determines the activity of reason toward action. Only when desire acts under the sole order of reason, unaffected and not subdued by any kind of external influence, one can speak of true liberty. This condition does not always occur within limited social institutions, because corrupt governments— tyrannies, oligarchies, and demagogies—subdue people to their goals. Only the monarch, who loves equally all people and wants all of them to become good, can assure justice in freedom. Within the monarchic framework, also the minor states remain incorrupt and govern fairly. The citizen is no longer dependent upon the magistrate but the magistrate upon the citizen: "In truth, the citizens are not dependent upon the consuls, nor are the people dependent upon the king, but, on the contrary, consuls depend upon the citizens and the king upon the people." From this point of view "the consul and the king are the servants of the others, for they interpret and fulfill the law," and "especially the monarch who is without doubt the servant of all." Politics and morality, that had dangerously become disso- ciated in the tainted and twisted ordinances, are newly identified "*in recta politia,*" according to Aristotle's principle, "*bonus homo et civis bonus convertuntur.*"

If we take into account the large difference between the juridical foundation of the universal authority that the medieval theoretitians, including the author of the *Monarchia,* assigned to the emperor and the somewhat narrow limits within which such authority had been reduced in the historic situation of the fourteenth century, it would be futile to try to define precisely the way Dante envisioned the concrete realization of his ideal on practical grounds. And he proceeds logically, disregarding the actual situation, not differently from the other treatise writers favoring the emperor, the king or the pope but with a higher scorn for the contemporary cases as he limits his observation within the borders of a highly speculative proposition. It is certain, however, that in his mind the monarch's authority does not eliminate but incorporates the individual autonomies in their specific limits. "Nations, kingdoms and cities have their specific characteristics that ought to be regulated by different laws. They receive from the emperor the generic law, the *comunis regula* that must be applied to the individual case from time to time, and they are obliged to abide by that law."

In conclusion, it is in the monarch that is embodied the rule of justice and the need of a supreme judgment, a need which still lasted in that twilight of the Middle Ages and was commonly felt and persistently invoked in different times, even during the evident and rapid decline of institutions, such as the Church or the Empire, that were supposed to represent it in theory and to carry it out in practice.

The difference between doctrine and the actual situation reappears in another form related to the problem developed in the second book: whether the responsibility of monarchy is by right the duty of the Roman people. In reality, at Dante's time, the task of designating the emperor had been transferred for several centuries to the German nation. But, on the other hand, Rome, that was the nominal capital of the state, had been removed from the regular sovereign's jurisdiction to the point that, in order to enter the city and be crowned there, he had first to negotiate with the pope and the commune, as in the case of Harry, and swear to recognize its autonomy and renounce his power while he resided in it.

This opposition and particular resistance, however, had to seem, in Alighieri's mind, insolent enchroachments that could not be considered in a rigorously theoretic view and, as far as the designation, the choice and the confirmation of the emperor were concerned, they were attributed to God and the so called electors, in a manner that resembled the procedure followed by the cardinals when they designated a pope, who were considered intermediaries and revealing agents of divine providence, "*denuntiatores divine providentie.*" Having done that, he was able to set about his task of explaining the rights and dignity that had been acquired in history by the "*populus romanus,*" by resuming the topics that he had discussed in the *Convivio* concerning virtue, nobility and civil wisdom that predestined naturally the Roman people to subdue and rule over the other peoples.

The religious principle of historic tradition that continues to exist from the Romans to the Italian nation, the evidence drawn above all from poets and philosophers (from Ovid to Lucan, from Cicero to Seneca and Boethius), and even more, that full confidence that unites myth and truth, poetry and history and Virgil, "our poets", "our major muse," disclose and accompany themes and positions that play important roles in the *Commedia*.

And there will equally be an ample treatment in the *Paradiso* of one of the major topics: Christ himself recognized the emperor's authority both when he wanted to be born during the edict issued by him and when, upon his death, he submitted to a sentence pronounced in his name. In fact, if the imperial authority had not been considered legitimate, that sentence would not have represented the rightful punishment that it was supposed to be and if his jurisdiction had not involved all humankind, it could not have punished a fault that was shared by all humans.

In the third book Dante finally tackles the theocratic thesis whereby imperial authority is subordinated to the Church, a thesis asserted by excess of zeal by the pope and by many leaders of the Christian flock, in bad faith by the politicians who used it as a convenient tool to avoid the protection and justice of an international sovereignty and because of ignorance by the jurists of the Curia who strove to offer the papal ambitions a justification on theoretical ground by corrupting and debasing the revelation of the original tradition of Christianity.

The latter people were wrong in that they attributed to the popes' decrees the same value that is due the Holy Scriptures and the decisions of the earliest ecumenical councils where Christ himself attests the priority and pre-eminence of the "*mandatum Dei*" compared with the later tradition of the Church. As for the politicians, their attitude had no other motivation but the defense of their greed. False allies of the Church as they proclaimed to be her faithful subjects, they were in truth Satan's progeny.

Only the reasons that excessive zeal and good faith inspired popes and religious leaders deserve to be refuted specifically. First the scriptural issues, such as the allegory of the "*duo luminaria magna*," that is superior and endowed with its own light, the sun (the Church), and the inferior, having a partially reflected light, the moon (the Empire).

Dante, who had used this allegory in his epistles, does not reject it even here, but he refuses to draw from it the same conclusion stated by the decretal officials: unlike the case of the moon and the sun, the Empire does not derive its existence from the Church's characteristics or actions, but only its capacity to function more effectively "*per lucem gratie, quam in celo Deus et in terra benedictio summi Pontificis infundit illi.*" And similarly, it is not true that incense and gold offered to Jesus by the Magi, or the two swords given by Christ to St. Peter, according to the gospel, should be understood as the representations of the two powers, temporal and spiritual. And it is arbitrary to attribute to political power the authority to bind and unbind, that had been granted Peter by the Redeemer concerning exclusively spiritual matters.

Among the historical topics, the most important is the donation of Constantine. Dante does not question its authenticity, but he proves juridically that it is not valid. The emperor had no right to transfer a portion of his jurisdiction, nor could the pope receive material assets *"per modum possessionis."* At the most, he would have been able to act as an usufructuary in order to distribute them to Christ's needy. Nor more valid is the other argument about the *"translatio imperii,"* whereby Charlemagne received from Pope Hadrian the title and the dignity of the Empire. That action was a mere usurpation similar, yet parallel and contrary, to the way in which Otto I restored the papacy to Leo after deposing Benedict V and *"usurpatio iuris non facit ius."*

There remain the considerations of a more philosophical nature, most importantly the Aristotelic principle of the *"reductio ad unum."* But it would be purely sophistical to deduce from it the subordination of the Empire to the Papacy, while it only implies that both powers derive from God, the primary source of all power. In reality, the Empire did not obtain its power from the Church because it carried out its activities before and independently from it, *"Ecclesia non existente aut not virtuante."* According to Aristotle's thinking, the foundation of the state is natural and rational: *"ius humanum"* and its mission is distinct and parallel to the Church's. The one and the other are *"remedia contra infirmitatem peccati,"* or means established by Providence to lead mankind back to the right way, for its nature has become corrupt as a result of Adam's fault. In any case, the area of temporal power does not coincide with the papacy's because the realm of the Church, like the realm of Christ, is not of this world.

At this point, the analysis is brought back to its fundamental theoretical basis and connected with the speculative premises established in the early paragraphs of the treatise. Differently from any other being, man, who is endowed with a twofold nature that is corruptible in body and incorruptible in soul, was given by God a double goal, "the blessedness of this life consisting of human virtue represented in the Garden of Eden, and the bliss of eternal life consisting of the enjoyment of the vision of God, that mankind cannot reach without the soccour of the divine light that is envisioned in heavenly paradise. Humankind, therefore, needed two rulers concerning the two goals, the supreme Pontiff to lead humankind to eternal life according to Revelation, and the Emperor, to lead it to temporal happiness according to the philosophical precepts." The two authorities, as the two ways, are naturally independent and autonomous: the sphere of philosophy, that by means of the intellectual and moral virtues leads to happiness on this earth, and the sphere of revealed doctrine that through the theological virtues, provides salvation in the beyond.

This concept that establishes the Empire as the instrument that must accomplish the end assigned the *"humana civilitas,"* distinguishes decidedly the two areas, material and spiritual, terrestrial and celestial, philosophical and theological, and is the point where the theoretitians of the Curia recognized the heretical focus in the *Monarchia* and the *Commedia* because, in orthodox Christian thought, it is not licit to assign an autonomous purpose to the *"beatitudo huius vite,"* that should be subordinated, rather, to the ultimate aim of celestial salvation.

Nor can the boldness of Dante's proposition be lessened by the amendment introduced by the author in the last lines of the treatise, that appears awkward and philosophically not quite accurate. He states that the essence of what he expressed should not be taken *"sic stricte"* so as to exclude any form of dependence of the emperor from the pope. In fact, "mortal happiness is ordained *'quodam modo'* by the immortal one, and it is proper for Caesar to adopt toward Peter that reverence that the eldest son owes his father."

This correction seems a retraction imposed by some scruple or a last minute caution or more probably by a compromise on a practical ground not so different from the many that will be devised through the centuries to solve temporarily the problem of the relationship between Church and State.

Dante's adversaries in the Curia could rightfully expect a coherent logical approach, when they rejected the subordination, recognized *in aliquo*, of the ruler to the vicar of Christ, a subordination *"quodam modo"* of the terrestrial and philosophical order to the heavenly and theological one. What is exactly uncertain and imprecise in these formulations is the hesitant and contradictory attitude that they reveal. They do not allow us to overestimate that phase of Dante's theoretical distress by exaggerating, as often happens, its importance on the ground of speculation.

We do not try to discover in the *Monarchia* new and vigorous concepts and even less the unforeseeable anticipation of a modern lay spirit (where there is, essentially, a not quite conscious activity of heretical tendencies to be considered within a purely medieval controversy). For us the book represents above all a revealing document regarding the structure of the *Comedy*. It reflects a phase of intellectual concentration that follows his disappointment and indicates a definitive renunciation of political activity. It is proof of an already advanced solution of the political theme with a religious and messianic hope, particularly through his persistent attention to the entirely spiritual mission of the Church, his repeated references to the evangelic sources with a significant statement concerning the providential and reforming mission entrusted to the Empire.

*

In the late years, the fame of high erudition and expert artistic mastery surrounded the image of the poet and theoretitian of the *Monarchia*. The cases, undoubtedly relevant from a biographical and cultural point of view, of the *Egloghe* and the *Questio*, are indicative in different ways of this fame and circumscribe it even geographically within the Aemilia-Venetian area from where only at a later time he was to direct his attention to the Tuscan cities and ultimately even to Florence, after he overcame the not so minor obstacle of his constant political grudges.

Along with these episodes we could mention others, not as significant but equally relevant, such as his connections and literary correspondence with a group of poets from Veneto and Aemilia headed by Giovanni Quirini, the evident and proven influence of method and exegetic forms in a letter to Cangrande in commenting on Mussato's *Ecerinis,* written around 1317 by Guizzardo from Bologna and Castellano from Bassano, as well as the commentary of Ovid's *Metamorfosi* written by Giovanni del Virgilio around 1323.

It is probable that Dante followed with concern and anxiety the events regarding the renewed success of the Ghibelline party in Tuscany with Uguccione della Faggiola, who had become the Lord of Pisa and Lucca as well as the chastiser of the Florentine pride at Montecatini, and in northern Italy with Cangrande della Scala who had been given by Harry the title of imperial vicar over Verona and Vicenza in 1312 and was pursuing tenaciously his political plans by foiling the scheming of the Guelph cities and the Angevin Robert as well as the spiritual threats of Pope John XXII.

Perhaps already in 1316 or in the previous year, after the death of his powerful protector Moroello, he had to decide and accept Cangrande's hospitality in Verona. At that time, he wrote a letter where he dedicated to him the third canticle [Paradise] that he had recently begun composing. In his letter he expressed his gratitude in the solemn style of praises: *"I came to Verona to see with my own eyes what I had previously learned about you and I witnessed your munificence, I saw and experienced your generosity and as, at first, I considered suspiciously your extraordinary fame, I later realized that it was indeed below reality. So that if the public renown had influenced me benignly towards you, after I met you, I became your most devoted friend in sincere respect."*

The poet's stay in Verona, where the munificent lord welcomed courtiers and political exiles from every country, had to be somewhat long if it gave rise to numerous anecdotes and legends that Petrarch heard directly from people some decades later. The presence with him of his two remaining children and perhaps his wife and the need to provide for them decorously, drove him to find a more stable settlement, or less precarious, for his living. And he continued to have a relationship of friendship and devotion with Cangrande till the end of his life, by sending him, according to their agreement, the cantos of his *Paradiso* as he was composing them.

It is not known when he moved from Verona to Ravenna under the protection of its ruler, Guido Novello da Polenta, whom he had probably had the opportunity to meet first as a military leader in Reggio Emilia, then as podestà in Cesena, and whom he probably esteemed also as a fine judge and an amateur poet. Although the tradition of Dante's public teaching in Ravenna appears unreliable, it is certain that in that city he enjoyed a coterie of admirers, disciples and jurists, such as Dino Perini, Pietro Giardini and Menghino Mezzani whose information was gathered later by Boccaccio in his attempt to prepare the poet's biography.

At the same time, Dante's connections with pre-humanistic centers in Veneto, Aemilia and Lombardy, Verona, Padua, Mantua and Bologna remained active. While he was in Ravenna, he received from Bologna, in 1319, a poem by Giovanni del Virgilio, a grammarian, teacher of classical poetry at the university, and an important cultural personality who was closely connected with Mussato and the Paduan classical school. Along with the highest and sincerest praises for Alighieri's poetical genius, the poem contained a disapproval and an invitation both in accordance with that spirit of cultural aristocracy that was already making its way in the schools and would end up in the pre-humanistic fervor of the Petrarchan era: Why did Dante, in spite of his great ability, persist in wasting its fruits in behalf of the common people? Why did he insist on dealing with sublime concepts in popular terms and in a plebeian language, "*carmine laico? Clerus vulgaria tempnit;*" "scholars spurn writings in vernacular tongues." "Indeed no one of those poets, in whose company you wanted to be the sixth, nor the other one, Statius, in whose company you journeyed toward heaven, has ever seen fit to use the lowly language of the common people ... Desist, then, from lavishing pearls on pigs and forcing the Castalian sisters in unworthy garments." "If, from now on, you will not be content with mediocre fame and the praise of the common people and will undertake to celebrate in a lofty style some worthy event of contemporary history—Uguccione's war against Florence, Cangrande's siege of Padua, the Visconti's fight against Genoa,—I myself, the humble scribe of the Muses and the slave of Maro, will be glad to introduce you to the honoring schools, your head adorned with the Peneian wreath, in the manner of the riding herald who rejoices in handing to the people the trophies of the victorious leader." Unexpectedly, Dante responded to the poem with an eclogue where he resumed the motives, references and the pastoral scene, of the *Bucoliche*. Thus, while he reaffirmed his intention to attain poetic renown by way of a literature that was modern in content and language, he gave proof of his humanistic knowledge, of his extensive study of the classics and of the artistic degree that he would have achieved, if he wanted to, on the basis of that refined, utterly imitative and literary style that the Bolognese master had shown him. He pretends to have a conversation between himself, Titiro, and another shepherd, Melibeo, and he introduces them in a lively scene as they converse about the recent invitation of Mopso who is watching over his herd in the shadow of the towering Menalo and "*dum lenta boves per gramina ludunt,*" he lingers to observe pensively "*hominum superumque labores.*" He reveals how pleasant it was to receive Mopso's praises and the promise of poetic glory. He returns his praises but he states that he hopes to receive his laurels for the composition at which he is tirelessly working when also the canticle that celebrates the rotating celestial spheres and the inhabitants of the starry kingdom is published, as *Inferno* and *Purgatorio* were. Then it will be good for him to wear a crown of ivy and laurel not in Bologna but on the banks of his native Arno:

> *Nonne triumphales melius pexare capillos*
> *et patrio, redeam si quando, abscondere canos*
> *fronde sub inserta solicitum flavescere Sarno?*
> *... Cum mundi circumflua cospora cantu*
> *astricoleque meo, velut infera regnat, patebunt,*
> *devincire caput hedera lauroque iuvabit.*

Welcoming the bucolic style that Dante had used in his eclogue, but using it in a clumsy way, lacking the creative elegance that embellishes the Florentine poet, Giovanni del Virgilio reiterated once again his invitation: in Bologna the "divine old man" will find a group of disciples eager to find their pleasure in the style of the new and the old art: "*Parrhasii iuvenesque senes, et carmina leti/qui nova mirari cupiantque antiqua doceri.*"

Dante answered with another, even more exquisite eclogue: where he is residing at present, a host of admirers and faithful friends assures him a serene sojourn and they would see with great concern his departure for a place where perhaps he would face uncertain dangers and the presence of a Polyphemus thirsting for human blood would be threatening him. And Titiro can only agree with their foreboding trepidation and loving pleas.

Reservations and misgivings concerning the authenticity of his bucolic correspondence have been repeatedly expressed, even in recent times but it is difficult to consider purely invented a number of documents that, in their totality or singularly, fit so naturally in the framework of confirmed biographical data belonging to an early period of cultural differences that were going to reach the intensity of a polemic at the time of Petrarch. And, on the other hand, the novelty of a return to Virgilian styles, and above all the artistic liveliness that is noticed in that imitation when compared with the clumsy attempts of the Bolognese writer, agrees with the endless fervor for technical experiments typical of Dante's genius.

More serious, undoubtedly, and also more obvious, are the reservations that were put forth even at the time of Tiraboschi and resumed more intensely at our time against the authenticity of the *Questio de aqua et terra*. From the context of the book it would appear that, after witnessing in 1319 a debate in Mantua on the issue of whether water, in its sphere, may be higher than the land emerging from it, Dante may have been permitted to define publicly the issue in Verona, in St. Helen's Chapel, in the presence of the city's clergy, on January 20, 1320 and, later, he might have put in writing the topics of his oral discussion. After presenting the opinions of those who asserted the greater height of the water, the author of the *Questio* confutes them, demonstrates that in every place the earth is higher than the surface of the sea and determines the immersion of the "inhabitable fourth," in the approximate shape of a half moon, in the attractive and drying power of the constellations. The deniers of the *Questio*'s authenticity bring out the differences between the physical theories of the Latin treatise and those that appear in some places of the *Commedia*, especially C. XXXIV of the *Inferno*, and in defense of their opinion is the fact that the composition reached us only in a print of the early sixteenth century, while it is completely ignored by the earliest annotators of the *Commedia*. Although the written compiling of the treatise is not indicated, mention is made explicitly of the Verona debate in the third writing of Pietro Alighieri's commentary, composed around the year 1350: "*Dantes auctor iste, disputando semel scilicet an terra esset altior aqua vel e contra ...*" In that passage, Pietro explains, but with different words, Dante's reasoning and points out their source in the doctrine of an Aly, "*summus astrologus et naturalis;*" and as far as the differences noticed between the *Questio* and the poem, one may adduce that they do not constitute a real contradiction while they may be easily explained by taking into account the difference between a scientific explanation and an imaginary creation, such as the last canto of the *Inferno*, where Dante speaks "*ficte et transumptive,*" expressing himself "poetically, pretending in order to render his poetry more believable." On the other hand, it is not easy to credit a forger with the numerous references and mentions concerning Dante's ascertained scholarship that emerge from a careful reading of the *Questio*. It is equally difficult to give proper credit for some stylistic details and the strictly medieval use of *cursus* as well as some more sentimental and personal impulses of the style that break its rigorously scholastic structure in a manner not quite different from what occurs in the *Monarchia*, as the writer's "inter vere phylosophantes minimus" and the autobiographic reference in the preamble: "cum in amore veritatis a pueritia mea continue sim nutritus," and also in paragraph xxi and xxii, the touching praise of God, splendid architect of the universe, as well as the polemic digression, entirely built on biblical citations, against the foolish who presume to investigate the truths that transcend human intelligence:" Desinant ergo, desinant homines querere que supra eos sunt, et querant usque quo possunt, ut trahant se ad immortalia et divina pro posse, ac maiora se relinquant."

If one accepts the authenticity of the *Questio*, the episode assumes the value of an important evidence of the fame reached, at least in some circles, by Dante as a philosopher, just as Giovanni del Virgilio's invitation is proof of the great fame that Dante had achieved as a poet. Although not quite impossible, it was not a common occurrence to allow a lay person without academic titles to define publicly a doctrinal topic.

In Verona and then in Ravenna, Dante dedicated himself mainly to the completion of his poem. He had just finished it when he was sent by Guido Novello as an ambassador to Venice. On his journey back he got ill and died in Ravenna the night of September 13, 1321. As the chronicler Villani indicated, he was entombed with a solemn funeral, as a poet and great philosopher, in a stone sarchofagus situated in a chapel near the church then called San Pier Maggiore, and later San Francesco.

The author of the *Ottimo commento* states that the funeral was attended by a multitude of "doctors of science," and the personality of the deceased—*"theologus nullius dogmatis expers ... Gloria Musarum"* —was soon honored with heartfelt celebrations in Latin epigraphs, among them one by Giovanni del Virgilio, and in poetic compositions, such as a canzone by Cino and a sonnet by Giovanni Quirini. Many years later Boccaccio composed a physical and moral picture of the poet, after the descriptions of those who had known him in his late years, with those traditional characteristics of a somewhat rigid composure, austerity and solemn decorum where one may notice a still powerful natural vitality even in his precocious old age. "Our poet was a man of medium height, with an oblong face and an aquiline nose, pronounced jaws and the lower lip protruding somewhat over the upper lip. He had rounded shoulders, rather large than small dark eyes, thick, dark frizzy hair and beard, always somber and pensive ... His clothes were always most simple and his attitude befitted his maturity, his walking calm and grave. In both private and public appearances his manners were modest and courteous ... Although he was most eloquent, he spoke rarely and only when invited. He was mostly solitary and close only with few. He was devoted to studying for the time he could dedicate to it. Eager of honors and formality ... his nature was noble and most disdainful."

*

The biographical events briefly outlined thus far and the minor works mentioned chronologically and presented in a form that appears compatible with contemporary situations, feelings and opinions, help only in part to explain the origins and greatness of the *Commedia*, and to fill the difference between the poetical masterpiece and its cultural predecessors, including those very minor works that are significant in themselves but not substantially different when considered within the framework of a rich literary production of an uncommon doctrinal and artistic level.

That biographical story and textual analysis, however, observed in their contents and forms, indicate both the constant broadening and enriching of the writer's moral and cultural horizon and his growing isolation within a historical situation that contradicts and revolts the frame of his mind and drives him into a tense polemical condition where the idea and structure of his major work are defined. The poem, that summarizes in a supreme synthesis the entire civilization of the Middle Ages, is also the element where one can perceive the advanced crisis of its institutions, ethic norms and intellectual framework and it ripens in a period of time that is already aiming at the overturning and rejection of its ideals. Hence, the attitude of incomprehension and surprise noticeable in its contemporaries or at least in the generation immediately following as regards that miracle, both strange and anachronistic yet stimulating and fascinating, of knowledge and style.

And it is possible to grasp the precise historical condition of the poem, its genesis in time and its doctrinal and moral principle exactly in the manner in which Dante feels painfully and polemically the break between the ideal system of scholasticism and the actual reality of his time without denying its ideology, rather by adhering to it with a resolute faith, as if it were the only means still valid and irreplaceable to understand, evaluate and correct in its aberrant reality.

Far from rejecting the contradictory complexity of the elements that arise in the intellectual, social and political experience of the crucial and troubled years between the end of the thirteenth and the early years of the fourteenth centuries, the author of the *Commedia* intends to reconstruct and reinsert them in the complex body of the system. He deals with those clouded and reluctant issues with all available means of reasoning, eloquence, invective and satire, with a constantly menaced confidence that revives every time bolder and more combative, in the possibility of creating an intellectual synthesis that might constitute an infallible instrument of reason and steady guide of human actions.

His philosophy was opposed to the attempts of reducing it to conceptual abstractions and was always ready for new applications and compromises in the area of reality, open to the lay world and more and more concerned with ethical and civil problems. It ignored, however, any fideistic withdrawal, irrational polemic and the monkish moralism that celebrated their triumph with the decline of scholastic thinking, following Duns Scoto and varyingly continued by Occam and his disciples. It adheres with faith intact to the assumption of a substantial concord and coherent continuity even in the distinction between reason and faith, Aristotelism and Christian revelation, dialectical and natural science as well as theology.

On the other hand, his concept of poetry that forebodes a humanistic view of art as a conscience and autonomous value of form as well as restoration and imitation of a classical tradition, remains otherwise medieval, allegorical and didactical, intended to put the contingent back in the sphere of the absolute, to reduce the varied matter of sensitiveness into a rigid framework of ideas and synthetize in a universal plan the writer's moral and mental experience so that it may be proposed to the readers as a precise educational and exemplary function. While the balance created by the great scholars and systematizers of scholasticism is almost ready to break up, the *Commedia* resumes its process by transferring it to a more direct application and broader emotional and pedagogical ability and it seems to aim at becoming a continuation as well as a replacement of the *summae* and encyclopedias but with a more intense and ample force of its persuasion, exhortation and drive.

It will also avail the modern critic who has become aware of the inadequacy of an impressionistic and fragmentary reading of the poem, to start again from the exegetical criteria specified in the already mentioned dedicatory letter of the *Paradiso* to Cangrande della Scala. The Dantesque origin of the poem, confirmed recently by strong philological discussions, is confirmed also by the precise adherence of the poetry to the textual characteristics, a poetry that is defined within a cultural situation determined by its time to the point that already in the earliest commentators, Lana, Ottimo, Pietro Alighieri and Guido da Pisa, it is echoed, often literally, yet also altered and misunderstood in its most personal aspects. It is there that the purpose, the *"finis"* of the *Commedia*, conceived in its specific character of *"opus doctrinale,"* is shown in the intention of *"removere viventes in hac vita de statu miserie et perducere ad statum felicitatis."* One should consider also that the philosophical discipline, the *"genus phylosophie,"* in which said purpose is framed, is the *"morale negotium,"* an ethic entity as the consideration of the behavioral foundations and active instrument of action, so that the entire book, in its complex and varied structure, may be considered *"non ad speculandum, sed ad opus inventum."* Also, the elements of a strictly philosophical and scientific knowledge that operate in it should not be evaluated autonomously but in relation to its practical aims, *"non gratia speculativi negotii, sed gratia operis."* Only such definition, when it is understood in its entire significance, is truly comprehensive of the main purpose, of the development in time and the personal and historical development of the poem as a marvelous organization of doctrinal frameworks that, when applied to the poetic material and the author's autobiographical experience turned into an exemplary concept, that constantly tends to become a sharp instrument of individual social, moral and political behavior.

It is important, for Dante, to rediscover the essence of human *"felicitas"* in the present reality and in eternity, according to the twofold goal indicated to humankind in this world and beyond, within the scheme of a blessedness to be reached on earth, in a just and peaceful civil order, through the help of philosophy, and a higher blessedness promised in heaven, through the assistance of Revelation and Grace.

When Dante begins to compose his poem, he intends to clarify in his conscience and beyond the world's reasons of its *"status miserie."* On the one hand, then, it involves a strongly polemical interpretation of the historic situation and the will to intervene in that situation to modify it and bring it back to the right way. That "right way" means the need to reestablish the solidity of an intellectual and normative order consecrated by a century old cultural tradition and, on the other hand, it involves a reconsideration of the author's intellectual and practical autobiography where that extreme crisis of Christian civilization is reflected and resolved, as it were, in a personal form. From such a number of life experiences and moral reasons where repentance and the individual's conversion is nobilitated and broadened to reflect the revival of the whole of mankind, arises the poem in its two-fold nature, personal and universal, lyrical and doctrinal, and the meeting point where the two fundamental components of Dante's inspiration converge; it is the ethic-political theme that drives its roots in the actual experience of the man of action and the exile and builds on that basis the terms of a universally valid doctrine that is never conceived in abstractions but is always involved in a plot of feelings, grudges, anguish and polemics, hopes and nostalgia, impulses of scornful anger and distressed, contemplative reflections. Hence his polysemy, explicitly defined in the letter to Cangrande and extended to the interpretation of the whole poem which, together with its literal and historical meaning, includes in its entirety also a meaning that includes allegorical, moral and anagogical values.

Yet, in this case, the alternative sense is no longer applied from the outside, to the letter and mechanically, as in the case of the allegorical canzoni for Philosophy, but it exists internally in the story that assumes the function of *"exemplum"* but maintains its political, real and poetic substance intact. Because, in this case, said story is, first of all and immediately, I mean with all the importance of its events and determining psychological reactions, the transcription, albeit stylized and exalted, of an individual man's book in the very writer, the author-protagonist, Dante the poet and the character, who is present throughout the composition, but also the other fundamental personalities that represent the allegorical setting, Reason and Revelation, the *"phylosophica documenta"* and the *"documenta spiritualia,"* the two guides that are necessary to reach the *"beatitudo huius vite"* and the *"beatitudo vite eterne"* before representing symbols are characters of a reality experienced in its two-fold substance, intellectual and sentimental. Virgil, the favorite poet, master of style but also witness and prophet of a solemn ideology and Beatrice, the exclusive love, are the image of a youthful purity briefly perceived, lost, mourned and finally recovered laboriously in painful recollections and repentance.

Not otherwise is based the relationship between the two views, if one considers the book's material, the *subjectum,"* according to the author/commentator's terminology. In its literal meaning it is the *"status animarum post mortem,"* the representation of the three realms of the other world, a theme the poet derives from a century-old tradition and mainly, at first, from the Virgilian inspiration but that he innovates deeply by transforming it into a real journey and a personal experience.

From an allegorical perspective, it stands for man's condition in that, by acting freely, he becomes worthy of punishment or reward, in our time and in eternity: "*homo prout merendo et demerendo per arbitrii libertatem est iustitie premiandi et puniendi obnoxius.*" The link between the two meanings is quite close, almost inextricable, with respect to allegorical medieval literature and even Dante's preceding attempts. Yet, at the same time, it is more flexible and free because it allows both elements complete actuality. If one sets totally aside any possibility of dual interpretation, the reader must be ready in every situation and for every character, to grasp simultaneously the historical value of the episode with its chronological and sentimental essence as well as its symbolic function, the imaginative and didactical/moral elements blended together and indissoluble in the peculiarly medieval structure of the "*exemplum.*" Should one consider this fact carefully, it would imply the absurdity of an allegorical interpretation, applied pedantically (as in the case of readers having scarce poetic sense) in order to give any detail of the narration, facts or word, a tacit meaning.

As in the case of the Bible, the hagiographic texts and, for Dante, the Virgilian story of Aeneas' journey in the underworld, the narrative material here is far from being "a pleasant lie," whose concealed meaning must be reached through the veil of false images. It is, rather, a story of real facts that assumes immediately a symbolic value, or better, a revelation that sets the mutable story into the stillness of absolute values while it captures the eternal in the contingent. This approach limits completely the importance of allegory, conceived in its most obvious sense, and allows a nearly unlimited freedom to poetic imagination. Far from being reduced to a mechanical exercise of the mind submitted to a didactic purpose, the "form" of the composition, envisioned in its most essential aspect, may be expressed in a variety of procedures spreading over a very broad gamut, from the poetic creation and description to the theoretical digression, the moral exemplification, doctrinal polemic and satire: "*modus tractandi est poeticus, fictivus, descriptivus, digressivus, transumptivus, et cum hoc diffinitivus, divisivus, probativus, improbativus, et exemplorum positivus.*" (Note: Out of the six items that are considered in the letter to Cangrande, we have selected five and have included them in our analysis:" subjectum," "agens," "forma," "finis," and "genus phylosophie." What was left out is the "titulus," that reads as follows "Comedia Dantis Alagherii, florentini natione, non moribus." The reservations of the deniers of the letter's authenticity are focused with a keener sharpness exactly on the title, for it appears to them to be outrageously conflicting with the "sacred poems." But it is in accord with the terms of Dante's specific culture, according to the values the two terms, tragedy and comedy, had assumed in the medieval dictionaries, both concerning the matter of the work "in principio horribilis et fetida, ... in fine prospera et grata," and with respect to its form, that is the vernacular, the language of the uneducated and even of women, "locutio vulgaris, in qua et muliercule communicant." After all, the letter's words echo almost identically in the eclogue to Giovanni del Virgilio, where there is a reference to the poem as "comica verba," that "femineo resonant ut trita labello."

When one says, according to a formula that is mentioned frequently by modern Dante scholars but whose origins one can trace back in some of the earliest comment writers, such as Guido da Pisa, that the *Commedia* is a vision, a revelation, and a prophecy, it assumes the writer is convinced to have a providential mission whereby he can appear as a new Aeneas or Paul ordered, when still alive, to know and divulge the secrets of the beyond, or even a forerunner appointed to prepare the way for the nearing arrival of the Veltro, "God's messenger," who will come to reinstate justice on earth, and by assigning, within order, the duties of the monarch and the pope. He will prepare the conditions for a perfect accomplishment of the twofold goal entrusted to humankind, as when one says undoubtedly something essentially and profoundly true or greatly near truth. In fact, while one circumscribes more exactly the literary genre where the work belongs according to the author's intention, namely, the "prophetic" genre (although he deals with it in a grand vision and with artistic developments that have no examples in the confused mysticism of similar compositions of its time and before it), one would remark the value of absolute truth concerning the solidity of its principles. As for the general plan of the poem, religious faith allows the author to attribute to the world of the beyond a reality that appears as complete as the one experienced on earth. Finally, concerning details, it is viewed in each one of its components with an equal, integral and firm conviction.

It is mandatory, however, to establish clearly the limits within which that definition may be considered valid and useful for the critic, beyond which one may conceive the absurd idea of imagining a Dante naïvely identified and possessed by his prophetic function, convinced of reproducing the substance of a vision and an ecstatic rapture experienced in reality, called to act passively, that is, rather than to create and control the product of his imagination.

As we have mentioned previously, prophecy is, by itself, a literary genre that the writer derives from the biblical tradition and is resumed and renewed with great success especially among the Joachim followers and the Franciscan spirituals as it meets some essential requirements of medieval aesthetics. In fact, it emphasizes subjectively the notion of a transcendental character of inspiration whereby the poet may appear as a *"scriba,"* the humble and faithful recorder of an order from above and he objectively guarantees the truthfulness of the contents, its cognitive value and pedagogical effectiveness. But it never excludes from the author, poet or artist endowed with a terse and strong mental disposition the vivid consciousness of building a *"fictio poetica"* and of engaging in the constructing endeavor by adopting at the highest degree all the resources of his rhetorical technique, inventiveness, knowledge and education.

From this there stems not only the necessity but the special importance of a work such as the *Commedia*, composite par excellence and deliberately architectonical, the so called structure, that Croce called "theological romance," namely the invention's division into a plan and on the line of a framework of conceptual outlines that tend to reduce to the least the irrational components of the fictional process.

The first narrative opportunity is offered by a biographical aspect, a phase of moral and doctrinal straying in the life of the writer/character, at the beginning although it is taken as a meaningful function of universal value framed into a precise chronology, such as the death of the woman who, by enamouring him for her, keeps him in a condition of purity and leads him toward heavenly matters. The poet is lost in a dark wood and, reaching the age of thirty-five, at the apex of the approximate duration of human life, he is at the edge of a spiritual death. Beatrice and, indirectly, St. Lucy and the Virgin (the three ladies who look after the poet's destiny), send Virgil to help him in his extreme peril. Virgil will guide him through Hell and Purgatory as far as the Garden of Eden whence Beatrice will lead him through the heavens to the Empyrean. The journey takes place in 1300, in seven days, beginning April 8 (Good Friday, the day of Jesus' death), or March 25 (according to the tradition that caused the creation of Adam and the Redeemer's death to coincide), at a time, somehow, near the spring equinox.

Considered in its reality, the journey has the purpose of healing Dante's soul through all those means that can be offered by a mind controlled by knowledge and faith and make him worthy of beholding God's splendor and of revealing to humankind the substance of his amazing vision.

From an allegorical point of view, it portrays the process of purification by means of which man becomes worthy of the eternal reward, by reflecting on the consequences of sinning and the conscious experience of repentance and mortification. Furthermore, it indicates the arduous way of humankind, assisted by philosophical doctrine and governed by imperial authority toward happiness on earth (Garden of Eden), inspired by Revelation and enlightened by the Church toward the supreme beatitude (Empyrean).

The primary concept of the pilgrimage implies, first of all, a physically reliable topography of the spiritual realms. Hell is conceived as a large conical abyss, divided in nine circles that opens near Jerusalem and descends to the center of the earth where Lucifer is implanted. Purgatory is a very high mountain rising in the southern hemisphere in the middle of the ocean, on the opposite pole of Jerusalem. It is also divided into nine sections and its top, where Eden is located, reaches the highest region of air, beyond the zone of meteors. Finally, Paradise consists of the nine heavens of the Ptolemaic system that are translucent spheres rotating around the earth and, beyond them, is the Empyrean, the heaven of pure light, outside space and time, where are God and the blessed souls. If for the concept of Empyrean and the nine heavens, with the doctrine of the influence that they exercise on the sub-lunar world and of the moving intelligences, it is evident to notice the close connection with current science and theology, also concerning the position and configuration of the first two realms the writer does not resort to summary indefinite inventions, such as those that one would find in the ample literature on the hereafter, but he carries out a rigorous selection of the data that he could obtain from the biblical, patristic and scholastic exegesis and introduces them in a great cosmological hypothesis which, although imaginary, may aspire to a certain scientific rigor, as, for example, in the case of Lucifer who, when he was expelled from heaven, precipitated toward the center of the physical universe and caused the infernal abyss. The land that emerged in the southern hemisphere, "fearing him," withdrew under the water and formed, in the other hemisphere the "great dry land," namely the inhabited continents and perhaps another mass of land, in order to avoid any contact with the monster's enormous body, emerged in turn to form on the other pole the very high mountain of Eden, a solitary island in the immense ocean.

A no less rigorous and precisely defined doctrine inspires the moral and juridical order of the three realms with the respective classifications of sin, sinful predispositions and virtuous tendencies.

In hell, the condemned souls are distributed according to the Aristotelic distinction of incontinence and malice: the incontinent souls, whose reason was overwhelmed by uncontrolled passions, are situated from the second to the fifth circle. In the last three circles, from the sixth to the ninth, are the sinners of malice, divided according to their unjust actions expressed through violence (against God, the self and/or one's fellow human beings), or through fraud (against one's trust or mistrust). In the sixth circle and out of the Aristotelic classification, are punished the heretics. The first circle is Limbo where are placed the infants who died un-baptized and the just souls of those who lived outside or before the Christian revelation. At the gates of hell are relegated the neutrals "displeasing to God and to his enemies." In Purgatory, the classification of the penitent souls is no longer determined by the sins actually committed but by their sinning predispositions following the ideas of a psychological analysis based on the concept of love innate in every creature, generating all virtues and defects of created beings. Since love involves a voluntary and conscious choice, it may err because of an evil object, in that it wishes for others' suffering (pride, envy and anger, from the first to the third terrace of the mountain), or because of "too little vigor," in that it operates lukewarmly or negligently in pursuing true good, that is God (slothfulness, on the fourth terrace); or, finally, through "too much vigor," in that it pursues excessively finite and imperfect good (avarice, gluttony and lust, in the last three terraces). At the foot of the mountain is Ante-Purgatory, where those who delayed repentance for their sins to the very last are waiting to begin expiation. In Paradise, finally, the rank order of the spirits dictated by artistic reasons and symmetry with the other canticles, has almost exclusively a symbolic value and entails a reality of a spiritual order.

Granted that all blessed souls reside in the Empyrean, Dante imagines that they come to meet him in the lower spheres to show him the image of their different degrees of blessedness, according to the various influences that the spheres have in determining the character of every human being. Thus, in the heaven of the Moon he sees the souls that, being naturally inclined to chastity, broke their vows, by giving in to external violence. In the heaven of Mercury reside the souls who acted virtually for the exclusive desire of glory. In the sphere of Venus are those whose devotion was directed toward love and who succeeded, although laboriously, to convert their inclination toward earthly matters to the supreme Good. In the sphere of the Sun are the wise ones, in Mars the soldiers and martyrs of the faith, in Jupiter the rulers inspired by justice, in Saturn the contemplative and ascetic souls. In the sphere of the Fixed Stars he contemplates Christ's triumph and the Virgin's coronation, in the Primum Mobile he sees the angelic orders like fiery whirlwinds rotating around an extremely intense light and finally, in the Empyrean, he has a vision of all saints distributed like the petals of an immense flower on which pure intelligences descend from God and return to him eternally. There, through the intercession of the Virgin invoked by St. Bernard, he prays for the supreme grace of seeing the divine Essence and to comprehend the mysteries of the Trinity and Incarnation.

It would not be helpful to dwell on the intellectualistic aspect of the topography and the ethical/juridical order of the other world, as it would not be the case to linger over the course followed by abstract intellect in devising the punishments of the sinners' categories according to a qualitative correspondence between the sin and its eternal retribution, the prayers and examples of rewarded virtues in Purgatory or to modify the atmosphere of the third canticle with spectacular and symbolic inventions, such as the crowns of dancing and singing lights in the sphere of the Sun, the luminous cross in Mars, Jupiter's eagle, the immense ladder in Saturn and so on. Everybody knows that such an abstract devise is envisioned by a prodigious, imaginative power that creates step by step the illusion of a real journey with its horrid, hallucinating, idyllic, elegiac, and ecstatic scenes, the variety of the encounters, its time, the concrete representation of pain and pleasure, despair, hope, resignation and total spiritual fulfillment. Only an abstract and *a posteriori* analysis can isolate the poem's structural framework from the human matter, characters and feelings that converge and settle in it.

In reality, the concrete study of the book in its totality and the most reliable reconstruction of its genesis shows that its structure is created and developed in close connection with its poetic content and with the tools of the writer's narrative and dramatic technique. Not only the details but also the general structure take shape by degrees along with the inspiration that evolves and becomes complete in time while, along with a building up that lasts about fifteen years, it becomes progressively clearer broadening his experience, polemic reasons and theoretical premises.

Those who read the first cantos of the poem with an open mind, will certainly recognize some uncertainty in its ethic-political ideology together with a relative technical unpreparedness and, by going further on in the reading, they will notice that the poem modifies and defines itself under the influence of chance elements while cleverly avoiding the danger of sudden and serious contradictions in the first canticle and in those that follow.

It may be opportune, at this point, to mention the issue of the poem's chronology. Among the diverging opinions of those who attribute the composition of the entire work to the last years of Dante's life, after the failure of Harry VII's intervention, and those who think that it had been initiated already around 1307, when he gives up the completion of the *Convivio* and the *De vulgari eloquentia*, or even in 1304, along with the writing of the two treatises, the second opinion appears the more reasonable at least for the greatest margin of time that allows the construction of such an ample and complicated body of work. (Note: Indisputable data are scanty and not quite probatory. It is known that around 1314–1315 people had knowledge of a book that Alighieri was writing, that dealt, among other things, of the infernal realms. This much and no more one can infer from an indication of Francesco da Barberino in the Latin commentary of his *Documenti d'Amore*. Reliable documents attest to the already occurred divulging of the first canticles in 1317 and 1319, while from the eclogues to Giovanni del Virgilio and other agreeing evidences it emerges that the *Paradiso* was a labor of the latest years and was divulged posthumously. From the internal elements one can obtain only generic, and partly contradictory indications also because one will have to consider the possibility, in some places, of late reconsiderations and emendments on the already completed text.)

To incline us to prefer the second opinion involves a careful comparison of the various parts of the book and the consequent opinion of a partial modification and enrichment of the moral, political and religious ideas of the writer, of the gradual evolution of his psychological and sentimental conditions from which derives a twofold process of perfecting doctrinal patterns and clear-cut ethic-political ideals on the one hand, and, on the other, of a progressive softening and refining of his initial satirical and polemical impulse.

It is appropriate, in fact, to consider the *Commedia* an *in fieri* work, rather than a single block of pre-established concepts and forms. In this manner we will better realize the presence of some perspective and tonal variations that an experienced observer cannot fail to notice as his reading progresses, and that can be explained only in part along with the changes of the contents, while, on the other hand, they reflect and accompany the development of a laborious, personal experience representing the entire final phase of the poet's life.

And by pursuing this direction one does not challenge in any way the principle on which rests the unity of the poem, which is based on a general concept, the vision of the beyond, and an original intuition that supports that concept and develops it in a complex and coherent series of figures, so that from a deep root grows an immense tree that progressively expands in time with its trunk ramifications, branches, flowers and fruits without any arbitrary aggregation, stratification or mechanic superimposition but with a totally natural and organic developmental procedure.

It is also true that such early root, the fundamental core of his inspiration, penetrates in time quite beyond the programmed initial phase of the composition, but it comes to life and grows, one might say, with Dante's biographical development, with the maturing of his intellectual and moral personality, so that one may perceive its earliest, uncertain signs in the writings of the poet's youth (in the last paragraphs of the *Vita nuova*, Beatrice's vision in the Empyrean is, in fact, announced), and, on the contrary, in the supreme phase of his development, it appears capable of enclosing and synthesizing, although transfigured and enriched, even the most remote moments, as well as the faintest and most fragile residues of that experience.

If it is conceived in this sense, the genesis of the work entails not only a close and constant connection of logical structure and fictional matter, but also the essential and determining function of the former in comparison with the choice and the way of accepting that matter and elaborating it poetically. The function of the structure of the *Commedia* is far from being reduced to a mere extrinsic and negligible connective tissue, it establishes the form of the representation and even the narrative technique. The content of Dante's imagination sweeping over a horizon of unheard of breadth involves all aspects of reality, from the humblest to the noblest ones, from the simplest to the most complex and all the facets of an experience into an organic vision, past, present and foreseeable future, the current events and the univocal reality of history, poetry and myth. It contains, therefore, an infinite number of variations that already amazed its contemporary readers, ranging from the comical to the elegiac and tragic, from the satirical to the didascalic and epic (*omnis pars poeticae*, according to the keen definition of Benvenuto da Imola), and derives every one of its elements, in its least details, its wonderful vitality, its tone of truth from its projection in space and time "against the background of a changeless reality" (Hegel), from the original choice of the particular perspective adopted by the writer by whose virtue the topic of the book is, as De Sanctis ingeniously defined it, "God's city, in which is reflected man's city in all its reality of such place and time, the one (being) the exemplary model and judge of the other."

What stems from it is a constant, common presence and mutual conversion of the moral themes and poetic invention. The reader who, rather than accepting obediently the poet's assumption, naively gives himself up to the wave of immediate impressions, forgetting or neglecting the primary issue of the spiritual condition and the continuity of the narration as an active, progressive, intellectual and moral experience, runs the risk not only of missing too much of Dante's creation but also of misunderstanding and impoverishing the poetic substance of those very pages where the writer's humanity shines through the most and acquires prominence.

The entire history of the poem's fortune and criticism, from the Renaissance men of letters to Croce, proves that the above does not constitute merely a hypothetic risk. The fact being that a more careful reading reveals the impossibility of distinguishing and separating, even ideally, the fundamental components of Dante's genius: the earnestness and greatness of his ethical project as well as an extraordinary mold of figurative inventions and a prodigious wealth of stylistic and verbal solutions. The poetry of the episodes that are introduced as more independent and removed from the "theological romance," develops into more or less explicit moral reasons and, to be well understood, it requires continued attention to its structure. And, on the contrary, the vigor and intensity of an imagination naturally inclined to transform into sensitive and substantial terms even the most intellectual and abstract of its experience, intervene everywhere to embellish poetically every detail for the composition and even the most obviously didascalic or allegorical situations.

Those who isolate, in the tenth canto of the *Inferno*, the majestic figure of Farinata and the pathetic one of Cavalcanti or the themes of political passions and paternal love, while they come inevitably to an arbitrary and anachronistic interpretation of the episode, deprive themselves of the possibility of understanding it in all its complexity and in its dramatic movement, they immobilize and weaken the poetical substance that originates from the converging and contrasting of differing feelings, with the active presence of Dante the character and unfold entirely under the sign of an inflexible justice, whereby it becomes brighter and more apparent in its nature and, at the same time, is punished and overcome in the conscience of the pilgrim, the sin of the Epicureans. And similarly, the episodes of Francesca and Pier della Vigna are misunderstood by those who in the first case concentrate on the image of the loving woman and in the other on the image of the faithful and unacknowledged minister, whereas in both situations the stress is exerted on the moral experience of Dante the character and it reaches its peak in the reconstruction of the origin of the sinful actions, showing us the convoluted ways (the theory of the gentle heart and the natural resentment of the scorned and violated justice) the soul works in itself with the intention to sin and creates progressively the bases for that instant when its damnation will become reality. Thus, the very wealth of the dramatic and pathetic developments, in one with the representation of the punishment and the damned souls' unchangeable damnation, far from contradicting the moral condemnation, it prepares and justifies it by freeing it from the burden of abstract, moralistic pedantry and enriches it with an abundant, psychological casuistry.

Not differently, the moving and cordial sadness of the encounters with the master and friend in the episodes of Brunetto and Forese is determined by the contrast with the punishment that disfigures horribly their faces and renders them unrecognizable. By becoming impressed in the pilgrim's mind, it enters, with its burden of affection and memories, in an actual cathartic process of a progressive spiritual redemption.

Nor is it possible to separate the human poetry of the dialog with the ancestor Cacciaguida, the polemic recollection of the commune's happy times, the celebration of the prophetic mission and the sad commemoration of the exile's sufferings, from the heavenly and theological atmosphere of the *Paradiso*; and it is not possible to isolate the most intensely dramatic passage of the entire poem, the story of Ugolino, with its inextricable knot of pity and hatred from its background of gelid and cruel horror, of implacable and ferocious justice, of Cocitus' ice.

Not even Ulysses' episode which, more than any other one, seems to hover in an atmosphere of poetry and independent human character and almost to establish a contrast between the judgment of the theologian who condemns and that of the poets who unconsciously admire, really escapes the inflexible, ever vigilant moral reason of the writer. In fact, it draws from it, with its development and its manifest exemplary function, the tone of the story that is not celebratory but tragic.

On the contrary, even in the pages where the medieval technique of the *exemplum* appears more openly, the writer's human sensitivity is never entirely absent, with his warm attitude and concrete vision. Simply to mention one case, there is in Canto XIX of the *Purgatorio* the typical *exemplum* of Pope Adrian's story but, even within the boundaries of a moralistic inspiration, it is developed with a moralistic rhythm that stresses the intense notes of disappointment and sad loneliness of the ambitious man who has reached the peak of his fortune.

Poetically intense, along the terraces of the *Purgatorio*, are the examples of vices and virtues that sometime adopt the thin technique of the *Novellino* (such as the episodes of Micol and Trajan, Pisistratus and Stephen Protomartyr), other times condensing in the power of an epithet or verb the human and dramatic substance of a fable (as in the rapid images of Lucifer and the Giants, Nimrod, Arachne and so on). The elements of an extraordinarily broad, complex and manifold literary, philosophical and scientific culture are never reduced to idle or merely decorative ideas but, for the most part, are endowed and enlivened by the fervor of lively and quick imagination, while the more strictly didascalic elements that become more and more frequent in the second and third canticle, are dramatized in the dialogs and made to fit an instrumental purpose vis-à-vis the general plan. One should keep in mind the manner in which the themes of Dantean politics are taken and transformed into functional elements of a broader poetic view in many pages of the poem (for example, in the canto of the simoniacs or in those of Sordello, Mark Lombard, Justinian or in St. Peter's invective). One should also observe how, in the central cantos of the *Purgatorio*, the accumulation of a doctrinal subject that concerns the fundamental problems of moral life and human liberty, and then in the *Paradiso*, the constant resumption of the predestination theme and divine justice and, finally, the interrogations, scholastic only on the surface, on the three theological virtues, correspond to a precise structural reason and originate from the impulse of concrete experience, enlightening the moments and essential pauses of the interior process of liberation and ascension of the pilgrim. Even the discussion on the lunar spots, the most dry reasoning of the entire poem, where a problem that appears limited at first, of pure curiosity and somewhat archaic, is dealt with in the form and method of a scholastic *quaestio*, arises from a strong structural requirement and is connected with the theme of a much broader and intrinsic function: the great and moving celebration, at the gates of the heavenly kingdom, of the physical and spiritual order imposed by the divine will upon all parts of the universe. Thus, by superimposing on the eternally unchanging background of the beyond the present, infinitely variable reality of human history, the *Commedia* may be, in the whole, an encyclopedia concerned with every aspect of knowledge, a complete system of ethics and psychological casuistry, the impassionate statement of a political ideology whose roots reach a grand, unitary concept of the history of mankind first and, after Redemption, the production of an ideal autobiography, the supreme effort of the art that aims at obtaining and reproducing all elements of physical and spiritual experience of life and culture. Every part corresponds to another; each one develops from another naturally and returns to it in a circle of ever expanding breadth and complexity.

The imposing structural system that develops and progressively takes shape from the basic nucleus of the vision of the beyond as the narration progresses, explains the gradual change of the tone, the feeling and the poetic perspective. Originally it constitutes a lively polemic, the scornful anger of the exile *"exul immeritus,"* the violent rebellion of an offended conscience. This original impetus is never totally extinguished and it constitutes to the very end, to the terrible invective of Peter against the degenerate popes the power spark of Dante's poetry. Yet it changes and moves from one to the other canticle, it develops along a line of progressive detachment from the present to assume the character of a metaphysical judgment and the urgent solemnity of a heavenly condemnation. In the *Inferno* polemics tie, in an inextricable knot, the earthly experience with the world beyond. In the following canticles, the two levels of reality tend to dissociate, to increase their contrast until, at the end, the life beyond prevails and grows separated, in an attitude of pity and annoyance for the petty turmoil of worldly quarrels, "the little threshing-floor which makes us so fierce" and the "false reasonings" behind which the foolish bustle of mortal beings goes astray. A graphic ideal of the material that the poet of the *Commedia* is using shows a toning down in the commitment and interventions of the writer concerning the political and ideological debate. On the other hand, it reveals an increase in the intensity with which he notices and emphasizes the contrast between the earth and the other world, the "human" and the "divine," "time" and "eternity," the "example" and the "exemplary." The nature of the theme that requires a progressive spiritual growth and, consequently, the refining of the realistic components of Dante's imagination whereby the initial dramatic violence diminishes progressively and becomes elegiac and finally pure lyricism predicate objectively such a twofold line of tension.

On a biographical ground, it reflects and seconds the growing loneliness of the poet, the waning and disappearance of his hopes, or better, their shifting from the present to a more and more remote and indefinite future in space and time, although most certainly and inevitably in his mind. But, from the very beginning, the structural creation and the spiritual vision that Dante conceives assume the continuity and unity of the poetic body as a criterion of "figurative" interpretation (according to a penetrating formula of Auerbach) and of judgment of earthly and historical reality compared with a meta-historical and ideal model. It is, then, an attitude of the writer concerning the substance of experiences that were made in his feelings and mind, which is, at the same time, a definite antithesis and a tormented, painful and scornful participation where the opposing attitude constitutes a primary element and a constant assumption that presupposes the fundamental break caused by the unforgettable experience of being condemned to exile.

On the other hand, his participation, although reduced considerably, remains lively to the end and echoes even in the remote and rarefied atmosphere of the *Paradiso* the voice of earthly polemic and anguish.

To the dramatic and dynamic inspiration of Dante that is developed within the framework of a broad and relatively rigid conceptual design, correspond, on the artistic ground, the ways of conceiving and portraying through quick visions and powerful syntheses that express the emotional charge of an event or of a character by means of a gesture, a brief dialog while, at the same time, they subject it rigorously to the continuity and the rapid flow of the narrative rhythm which, in turn, coincides with the impetuous presence of moral reason.

As the quality of his art changes and progresses along with sentimental attitudes and the mellowing of polemic issues, it becomes gradually more difficult and refined; it interiorizes its dramatic and inventive resources from the powerful and showy devices of the first canticle to the intimate tension and dynamic movement of the *Paradiso*.

It is obvious that such broadness of mental and imaginary views is accompanied by the endless gamut of details that are involved and echoes an attitude of extreme liberty and multiplicity of expression, that stylistic and linguistic eclecticism that is one of the peculiar and important characteristics of the poem. The criterion of the relationship between form and subject matter remains a constant rule of Dante's and the medieval poetry, but as this changes in an unlimited series of experiences, so does the rule become diversified into endless degrees between the extremes of linguistic requirements and the demand for softer, veiled patterns. The experimental restlessness that characterizes Dante's artistic experience in the minor works is resumed and synthesized in the *Commedia* where one witnesses the emerging of the rhetorical process that is prolonged and intensified by overcoming obstacles of all kinds for the pure pleasure of confronting and overcoming them through the maximum use of his intellectual and technical possibilities.

The adoption of the "comic" style, with its relative freedom of variety of tones, enables the poet to elude and overcome all barriers imposed by a rigorous and exclusive theory (that in the *De vulgari eloquentia* reaches its most explicit and firm expressions), whereby in the pages of the *Commedia*, the refined style of courtly lyrics and popular verses alternate and proceed together joined by the fruit of a more mature and keen study of the ancient poets, such as Virgil, above all, but also Ovid and Lucan, that the writer translates, imitates and modifies in a demanding challenge. All these elements meet and blend with each other in a constantly mutable and hard balance, sometimes within a single episode or in a single page.

The vocabulary, free from pre-established limitations, spreads in an area of unforeseeable proportions because not only is it able to include all the contributions of the literary tradition, from the Sicilian school's to the "stilnovista" group's, but it includes also Tuscan vernacular forms, such as *manicare, introque,* that had been rejected in the treatises, and even other regions' idiomatic forms (sometimes in the form of quotations, other times even assimilated in the context). It acquires distinction and richness with an unusual frequency of classical and medieval Latinisms and reaches even beyond the norm and linguistic usage by drawing from the virtually inexhaustible wealth of the most daring neologisms, such as *intuarsi, immiarsi, inluirsi,* and *incinquarsi, intrearsi, indovarsi,* as well as *insemprarsi* in the last canticle.

Not otherwise does the syntax vary in an unheard of number of forms, transitions, unions, word orders from sentence to paragraph, now adapting to the movements and the surprise of narration, now concentrating in a powerful space of complex images, following closely, according to his inspiration, the most varied epic and dramatic forms, the solemn eloquence, the apocalyptic invectives, the scholastic *quaestio,* the courtly conversation and everyday speech.

The extreme creativity and variety of Dante's language that may range from brutal realism to vulgar comic spirit and grotesque virtuosity as well as to solemn abstraction in metaphysical passages on the universal order, predestination, angelic orders and the mysteries of the *Paradiso;* that language that alternates violence with idyllic gentleness, sarcasm and anger with moments of mystic abandonment, this extraordinary world of stylistic and verbal resources, is justified by the ever present "seriousness" of the writer, the constant moral and polemic engagement that touches all spiritual varieties and it envisions at once all levels and correspondences, all oppositions and relationships of a subject matter that encompasses the entire physical and metaphysical reality, the single and complex, the human individual and God.

This is the mark of Dante's genius but also the genuinely medieval character of his book and the reason of his dignified loneliness in the new culture that was developing in our country at the beginning of the fourteenth century and that in its progress along with the great personality of Petrarch, will leave its mark for centuries on the entire Italian and European civilization, a culture that rejects Alighieri's encyclopedism and universalism, disdains ambitious syntheses, reduces the limits of poetry, excludes linguistic and stylistic excesses both within the lowly and the sublime material in order to concentrate entirely on the patient and refined exploration of a lexical, formal and emotional patrimony that is limited yet homogeneous. For certain persons, Dante becomes an archaic model already at Petrarch's time, for others, the occasion for a totally exterior and conventional admiration, but he is not understood by anyone in the ample and full nature of his undertaking and poetic discipline. Only after five centuries of a contrasted and unfeeling admiration, romantic and post-romantic experience will open progressively the way to a more congenial and gradually more intense understanding of his classical yet not classicistic spirit.

CHAPTER THREE

Between Dante and Petrarch

Among the questions that erudite criticism likes to revive from time to time and are developed on the weak ground of a thin hypothetical framework of conjectures that seem destined to remain unsolved for lack of convincing reasons is also one concerning Dante's possible authorship of the *Fiore*. This little poem consisting of 232 sonnets, is essentially a translation, or better, a reduction of the *Roman de la Rose,* stripped of doctrinal and encyclopedic digressions and rendered in its original inventive and narrative nucleus. The person who composed it toward the end of the thirteenth century in a Florentine language that is strongly speckled with numerous and often crude Gallicisms, drew its subject matter both from the first part of the romance written by Guillaume de Lorris between 1225 and 1240 and its continuation by Jean de Meun composed between 1270 and 1280. But [the Italian writer] developed it not so much on the lyrical and dreamy style of the former, but rather on the skeptical, licentious and free style of the latter, emphasizing above all the misogynic and anti-clerical elements.

A close and objective investigation of both contents and language does not allow one to accept the identification of a "ser Durante" (noun or pseudonym that it may be, used twice about himself by the author) with our Dante for, among other things, we cannot envision how and when such an experience of harsh anti-monastic attitude and representative technique roughly patterned on the French original, might enter the sufficiently coherent direction of the culture and youthful poetry of Alighieri.

Certainly the author of the *Fiore* is an artistic personality of uncommon importance, whose development follows two distinct yet complementary directions: its taste which, as we said, is that of a sharp satire in the two episodes of the advice of Amico to Amante and of Vecchia to Bellaccoglienza (two sides that complete each other in an ambiance of purely bourgeois attitudes, quite removed from the chivalric concepts of love relations) and in Falsembiante's confession and the liveliness of the narration, that is free and quick almost always carried out through images and actions of a remarkable realistic power. This well defined orientation of the writer justifies reducing the allegorical elements to a mere pretext and decorative function as well as the drastic elimination of the moralistic and doctrinal structure that are amply developed in other elaborations or derivations of the *Roman de la Rose* done at that time or shortly afterwards in Tuscany.

As it is evident in several similarities and images, ideas and linguistic material, we should credit the same author with the creation of the *Detto d'Amore*, which is also a free transcription of the French romance in septenary lines in couplets, according to the device that was favored by Tuscan poets at the time of Guittone. One might even suppose that the *Detto* represents an early attempt, which was subsequently abandoned perhaps because the writer grew weary of forcing a fertile and lively topic into the limits of a dry and formal virtuosity. The poet, however, aptly manages to exhibit a rare ability even within the limits of the chosen metric scheme, and succeeds in expressing at times his witty imagination and his lively and unbiased intelligence.

Much less gifted are two other writers who share that allegorical/didactical taste that, in one with the ambitions of an encyclopedic culture, had been introduced, on the pattern of the great French examples, in the Florence of the end of the thirteenth century, particularly at the hand of Brunetto Latini, the anonymous author of the *Intelligenza* (identified groundlessly as Dino Compagni) and Francesco da Barberino (1264–1348), with his *Documenti d'Amore* and the *Reggimento e costumi di donna*.

In both writers a weak and shaky symbolic framework contains the didascalic material that constitutes the true substance of the work. But in the former the naïve intellectualism of the structure is more obvious and more limited in the scope of the cultural sources while the writer's contribution is minimal and the limitation and rigidity of imagination as well as the lack of synthetic ability go along with a faulty technique, uncertain language and an inadequate, limited syntax. Only in a few cases one can notice a more genuine tone within the limits of the reproduction of a bookish material that the author experiences with an alternatingly intellectual and sentimental fervor, such as in the prelude, with the spring portrayal and the image of the angelic woman. In these cases also the meter (which is the nine-hendecasyllabic stanza, rhyming ABABAB, CCB) helps with its indefinite narrative cadence, a forerunner of the octave form.

Compared with the author of the *Intelligenza*, Francesco da Barberino shows certainly a more definite personality. But he lacks the sense of unity, in general and in particular, yet the structure of his works is more complex and varied, more unified and balanced in its order and in the internal relationships of its abundant and, at times, overflowing subject matter. His interests and intellectual and moral curiosity, however, range over a broad and more concrete scope. His culture is richer and more varied. To his juridical and rhetorical knowledge as well as ample readings in classical and medieval Latin and patristic and scholastic philosophy one should add his awareness of the most recent contemporary contributions, from Brunetto to Guinizelli, from Cavalcanti to Dante and Cino, his vast knowledge of oc and oil literature acquired directly during his long stay in France and his close experience with the customs and institutions of different peoples. Even his technique as a verse writer and commentator, although affected by a commonplace, simple and prosaic form, reveals a quicker mind, a multiplicity of attitudes and experiments from the *Documenti d'amore* (in quatrains of alternating seven-syllable and hendecasyllabic lines rhyming aBbC, cDdE, etc.) to the sequences of coupled seven and eleven syllable lines, to the various metric structures of the "rules" and the "sayings" patterned on the Provençal *coblas* and the rhythmic prose of the *Reggimento* that, at times, resemble a free verse style and in the most intense parts becomes a long series of unrhymed hendecasyllables. Even for a contemporary reader, the characteristics and the interest of the Florentine magistrate's two books are determined by the conversion of two apparently contrasting tendencies yet complimentary, in reality, due to the common ground of his curiosity that consists on the one hand of the gnomic subject matter and, on the other, of an inclination to assimilate and elaborate fable-like, descriptive points until it reaches the apex of his modest poetic ability as in some sections of the *Reggimento* where the influence of the French romance style is evident from the picturesque and gentle description of the regal nuptials to the fervent lament of the inconsolable widow and the dramatic story of the other Castilian widow who defends with weapons her imperiled honor.

All the works mentioned here flourished in a cultural and literary atmosphere that is the same where Dante developed his knowledge and, perhaps before being exiled, he could draw from it the general intention of a large allegorical/didactical composition destined to come to maturity and precision much later on firm and organic bases in the concept of an ultramondane vision. At any rate, as they appear now, with modest structural possibilities, the archaic elements of their inspiration and style and their weak didascalic ambitions are apt evidence of a certain affinity and, even more, of a deep difference between a mediocre composite culture and a noble and valiant culture engaged in the organization in clear patterns, on the wings of a vigorous imagination, of a very rich body of intellectual and affective experiences. They were all conceived and composed quite independently from the great model of the *Commedia*, including the two books by Francesco da Barberino who, in a passage of his Latin commentary, gives evidence of possessing a vague knowledge of it, and whose life lasted long enough to become personally acquainted and even mentioned, with a moderate consent, by Boccaccio.

A direct and sufficiently precise knowledge of at least the *Inferno* is documented in the poem of Francesco Stabili, from Ascoli, an astrologer, tried for heresy and sent to the stake in 1327. The very metrics of the *Acerba* (double three-line endecasyllables ABA, CBC ... DD) echoes, but for a small variation, Dante's tercet. But his poem stands entirely by itself, with its clear intention of pursuing a scientific, physical and moral propagation, its intended prosaic language and its absence of allegorical contrivances. It does not intend to become part of the repertoire of poetic inventions, in fact it opposes and repudiates it in Dante himself, as a frivolous and dangerous play, "here we do not sing like the poet/who, imagining, pretends empty things ... I leave behind all rubbish and return to truth:/fables never agreed with me."

It is true that, when considered in their totality, all these writings constitute a background for the *Commedia*, they indicate an inferior culture (Dante would have called it "municipal"), but substantially not dissimilar. Reading them one understands better if not their poetry at least their doctrine, the moral themes, symbolism and the composition structure of the poem. The ensuing fortune of the allegorical/didactical taste that continued for the entire fourteenth century and spilled into the fifteenth develops into a radically different atmosphere and it seems a late product, a fruit out of season. Naturally, the authors who proceed in the direction of an antiquated taste cannot avoid taking into account Alighieri's masterpiece, which, as a genre, is considered the example par excellence. First of all, they take up its metrics and then a series of different elements concerning structure, invention, individual episodes and language. Yet, their imitation is entirely external; it concerns details, not intimate and general concepts. While the scholastic synthesis is slowly crumbling and the interest for the great philosophical, theological, ethical and civic questions that had filled Dante's mind with passion and enthusiasm declines together with the unitary concept of reality, the constant connection between ideas and symbols, faith and reason, earth and the other world, that superficial and fragmentary imitation seems to have the sole purpose of emphasizing the difference between intentions and results. The ideal, imaginary organism breaks up, its individual components, moralizing and didascalic, narrative and figurative, prevail alternately with strangely incongruous and contradictory results; the actual instrument of allegory and vision is seen only as a convenient tool, little more than a play, a pretext to gather and put together a number of minute life experiences and, quite often, of literary erudition.

Moralism and bookish doctrine of a strong medieval character prevail, for example, in Jacopo Alighieri's *Dottrinale,* which, among all these poems, offers the most archaic and confused appearance even in its metrics that imitate Latini's *Tesoretto,* as well as in the *Ristorato,* composed in 1363 in Bologna by the Florentine Ristoro Canigiani on the pattern of the *Fiore di virtù,* and also, toward the end of the century, in the anonymous *Virtù e Vizio* that picks up the theme of the dialog of Soul and Body and elaborates in rhymes the matter of Guillaume de Perrault's *Summa virtutum et vitiorum.*

The decorative elements that are often used in the attempt of raising and idealizing an autobiographical, flattering or occasional theme in one with the presumptuous forms of the new, classical, pre-humanistic culture, prevail, on the contrary, in the attempts made by the masters of the new generation, from Boccaccio's *Amorosa visione* and Petrarch's *Trionfi,* that become, in turn and almost immediately, examples of the "gender" that go along and integrate with the model, still fundamental and predominant, of Dante.

The threefold influence of Dante, Petrarch and Boccaccio clearly appears in the poems written in the late decades of the fourteenth century, such as Zenone da Pistoia's *Pietosa fonte,* an elegy for Petrarch's death written at the court of Francesco il Vecchio, Lord of Padua, the *Leandreide,* composed perhaps shortly after 1380 by the Venetian patrician Giangirolamo Natali who developed in a delicate allegorical plot the myth of Hero and Leander containing a long digression that offers a list of all Greek, Latin, Provençal and Italian poets of love, the *Fimerodia,* by Jacopo del Pecora from Montepulciano, written after 1390 to celebrate Luigi Davanzati's love for Alexandra de' Bardi that combines "stilnovo" and humanistic motives, religious spirituality and mythological reminiscences, and finally, the *Quadriregio,* completed near the beginning of the fifteenth century by Federico Frezzi, a bishop from Foligno, who was part of the world of fervid cultural and artistic practice of the Trinci's court. The latter poem may aptly represent a synthesis and example of the "genre's" characteristics. It has a complicated and obscure intellectualist structure. One can hardly perceive the author's intention. Starting from the allegorical representation of his youthful passions, he strives to attain a teaching of universal value. In the first book under the sign of the kingdom of Love, he narrates the loves of his youth with the idyllic and mythical forms of the Ovidian poetry and the ingenious and cerebral allegorical disguises that Boccaccio had made popular with his vaguely autobiographical romances and poems. In the other books, the kingdom of Satan, that corresponds in part to Dante's *Inferno,* that of Vices (which is, so to speak, Hell as seen in the corruption of world orders), and Virtues (ending in a portrayal of heavenly bliss), are represented with an extreme simplicity of forms ending almost everywhere in an endless series of cold and abstract personifications, mingled here and there with lists of ancient and recent illustrious personages. In its totality, the poem constitutes the late representation of a mind strongly influenced by medieval scholasticism in spite of the superficial contributions of the new end-of-the century culture and the stylistic and grammatical dignity of a rich, easy and monotonous language.

Besides the imitation of the *Commedia*, that affects both the contents and the language, one discovers also the influence of the entire tradition of didactical and allegorical literature, from the *Roman de la Rose* to the *Trionfi*. But this intentional and archaic attitude, this effort of a total and concise revival of a wealth of traditional forms and contents that characterize the anachronistic aspect of the *Quadriregio*, show more clearly the deep change of the mental scope that occurred in the space, more or less, of a century, that sets apart this late and ambitious resumption of the allegorical genre intentionally adapted in all its power of structural rigor and imaginary suggestions by the Dantean ancestor.

Also for Frezzi, in spite of his intention of a global imitation, the *Commedia* is an unreachable example not understood but in fact misunderstood in its philosophical foundations and ethical/political inspiration. His work reflects, in the mirror of a mediocre and a bit arid intelligence, the crisis of a culture where the medieval residues of a simple and prosaic moralism alternate with the ideas of an entirely literary, idyllic, descriptive and decorative taste.

Perhaps one may find a closer, truer adherence to Alighieri's ideal world in another poem almost fifty years prior to Frezzi's, namely the *Dittamondo*, the "heavy work," that kept the Tuscan exile Fazio degli Uberti busy in the last twenty years of his troubled, wandering life, and was interrupted by his death in 1367.

A previous renunciation of two ambitious intentions and the limiting of his imagination within modest yet sufficiently precise proportions allowed Fazio a more cautious but genuine assimilation of some aspects of Dante's language and syntax, with the intention of elevating and dignifying on a stylistic level the "prose" of his creation. The scheme of the allegorical vision offers in this case only the start and the frame of the work. While the understanding becomes humbly and rigorously didactical, an out and out treatise of descriptive and historical geography conceived as an imaginary journey in the three parts of the world known at that time, under the guidance of an ancient geographer, Solino, a part of the commitment, at least doctrinal, if not poetic, of Alighieri, survives in the intention of trying, by facing "hunger, thirst, and sleep," to conclude the difficult enterprise "of searching and wanting to see/the entire world and the people it contains/and wanting to hear and to know/where and how and who were those/who tried to excel by a virtuous life."

Dantesque are also some ethical and civic themes that, at times, expand the narration to sudden bursts of touching eloquence: Rome, as a decayed and humiliated queen; Florence, the fatherland, contemplated in dreams and desires; the

Church, corrupted because of Constantine's donation; the depraved lives of the popes and the Avignon curia; emperors unmindful of their dignity and mission and the holy lands, fallen in the infidels' hands because of the shameful apathy of Christendom's spiritual and temporal leaders.

*

On the other hand, all those elements that contribute to cause, almost after Dante's life, a profound transformation of the culture, mentality and taste, are most manifestly reflected in that literature, considerable in quantity and quality, that indicates more exactly the continuity and integrity of the *Commedia*'s fortune. I am referring not so much to the number of citations, particular echoings, praises and commemorations of fourteenth century civilization, but to the writings that were specificly directed to establish the precise exegesis of the poem.

As everybody knows, as soon as it was published, the poem was glossed and commented. In the early third decade of the century, there appeared the commentaries of the *Inferno* by Jacopo Alighieri and Graziolo de' Bambagliuoli from Bologna and, in the early fourth decade, the complete work of the other Bolognese, Jacopo della Lana, the explanation of Guido da Pisa, and the anonymous that a late tradition designates as Ottimo, not to mention the summaries, limited or in verse, similar to those by Jacopo di Dante, Bosone da Gubbio, Mino d'Arezzo, Cecco degli Ugurgieri, Jacopo Gradenigo, and so on.

Soon the book was introduced also in the schools and was honored with "lectures" as it was done traditionally for the texts of classical poets. There even came the time, in some cities, to discuss the establishment of special professorships in the universities or in otherwise designated places for the benefit of a larger public, even of illiterates.

Besides the most outstanding monuments of this imposing exegetic activity, such as the various compilings of the commentary by Pietro Alighieri begun, at first, around 1340, Boccaccio's lessons at Santo Stefano di Badia and those of the Anonimo Fiorentino (Florentine Anonymous), the Bolognese commentary of Master Benvenuto da Imola, re-elaborated later and dedicated to Niccolò III d'Este, and the other by the grammarian Francesco da Buti in Pisa, all attributable to the last thirty years of the century, we are more or less aware of similar projects entrusted, in Florence, to Parson Antonio di San Martino a Vado, in Pistoia, to Nofri di Giovanni from Siena, in Verona, to Gasparo Scuaro de' Broaspini and in Siena to Giovanni di ser Duccio from Spoleto.

Leaving aside the different degree of commitment, preparation, cultural maturity as well as the intellectual and rhetorical stature of the single commentators, such as Bambagliuoli, Ottimo and Francesco da Buti, who reveal uncommon ability in their analysis, others, such as Pietro Alighieri, Della Lana and, above all, Benvenuto, without mentioning the old and a bit tired Boccaccio and the Florentine Anonymous, there appears, more or less in all of them, the changed aspect of the culture, thought and spiritual interests whence the growing inability to understand fully the content and the form of a poetry that had the tendency to become progressively more remote and that was locked in its compact and arcaic image, at once fascinating and mysterious.

Pietro Alighieri's adherence, albeit a partial one, to philosophical, religious and political themes and a complex, already eroded and faded of family recollection, remains an isolated instance, similar, from certain standpoints, to the attitude of Fazio degli Uberti, in the area of allegorical and didascalic tradition. In most of them, the sentiment of personal experience and historical situation where the *Commedia* originated tends to disappear. Importance is given, instead, to individual aspects considered in abstraction of a composition that, because of its extensive and imposing form, continues to dominate the minds forcing them to pay a tribute of respect and admiration. Dante's concrete morality, reflected in the short-sighted and fragmentary analysis of the fourteenth century exegetes, turns into a generic, cathechistic moralism and especially in the earliest ones, it presents the sterile subtlety of allegorical interpretations. The philosophical and theological passion breaks up because of the demands of a mediocre, encyclopedic curiosity. The vast human subject, images and drama, is lost in a mass of situations, along the lines of a by then remote and rarely understood criticism or of an idle, dispersive erudition.

Several factors contribute to determine this process of progressive misunderstanding and impoverishment within the florishing exegetic literature: the crisis, or better, the evolution of scholastic thought, the changed nature of political clashes and their ideologies, the modified direction of taste and culture in a humanistic sense. One should add a certain atmosphere of diffidence and suspicion that grew little by little around the poem, with its apocalyptic message and prophetic stance ending in the treatise *De reprobatione monarchie* of the friar Guido Vernani from Rimini (1327) where the allegation of heresy is explicitly implied even concerning the *Commedia* and in the public burning of Dante's *Monarchia* by order of Pope John XXII, which did not lessen even at a later date. It then became customary, for commentators, to make a preliminary statement of respect for orthodoxy accompanied by a precise distinction between theological and poetic truth that had the hope, first, to justify the text and, secondly, to safeguard the commentator's responsibility by circumscribing it. Such statement, that is repeated often at a later time, is already present in Guido da Pisa: "If in some place or passage it seems that the poet expresses himself in a way that is contrary to the Catholic faith, it will not be a reason for surprise, because in his dealing with the topic he proceeds according to poetry's human reasoning. And also I, commenting and exploring in a similar fashion, am doing nothing but following in his footsteps. In fact, where he speaks like a poet, I explain him poetically; where he speaks like a theologian, theological, and so on. I do not intend to affirm anything contrary to the faith or Holy Church. If, on the other hand, in attempting to explain the text in every one of its places, I happened to express myself foolishly, I, from this very moment, retract and annul my words and declare to submit to the Holy Roman Church and the correction and discipline of its officers. Because, should in this *Commedia* be found anything heretical that could not be justified from a poetical point of view or otherwise, I do not intend to defend or approve of such a point, rather I intend to reject it with all my power."

But over all prevails the deep difference in tastes between Dante's generation and that of Petrarch, Boccaccio and pre-humanistic grammarians. It is not just the proud opposition of the renewed Latin culture against the vernacular one, but also, even within the vernacular, of an exclusive poetry and a tendentially classical rhetoric against the priority of contents and style of the *Commedia*'s eclecticism.

This attitude may have favored, on one hand, a growing attention for the more strictly poetic aspects of Dante's masterpiece, and even in the commentators of the end of the fourteenth century, the attempt to underscore the classical elements of Alighieri's culture with the purpose of assimilating his poem in the modern tendency toward sensitivity appeared, but, on the whole, it contributes to alienate, even in a reverential way, the greatest monument of a culture that has no equal in the conscience of a new era. The most coherent expression of this opinion is noticeable in the hurried, indifferent homage expressed by Petrarch in his famous letter to Boccaccio (*Fam. XXI, 15*) concerning a poet whose "content is doubtlessly noble," but "the form is lowly," although "his style is excellent in its 'genre.'"

More frequently, however, the reaction of the pre-humanistic commentators is expressed in more uncertain and indefinite terms and, particularly in the Florentine world, from Boccaccio to Filippo Villani and Salutati, it does not exclude sincere admiration mixed with parochial pride that will continue in the following century with Bruni and Landino.

But the sense of lively unity of wisdom and imagination, poetry and theology that can still be seen in the ideas of Bambagliuoli about Dante ("philosophye verum alumnum et poetam excelsum," "sacre theologie, astrologie, moralis et naturalis philosophye, rectorice et poetice cognitionis peritum") has a tendency to break up: from one side there continues the amazement for the immense wealth of knowledge, the ample structural setting and, from the other, the regret for an inadequate rhetorical knowledge, although still noticeable, for those uncultured times.

It is exactly in the fourteenth century that one ought to search for the documents of a critical attitude that will develop in the humanistic world and later on in the Renaissance, a varied attitude of detached admiration for the greatness of the inventive genius and the vast knowledge of Dante as well as a moderate disapproval for the unrefined and not coherent means of expression.

In the case of Benvenuto, for instance, this attitude may even develop into an antithetic formulation that distinguishes and sets poetic genius against art, imaginative height and formal knowledge, the "poet" and the "orator," and thus it saves "in extremis" Dante's greatness when compared with an idolized Petrarch; the *stile* of the *Commedia*, certainly is, in terms of its language, "humble and common," even though it is sublime and excellent in its own kind. But Dante's poem is an extremely complex work, that includes "all the philosophy and all the elements of poetry," and manages to be, at the same time, "tragedy, satire and comedy." Therefore, if Petrarch surpasses Dante in eloquence and style, "copiosior in dicendo," he is inferior for the broadness of themes and the fertility of inventiveness. One is a major artist, the other a greater poet. "Quanto Petrarca fuit maior orator Dante, tanto Dantes fuit maior poeta ipso Petrarca, ut facile patet ex isto sacro poemate."

*

With the names of Benvenuto, Francesco da Buti, Filippo Villani, Broaspini and the very Pietro di Dante, we already enter that world of grammarians and teachers, disciples and friends of Petrarch and Boccaccio, and with these, collaborators more or less intelligent in the wise activity of renewal and cultural modernization that prepares the tools and defines the fundamental directions of humanistic civilization. But the archetypes of this movement must be sought further back in time, in the old, unbroken medieval tradition of conventual and capitular traditions and of the universities and, more specifically, in those coteries that are usually called humanistic that flourished in northern Italy at the time of Dante. The already mentioned case of the poetic correspondence between Alighieri and the Bolognese master Giovanni del Virgilio, takes an almost symbolic significance as one of the early evidences of the culture's and tastes' transformation, and it is so typical to drive some to doubt the authenticity of the texts that document it and consider it an anecdote entered arbitrarily much later in time in the Florentine poet's biography. Such hypothesis is unproven and unlikely, all the more so, for if one considers matters closely, these texts offer not only contrasting elements but also those showing continuity in a well indicated transitional phase between two generations and two schools. In Giovanni del Virgilio's lines there is indeed the contemptuous attitude toward the vernacular and the nostalgia for ancient poetry, but there is also a sincere admiration for the noble and grand inventiveness of the *Commedia*. On the other hand, Dante's eclogues reveal, next to the proud awareness of the novelty and modernity of the sacred poem in vernacular also the not broad but intense Latin culture of Dante and his participation in some aspects of the pre-humanistic movement, that is marginal only in relation to his multiform personality and not to the movement itself.

The most important center of propagation of the new cultural trend that saw its development during the fourteenth century is, as the humanists of the following century recognized, (consider, out of all of them, Sicco Polenton,) Padua where, since the late decades of the thirteenth century, worked the judge Lovato Lovati (1241–1309) and where excelled the strong personality of Albertino Mussato (1261–1329) around whom gravitated other minor people, such as Rolando da Piazzola, Giambono d'Andrea and Geremia da Montagnone. Giovanni del Virgilio himself has a Paduan background and sent an eclogue to Mussato. Masters from Verona among whom the noted Guglielmo da Pastrengo, who will become a friend of Petrarch and those from Vicenza, Benvenuto Compaesani and Ferreto Ferreti (who died in 1337), established close connections with the Paduan group as well as with others, prominent in different degrees during the bitter struggles among Venetian towns, in the shifting from communes to signiories, such as Pace del Friuli, Giacomo da Piacenza, and Castellano da Bassano who authored, among other things, a commentary of Albertino's tragedy. In all these writers continue to exist strong ties with the spirit and the themes of medieval and romance civilization (Lovati composed in Latin a poem on the story of Tristram and Isolde), and perceive them as Dante's contemporaries in the fervent and polemic passion concerning the current political trends, as evidenced by their poetical and historical works and not rarely by the actual events of their lives. Again, by Lovati, a short poem, now lost, *De peste Guelfi et Gibolengi nominis,* Giacomo da Piacenza, deals with the war of Venice and the Scaligeri family, from Bassano, Castellano recalls the clash between the Papacy and Empire and exalts the peace of Barbarossa and Hadrian III. Ferreti, the author of a poem *De origine gentis Scaligerae,* summarizes in the seven books of his *Historia* Italian events from 1250 to 1318, and finally Mussato who also from this standpoint stood out among the most prominent personalities, plays an active role in councils, legations and fights in defense of his commune against Cangrande and Marsilio da Carrara. He entertains enthusiastically the hopes of a new, peaceful order in Italy at the time of Henry VII's expedition, a man that he venerates and celebrates in the *Historia Augusta* and in *De gestis Italicorum post mortem Henrici VII.* Then, as a combative message, of a vigorous incitement to fight for the communal freedom, threatened by tyrants, he composes and presents his tragedy, *Ecerinis,* where he exalts the victory of the united cities over Ezzelino and Alberico da Romano and when, at the end, Padua falls under the control of the Carraresi, he is banished and dies in exile and poverty in Chioggia.

Because of his civic engagement as a man and a writer, even in some biographical details and political ideology, Mussato has often been placed along Dante with whom he has in common, if not a great intelligence and poetic art, certainly the pride of the time and a polemic spirit. But it is also true that other facets of his work and that of his friends and colleagues from Veneto and Aemilia seem to forebode Petrarch in the new way of approaching the classical texts with mainly grammatical, metrical and rhetorical interests, the imitation of Seneca that, in *Ecerinis,* prevails upon the angry and oratorical inspiration, the structural and stylistic intentions of historical works which, in the case of Mussato and Ferreti, show the ambition of adapting to the models of ancient historiography and recreate Livy's greatness and Sallust's rich vigor, the first example of autobiographic genre, in the now lost *De vita et moribus suis,* and even in the *Soliloquia,* which express a religiosity that hearkens to the Fathers of the Church and St. Augustine more than to the recent scholastic thought.

The essential point where one notices the difference between Dante's mentality and the sign of a new attitude, consists in the character of a culture that refrains from centering on a philosophical and theological nucleus, and is, instead, mainly a literary and philological subject, consequently subject to manifold, decentralizing influences yet ready to affirm the importance of human values inherent in the poetic tradition against the systematic demands of the surviving scholasticism. Therefore, the most significant moment of Mussato's activity is to be seen, perhaps, in the texts that kept his polemics against the friar Giovannino da Mantova and the judge Giovanni di Vigonza who condemned the poetry and cult of the classical models as dangerous deviations from Christian theology and a return to pagan ideals. In these texts one is to find, more than a rough draft, almost the whole plan of the discussions around which there will develop the "defense of Latin poetry," mythology and eloquence, of the *"humanae literae"* against the recurring and concentric attacks of doctors, jurists, dialecticians and theologians, in Petrarch, in Boccaccio and Salutati, all the way to the humanists of the fifteenth century. Besides being an enemy of theology, poetry is itself a kind of theological revelation under the veil of allegory; *"altera philosophia," "a summo demissa scientia caelo."* Even Moses won divine favor for his people singing in hexameter lines; Job expressed his lamentation in heroic verses, if we have to go by St. Jerome's authority; David placated God's anger with melodious rhythms and Solomon's canticle is entirely enriched with poetic figures. And the ancient writers, apart from a few profane and wonton expressions, should not be repudiated but, rather, considered masters of truth and morality, "Let at least the eternal fame of the greatest, Virgil, Ennius, immortal Homer be spared, that neither Jupiter's wrath nor fire nor iron or ravenous time could destroy. Even modern philosophers, jurisprudents, those who investigate the secrets of nature cannot avoid mentioning them, and defend themselves with their arguments, no art can refuse the help of our muses and even the Church expresses itself by singing with our own lines." The scruples of the enemies of poetry are based on timidity and ignorance. Their refusal originates from a crudely utilitarian and venal concept of culture. It is true that poetry does not produce conspicuous gains, like jurisprudence or medicine, yet it cannot be considered useless, rather, it performs an essential function by establishing in lasting forms the expression of the highest values of the human spirit, the "history of the world," "the heroes' great exploits," religious longing: "its music rises to the throne of the Supreme God."

What gains prominence in these polemic texts of Mussato is certainly the novelty of his doctrine. His dwelling on allegory is entirely medieval and the very topic of poetry as theology is somehow adapted to his foe's theses, the Dominican Giovannino da Mantova who, considering the close ties between classical poetry and a determined mythical conception of religion, logically inferred the necessity to reject entirely that poetry, which agrees *"cum dictis primorum theologorum,"* but not *"cum nostris scripturis."* What counts, and justifies the fortune of these ideas, and of those somewhat approximate structures in which they are expressed, that were to be resumed, developed and amplified later by way of Petrarch in the *Genealogia deorum gentilium* by Boccaccio and in the *De laboribus Herculis* by Salutati, is the new character that inspires them, namely the shifting of the dispute from the doctrinal to the literary ground, when the intention is no longer directed toward the defense of a substance but mainly of a form, a linguistic and stylistic pattern and only in a subordinate manner of the substance inherent in that form, which must necessarily be presented as an intuitive revelation of the eternal truths that are constantly latent in human hearts.

Petrarch's work and that of the minor literary figures of his generation developed and based a moral justification on these foundations, in order to pursue the critical re-evaluation of the classical authors, an action that represented the premise of the great discoveries and philosophical assimilation that was going to leave its mark in the humanism of the fifteenth century. Only in the most recent years, the fruitful investigation of a group of historians and scholars, among whom Billanovich stands out by continuing to explore more systematically a trend indicated in past times by De Nolhac, and through a patient and meticulous investigation of the manuscripts scattered in all the major and minor European libraries, brought back to light and put together the loose and fragmentary evidence of this imposing philological activity of the humanists of the fourteenth century and redeemed for them the importance that they deserve in a more articulate and rigorous history of the various elements that contributed to bring about a profound cultural renewal and shift the hegemonic function of the European cultural movement from the regions beyond the Alps to Italy. The renewal was realized both through the numerous findings of texts that had remained unknown until then or had been considered lost (extremely important, at times, such as the rediscovery of

Livy, Tacitus, of some works by Cicero, Pliny the Elder and so on), or through a meticulous work of collation and editing of new and old texts.

By virtue of this twofold activity, the aspects of the traditional knowledge of Latin literature had to become greatly expanded and restored to their genuine essence, freed at least in part of the distortion of medieval exegesis. Historical circumstances of different kinds favored then a process that drew its impulse from the new intellectual alacrity, the growing thirst for knowledge, the exuberance of the spiritual life of the bourgeois and commercial activity that had been flourishing in the cities of northern and central Italy since the last decades of the thirteenth century.

The transfer of the papal see from Rome to Avignon brought the most enterprising Italian masters (who rushed in large numbers to occupy positions and curial offices and secure for themselves the benefits even in the remotest regions of Europe) close to the wealth of books of the monasteries and chapters of France and Flanders, far richer in holdings and discoveries when compared with the scarce resources that our country could offer in this respect. Avignon became, then, the center of intellectual exchanges, the focal point of the various cultural trends and one of the primary junctions of European diplomatic activity as well as economic and political life.

In that intense activity, the contributions of Italian prelates, functionaries, experts of notary and chancery, rhetoricians and jurists gained almost immediately a prominent place. The wealth accumulated by Tuscan and Lombard bankers and merchants helped in part to convey to Italy precious collections of manuscripts, while in the country itself the main centers of libraries, such as Verona and Montecassino, were identified and explored again after a long oblivion.

And it was a great fortune that in that movement there entered in the capacity of a guide, widely and immediately recognized for an uncommon attitude for leadership and organization, a cleric of genius such as Petrarch, endowed with a restless and sensitive personality, a man of letters and a poet, erudite without pedantry, a moralist without dryness, a free master inclined to develop his active ability above every scholastic and professional pettiness and limitation, in a very broad ambiance characterized by spontaneous relationships of friendship and collaboration.

The Aretine poet's constant changes of residence from Avignon to Parma, Milan, Padua and Venice, his travels, the acquaintances made on the occasion of his various duties and diplomatic activities became, among other things, the tools of a habitual cultural enrichment and improvement that drawing from different sources enriched a broad and meticulous expansion of the doctrinal material that he had learned and retained. More than the literary treatises and elaborations, more than poetry itself (that, in any case, works on a different and narrower basis), epistolography is Petrarch's means that influences his immediate followers in Italy and in all of Europe and whose practice he caused to prevail through his example.

Persons who by themselves were not prominent, the men who personify the fourteenth century humanistic cultural movement, are to be sought above all among the direct or indirect recipients, collectors, copyists and transcribers of Petrarch's letters, grammarians and teachers, such as the Roman Landolfo Colonna, the Florentine Zanobi da Strada and Bruno Casini, Donato Albanzani da Pratovecchio, Rinaldo Cavalchini da Villafranca, Benvenuto da Imola, Moggio de' Moggi from Parma, Gasparo Scuaro de' Broaspini from Verona, Giovanni Malpaghini and Giovanni da Conversino from Ravenna, notaries and jurisprudents, such as Guglielmo da Pastrengo, Lapo da Castiglionchio, the Venetian Paolo de Bernardo, the Bolognese Pellegrino Zambeccari, the Venetian chancellor Benintendi de' Ravagnani, the high officials of the Neapolitan court Barbato di Sulmona and Giovanni Barrili, learned clerics, such as Filippo Nelli and Dionigi di Borgo San Sepolcro, all the way to the founders of Florentine humanism (Boccaccio, Luigi Marsili, Coluccio Salutati) and Paduan humanism (Lombardo della Seta) and, beyond the Italian borders, Filippo from Vitry and Ludovico from Kampen, Giovanni from Neumarkt and Ernesto from Pardubitz.

It would be scarcely useful to study these persons' writings, distinguish their major or minor ability in the use of Latin and the various degree of their erudition, both still affected by somewhat archaic and medieval rhetorical characteristics and more so than the master whom they all imitate.

More useful, at least for the ends of a study that, like ours, aims at being a history of tastes and poetry, is the consideration and mention of all of them against the background of a large cultural, common enterprise, almost like a chorus that is addressed and that sends back the echo and lasting force of the message of the great poet from Arezzo.

CHAPTER FOUR

Petrarch

In Petrarch's case it would not help to try, as it was done for Dante, to link the story of his life with the description of his works, also because it almost never occurs that his writings may be arranged in a precise, clearly limited chronological order. The modern philologists' investigations have amply demonstrated how those works came into being and developed in a process of composition organized in successive layers that, at times, span an ample period going from his youth to old age. While the constantly increasing uncommon wealth of archival documents and, above all, the abundant information provided by the writer and his contemporaries allow us to follow the progress of his life in every phase, almost day by day, without major gaps and excessive conjectures, it increases, nevertheless, the difference between personal history and general anecdotes that seem to be interconnected only by rare and intermittent links.

Petrarch's spiritual journey does not present violent crises or sudden changes, as are those that occur in the evolution of Dante's life and literary works, that are determined by a vigorous speculative interest and an ardent ethical political passion, but, at most, a slow process of progressive enrichment and partial corrections that reflect the organic and meditated growth of a great cultural enterprise, mainly literary and philosophical, quite opposed from the very beginning to any excessive and improving involvement in events and contingent struggles.

Consequently it seems to lend itself not so much to an investigation and genetic reconstruction but rather to a global consideration of its historical significance or perhaps a detailed description of its individual components not along a chronological line but a thematic distinction.

The poet's father, Pietro di Parenzo di Garzo, originally from Incisa, in Valdarno, had a notary practice in Florence, as his father and grandfather did, who is almost certainly identified with "Doctor Garzo," who affixed his signature to four compositions of the Cortona laudarium. In some documents his name recurs as "Petracculus de Ancisa," but in a document of 1312 it is already indicated as "Patrarca," that is approximately the form of the surname adopted by his son. As the chronicler Marchionne Stefani states, between mid-December 1300 and mid-February 1301, somewhat close to the period of Dante's priorship and the late phase of the struggle between Whites and Blacks, Pietro held the notary position in the Board of Priors.

It is believable, therefore, that he kept with Alighieri relations of friendship and common cultural interests "studiorum and ingenii multa similitudo," as we learn from his son who adds also that he was a great admirer, "venerator ingens," of Cicero's writings, the rhetorical ones in particular, and he credits him for introducing him since his adolescence to the love for Cicero's books, notably, and Virgil, respectively "pro adminiculo civilis studii" and "pro solatio quodam raro animi." It is not true, on the contrary, that, similarly to Dante, he was immediately involved in the persecutions against the enemies of the Donati party. He was forced to flee from Florence only in October 1302, after being sentenced to a fine of one thousand lire and the cutting of a hand, for incurring in the wrath of the powerful Albizzo Franzesi. He had then to join the vanquished party, and, in the capacity of the exiles' representative's secretary he participated in the spring of 1304 in the precarious attempt of an agreement promoted by Cardinal Niccolò da Prato. In February 1309, when his innocence was recognized, the sentence was revoked, but he rejected the available opportunity to return to his land.

He had spent the early years of his exile in Arezzo, where, on July 20, 1304, his wife Eletta Canigiani gave birth to his first born child Francesco, who was followed, three years later, by the other child Gherardo. After he wandered for some time looking for a more stable situation, he could rejoin his wife and children in Pisa, at Incisa, only in 1311. From there the entire family moved to Provence following the large migratory flow caused by the recent transfer of the papal curia. They probably arrived in Avignon in the early months of 1312 but the city was overcrowded and offered no lodgings so that Eletta and the children had to settle for the near Carpentras where Francesco was entrusted for his early schooling to the care of master Convenevole da Prato. In the autumn of 1316, the boy moved to Montpellier to initiate his legal studies that he continued between 1320 and 1326 in the more important University of Bologna but reluctantly, it seems, and with little enthusiasm, so that he was glad to give them up for good "as soon as he was no longer under the guardianship of his family."

His mother had died while he was still in Montpellier, and on that occasion he had composed a Latin poem that is the earliest evidence of his literary vocation that reached us in a form that was probably revised at a much later date. He must have learned of his father's death when he was in Bologna, in 1326, and that occurrence induced him to return, with his brother, to Avignon where the numerous connections established by Ser Petraccolo and by himself with influential persons of the curia offered a quicker and honorable employment with the provision that he accept, as he did very soon, to adopt the ecclesiastical life by taking the minor orders that opened the way to offices and profits.

The international environment and the intense rhythm of activity of the pontifical see offered his already eager and restless mind ample prospects, the broadest that one could have conceived, for human experience and cultural exchanges.

Avignon and the lands of the lower Rhone and Sorgue were, until 1353, for a little less than thirty years and with more or less protracted intervals, the main residence and the center of his multiform activities and relationships. He resided there more permanently in the first ten years, from 1326 to 1336, that correspond to the time of his youth that, in his epistle to posterity, he portrayed under the sign of frivolous pleasures and wasteful worldliness, "sub vanitatibus," that in a late letter to his brother he recalled with terms of bitter irony and repentance, dwelling on the details of the fashion of that badly wasted time. Clothes of choice elegance, changed repeatedly in a single day, shoes so narrow to become as painful as torture, hair set in artificial curls, banquets, long nights, conversations, love affairs, gallant life. Experienced completely and secretly were his sexual adventures, that he always considered humiliating and vulgar, as a grave fault, from which he freed himself when he was nearly forty, when, in 1337 and 1343 respectively, he had two natural children, Giovanni and Francesca, his favorite, that he legitimized later and provided with financial assistance and education.

Within the framework of his worldly life there entered naturally and held a prominent place as means of acquiring fame and fortune the practice of poetry in the vernacular, that he had learned perhaps in the years of his studies in Bologna, and had been resumed with increasing diligence and deeper dedication in an environment where abounded Tuscan poets, late imitators of the "stilnovo" writers, such as Franceschino degli Albizzi and Sennuccio del Bene, just to mention the only ones with whom he struck up a friendship and exchanged correspondence in verse.

To the practice of that poetry belonged also the rule, recently confirmed in clearer terms by Dante and Cino, of leading all occasions and varied modes of inspiration to the exclusive ardor of a single image and name that for Petrarch was Laura, the woman he saw for the first time in the church of Santa Chiara on April 6, 1327, who died twenty years later on April 6, 1348 and that he mourned and exalted even after her death.

The main dates of this event are significant because they coincide, deliberately or by chance, with the recurrence of the passion of Jesus, but Petrarch stresses and adapts them in the thread of a detailed chronology with the intention of emphasizing the real nature of the event.

As it is always significant in the medieval tradition of love poetry, the name lends itself to various references and images of a subtle rhetoric, *Laura—Aurora*, in an extravagant sonnet, written perhaps in his youth, *Laura—lauro, laurea*, Daphne in mythology, poetic glory symbolically, and finally, *Laura—aura* in the wake of a mere verbal echoing, that Arnaut Daniel had already liked. Yet, the poet is inclined to avoid reducing the name to a simple *senhal*, and since the last compilation of his "canzoniere" he includes the sonnet that uses twice the local, endearing version of a real name, *Laureta*.

The writer's determination of establishing a connection, if only emblematic, of his lyrical confessions with reality is evident in these processes as well as in the wealth of anecdotal elements, situations, fiction and landscapes with which he portrays his story. Even in the Latin of his epistles, the reality of his passion is asserted against the suspicions and insinuations of his contemporaries who inclined to see in them nothing but the literary transposition of his desire to receive the poetic laurel. Still, the entire story and the character that embodies it, are unable to achieve a real consistency in the mind of the biographer, not in their existence, where that love will be nothing but an ephemeral episode, and not in poetry, where it has the function of coordinating and, more often, of symbolizing in perspective a complicated psychological experience that is not entirely and solely determined by love. The hypotheses and repeated attempts of scholars and exegetes from the fifteenth to the nineteenth century to give a face to Laura in history or in the chronicles, have never achieved convincing results and remain an aspect, among the many, of the century old cult dedicated to the excellence of poetic imagination.

Worldliness, passions endured in a constant alternation of instinctive weakness and contrite reflections, and, against that dark background, the blossom of poetry that enlightens and softens it, constitute the restless, mutable and whimsical (feminine, as it were) side of his character. This was balanced by the precocious presence of a solid common sense, a natural inclination to use wisely the qualities of his mind and the good opportunities, along with a modest need of security and comfortable peace of mind that found its justification and dignity in the awareness of a noble, cultural mission.

The fame of elegant poet and brilliant conversationalist as well as the friendship he struck up with Giacomo Colonna during his sojourn in Bologna helped the young cleric to enter the circle of the powerful Roman family. When Giacomo became bishop of Lombez in Gascony in 1330, he invited him to spend summer in that remote seat, on the slopes of the Pyrenees. When he was back in Avignon, Petrarch became one of the assistants of the bishop's elder brother, Cardinal Giovanni, and continued in that position until 1347 "not under the control of a superior, but in the company of a father or better a very loving brother."

Since the beginning, he managed to establish somewhat flexible relations with the powerful people who protected him, so as to consent him ample possibilities for his studies and literary activity. Familiarity with great personalities was a means, not an end, for him; he had to be able to live with them as if he had been by himself and in his own house, "mecum et propria mea in domo," and obtain from his clients a minimum of duties and a maximum of advantages and opportunities for his personal career, "nullum tedium, commoda multa."

Especially in those years he built, through careful diplomacy, the solid foundations of his fame: he defined the direction and the substance of his vocation as great intellectual, and drew the broad picture of that ideal image of himself that he was to impress upon the devout admiration of his contemporaries. At the bottom of this lies a vivid awareness of the possibilities and limitations of his nature, that is more inclined to absorb a large amount of knowledge rather than organize it within rigorous scientific lines, not as a philosopher but as a man of letters, in whose mind even the keen meditation of ethical problems takes heed of the impulse and attitudes of a variable psychology and proceeds along the path of an entirely personal experience (*ingenio fui equo potius quam acuto, ad omne bonum et salubre studium apto, sed ad moralem precipue philosophiam et ad poeticam prono.*)

At the center lies the coherent delimitation of a congenial cultural area that is vast but not encyclopedic, based on a progressively expanding and deep, minute and thorough knowledge of the great minor and small figures of the Latin classical age, the "notitia vetustatis," that uses a growing philological ability and is, above all, an instrument of stylistic learning; and the literature conceived humanistically as a form of life, a principle of practical existence, an intellectual and moral dignity which does not oppose but continues ideally the supreme Christian message so that, within the framework of that culture, there converge in perfect harmony the ancient moralists and the Fathers of the Church, Cicero and Seneca with St. Augustine, Jerome and Ambrose, the high biblical and evangelic tradition leaving out, as objects of diffidence and dislike, systematic theology, dialectical disputes, the analytical method of Scholasticism and, even more, the strange investigations of natural philosophy.

At the summit appears the image of the wise man that embodies this form of culture on whom Petrarch tries consciously to shape his activity as a writer, his conduct and even the details of his tastes, preferences and feelings. He is like a wise man that avoids the ordinary aspects of vulgar interests and passions and judges severely and scornfully the people and customs of a decayed age where his fate destined him to live and where he feels alienated. He then secludes himself in order to converse with an ideal, selected society of illustrious dead personalities and noble spirits, the ancient wise men, and with the selected group of friends and collaborators that he honors with his familiarity and enjoys their devotion.

His fame as a man of letters and the recognition of his exemplary and determining function in the transitional phase of the establishment of a new culture grow and prevail rapidly while the formative process of his personality is still taking place. The sporadic disclosure of the first poems and epistles, the relations with other literary men and scholars residing in or visiting Avignon, his travels (in 1333 all over France, Flanders and the Rhineland, and in 1337 in Rome as a guest of the Colonnas) that widen the number of his acquaintances and favor the first discoveries and successes of his erudition, the skillfully divulged news of the great works projected and initiated around 1338 but never completed (*De viris, Africa*), the myth of an active isolation, favored and practiced in the country retreat of Vaucluse, near the springs of the Sorgue where he spends long periods of time from 1337, all contribute to establish that extensive renown that reaches its peak, albeit prematurely, as he himself quickly recognized, of his public poetic crowning.

Probably upon request, he received the invitation simultaneously from Paris and Rome in September 1340. He chose Rome, and in February of the following year he went to Naples in order to be examined, according to the rules, by the learned King Robert. On April 8, 1341, he was solemnly given the laurel crown in the Capitol by the senator Orso dell'Anguillara. The function, in its uncustomary, celebratory form, was intended to represent an authoritative recognition of the new, classical, cultural direction and went back to Statius' crowning. But it also signified, as in Mussato's case, an academic consecration in that the *privilegium*, composed as it seems by the writer himself, conferred on him the *nomen magisterii*, with all the exemptions, honors, symbols and prerogatives enjoyed by professors in the arts.

Those were also the years that showed Petrarch's early signs of a participation, not exclusively literary, in public events: in 1333 he wrote a canzone and a sonnet in support of a crusade against the infidels; in 1335 and 1336 he composed two epistles in order to exhort Benedict XII to transfer the papal see back to Rome; in 1341 he took part in the diplomatic maneuvers intervening among the Colonnas, his patrons, the Angevin king and the Viscontis, whereby Parma, removed from the Scaligeri's control, was placed under the rule of his friend Azzo da Correggio.

Returning from the Roman ceremony together with Azzo, the poet went to Parma and there he composed a canzone to celebrate that city's regained freedom but very soon he escaped the troubles and turmoil of urban life to find the solace of his studies in nearby Selvapiana, on the hills along the Enza.

Having returned to Avignon in the spring of 1342, he addressed another metric epistle to the new pope, Clement VI, beseeching him to restore "Rome to himself, peace to Rome, and the end of all misfortunes to Italy and to the whole world."

The dream of the greatness and historical mission of Rome, enriched by classical memories and religious hopes, the picture of the city's decadence, swept under by anarchy and the arrogance of aristocracy's factions, the fascination of spreading ideologies that foretell and invoke the approaching arrival of a renewed Christianity restored to its origins, the vexation brought about by the corrupt and busy life of the curia with its intense interplay of ambition, greed and jealousy, from which he was not entirely alienated, contribute equally to determine the somewhat constant, albeit varied, themes of his ethical and civil work: the restoration of a religious and political universal order based in Rome for ideal and historical reasons, the *renovatio*, in an evangelical sense, of the Church and Christianity, and the peace of Italy gained through a spontaneous or enforced repression of the countless factional interests.

These attitudes may adapt themselves, depending on the situation and in a larger or smaller measure, to his official obligations and diplomatic functions, and coincide with his friends' and protectors' demands (the Colonnas, the curia, and later on, the Viscontis, Venice and the Carraresi) but they involve, in a practical sense, glaring contradictions, sudden changes, uncertain and mutable judgments according to times and events, such as, for example, the importance and the function to be given to the universal authority of the empire or the Church.

In reality, they never engage him thoroughly in a struggle that may jeopardize not as much his destiny as a man, as in Dante's case, but even his personality as a scholar, the deepest reasons of his being. His rare commitments, contradictory decisions, too frequent agreements, do not escape even the judgement of his contemporaries. He will be harshly and justly blamed for them by the critics and biographers of the Romantic and Risorgimento age.

It is necessary, however, to recognize the sincerity and even the fundamental coherence of a sentiment that, in its essential motives, and even in the refusal to determine itself in a linear action and a total and exclusive devotion, reflects the conscience of a tired generation, the rapid failing of a number of institutions, customs and ideals that were typical of them, the widespread inclination to fall back on individual and asocial positions, as well as the desire of a peace secured by any means and cost. Not by chance this feeling will end with the idea of the uselessness of political struggle, factional passions, the very love of country and earthly city for which an individual sacrifices the important concern for one's destiny in time and in eternity.

Meanwhile, particularly in the last decade of the Avignon period, between 1342 and 1353, Petrarch's hopes and utopist expectations became more frequent, intense and daring, even compromising, in the world of politics and merged with the others, no less significant, of a subtle intimate, moral and religious crisis. The most notable episode of this period is his open support for Cola di Rienzo's plans, both in the area of a popular reform of the internal rules of the Roman commune and in the other, more important issue, of the function of Rome as a unifying center of Italy's political life and all Christianity and, finally, in the doctrinal foundations whence there originated that action connected with the renewal of religious institutions and the return of the Church to its origins.

Already in 1342 Petrarch did his best with the curia in behalf of the popular government established in Rome in order to obtain the pope's favor. In 1347 he exalted publicly the tribune's revolutionary activity and entertained briefly the idea to join him in order to support his deeds with exortations and advice. Even though Cola's defeat suggested a more prudent attitude, it did not cause in him a change of mind nor did it prevent him from expressing his opinions in writing. The ideas brought forth in the famous *hortatoria* and in the other epistles addressed to the tribune are confirmed, again, in 1351, in his letter to the cardinals on the reform of the Roman magistracy, on the necessity to entrust the government to the people and eliminate the factions of the aristocracy that were the major causes of anarchy.

His sonnets addressed against the Avignon situation, the *Sine nomine*, that were composed mainly between 1351 and 1353, show how polemically and sarcastically he considered the present condition of the Church and the curia and accepted the widespread ideals of an imminent *renovatio*.

Another important event in the writer's biography of those years is the conversion of his brother Gherardo who became a monk in the Charterhouse of Montrieux in April 1343. It signals the beginning of a period, neither unique nor decisive but particularly intense and prolonged extensively, of painful meditations, a slow and tortuous crisis of his moral and religious conscience, characterized by alternate phases of ardor and weariness, sudden moments of repentance and gloomy sadness that were enticed by events of his daily life, such as his frequent visits to his brother, in 1347 and 1353. These visits portrayed for him a very different tenor of life, absorbed and appeased in the thinking of God and ascetic practice, the frequent, grievous losses that caused a void among his friends, acquaintances and protectors, mainly during the tragic years of the plague, between 1348 and 1349, the long stays in Vaucluse where he withdrew in search of concentration and peace (1342–1343, 1346–1347, 1351–1353). In those pauses of solitude were born the *Secretum*, *De vita solitaria*, *De otio*, the *Salmi penitenziali* and many Latin and vernacular poems, the writings, in sum, that represent the most notable and conspicuous indications of his crisis.

Examining one's conscience, however, even when it is done deeply and with implacable sincerity, is far from exhausting the complexity of a life affected by different and sometimes, contradictory factors, such as longing for spiritual purification, painful repentance and the intention of spiritual reformation, because these could coexist with an unappeased desire of glory and worldly interests that may not necessarily cause breaks and final solutions in a literary man's conscience.

His interest for the large moral and political themes and the need that in those years became more acute of isolating himself as well as a firm judgment of the most disquieting aspects of his inner nature tend to materialize as important but not exclusive components of that image of great master that Petrarch intends for himself and in which play a role also his civic activity and the concept of ethical and religious values.

One must acknowledge, however, that these motives, by acquiring a predominant importance in this period of his life, contribute to determine the most striking changes in the writer's life, such as the end of his relation with the Colonnas in 1347, caused by his public support of the democratic program of Cola di Rienzo, and his definitive parting from the Avignon environment that he began to hate because of its corruption, gossips and scandals, relentless careerism and rancorous controversies.

For quite some time he had turned his attention to Italy for an arrangement more suitable to his needs of personal independence and peaceful studies. In 1345 and again in 1348, he was the guest of the Scaligeri in Verona; in 1348 he went to Parma where the good offices of its lord, Giacomo Novello da Carrara, had provided him with another canonry; in 1350, on his way to Rome for the jubilee he stopped in Florence where he was enthusiastically received by his admirers, Boccaccio, Nelli, Lapo da Castiglionchio. From Florence, upon the suggestion of his friends and presented to him by Boccaccio himself, the following year he received in Padua the invitation for a professorship in the Studio that was being restored, together with the promise of the restitution of his father's confiscated property.

In May 1353 he returned to Italy to live permanently there and from the hills of Monginevro he greeted his fatherland with moving and fervent words: "Hail, most sacred land, dearest to God, land of salvation for the good, formidable for the proud, the most fertile, the most beautiful of all regions, surrounded by twin seas, proud with famous mountains, venerable seat of arms, laws and the muses ... Nature and art vied to bestow on you supreme gifts and made you mistress of the world. After a long time I come back to you, yearning to live here forever. You will offer a shelter of consolation to my weary life, you will give me sufficient soil to cover, at the end, my lifeless remains."

Unexpectedly, he took up residence in Milan, accepting the invitation of Giovanni Visconti, the archbishop and lord of the city. He remained at his service until spring 1361, and did not sever his ties with that court even later on when he moved to Venetia, the center of his activity, until the last years of his life. Soon he had to defend himself against the indignant accusations of the curia officials and his Florentine friends who faulted him for accepting the protection of a tyrant, in fact, the most powerful and dangerous among Italian tyrants, leader of the Ghibellines and perpetual enemy of the surviving communal freedom of Tuscany. In truth, he rebutted, of the only freedom that counts, that of the soul vis-à-vis itself and God, he had never been deprived; one's obedience to political authority that varies according to place and situations, is the price that must be paid to secure the possibility of attending peacefully to one's own activities and it was in Milan, as it was in other places, that he would have the opportunity of remaining apart, devoting himself to his studies. On the other hand, nobody in the world is free, not even the princes who are feared by their subjects and, in turn, are afraid of them. Nor do the differences in the political order have any importance, and the communes' cannot be called true freedom: "There is no place on earth that does not have its tyranny, where the lords do not rule, it's the people that oppress, and when you are under the illusion of having escaped the tyranny of a single individual, you run against that of the many."

At the Viscontis, first with Giovanni and then with Bernabò and Galeazzo, Petrarch was not given specific tasks. He was, at times, employed as a secretary and orator in the most solemn occasions or sent on diplomatic missions: to Venice in winter 1354, on the occasion of the peace between that republic and Genoa, to Mantua in the same year and again in Prague in 1356, where emperor Charles IV bestowed upon him the title of Palatine count, and to Paris in 1361 to congratulate King John for his liberation from English imprisonment after the peace of Brettigny. He was always considered an illustrious guest whose presence lent the court of Milan dignity and splendor.

It is not easy to establish nowadays the concrete results of Petrarch's diplomatic activity. It is probable, for example, that he repeatedly contributed effectively to sedate the disagreement between the Viscontis and the emperor. It is more important to stress, in this regard, the prestige of the man, the authority of the great intellectual who, even in his contact with powerful rulers, is able to maintain a considerable degree of independence, remain above individual interests, become the arbitrator and judge in their contentions in the name of noble, ideal principles, and writes in the same manner to the Venetian and Genoan doges exhorting them to put an end to their fratricidal war, addresses all Italian lords to support peace and the removal of mercenary troops, deals face to face with popes and the emperor, alternating advice, exhortations and searing reprimands.

It is certain that in the mind of the writer and the public opinion of his time it would be difficult to reduce the significance of this activity to mere courtly function. And it is equally inappropriate in this sense to consider the action that seemed disconcerting to some individuals, but is easily part of the entire concept of Italian politics of the time, of lending his writing ability to the ferocious polemics of the Viscontis against the friar Jacopo Bussolari, who, after liberating Pavia from the tyrannous rule of the Beccarias, had taken the leadership, in 1359, of the fierce resistance of that commune against the deceit of the Milanese lords. It is true that if he had envisioned Cola as the founder of a new order for Rome and all of Italy, he had to see in Bussolari only a representative of that factious communal spirit that he disliked and tended to consider responsible for the present anarchic situation of the peninsula.

A much later episode may help to understand better what opinion he harbored and impressed upon contemporary politicians about his function as a free mediator. When in April 1368 Emperor Charles VI returned to Italy as a member of the league furthered by the pope against the Viscontis, he met him in Udine and immediately afterwards went to the court of Milan, whence he returned to Padua in July as a messenger of peace, honorably received by both parties, having harmlessly crossed the territory occupied by both armies.

It is certain also that the Viscontis fulfilled their promise to provide him ease and freedom to study. The writer's Milanese stay, divided among the suburban residence of Sant'Ambrogio and then of San Simplicio, as well as the summer vacations near the Charterhouse of Garegnano, is one of the most active and productive periods of his life. This is when he continued the re-arrangement started in Vaucluse of his lyrical poems and epistolary collections and began the composition of the *De remediis* and the *Trionfi*. In 1361, escaping from the new epidemic of the plague, he took refuge from Milan to Padua and then Venice where the republic generously supplied him with a house on the Riva degli Schiavoni on the promise, that was never carried out, of bequeathing his large library to the city upon his death.

In his Venetian residence he carried out the definitive organization of the *Familiari*, the new collection of the *Senili*, the completion of the *De remediis*, and the dispute with the Averroists that inspired the important pamphlet *De sui ipsius et multorum ignorantia*.

Leaving Venice in 1367, he was the guest of Francesco da Carrara in Padua. In that city, and more often in Arquà, on the Euganean Hills, where he owned a "little, graceful villa surrounded by an olive-grove and a vineyard," he spent his last years "in complete spiritual serenity in spite of his illnesses, far from turmoil, noise and things, reading constantly, writing and praising God."

In Milan and then Venice, Padua and Arquà, he continued tirelessly to put together his great work of cultural renewal, attending to his numerous connections and establishing new ones among which was his friendship, that had become closer and closer in those years, with the most loyal Boccaccio.

He did not renounce traveling until almost at the end, when he was in bad health. Between 1363 and 1369, he spent part of summer every year in Pavia, as a guest of Galeazzo Visconti. In 1370 he started out for Rome, to greet pope Urban V, who had moved back the papal see but, struck by a syncope, he had to stop at Ferrara. In 1373 he accompanied Francesco Novello, the new ruler of Padua, to Venice where he was going to submit to the rule of the republic. He gave a speech in the Senate and on account of his illness and old age "his voice trembled a little," as an old chronicle refers. He died suddenly at Arquà in the night between July 18 and 19, 1374.

The episodes of his successes and exceptionally broad influence over every part of Europe began immediately. The collection of the precious manuscripts of ancient authors, amended and annotated incunabula and models of the humanistic philology in the following century, migrated as war booty from the Carraresis' to the Viscontis' library, then to the Sforzas' and from there to Blois and Paris. In the meantime, the Paduan and Florentine disciples competed to provide the transcription and publication of unpublished or partially unfinished writings. More and more numerous copies of his works, particularly those in Latin, reached friends and admirers in every Italian region, in France, the Flanders and Bohemia, while the eager curiosity of a less educated but larger public was soon gratified by translations of the *De viris* by Donato degli Albanzani and of the invectives of the *Contra medicum*, edited by Domenico Silvestri, and, a few decades later, the *De remediis* at the hand of Giovanni da San Miniato. In the meantime, there appeared the first signs of the enormous success of the rhymes in vernacular that established Petrarch's European triumph between the fifteenth and the seventeenth century, in the wake of the imposing expansion of Italian culture in the Renaissance.

*

A statement in the epistle *Posteritati* that, in preference to many others sharing a similar thinking and manner, might help us to enter Petrarch's personality and show us the meaning and direction of his work, its "historical function, the man's nature and the dialectics of his relationship with the times is this: "*Incubui unice, inter multa, ad notitiam vetustatis, quoniam michi semper etas ista displicuit; ut nisi me amor carorum in diversum traheret, qualibet etate natus esse semper optaverim, et hanc oblivisci, nisus animo me aliis semper inserere.*" At the root of several and varied aspects of a cultural enterprise that was destined to modify profoundly the course of European civilization well beyond the confines of literary taste and style, lies mainly this annoyance with the world, namely the deep conscience with which the writer experiences and reflects the crisis of civil, moral, philosophical and cultural traditions and institutions of a historical situation that was deeply troubled and entangled. From this originates doubtlessly the need of a passionate study of the ancient world, the "notitia vetustatis," Petrarch's philology. And it was from these elements that came also his polemic flare-ups, his ethical and political eloquence, even his attitudes and positions as well as an anxiety to evade, the awareness of a deep separation that subsides only by mirroring itself in a terse web of vivid confessions which places ideology near philology, written and experienced rhetoric, literature as well as, and most importantly, poetry.

It is certainly wrong to refer to the conventional and overused characterization of the romantic critics and imagine a Petrarch entirely alienated from contemporary political life. In reality, all themes, clashing forces, doctrinal patterns of that political strife are present in his mind and are found in his writings, often expressed in ways that echo closely those that appear in Dante's treatises and invectives but characterized by corrections and mitigations that reveal mainly a more realistic and disheartened view of what is real and possible.

The inadequacy and contradictions of the communal laws were as clear to him as they were to Dante, and since the very events of his life contributed to keep him free from any petty municipal interests, he could observe with scornful detachment the spectacle of mean and bloody rivalries. Out of these observations arose quite strongly the ideal of the cultural and civil unity of the nation. He also invokes, in the name of restoration, order and justice, the emperor's intervention but the intrinsic weakness of the empire does not go unnoticed when it is compared with the ancient greatness for the sake of Italy's hoped for renewal. He will say that: "If the Roman Empire does not have its seat in Rome, it cannot be called empire of the Romans but only of those peoples where fickle fortune placed it." Eventually he will recognize that imperial authority is reduced merely to "an empty word, replete with the echoes of the ancient fame yet deprived of all value, based only on the shadow of the ancient power."

Concerning the Church, he goes back to the image of its early purity and he harbors the ideas of Franciscan spiritualism, he wishes for the coming of a restorer sent by God to liberate the Christian world from vice and superstition and establish a new golden age. At times he even seems to indulge in the hypothesis of an imminent palingenesis, a sudden, "terrible change," already foretold by recent portents.

One cannot consider that work as a portrayal of the commonplaces of an already trite polemic. His experience of the curial world was vivid and direct and it would be difficult to point out, in the literature of the time, pages where the corruption of ecclesiastical life is represented with similarly intense apocalyptic tones, vehement invectives, sarcasm and irony together with cruelly concrete details and anecdotes, scandalous narration, sapid characterization of events and persons as in the Avignon sonnets, in several places of his letters and, above all, in the most lively *Sine nomine.*

With uncommon clearness and the customary adherence to concrete facts, Petrarch considers the actual conditions of a divided Italy in conflict internally weak because of its inability to establish a solid civil order, and equally weak abroad against the forces of foreign powers that grow and consolidate rapidly. It is not only due to a mere rhetorical suggestion that some of his words represent, with the value of a synthetic epigraph, the feeling that will inspire Machiavelli's stern investigation; indeed, it is not impossible to recognize a pre-Machiavelli sense in some of his addresses, as in the one where he reproaches Cola for his clemency shown toward the vanquished noblemen, the error of not eliminating, when he could have, the potential enemies of the new order. The common motives of the anti-tyrannical polemics echo also in Petrarch's lines: the longing for freedom, "sweet, desired good,/not known well by those who do not lose it,/the tears of oppressed peoples, of the afflicted and scattered groups," worn "to the bone" by the "insatiable hunger/of the hounds that keep their sheep in misery."

And he certainly does not adhere to these polemic principles with the attitude of the threatened mercantile oligarchies and the Tuscan Guelphs but he considers the possibilities offered by the new age and analyzes the lords' and princes' politics whose fortune grows all around over the disintegration of the communal institutions and declares that "the rule of the single person is the most suitable to unite and restore Italian strength that the protracted fury of civil strife has scattered," applying generally his principle to the ambitions of Robert of Anjou, Charles IV and the "tyrants" of northern Italy.

He tends, in fact, to avoid the urging of current struggles and safeguard the relative freedom of his judgment within clashing animosities while, amid the contrasting arguments of the political literature of his century, he chooses for himself only themes of solemn morality and compassion that constitute the deepest and most common aspects of that literature: the anxious demand for justice and peace that arises everywhere even from the lowest and most neglected levels of society, the stern admonishments to the rulers to rise above greed, hatred and individual ambitions and conform the exercising of their authority to a truly human and Christian concept of life.

Who, among the numerous courtly or popular poets, was able to find, as he did, sincerely moving expressions in portraying the wretched conditions of the common people, "the poor, dismayed people," "the tears of the sorrowing people?" Who commiserated, as he did, the destiny of those who bear, unrewarded, the burden of anarchy and misgovernment: "Le donne lagrimose e 'l vulgo inerme/de la tenera etate e i vecchi stanchi,/c'hanno sè in odio e la soverchia vita"? Where does the general moralism of a great part of contemporary literature find such fervently pure expressions but in his verses that exhort the powerful to consider the limits of their earthly function and the duty of exercising it with Christian spirit before the approaching divine judgment? "Lords, see how time flies/and how our lives flee,/ and our death is at our backs .../And that time you spend/in giving others pain/let it be spent in some more worthy action,/of the hand or the mind,/in some lovely praise,/in some noble study ..."

Petrarch's political discussion (not only in the famous canzoni but also in his epistles and treatises) shifts between two attitudes that are both forms of escape: his taking shelter in the utopia of the restoration of a glorious past of virtue and greatness and the withdrawal in God, elimination of time in the concept of eternity, the humanistic dream and the ascetic rejection of struggling. Among the many who dealt with the former theme and liked to go back to the examples of the great Romans, no one expressed it with words so pervaded with sincere emotion: "The ancient walls the world still fears and loves and dreads when it remembers/time past and the days of yore." And, on the other hand, nobody expressed the vanity of political strife with so firm and harsh words as in *De remediis* where the very fundamental concept of love of one's own land and tradition is analyzed and criticized: "Arrived at the threshold of death, you yearn to know what will happen to that which you call fatherland. It will do what it always did, what all do: It will be beset by tumults and factional strife, it will change rulers and laws for the worse. It will end as many great cities finished, in dust, ashes, scattered stones, empty names ... Why do you wear yourself out in anguish? When you will rise to heaven, you will feel pity for it as of any mortal thing."

To rid oneself of his duplicity and attitudinal inconsistency by constraining both terms within a literary play would be too simplistic. It will be necessary, instead, to find the meaning of that literature in the writer's personality and in the culture of his days and its combining motives, at once opposing and heartfelt, carried out with the same intense participation. For if, on the one hand, Petrarch's position within the framework of a political situation may be defined abstract and beyond time itself, on the other hand it is quite true that the intensity with which he perceives and expresses its deepest voice is sufficient to define his as the most lucid conscience of the anxiety of his century.

*

If the writer moves from the consideration of external reality to that of intimate life, of his soul's content, his search goes through a no less painful ground, filled with distressing perplexity and reaches equally evasive conclusions. A long and unanimous critical tradition had always recognized Petrarch's most courageous and penetrating effort in the direction of an unbiased analysis of his inner nature in that book that he titled *Secretum*.

Composed in a straight off manner, between autumn 1342 and winter 1343, it reflects the culminating point of his moral crisis even though the author repeatedly revised it from 1353 to 1358, with more than formal additions and revisions.

A caption clarifies that the topic of the work is the description of the constant clash of his affections, "de secreto conflictu curarum mearum," and adds the promise, that he could never keep, to resume his elaboration in order to describe, if and when it might occur, the conclusion of that conflict in a peaceful and serene conscience, "facturus totidem libros de secreta pace animi, si pax erit unquam."

The confession is developed in the form of a dialogue between Francesco and St. Augustine. The latter reveals progressively the error and weakness of the poet, he reproaches him and tries to remove him from his spiritual idleness and culpable weakness and shows him the way that he should follow suggesting the means to reach it and proceed on it with a strong and resolute mind. Truth attends the three-day dialogue, constantly present but speechless. From the beginning, St. Augustine touches the most painful points of Petrarch's illness: his lack of a firm, vigorous resolve, the absence, or corruption, of his will. It is true that he has often entertained the desire to lead a pure and virtuous life, but that desire remained a vague fancy, an uncertain, precarious aspiration, as it never turned into one of those profound, unshakeable resolutions that generate solid and lasting moral conversions: "The man who wishes to rid himself of his own wretchedness, cannot be frustrated in his longing provided that he pursues it truly and completely … Nobody is unhappy but for one's own fault: 'sine peccato nemo fit miser.'"

Such a situation reappears unchanged at the end of the long dialogue when the poet admits how much more profitable it would be for him to interrupt all those plans that deflect him from the right way to salvation and being still unable to control his emotions with prompt and firm decision. The saint repeats the initial concept of the will, that can always do what it really wants: "in antiquam litem relabimur: voluntatem impotentiam vocas."

In the second and third book of the *Secretum*, Augustine's reproach concerns a number of concrete and detailed charges: Petrarch relies too much on his intelligence, he is excessively proud of his eloquence, knowledge and even physical appeal; he loves and pursues honors, ease and wealth; gives in very often to the drives of lust and the dangerous fascination of indolence. And there are in his soul two serious and secret faults, the more dangerous and deceitful, because they are clothed in a virtuous appearance, his love for Laura and the desire for glory. The image of the beloved woman has deflected his soul from heaven, it has driven his desire from the Creator to the creature, and it has marked the decadence of his moral life and the loosening of his behavior. Similarly, the attraction of worldly glory impedes his progress toward true immortality; it distracts him from the thought of eternity.

The entire book is an inexorable and marvelously lucid analysis that delves deeply into the maze of his soul and sheds light on the innermost spots, its darkest and most intricate corners. At times, it even brings to the surface the turbid essence of sin and despair that is presupposed, but only rarely revealed, in his verses.

From this point of view, the passages that demolish the concept of honest love, instrument of purification and introduction to virtue are exemplary: it is not true that the thought of Laura has taken away, as he says, his youthful mind from every vile attraction, forcing it to look up to heaven, and scorn all lowly concerns and ambitions. And it is also not true that the object of his passion was not her body but only her soul for, if he wants to look with open eyes at the truth of his situation, he will have to admit that the first appearance of Laura in his life coincided with the beginning of his going astray, the image of the most honest woman has unsettled his mind, it sowed the seeds of carnal temptations that he had to satisfy otherwise, it even led him "to feed himself with grievous pleasure on "tears and sighs," and instilled in him "the loathing of everything, the hatred of life and desire of death, the sad liking of loneliness and the escape from human company." Rather than directing him toward God, that love contributed to drive him to the edge of an abyss: *"Ista quoque, quam tuam predicas ducem a multis te obscenis abstrahens, in splendidum impulit baratrum."*

Equally exemplary and more famous are the other pages which describe that grievous illness of the soul the ancient called *aegritudo*, and the modern *accidia*, the worst of passions, because "while something sweet is always mixed with the other ones, everything in it is harsh, wretched and horrid," "a way open to despair," on account of which every day is deprived of light and liveliness and changes into "a hellish night and most bitter death," and one is led to "feed on tears and sorrow with I do not know what obscure enjoyment, so that one turns away from it against one's will."

Because of this *accidia*, one feels like "a person who is assailed all around by countless enemies, without escape and any possibility of relief, threatened from every direction." The sores of misfortune, unrelieved by time, heap up on him, "all recent, open and untreated." The awareness of an unsufferable destiny imposed upon man adds to it, "humane conditionis odium atque contemptus," forcing him to perceive as irritating "everything he sees, hears and feels."

Although entirely confined, and awkward at times, in the schemes of a terminology that still belongs to the Middle Ages, his analysis cuts deeply into a concrete psychological matter and the substance of personal events in order to open views of disconcerting modernity. The soul's reality is portrayed against its gloomy, restless and dramatic background, an always open, insoluble conflict between the principles of heaven and earth, body and soul, passions and God. But what counts most is, above the conflict, his clear and firm vision that observes, dissects, analyzes and describes it. Instrument and assumption of his intellectual clarity is his moral and poetic wisdom drawn from patient readings, merged in a repertory of examples and definitions, as the strength and comfort that is never lacking in literature.

It is precisely St. Augustine who invites the poet to read over the exemplary texts of the ancient writers, citing Seneca, Cicero, Horace and Plautus, and take to heart their precious maxims. "Every time that, while reading, you come across some beneficial statement capable of inciting or restraining your mind, do not trust only the strength of your soul but place it in the deep corners of your memory, make it yours most carefully so that, like an expert physician, you may have available and well set in your mind the remedies when, at any time and place, an illness comes that requires prompt treatment."

Thus, also from the *Secretum*, along with an ascetic tendency nourished by the sadness of an infirm conscience that frustrates all aspects of life in the steady thought and the tormenting comparison of death and eternity, originates this exhortation to find safety in the wisdom of books, that is itself an evasion from the real world, and, at the same time, a conquest of a higher reality, a moral balance that, although precarious, may justify life and constitute the mission and authority of the man of letters and the poet, the sole person endowed with clear-sightedness in a sightless world.

*

The Christian motive, medieval as it were, of introspection, repentance, disesteem of worldly interests and the other motive, humanistic in nature, of the trustful recourse to the ancient's wisdom and restoration, not exclusively philological, of a cultural heritage which represents at once a model of life and a new criterion of evaluating values, pervade all of Petrarch's minor works, and only a very superficial distinction could assign them to groups characterized by various tendencies, because all of them contain, in various measure, that dichotomy that never becomes a real contradiction of attitudes.

It is true that the humanistic theme seems to settle more strictly, both as content and as form, in the writings that reflect a youthful enthusiasm in the earliest phase of the rediscovery and assimilation of the classical world: in the *Africa*, the poem that celebrates Rome's greatness, and in the first version of the *De viris illustribus*, conceived as a series of biographies from Romulus to Titus, aimed at offering a wider and more documented view of that great history from its origin to the early stages of its decadence. Virgil and Livy and, later, also Valerius Maximus, because of the fragment of the *Rerum memorandarum libri*, stand out as exclusive examples. Thus Roman history acquires exceptional and exemplary importance, preceded and followed as it is by centuries of darkness and uncivilized conditions.

An intention to imitate and emulate inspires the conception of far-reaching writings, intended to renew the examples of antiquity in the two noblest genres of poetry and prose, epic poetry and historiography. First of all, however, we should consider the fact that that initial celebratory and imitative attitude ended very soon, and grew fainter with the writer's broadening of his cultural and philological views where he included, more and more abundantly, together with the classical texts, the biblical and patristic ones as well as the large elaboration of medieval scholars thus forcing himself to re-evaluate the inheritance of ancient experience in its values and limitations in a comparison with the modern, Christian one. But the *Africa* remains unfinished and although the author went back to it repeatedly to fill its gaps and refine it, he remains unsatisfied to the last and never decides to publish it.

The project of the *Rerum memorandarum* is abandoned almost immediately and forever. The early plan of the *De viris,* that ends with the lives of Cato the Censor, is resumed later and amplified in order to include all illustrious characters from Adam to the modern ones. Eventually also this new project is discontinued, although the two great biographies of Scipio and Caesar stand out for their nature, psychological investigation and historical opinion.

It should be noted, on the other hand, that since the beginning, in the humanistic framework of these writings, enter motives that contradict in part and alter their character of confident admiration. The most spontaneous pages of the *Africa* are not certainly those that derive from an epic intention and end up in a tired versification of Livy's text but the pondered and lyrical ones that are developed partially and marginally in the narration; they are the expressions that convey the fleeting quality of glory conquered on earth at the price of countless labors and lives (… facili labuntur secula passu; tempora diffugiunt; ad mortem curritis; umbra, umbra estis pulvisque levis, vel in ethere fumus exiguous, quem ventus agat. Quo sanguine parta gloria? Quo tanti mundo fugiente labores? Stare quidem vultis, sed enim rapidissima celi vos fuga precipitat); the vanity of conquests and power that death obliterates, (… Quid tot valuere rapine? Raptor raptorem spoliat. Nunc ite per ampla equora, nunc validas prosternite turribus arces, nunc aratrum antiques insultet minibus; omnes unus habet predas hostis); as well as the distress and apprehension of mortal life opposed to heavenly beatitude: (… Numque hactenus ire et dolor et gemitus et mens incerta futuri … Illic pura dies, quam lux eternal serenat, quam nec luctus edax, nec tristia murmura turbant.)

The only place in the poem that gets close to poetry is that lamentation of Magon that a few fourteenth century readers had already accused of being inappropriate and improbable because it had a pagan, and a barbarian at that, utter the most disconsolate words of Christian asceticism: "Mors, optima rerum,/tu retegis sole errores, et somnia vite/discutis exacte … Moriturus ad astra/scandere querit homo, sed mors docet omnia quo sint/nostra loco." Responding to such charges,

Petrarch warned that those concepts could not be considered exclusively Christian, but rather appropriate for man at any age and condition, for man in whom the sense of death, the awareness of his frailty and repentance "in extremis" of faults and wrong ambitions are inborn. Through these thoughts the poet revealed the true direction of his humanism, envisioned not to contrast but to reconcile the teaching of pagan wisdom and the revelation in the light of a "pietas" opposed against any form of polemic harshness and open to the most deep aspirations and unchangeable suffering of humankind.

Similarly, painfully thoughtful interventions that have their roots in a strongly autobiographical ground, may be seen, often enough, also in the *De viris,* and already in the first version of the book: "O tremula semper et fragilis humana potentia," "O humanum animum inconstantem et passionibus semper obnoxium!" "O mortalium semper laboriosa conditio!" "Preceps hominum genus et consilii inops," "Nulla est autem in terra inconcussa felicitas." Besides, the entire tormented elaboration of his work shows a progressive detachment from a rhetorically commemorative historiography to the advantage of a psychological penetration that is acceptance of humanity in its real dimension, where merits and faults, greatness and failure, are measured in the same way as are the opportunities offered by nature and destiny.

If in the writings inspired by an early enthusiasm for classical restoration we notice tones of ascetic pessimism and lyrical restlessness, the awareness of a cultural, humanistic mission is also present, giving them a specific moral and Christian purpose. Conceived a few years after the composition of the *Secretum,* the two treatises *De vita solitaria* and *De otio religioso* arise from the same need of spiritual introspection and religious meditation. Both develop the theme of renunciation and overcoming of worldly ambitions and outline an ideal evasion and monastic peace. In both writings also the body of citations derived from the Bible and the Fathers of the Church grows enormously and acquires a distinct importance. Yet, the awareness of even the ancient culture as comfort and direction of moral progress does not fail. The concept of ascetic or recluse life remains in the two treatises as a remote ideal that the author observes with an admiration not deprived of fear. It is the kind of perfect life that he perceived and envied at times on the occasion of his visits to his converted brother in the Charterhouse of Montrieux. Those friars were like "God's angels on earth," free from the burdens of desire, anxiety, and ambition, alert in the expectation of heavenly peace whose unutterable joy they were already anticipating.

Perhaps divine grace may elevate him to such condition. For the time being, it remained an unreachable goal for the worldly and sinning man. The loneliness that he contemplates is a separation from the daily concerns and troubles, a total immersion in reading, meditating and studying, the seclusion of the man of letters above which reigns the concept of an idea of religion that is neither sharp nor intransigent, but entirely imbued with and embellished by the learning contained in books. From many standpoints, it is Cicero's and Seneca's ideal of the literary "otium," adapted to the type of a Christian scholar: "Solitudo sine literis exilium est, carcer, eculeus; adhibe literas, patria est, libertas, delectatio." It is the idealization of the poetic and erudite leisure of Vaucluse, where all the hours of the day are wisely distributed in refined and congenial occupations; the turmoil of vain attractions is appeased in the silence and peace of nature and even devout thoughts and the gratitude for God acquire greater spontaneity and taste amid a pleasant and peaceful scenery, along with the "gentle murmur of a waterfall and the birds' harmonious laments."

In this sort of solitude, the writer believes to find a meeting point for his humanism and Christian spirituality because, on the one hand, it does not oblige him to reject a realm of doctrine that is so dear to him, and, on the other, culture envisioned in this fashion is no longer an instrument of refined sophisms and futile eloquence but a way to superior morality. Drinking deep with equal love from the fountains of the classical sages and the holy fathers, he will strive to become "non disertior, sed melior ... neque disputator maior sed peccator minor."

But also these books where he exhibits the fruit of his meditations, of his contrition and resolution for an ethical renewal, are themselves documents of doctrine and wisdom, if not of virtuosity, important evidences of literary skill in the style of their structure, in their ample and varied scope, in the endless care for style, in the wealth and display of their historical and scholarly apparatus. Their artistic intention is never separated from devotion. Even in the *Psalmi penitentiales,* the bitter confession of the repenting sinner, the prayers' sincere and strenuous labor, the deeply Christian instinct of the soul groping in the terror of a loneliness imperiled by hopeless temptations and deprived of the light of grace, are accompanied by the exquisitely literary intention to follow and renew the forms of an unusual poetry, the tones, metaphors and rhythm of biblical Latin.

The process that leads Petrarch from the works that were conceived in the early fervor of a limited classical ideal to those completed between 1342 and 1347, in a period of crisis and reflection—from the *Africa* and the plans of historical compilations to the *Secretum, De vita solitaria, De otio* and the *Psalmi*—certainly implies an enrichment of his cultural standing, an increased awareness of the Christian scholar's mission, progressive adaptation of cultural elements to the needs of his personal experience and the problems, not the achievement, of an orderly and coherent ideal and less than ever, the subordination of the literary man's restless fervor to the superior ends of a precise, ideological trend.

The early conception of the two works goes back, as it seems, to his sojourn in Milan, when the author tried in his way to organize in a definitive structure, capable of representing an example and in a completely persuasive form, the totality and results of his human experience and erudition.

They are the vernacular poems of the *Trionfi* and the treatise *De remediis utriusque fortune*, begun around 1354 whose elaboration continued far later in the poet's old age. Both works prove the impossibility of reaching a stable synthesis of harmonizing thoughts and affections from the infinite, indefinite and contrasting wealth of analytical data. As he endeavored to emulate Dante's poetic manner, Petrarch, in his *Trionfi*, tried to present a picture of his autobiographical experience meant to signify, in symbolic terms, generically human values of universal significance: from the anguish of love passion to the feeling of modesty that contrasts and humbles that disorder of passions and the contemplation of death that annuls the longing of the flesh and exalts the splendor of chastity; from the desire for worldly glory that is under the illusion of triumphing over death to the awareness of time that destroys all glories and, finally, of eternity, promised to the Christian believer but in a better world, where time disappears and also human hopes of glory and love acquire a new and true meaning of their own. Yet, on the other hand, this concept grows scanty through a number of abstract symbols, vaguely connected the one to the other by schematic, forced connections and it becomes dissolved in a myriad of details that are rarely poetic and, more often, erudite. Rare gnomic expressions of a peculiar intensity emerge from the moral intention such as the clear and distressed definitions of love:

> *(diletti fuggitivi e ferma noia ...*
> *stanco riposo e riposato affanno ...*
> *dentro confusion torbida e mischia*
> *di certe doglie e d'allegrezze incerte ...*
> *E vidi a qual servaggio ed a qual morte,*
> *a quale strazio va chi s'innamora);*

the inexorable passing of time and the vanity of human dreams:

> *(ciechi, il tanto affaticar che giova?*
> *tutti tornate alla gran madre antica,*
> *e 'l vostro nome a pena si ritrova ...*
> *Che più d'un giorno è la vita mortale?*
> *nubil'e breve e freddo e pien di noia ...*
> *Passan vostre grandezze e vostre pompe,*
> *passan le signorie, passano i regni;*
> *ogni cosa mortal Tempo interrompe ...*
> *O veramente sordi, ignudi e frali,*
> *poveri d'argomenti e di consiglio,*
> *egri del tutto e miseri mortali! ...*
> *O mente vaga al fin sempre digiuna,*
> *a che tanti pensieri? Un'ora sgombra*
> *quanto in molt'anni a pena si raguna.)*

From the tediousness of the bulk of bookish knowledge, very few images escape that are defined succinctly with classical clarity: "Giaufré Rudel, who used sails and oar, in search of his death," "Andromeda" virgin with black hair and fair eyes," and dead Laura's unforgettable portrayal, her "sweet sleep" that seems to render her more beautiful.

It is in the failure of the intended synthesis that the expression of a stylistic force remains; it is the effort, in short, of the man of letters that wants to raise to the level of classical examples also the type of medieval, didascalic and allegorical poem, by emending and refining the unmentioned models of the *Commedia,* of the *Roman de la rose* and perhaps also of the *Amorosa visione.*

On a more directly rational level, also the *De remediis* is written as the synthesis and definition of an experience, the attempt to gather and arrange a rich number of situations in some kind of manual or handbook that may be helpful to control man's behavior at any moment and in any circumstance.

The book is divided into two parts. They are meant to suggest respectively remedies in order to resist the lures of good fortune and the deceptions of the adverse one. They are distributed in little more than two hundred fifty dialogues, where reason examines and rebuts the arguments expounded in the first part by Joy and Hope and in the second part by Sorrow and Fear. Having reduced to a mere scheme also the dialogical device and minimized the intent to offer an organic development to a superficial structure that disguises the scattered and somewhat slight quality of the subject matter, there appears also in this case the remote and faint echo of a personal experience, the sharp novelty of some elegiac expressions that recur from page to page in an insisting and even monotonous treatment, such as the frailty of youth, worldly wealth, love and life itself as well as the futility of political passion, of freedom and mundane fame. What remains is the bulk of numberless examples drawn from classical literature and adapted to the individual conditions of human life, as well as the varied eloquence of sententious forms derived from ancient writings and then modified, a scholarly apparatus and erudite tone that were probably the cause of the enormous fortune of the book, particularly in the first phase of the transition from medieval to humanistic culture.

It is not fortuitous that exactly in the two works where he intends to arrange in a systematic way both his ideas and his feelings, Petrarch adopts the schemes of the unitarian structure from the mental and formal basis of the Middle Ages: the allegory of the *Trionfi,* the moral encyclopedism of the *De remediis,* both reduced to empty form where the foreboding of a new reality lives and vibrates. The fact is that both he and all men of his generation lacked the possibility of conceiving life in an organic and coherent manner, of having that strong trust in human nature that makes it capable of settling the elements brought about by experience that constituted the basis of scholastic thinking. Faith and reason tend to separate from each other, the validity of any systematic construction is doubted, and the very tools of dialectical and natural investigation are devalued and repudiated.

The philosophy, if it is allowed to be called it such, of the early founders of humanism—who act along and against the representatives of extreme scholastic speculation—reflects a crisis and ends in a series of critical and polemical themes that forebode but do not constitute the scheme of a new synthesis.

All aspects of daily experience, of historical knowledge and culture concur in representing life as a web of misfortunes and pains that, stemming from human conscience, reach a level of major intensity. In the first lines of the *De remediis* he states: "When I ponder over the events and fortune of men and on the uncertain and sudden developments of things, I cannot find a more fragile, more restless one than human life. Nature, with an admirable remedy, provided for all irrational animals by denying them knowledge of themselves. I see that only for us humans memory, mind, providence and the other divine and most noble gifts of our soul are turned into suffering and hardship."

The effort made by the mind to give a logical order to the ideas as well as the attempt to penetrate the essence and the laws of natural reality, reach no useful conclusion and, above all, do not satisfy the primary need of offering man a justification for life and a behavioral measure. Dialectics is child's play, sterile and inconclusive. Science is vain curiosity that distracts us from the most important problem. Religion and moral revelation that Christianity gives mankind, as the only valid remedy for its illness, is itself defaced and twisted by theologians' cavils, sophism and disputes. These people "speak of God, like nature's philosophers, making up stories in a reckless fashion. Some want to apply the rules of their ignorant insolence to God who laughs and derides them, others discuss natural mysteries as if they originated in heaven and had attended the Omnipotent's council." But "true knowledge is piety," true philosophy "is not that which flies on deceptive wings and with verbose arrogance wraps itself in the emptiness of useless discussions but the other one that aims deliberately and directly at the salvation of the soul." To this end, no comfort comes to us from the masters of logic, science and art. "Who is more foolish than he who, knowing nothing, does not want to neglect these trifles before sudden death comes upon him to hand him an unexpected end while he is still fully intent to meditate upon his petty conclusions? Meditating exactly on death, fortifying oneself against it with scorn and patience, going toward it, if necessary, in the name of eternal life, happiness and glory and endure this brief and wretched existence with strong spirit, this, finally, is true philosophy, that which was correctly said to be only the contemplation of death."

These words may be found in the first book of the invectives *Contra medicum*, written between 1352 and 1355, which, together with the small treatise *De sui ipsius et multorum ignorantia*, composed between 1367 and 1370, constitute the most eminent and organic expository effort on the doctrinal ground of Petrarch's thought.

In the *De ignorantia* the writer resumes and develops more extensively and with more numerous arguments the theme, quite familiar to him, of contemporary philosophers', theologians', and naturalists' vain subtleties, with particular reference to the Paduan Averroists. Against the latter's arid, curious and presumptious science, that tackles "topics that are dangerous and too difficult to investigate," he opposes the much more useful science of human heart and the good assigned to mankind: "What is the good of knowing the nature of wild animals, birds, fish and reptiles, and ignore or neglect the knowledge of human nature, why we were born, whence we come and where we go?" The great thinkers of the ancient time were precluded from knowing the secret of true happiness." Any pious little old woman, any farmer, shepherd or fisherman" knows much more about this subject today than Aristotle did. By reading the *Ethics*, one learns to distinguish moral problems clearly, but not to find one's way in practice and reform one's behavior, and we become "more learned, not better persons." Doubtlessly the philosopher "teaches what is virtue, but his explanation has, in a very small measure, those impulses, that warm effectiveness of eloquence by which the soul is urged and inflamed to love virtue and hate vice."

These impulses will have to be sought in Cicero, Seneca, perhaps Horace, in the great Roman moralists and poets and, among the Greeks, more than in Aristotle, in Plato, "philosophie principem."

Plato's praise (Petrarch had read only the few dialogues already known by the medieval scholars in Latin translations and could comprehend the speculative directions following the steps of St. Augustine and Macrobius.) is significant particularly for its polemic value in an anti-Aristotelic and anti-scholastic sense.

It is an element of the battle that the author is fighting with still inadequate means, along a rather sentimental than reasoned necessity, in order to shift the philosophical view from the logical, physical and even theological themes to those of morals, conceived as concrete experience as well as psychological knowledge of life.

In this sense, his referring to Plato and the refusal of dialectical subtleties and naturalistic curiosity are elements that the fifteenth century humanistic culture will reconsider and will cause to bear fruit. And in one with them, he will praise culture as an instrument of education and poetry, glorified in its unselfish values against the mechanical arts and applied sciences, a praise amply developed in a letter to his brother Gherardo and mainly in the third book of the *Contra medicum*, where the writer elaborates some ideas of Mussato and, in turn, transfers them to Boccaccio and Salutati who will adopt them in their ample apologetic treatments: the poet's wisdom is not certainly necessary, yet it is not useless, or better, its spiritual value does not fit the purposes of an immediate and common practicality, it transfers a high moral content into eloquent forms, it supplies the truly lasting verbal and metaphorical instruments to any type of expression so that not even true religion can operate without the assistance of the muses and style. Poetry is David's psalms and the gospels' parables, and even if one considers the Fathers of the Church, one will have to admit that in their writings "nullum pene mansurum opus sine poetarum calce construitur." They are all motives that will be applied and deeply developed in post-humanistic culture but in the works of Petrarch they remain points that are not truly organized in a theoretical synthesis.

In his mind, the very ideal of culture is still alternating between the ascetic solutions of moral treatises and the thought of *virtus,* of the *animi vis et acrimonia,* patterned on the Roman models that sometimes take shape in the image of the great heroes like Scipio or Caesar. More often, as it happens in a later epistle addressed to Marsili, he shows a tendency toward a reconcilement between the *studia humanitatis* and the *studia divinitatis,* the acquiring of a *pia philosophia,* of a *literata devotio,* that would not oppose proudly the fundamental value of the *devota rusticitas,* the humble faith of the little old woman, but would enrich and confirm them according to and with the help of a very large cultural basis.

The establishment of culture's educative value, and of the literature that is based on it and expresses it with images and expressions to which style confers the prestige of an absolute and definitive formulation, constitutes the most frequent motive for Petrarch's writings, the only one that is developed with a relative coherence and continuity, supreme constant element of the writer's personality. It is the most firm and dwelt upon because for him it represents a certain point of reference, the only means that is offered to him to grasp, portray and dominate in some way the restless and dynamic substance of his experience.

The praises of writing and reading resound everywhere in the large epistolary collections, from the dedicatory passage of the *Familiari,* where Petrarch affirms solemnly: *"Scribendi michi vivendique unus, ut auguror, finis erit,"* to the *Senile* addressed to Boccaccio in 1374, on the eve of his death, in which, speaking to his friend who had advised him to take care of himself and look after his own health by resting from his too laborious work, he answered by exalting in a moving praise the sweetness and necessity for him of the labor that was part of his very life: "If I listened to you I would die sooner. When I begin to rest or even slacken the rhythm of my work, I will cease to live. This reading and writing of mine, that you order me to discontinue, is a light burden, in fact, a sweet rest that generates oblivion of more serious worries. No burden is lighter or more joyful than the pen's. The other pleasures are fleeting, and even though they blandish us, they harm us. When the pen is picked up by our hand, it gives us relief; when it is put down, it offers pleasure and benefit not only to its owner but also to many others, even if they are absent, and to our descendants thousands of years later. Among many worldly enjoyments, there is no one that is more honest, sweet, faithful, than the one of literature."

Here we are in touch with the most intimate and sincere part of Petrarch's confessions, the very heart of his humanness, the special form of his intelligence. The passion for reading, in Petrarch, is quite far from being reduced to a faint erudite grammarian's habit. Books are his obsession but also his consolation and strength: *"Omne ferme laborum quies, omne solatium vite."* Particularly some books became part of his mindset to the point that a sort of mnemonic illusion brings back to his lips and to his pen their concepts and phrases as if they were his own, books that he read not once but a thousand times, not hurriedly but by engaging in a prolonged delay all the power of his intelligence, *"hec se mihi tam familiariter ingessere, et non modo memorie sed medullis affixa sunt unumque cum ingenio facta sunt meo."*

Just through this connection of steady and prolonged familiarity, he reached the time of finding in books not models to imitate as a mere stylistic exercise but a wealth of ideas and moral truths that he adapts to his needs and conforms to his personality of man and writer. He establishes with them an intimate, deep system of correspondences that is not exclusively formal and verbal.

Anticipating an image and an idea that Poliziano will repeat but that in Petrarch grows on a much richer, restless and tormented ground of human experience that is not exclusively literary, Petrarch reaches the formulation of his poetic style of *imitatio*, where the awareness of his poetic originality is affirmed and simultaneously, the fruit that comes from afar and ripens slowly, is justified and clarified in the work of a total assimilation of the classics: *"vitam michi alieni dictis ac monitis ornare, fateor, est animus, non stilum; nisi vel prolato autore vel mutatione insigni, ut imitatione apium e multis et variis unum fiat. Alioquin multo malim michi stilus sit, incultus licet atque horridus, sed in morem toge abilis, ad mensuram ingenii mei factus."*

Literature is, therefore, the knot where converge, albeit in different ways, the various aspects analyzed thus far of Petrarch's personality. Only this element can supply to us a criterion by which to define and characterize it. It would be in vain to search in him, as it is done for Dante, a solid and vigorous theoretical framework, a rational vision that includes all reality's expressions and harmonizes them on the basis of a coherent rule of moral behavior. His speculations are carried out by analyzing problems that are connected with a personal history. At the most, they hint at a kind of new philosophy that aims eventually at the field of introspective analysis and ethical thought, yet they are unable to form an organic system. His asceticism is only intentionally a desire of purity and an intention to rise to the divine. It mostly stops at the early stages of an engrossed, satisfied, voluptuous contrition and concentration on his errors.

Philosophy narrows within the limits of psychology, or better, autobiography and religion ends with an exam of his conscience. The substance of his mind is constituted by a series of intellectual principles that imagination, sensibility and his countless readings suggest to him but that do not reach a clarification and do not become orderly sets of ideas. Discordant aspirations and attractions that remain episodic and weak attitudes unable to change into convictions and firm intentions also constitute it.

In the absence of an ideal that may become the essence of life, the latter is divided and torn by the arising urges of the most disparate passions and seems to unfold in a constant contradiction, in a troubled alternative among the calls of the earthly and the divine, the love of material things and the keen awareness of their vanity, the murky air of anguish and perplexity and a constantly unsatisfied desire of purity and wisdom.

In the light of this radical malaise that is, at once, the mirror and conscience of the ideal crisis of an entire epoch and society, there become apparent the uncertain nature of some sorrowful and painful confessions, the apprehension, weariness and indolence of the man, that "dolendi voluptas quedam ... pestis eo funestior, quo ignotior causa, atque ita difficilior cura," in which the troubled sensitivity of the romantics recognized itself as well as the existential anguish of the later generations that grew up in a squalid, desolate world without light of faith or firmness of moral main lines. Yet, it is not difficult to realize how certain modern definitions that insist on this malaise and emphasize that intimate contradiction appear defective and inadequate in analyzing the real aspect of a literary work they are under the illusion of explaining. Searching beyond the layer of a static and vigorous wisdom, they do capture the storm that rages in the deep but are unable to explain how and why that storm dissolves every time in a peaceful and bright motion of waves barely rippled on the surface by the variable tension of the underwater currents. Something distinguishes the most sorrowful expressions of the fourteenth century poet from those of his distant and sad followers, something more firm and clear in the eyes of the writer who looks in himself as well as in the serene, flowing calm of his style. In this tumultuous dispersion of all spiritual energy, the clarity of his intellect remains integral, as does that steady need of examining his affections, of making them objects of meditation and description, of sizing and judging himself. That was Petrarch's strength and salvation.

To reach this goal, literature came as a necessary means, almost natural and spontaneous by a long tradition, through those forms and wealth of human sentiments that his sensitive philology was progressively uncovering day by day and caused to be brought to light from the darkness of ignorance and incomprehension that had obliterated or altered its true aspect.

When we say that literature is at the center of Petrarch's personality, we only want to emphasize the firm trust that Petrarch had given literature as the best instrument capable of comprehending and representing psychological life, thus partially overcoming irrational forces that emerge from the murky and obscure bottom of conscience. The books of the ancient poets, philosophers and historians, the Bible and the Fathers of the Church, become a mirror for him where he saw the reflections of the episodes and features of his soul. He would transcribe sentences and verses to turn into epigraphs and symbols of his anxieties and hopes. Writing styles consecrated by tradition and art became a means to know himself better and clarify in harmonious words his anguish and weakness. They were, in short, a way to moral awareness if not to perfection.

By writing and confessing in his writings, Petrarch detached from himself, from the shapeless and discordant matter of his experience; he observed himself from above and became the judge and biographer of himself, in a detached and serene attempt. Through the able and delicate weaving of his words, chaos gained form; the uncertainty of his intention and the discord of his feelings turned into limpid definitions, they found peace in patterns of penetrating and sharp psychological descriptions. His ideas, too vague to produce a whole philosophical design, defined themselves in phrases and objects of reflection that were formulated in a learned and artistic style.

Thus Petrarch, from day to day, marked and recorded the variable and fluid events of his life in notes and short compositions, more often in letters addressed to friends and confidants that he would re-elaborate with a more objective style in his poems and historical and moral treatises. At the same time, he was able to place his objective on a different and higher level where discordance softened, contrasts became smooth in the terse, uniform quietness of good style.

In this effort of progressive objectivation and sublimation of autobiographical elements that culminates ideally in his poetry, culture (that particular culture entirely literary and not philosophical) plays a determining role of clarity and order. It restores dignity to man, it even justifies his weakness, pettiness, contradictions that, at the very moment he observes and confesses them with relentless lucidity, acquire exemplary significance, giving an entirely human and modern meaning to the scholar's keen and endless curiosity, granting authority to his words and establishing the validity of his teaching.

From this standpoint, among the other minor works, those that correspond the least to an attempt of order and composition and clarify more closely the winding, somewhat occasional road of the writer's human and literary experience, achieve particular importance. They are the large prose epistolary collections and, more indirectly, the *Epistole metrice* and perhaps the *Bucolicum carmen*.

The former, especially, constitute a livelier, more varied and interesting group for the modern reader among Petrarch's Latin writings. Not, certainly, in the sense that one may recognize in them a closer and more personal kind of composition. For what we know, also the letters (not only the official and ceremonial ones or those concerning doctrinal or moral topics that constitute real treatises developed in a more rapid and succinct style but also those directed to friends and composed in a tone of free and amiable conversation) were originally written and constructed ingeniously and dedicated not to an individual friend to whom the poet intended to confide and narrate his actions, but to an entire public of readers that gathered around such friends curious and eager not so much of news as of stylistic elegance and uncommon erudition.

Furthermore, Petrarch planned very early to select and organize that material by building it into a unitary structure, a plan that he carried out completely for the twenty-four books of the *Familiari* and at least outlined in broad details and partially completed for the seventeen books of the *Senili*. The comparison, that is possible in several cases, between the definitive and the early version, or among the various intervening versions exhibited by the rich handwritten tradition, shows us how this selecting work proceeded, eliminating from the text all elements of a more casual and biographical nature, by re-arranging the text with an appropriate transposition of concepts and phrases, revising their style everywhere in order to conform it more to the classical models, enriching and perfecting the quotations, combining several letters into one or, at times, dividing one into two or more and even inserting new letters composed then and there and adapted to the chrono-logical and not quite rigorous order of the collection, so that from the seeming disorder there appeared to the careful reader the impression of a well distributed variety and secret harmony, a unitary structure, albeit troubled, of the work.

However, even if the style adapts itself here and there to the requirements of a solemn tone and the display of an inexhaustible knowledge, one should admit that no small part was left in these letters of the originally stated intention of using an essay writing style, "ostentemus nos in libris, in epystolis colloquamur." More importantly, the ample variety of topics and form, now scholarly, now of bitter confession, biographic information, literary exercise and lighthearted digression, present to us a broader, variable and detailed picture of the writer's personality, portrayed in all its facets and mirrored in its developments and contradictions with a spontaneity, freedom and richness of personal references that is not found elsewhere in equal measure.

It is not by chance that the imposing stream of the epistolography used by Italian and European humanists of the fifteenth and sixteenth centuries origi-nates from the great example of Petrarch. They drew from the *"corpus"* of the poet from Arezzo the suggestion and model for all the other widely used genres: the treatise, the dialogue, the invective, the *"carmen epistolare"* and so on. Precisely from the pages of his letters, through the accumulation of ideas and annotations suggested all along by the events of the public and intimate chronicle, in a sort of uninterrupted diary and confession, one may build up little by little the *effigies* of the writer. From it arises the model of the literary man on which were patterned, through the centuries, the humanists of the later generations, the scholar with his human richness, his faith in culture and ideal virtue but also with tastes of archaic magnificence, his posture of solemn and manly dignity, his imbalance and contradictions, his nostalgia for Arcadian peace and idyllic solitude.

There is, above all, the annoyance for the current time and the regret for the great deeds and splendid forms of the ancients (*inter scribendum cupide cum maioribus nostris versor uno quo possum modo; atque hos, cum quibus iniquo sidere datum erat ut viverem, libentissime obliviscor; in que hoc animi vires cuntas exerceo, ut hos fugiam, illos sequar*). There is the motive of the dwelling, modest but not squalid, and rich in books, *"libelli innumerabiles,"* the *"aurea mediocritas"* and the horror of heights that border the abyss, poverty without baseness and envy, humble but proud freedom, *"semper splendide servituti libertatem humilem pretuli,"* and the nuisance of city and court life, the pleasure of finding a refuge in the restful countryside, to find a rustic solitude together with the comfort of a friendly nature and an ambiance favorable to the cherished, calming reading of poets and moralists (*"utinam scire posses quanta cum voluptate solivagus ac liber inter montes et nemora, inter fonts et flumina, inter libros et maximorum hominum ingenia respiro!"*)

There are, finally, the parts that take us more deeply into the man's psychology. For example, in his famous letter to Father Dionigi da Borgo San Sepolcro on the ascension of Mt. Ventoux, [he makes] the description of his spiritual struggles, his constantly defeated eagerness for spiritual uplifting, the alternation of thoughts and attractions that are reflected in the changing aspects of the landscape (*hos inter undosi pectoris motus"*), the subtle representation of passion that, contrasted but never tamed, retreats progressively in more secret corners, and while it seems ready to die away, it becomes more tenacious and troublesome: *"quod amare solebam, iam non amo; mentior: amo, sed parcius; iterum ecce mentitus sum: amo, sed verecundius, sed tristius; iamtandem verum dixi. Sic est enim: amo, sed quod non amare amem, quod odisse cupiam; amo tamen, sed invitus, sed coactus, sed mestus et lugens.* And, elsewhere, there is the fear of worldly cares, that surround and oppress man everywhere (*"innumerabilia mundi mala, que ego miser sentio et quibus obsideor ac circumspiciens contremisco"*), and the anxious appeals for grace (*"Misereberis, Domine, ut dignus sum cui amplius miserearis; sine gratuita enim misericordia tua nullatenus potest humana miseria misericordiam promereri"*); the awareness of an interior rending (*"voluntates mee fluctuant et desideria discordant et discordando me lacerant"*), and the obsessive feeling of the vanity and frailness of all those things that fill our everyday existence and life itself: (*"video qua hic rerum caligine, qua errorum nube circumdati, quantis in tenebris ambulemus; video nichil esse quo passim gaudeamus aut dolemus in hac vita, nichil quod tantopere vel cupimus vel horremus; nugas meras quibus angimur, larvas quas pueri senes expavescimus auramque levissimam qua deicimur ac levamur prorsus arundinea levitate; video eam ipsam que vita dicitur fugacis umbram nebule vel fumum ventis impulsum denique vel confusum somnium esse vel fabulam inexpletam vel siquid inanius dici potest."*)

Not differently and in a progression of themes and less oratorical and more fanciful stylistic structures, also the *Metriche* contribute to this complex, varied and mutable definition of Petrarch's personality, and although indulging in secondary and marginal motives, they often sound notes among the most intense and poetic of his culture: passing of time, feeling of impending death, world weariness, discordant passions, the soothing of solitude and the tenderness of the country landscape, the obsessive presence, even in that loneliness, of the beloved, tormenting object [of his love].

More artistically elaborated than the *Metriche* that, in this regard, preserve some approximation, like a still uncertain and concise outline, with a more rigorous formal order, the *Bucolicum Carmen* penetrates the secret of the heart, albeit through the generally medieval style of the genre, the allegorical eclogue, that seems so bristly and archaic to the taste of modern readers.

Neither the evidence of the eclogues (the one, for instance, that refers to a comparison and competition among the elements of a religious and classical culture), or the other on the *"divortium"* of the poet from the Colonnas, his first patrons, or even that on Laura's death, might be neglected by the person who intends to become immersed in the study of the complicated genesis of Petrarch's poetry and retrace the intricate and twisted ways through which the varied, fleeting situations of a biographical history and the alternate feelings of sadness and exaltation, repentance and hope, were able to take shape in myths and fables till they reached the values and functions of lasting symbols.

By glancing through the volumes of the letters and minor Latin poems, it is possible to find, on the line of a solid literary work and of an assiduous combination of culture and autobiography, the pages that, in Petrarch's minor writings, indicate more intimately the attitude of a high poetic experience and prepare us to understand and appreciate it in the most correct manner.

*

It would be easy to illustrate with many examples the constant exchange of lyrical and cultural themes, images, moulds and constructions of Petrarch's Latin and vernacular writings. At times it is a matter of precise conceptual and verbal correspondences: *Deficio sub fasce ... nitensque fatisco (Ecl. xi)* Io son sì stanco sotto 'l fascio antico (Rhymes, lxxxi), *Mors roseo artus, mors candida colla genasque/sidereosque oculos tetigit, vultusque serenos/obscura demersit humo* (Ecl. xi), Oimè, terra è fatto il suo bel viso ((Rhymes, cclxviii), *Que' duo bei lumi assai più che 'l sol chiari/chi pensò mai veder far terra oscura?* (Rhymes, cccxi), *Dulcia sidereas iactabant ora favillas/ardentesque comas humeris disperserat aura* (Ecl. iii), *Erano i capei d'oro a l'aura sparsi …/e 'l vago lume oltra misura ardea* (Rhymes, xc), *Ventris amor studiumque gulae sumnusque quiesque* (Metr. ii, ii), *La gola e 'l sonno e l'oziose piume* (Rhymes, vii), *Nimia voluntas effectum necat* (Sen. 1, 6), *Men, per molto voler, le voglie intense* (Rhymes, xlviii); *Spectat hec Satan ridens … interque decrepitos ac paellas arbiter sedens stupet plus illos agere quam se hortari, ipse interim et seniles lumbos stimulis incitat et cecum peregrines follibus ignem ciet, unde feda passim oriuntur incendia* (Sine nomine, xviii) *Per le camere tue fanciulle e vecchi/vanno trescando, e Belzebub in mezzo/co' mantici e col foco e co li specchi* (Rhymes, cxxxvi); *Dies mei velociores cursore figierunt, et non viderunt bonum …/O curae huminum inutiles, metus supervacui, spes inanes!* (Senil., iii, I), *I dì miei più leggier che nessun cervo/fuggir com'ombra e non vider più bene/ch'un batter d'occhio e poche ore serene/ch'amare e dolci nella mente servo./Misero mondo instabile e protervo!/Del tutto è cieco chi 'n te pon sua spene.* (Rhymes, cccxix).

Other times there are more fleeting, almost elusive references, as are several details of the landscape or better, of the scenery, in which the love story unfolds. For example, the "lamentar augelli," and "lucide onde" of the famous sonnet cclxxix are echoed respectively by the *"volucrum dulces querele"* in *Metr.*, 1, 8 and the *"rivus lucidus"* in *Metr.*, 1.6 and with a wider concordance of images and sounds but more vague and light. The colors and appearance of shadowy woods and running streams, grass, flowers, bird songs among the branches, evoked in the two cited metric epistles, seem to echo the most beautiful lines of sonnet clxxvi: *Parmi d'udirla, udendo i rami e l'ôre/e le frondi, e gli augei lagnarsi, e l'acque/mormorando fuggir per l'erba verde./Raro un silenzio, un solitario orrore/d'ombrosa selva mai tanto mi piacque …*

Sometimes the correspondence occurs within a broader imaginary situation and almost offers the opportunity to analize the expressions concerning an identical theme, as in this appearance of Laura in the memory of the lonely man: *Invenient vix verba fidem …/dum solus reor esse magis, virgulta tremendam/ipsa representant faciem truncusque reposte/ilicis et liquido visa est emergere fonte,/obviaque effulsit sub nubilus aut per inane/aeris out duro spirans erumpere saxo/credita suspensum tenuit formidine gressum* (Metr. 1, 6) and: *Io l'ho più volte, or chi fia che m'il creda?/ne l'acqua chiara e sopra l'erba verde/veduto viva, e nel troncon d'un faggio,/e 'n bianca nube …/e quanto in più selvaggio/loco mi trovo e 'n più deserto lido, tanto più bella il mio pensier l'adombra* (Rhymes, cxxix), or in this sorrowful summary of the events of his life that occurs at sunset and renders more urgent and longing the sting of repentance: *Si meminisse velis, postquam genitricis ab aevo/nudus, inops, querulus, miser et miserabilis infans/emergens, tremulo vagitus ore dedisti,/et labor, et lachrime, et gemitus, et tristia cure/pectora torquentes habitarunt corde sub isto …/Vixisti in pelago nimis irrequietus iniquo;/in portu morere, et languentia comprime vela;/collige disiectos iam tempestate rudentes* (*Metr.*, 1, 14) and: *Vergine, quante lacrime ho già sparte,/quante lusinghe e quanti preghi indarno,/pur per mia pena e per mio grave danno!/Da poi ch'i' nacqui in su la riva d'Arno,/cercando or questa e or quell'altra parte,/non è stata mia vita altro ch'affanno* (*Rhymes*, ccclxvi), and: *sì che s'io vissi in guerra e in tempesta,/mora in pace e in porto; e se la stanza/fu vana, almen sia la partita onesta* (*Rhymes*, ccclxv).

Finally, it is possible, in some cases, to follow through its various phases the progress of an expressive scheme drawn from the humanist's cultural repertory used later in a literary context in Latin and, on a more poetic level, in the lyrics. In one of the most beautiful *Familiari*, the third of the tenth books, that was written in 1349 to his brother Gherardo, where his youth spent in dissipation and frivolity is recollected in the spirit of bitter repentance, among the many echoings and citations of classical, patristic and biblical texts, there slips in the motive of the lover who is unable to keep his ravings secret and becomes the object of gossip and derision of the common people: *Quanta nobis fuerit cura quanteque vigilie ut furor noster late notus et nos multorum essemus populorum fabula*. It concerns a well known Horatian motive: *Heu me, per urbem, nam pudet tanti mali, fabula quanta fui*, and Ovidian, *Fabula, nec sentis, tota iactaris in urbe*. It will appear in a passage of the *Secretum*, and it will return in the *Metriche* (iii, 27), but we may find it, transposed in a context of high lyrical reflection, in the introductory sonnet of his lyrics whose date may be conjectured to be after 1348 or perhaps later: *Ma ben veggio or sì come al popol tutto/favola fui gran tempo, onde sovente/di me medesmo meco mi vergogno.*

Even more peculiar is the destiny of a passage of the *Salmi*,—*Quis dabit mihi pennas sicut columbae, et volabo et requiescam?* that was to obtain a deep response and consent in the poet's heart, as the expression both of his desire of evasion and purification as well as of the anguished awareness of the worldly burden that clipped the wings of his flight. He resumes it literally, in reference to his brother, in the mentioned epistle to Gherardo; he then repeats it a bit awkwardly in the *Metriche* (1, 14), and renews it, finally, in one of his greatest sonnets, as if he had rediscovered in his soul one by one those words, polished by time and enriched by the contribution of his long meditations and a painful experience, no longer as the contents of his memory, but true substance of his own soul, a renewed, very personal voice of his yearning emotion: *Qual grazia, qual amore, o qual destino/mi darà penne in guisa di colomba,/ch'i' mi riposi e levimi da terra?*

Even when it is possible to try and find a precise chronological succession in this network, it helps very little in studying the thematic and formal relationship between Petrarch's two types of writings against the background of a broad field of culture assimilated from various sources. It is more significant to realize that the difference, which is the same in all cases, between Latin and vernacular texts is to be found everywhere, not only concerning degree but quality; it does not present a progression from minor to major poetry but actually a passage, in absolute sense, from literature used more or less properly to poetry, with a radical modification of its sentimental and linguistic character and intensity, because it is only in his poems where, free from the burden of dependence on illustrious models, the writer has the opportunity to acquire a form of expression that is no longer borrowed, as it were, but truly authentic. Yet, it is important that, in defining and characterizing that form of expression in its character, there remain between the lyrical texts and the verbal transcription the constant presence of humanistic culture and literary experience as a means and instrument of integral stylization and consideration of autobiography through poetic elements.

What is Petrarch's collection of lyrics, at least in its external form, is well known: a love story, the description and almost the diary of a constant and never tamed passion, in whose presence not only the other minor affections but even the noblest and highest ideals retreat becoming secondary and marginal. It is a human and worldly passion, a desire that engulfs the whole soul and the flesh, so much more deep and pressing when it is not granted and fulfilled, still alive when, because of Laura's demise, every hope is already dead.

This love holds in itself something dark and morbid in its very nature of perpetually unsatisfied desire, in its continuing beyond the woman's death, in its character of exclusive, tyrannical affection. Sometimes it seems the poet is resigned to the habit of desiring and dreaming, other times, instead, passion arises more dominant and makes him look for the reality of the beloved object, lament and beg for mercy, regretting the years that fly away without consolation and hope. And again, wearied of waiting and desiring in vain for so long, the poet asks to be relieved of his suffering but then precipitates in it anew and goes back to his vain anxiety, the morbid yearning of imagination, prayers and tears.

After Laura dies, he shifts his love to heaven where she has been taken and he recalls her in his dreams, still a magnificent woman, in fact, more tender, almost motherly toward him, more concerned for his sorrows and better inclined to soothe them. Otherwise, when he considers the harsh reality of death, he sees the world dismal and void, a field without flowers, a ring without jewels and he laments inconsolably the lost hope of his happiness.

Along the entire development of this love story, intertwined in this plot and in antithesis with it, there appears a process of repentance and contrition that emerges at times in the form of painful confession, existential weariness, and sorrowful prayer ending with the final appeal to the Virgin.

The choice of the lyrical genre, in accordance with the writer's disposition, with prevalent egocentrism and scarce ability for synthesis and precise organization, the burden of a tradition already established within that genre and its stated rules—the scholarly canzone, the sextet, the confession and exchange sonnet—led naturally Petrarch to place the origin and the development of his activity as a vernacular poet within the framework of a love story, with rare and hard inroads in the area of civic and moral polemics. Every diligent reader, however, notices that this story, in its most immediate and most biographical meaning, is far from exhausting the subject of the collection, not only because the poet included in it the most solemn compositions concerning his political ideas, the canzone for the crusade, the anti-Avignon sonnets and the prayer to the Virgin, but especially because the very love story expresses and suggests an otherwise rich and complex psychological experience, namely all the varied and intricate play of perplexities, fluctuations, contrasts, anguish, anxiety, the dark, irrational and unsound in that interior life that his Latin writings manifest more analytically and varyingly, catching it at its roots and with its implications of biographical nature and personal chronicle.

If Petrarch's entire work is, as we tried to clarify, the mirror of the profound ideological crisis of his time, his lyrical poems are the expression of that crisis in a higher, indirect form, its description in symbolic and mystic terms, poetic in a strict sense, that presupposes and absorbs the simple literary mediation already carried out in the minor writings. As it is known, this crisis implies the collapse of a moral and intellectual order and a serious break between the aspects of social life and the world of culture, therefore a new discovery of the individual and his loneliness, in a poetic sense. In other words, it was the discovery of lyricism conceived in a much deeper meaning than that of the Provençal troubadours and their Sicilian and Tuscan followers.

No literary reference is able to exhaust really the importance of such discovery. The attention paid by Petrarch to the moods of interior life is, potentially, much closer, direct and impassionate than it was in those uncertain and rigid models; it was more varied, free, productive and daring. He breaks, one by one, all patterns of conventional psychology, he interrupts the fragile balance of a rigidly stylized poetry, and rejects the intellectual assumptions of an ideal court of 'faithful of love,' the uttermost expression of the feudal world, where the early form of that practice of literary style had been followed in Provence and then in Sicily.

In Petrarch, the human being, his exclusive passions, intimate wounds and incurable pains are present in an unparalleled fashion, more tormenting and grievous, more genuine and intense. Yet, that crisis carried in itself, as we saw, a positive element, the premise of a future development entrusted entirely to the surviving pride of an intellectual prestige, the still intact trust in the comforting, guiding and enlightening function of literary culture as an instrument of intelligence and domination of passions, and, more noble yet, of poetry, "because by singing, pain becomes less harsh," and at the very moment that we observe it and transpose it in lucid and clear words, then irrational contents of the gained experience is completely acquired, overcome and redeemed. Consequently, even in Petrarch, although differently from the early lyrical tradition, confession is never strictly a direct one. With unmatched subjectivity, it has the tendency to transpose itself to an objective state, to draw from the personal case a norm, the framework of a doctrine.

The task of mediating and elevating the sentimental ideas after the elimination of the social and courtly patterns of the Provençal poetry is now assigned to the patterns of an essentially literary culture that had been applied by a long tradition to moral themes and is developed in absolute terseness and dignity, in integrally classical forms. Within this attempt, the presence of an experienced and productive rhetoric is justified, as is even the technical nature of the language.

Naturally, Petrarch did not achieve these results suddenly and without a long apprenticeship. Doubtlessly, it is at least inaccurate to dwell on a substantial immobility of his art. The few fragments of early and intermediate compilations of individual compositions that reached us in the Vatican Collection 3196, with their minute corrections, a group of minor variants confirmed by sixteenth century readers who knew manuscripts and documents that have been lost, the still unorganized and insufficiently explored group of poems that were rejected represent, in their totality, the precious documentation of this apprenticeship and exhibit the variety of the attempted directions that were abandoned later along the series of models that literary tradition offered him.

Among the compositions included in the first organization of the "canzoniere," one notices the stratification of distinct phases of the structural elaboration along the imitation, in some older texts, of the stilnovo, Dantean and Provençal patterns of the sextets, the oratorical syntax of the political and moral "canzoni," and the Ovidian speculation on love. But, on the whole, it is appropriate to say that the poems that were made a part of the book as the writer wanted it to be, have a constant voice that assimilates and blends, through delicate details, even the frequent residues of heterogeneous origin. As it came down to us, in the Vatican manuscript 3195, the book is the result of a long work of selection that was begun already before 1336, and then of a long process of organization, not mechanically chronological, elaborated until the eve of his death, where one can distinguish some conspicuous moments, from the edition dedicated to Azzo da Correggio, around 1358, (the present MS. Chigiano L.V. 176), and one quite close to the definitive text, compiled in 1373 for Pandolfo Malatesta, a copy of which is included in the Laurenziano XLI, 17.

The constant and close attention is proof of the intention to create a unitary composition, on the model of his collections of letters, and within the lines of the lyrical genre, that does not imply an actual order but only a juxtaposition according to some criteria of contents and art of various texts, each of which preserves intact its autonomy: *Rerum vulgarium fragmenta, "rime sparse."*

At any rate, it does not follow, as in Dante's case, a determined structure, and not even the somewhat uncertain line of a progress from passion to repentance, from earth to heaven, from Laura to God and the Virgin, but the topic's uniformity, the degree of the language's, and the style's, classical form, lends the book a precise and constant aspect and justifies the unitary plan of the collection.

Because it is the result of the combination of a secret and remote experience of passion with a firm determination to create a stylistic configuration and reconstruction, the "canzoniere" requires a reader that may be able to adapt the romantics' attention for the contents with the patient, rhetorical analysis of the humanists. These two modes of reading that reflect and synthesize the critical fortune of the book through the centuries, are, each in itself, insufficient, but if they are joined together, they permit a total comprehension of the text, eliminating the twofold risk of an indiscriminate admiration that confuses poetry and rhetoric and of an unjustifiable dislike that is unable to recognize, beyond the supreme formal decorum, the intimate reason of the heart.

It is not true, in fact, that at the root of Petrarchan poetry there is, as it has been repeated too often, a veiled and calm emotion lacking in dramatic force. On the contrary, it is true that what is cloudy and unseemly in the secret corners of the poet's soul, surfaces in the lines as if from a remote region, through a veiled modesty, already tamed, "repelled," as De Sanctis would say. This explains why Petrarch appeared as a model of linguistic and literary re-elaboration of spiritual experiences to the ancient readers and why later he seemed cold and artificial to the romantics and even to De Sanctis [who viewed him] "more an artist than a poet." The fact is that in a few poets among all literatures one can find lines like his, where human voice echoes so intensely yet always remote, almost whispered in simple, essential words that suggest it while, at the same time, they mitigate its motion in their terseness.

No poem of the "canzoniere," not even those that sound shaky and doleful or where their tone appears stronger and dejected, leaves in the reader an impression of violent pain and despair but rather a sense of tender elegy and sad wisdom. His anguished suffering, whose secret presence is felt in many poems, is, as it is sung, pervaded also by a firm and subtle intelligence so that no throb or dissonance, no sudden rush of his feelings comes to disturb the smooth melody of his poetry.

The apparent limitation of the Petrarchan world and its means of expression, especially if it is compared with the extraordinary scope and variety of Dante's thematic and structural experiences, allows an ample gamut of modes, tones and attitudes that converge to a common, fundamental source of intimacy and lyrical solitude.

For the romantic and post-romantic reader's taste, his agreement with those texts will be easier and closer because he will find in them the creation and development of an inexhaustible framework of sudden occasions, human relations with their alternations of anxiety, abandonment, hope and dejection, its natural background, the episodic variations of the situations and even its development, marked according to the actual calendar of days and places; and also from the effusive moments of enchanted contemplation of feminine beauty and pleasurable surrender to his feelings, to the compositions that portray the perplexity and mutation of affections, the "sweet error" of the mind. Or those on the theme of Laura's death's foreboding, and, after her death, of her appearing in his dreams or, finally, of the late and absurd loving at a late age when the poet and Laura, old but still in love, nurturing a less impetuous and overbearing affection, would come together to weave a web of memories and confessions.

From the commentators of the sixteenth century to De Sanctis, every reader of Petrarch's lyrical poems was able to create a precious selection of compositions and was always capable of retracing lines and words where the expression reaches levels of tenderness and affection seemingly more candid and spontaneous, a most refined and unforeseeable psychological analysis. The reader, however, who may even be an exceptional one, such as De Sanctis or Croce, always runs the risk of feeling disappointed and ends up by surrounding his admiration with countless reservations if he allows himself to materialize excessively or emphasize the human, fortuitous aspects of those imaginary situations and perceive in them the lines of a concrete story expressed through a narration, while the actual quality of this poetry tends toward an extreme stylization and softening of the biographical material and unfolds in a process aimed at transforming real elements into an unreal world.

The most famous myths of Laura's charm—it will suffice to mention *Chiare fresche e dolci acque*—do not enter a precise set of events and places, but emerge from a mysterious world of dreamy imagination, "with sighing I remember," "sweet in my recollection." The woman's beauty lives on more luminous when it is cast into the past and becomes the substance of memories:

> *Erano i capei d'oro a l'aura sparsi*
> *ch'en mille dolci nodi gli avolgea,*
> *e 'l vago lume oltra misura ardea*
> *di quei begli occhi ch'or ne son sì scarsi;*

or when it is pervaded by a bewildered suspense within the framework of an intimate dialogue between the lover and Love:

> *Amore e io, sì pien di meraviglia*
> *come chi mai cosa incredibil vide,*
> *miriam costei quand'ella parla o ride*

> *che sol se stessa e nulla altra simiglia ...*
> *Qual miracolo è quel, quando tra l'erba*
> *quasi un fior siede, o ver quand'ella preme*
> *col suo candido seno un verde cespo!*
> *Qual dolcezza è ne la stagione acerba*
> *vederla ir sola co i pensier suoi inseme,*
> *tessendo un cerchio a l'oro terso e crespo!*

Descriptive elements, landscape, scenery, barely hinted at with extreme modera-
tion, a "lonely bank," "a rivulet," a "spring," "high mountains," "wild woods," a "tall
pine tree and a hill," "clear water," "green grass," become in the other famous canzone *Di pensier in pensier,* mere symbols and external references of a psychological
condition or, in the sonnet *Solo e pensoso,* they become confiding and participant
of an intense, internal meditation or also, as it is mentioned elsewhere, witnesses
of his sorrows:

> *O poggi, o valli, o fiumi, o selve, o campi,*
> *o testimon de la mia grave vita,*
> *quante volte m'udiste chiamar morte!*

Not otherwise, in an air of remembrance and reverie, the image of the dead woman
reappears in his imagination, a motive he resumed and changed in a long series
of compositions that make the second part of the "canzoniere" more likeable and
touching:

> *Or in forma di ninfa o d'altra diva,*
> *che del più chiaro fondo di Sorga esca*
> *e pongasi a sedere in su la riva;*
> *or l'ho veduto su per l'erba fresca*
> *calcare i fior com'una donna viva,*
> *mostrando in vista che di me le 'ncresca.*

The process of stylizing, that in this case depends on the moderate choice of images
adopted in an entirely symbolic function, does not exclude elsewhere the use of
all devices, even the most timeworn, of a skilled rhetoric in order to enlighten the
corners and shadows of a tormented spiritual story: metaphors that became obvious due to prolonged usage like that of the ship overwhelmed by the storm or frequent and persisting antitheses that establish a bitterly autobiographical substance
within schemes of classical objectivity:

> *(lagrimar sempre è 'l mio sommo diletto,*
> *il rider doglia, il cibo assenzio e tosco;*
> *la notte affanno, e 'l ciel seren m'è fosco,*
> *e duro campo di battaglia il letto);*

sentences, in whose apparent banality is condensed the fruit of a long habit of reflections and experiences, the sagacious residue of a persevering exam of his conscience:

> e del mio vaneggiar vergogna è 'l frutto,
> e 'l pentersi, e 'l conoscer chiaramente
> che quanto piace al mondo è breve sogno.
> Or cognosco io che mia fera ventura
> vuol che vivendo e lagrimando impari
> come nulla qua giù diletta e dura.

Petrarch formulates through this progress a kind of language that might be defined as technical, not in the naïve courtly or scholastic terminology of earliest poets, but in that of the choice of a group of terms destined to signify emblematically the main situations of a totally personal condition explored and defined in an effort to carry out an almost scientific observation. They are words that acquire a weight that goes much further than their obvious semantic value, "error," "raving," "repent," "fear," "labor," "truce," "peace," and so on. Thus, at the end, the most genuine voice of the poet seems more recognizable just in those lines where such a language rejects any embellishment, sheds any metaphorical device and appears pure in its absolute essence, with those forms that, in the eyes of the commentators between the sixteenth and the eighteenth centuries, seemed plain and unimaginative, where, in fact, the entire poetic quality depends on the stylistic resources. There are sonnets of confession, *Io son sì stanco, La vita fugge, Quand'io mi volgo,* or of prayer, *Padre del ciel; Tennemi Amor; Io vo piangendo.*

Almost at the beginning of the "*canzoniere,*" Sonnet XXXII may be chosen to exemplify the modes of this less admired and perhaps greater Petrarch:

> Quanto più m'avvicino al giorno estremo
> che l'umana miseria suol far breve,
> più veggio il tempo andar veloce e leve
> e 'l mio di lui sperar fallace e scemo.
> I' dico a' miei pensier: Non molto andremo
> d'amor parlando omai, ché 'l duro e greve
> terreno incarco come fresca neve
> si va struggendo, onde noi pace avremo;
> perchè co llui cadrà quella speranza
> che ne fé vaneggiar sì lungamente,
> e 'l riso e 'l pianto e la paura e l'ira.
> Sì vedrem chiaro poi come sovente
> per le cose dubbiose altri s'avanza
> e come spesso indarno si sospira.

The intensity of the poetic situation is not apparent at first sight and does not impress the reader who received a romantic preparation. It becomes evident only by degrees to the person who weighs carefully the value of every word and becomes aware of the particular working of a style where the individual situations, reflections and moods cannot be accepted unless they are freed from their individual features and conform to a general form, a kind of Platonic idea that does not destroy their intimate value, rather, it multiplies it by giving it the illusion of a universal value.

The topic seems to operate on a plan of common, nearly obvious ideas. They are ideas that reappear persistently in every page of the book, govern its structure and offer the background to the varying situations—death, or better "the last day" (or "the last step," "the dubious step")—before which all life pales, a fleeting web of obscure "misfortunes," the "fast and light passing" of time and the futility of hopes that are always dashed. Each one of these thoughts is exactly a common place around which one might gather a number of quotations from the "canzoniere," and go back to the great maxims of the ancient moralists or of the holy books on which that easy and not uncommon wisdom is drawn up.

The educated reader is content with this somewhat empty solemnity, appreciates it in its splendid verbal manifestations, follows the thread of the many concordances and takes delight for centuries in repeating them in his mind, imitating them and varying them to repletion. But those who, nowadays, dig more deeply notice that, owing to so much repetition and insistence, those words had assumed in Petrarch a human voice that we would uselessly search in the major part of the Petrarchists. That ephemeral wisdom had been achieved during a painful and restless experience and only by degrees it had become the mirror where a real and never tamed sorrow was reflected and had become less sharp.

It will become clearer then why the poet approaches the painful points of the real condition that he wants always to express from afar through circumlocutions and word-symbols, his human sorrow then becomes the "earthly burden," the "ancient bundle," and love, the supreme apprehension, the tormented expression of his suffering is transposed in colorless, incorporeal words and, for this reason, more solid and meaningful: a long "raging," and then "laughter" and "crying," "fear" and "anger." The fact is that precisely those words, so bare and abstract, those relics of a language reduced to the pure essential, truly synthesize for the poet the meaning of his entire experience, and in the eyes of the person who reconstructed his cultural and biographical history they acquire weight, material substance of poetry. It is only by them that Petrarch confesses himself without the humiliation of an outburst, only in this manner the consideration for his misfortune and despair turns lyrical without being artificial.

This is how, among the other softer and less exacting voices, almost guided, sustained and introduced by them, there appears also the stronger word that, for a moment, seems to shatter the clear surface of the narration revealing in a flash the obscure depth of this poetry, its most painful, ashamed and secret "fear."

This is Petrarch's gift: intelligence surviving from the wreck caused by passions and hopes, the tenacious and valiant will of knowing himself and scrutinizing himself to the very depth of his soul.

In this steady concern, shorn of any gratification, without illusions but also without cynicism, tinged with regret, resides what we called the modern, deeply human discovery of lyricism.

The absolute coherence of the poetic world, exclusive to the point of monotony, and the consequent, rigorous choice of lexical and stylistical devices according to a classical pattern, the opposite of the extraordinary liberty, variety and formal independence of Dante, destined almost naturally Petrarch's poetry to acquire the regulative function of example par excellence in the area of lyrical genre and also, beyond that, of all cultured poetic literature.

After the rare attempts of the fourteenth century and the scholastic compositions of the fifteenth century poets that follow the surface of the rhetorical forms developing them in an utterly artificial and conceptual sense, the imitation of the "canzoniere" reaches its apex, as it is well known, in the sixteenth century, by assuming the character of untiring exploration and refined experimentation of a precious wealth of situations and linguistic constructions, thus establishing not only the Italian but the European fortune of Petrarchism.

But the most profound influence, although mostly indirect, of the authentic personality of the writer from Arezzo should be sought, beyond Petrarchism proper, among those poets that renew, with different attitudes and changed conditions, the absolute concept of form and the intensity of contemplative vision, from Gongora and the Spanish mystics, Shakespeare in his sonnets as well as the English metaphysics down to the masters of modern lyrics, Leopardi and Baudelaire and their followers of yesterday and the present.

CHAPTER FIVE

Boccaccio

In his relation with Petrarch, also Boccaccio kept during his entire life a secondary position not differently from the other numerous followers and disciples who were invited to collaborate, each one within the limits of his ability, in an operation of profound cultural transformation. He was, that is, a disciple among the many, although much more gifted with intelligence and enthusiasm. This did not happen only in the years of his early youth, when he became familiar with Petrarch, owing to his fame, and began to gather, transcribe and imitate those writings in Latin that he was able to obtain or were forwarded to him by his Neapolitan friends and acquaintances. At the same time he began to compose, with candid enthusiasm, a biography and a praise in *De vita et moribus domini Francisci Petracchi,* but also when, after the autumn of 1350, he could finally make his personal acquaintance in Florence and establish with him a deep friendship and mutual trust that was to end only after their death.

In a letter written in his old age, Boccaccio refers to him as his master and spiritual guide, "inclitus preceptor meus, cui quantum valeo debeo," and in another letter dictated a few months before his death, he refers proudly to his devotion that he harbored intact and fervent for more than forty years, "ego quadraginta annis vel amplius suus fui."

This humble attitude cannot be attributed only to his modesty that is, without doubt, one of the most genuine and pleasant qualities of Boccaccio's nature. It reflects objective reasons and, up to a point, a real order of historical functions.

In the mind of the scholar who intends to reconstruct the origin and development of the new humanistic conception, Petrarch's contribution appears more important and, above all, more organic and coherent. Boccaccio's intellectual interests contain always something eclectic and dispersive, his erudition remains muddled, his Latinity quite incomplete, with strong medieval remnants, and his philology, when compared with Petrarch's, is, by far, not as clever technically and often daring and clumsy. Nor could we find in his work (or not equally emphatic) that lucid, sorrowing conscience of the ideological crisis, both in its substance and in its modes of expression, that renders Petrarch, who experiences and portrays it in every aspect and phase of his intellectual activity, a historical figure.

Yet, a limited evaluation of Boccaccio's personality would be quite erroneous, if it aimed at refusing or even limiting its real contributions to a new feeling of life and the opening of new horizons in culture and taste, and would be under the illusion of defining it in an entirely medieval perspective, in that uncertain, crepuscular light after which the phrase "autumn of the Middle Ages" was coined, that is certainly valid for peripheral areas of western civilization between the end of the fourteenth and the early fifteenth century.

The lack of rational awareness is largely counterbalanced in his mind by instinct; his philological unpreparedness and scattered knowledge are compensated by an extraordinary vitality of sentiment and imagination. Also his serene and meek acceptance of reality, his obstinate optimism, that seems so simple and hardly problematic when it is compared with Petrarch's deeply pessimistic views, do not exclude the spark of a lively and daring polemics.

It is precisely his potential eclecticism, his renouncing the uncompromising and exclusive assertion of the humanistic ideal, with its intrinsic rejection of all the forms of a recent tradition, that allows Boccaccio to emphasize freer, bolder and unbiased aspects and even anticipate and draft ideas of sensitivity and art that will be fully developed in the most successful era of Renaissance civilization while, on the other hand, it allows him to keep closer ties with the pre-humanistic activities inherent in the culture of Dante's time and still vital, especially in Tuscany, in the second half of the fourteenth century. In his works, much more than in Petrarch's, it is possible to study the relationships and connections between the learned literature of a complex cultural background and that of the minor mediocre writers, without excluding expressions of a humbler and genuinely popular taste.

These aspects that mark the most illustrious representatives of the post-Dante generation and address also their art in almost opposite directions, may be understood, rather than as a difference of characters, as a difference in human condition and mental preparation that is, in other words, a difference of natural and historical background.

In the second half of 1313, Giovanni, the natural son of Boccaccio di Chellino, a merchant, was born in Florence, or better yet in Certaldo, where his father's family originated and lived, in the heart of that Tuscany where there remained and lasted for a long time the communal institutions and flourished there a bourgeois society inspired by a particular sense of its liberty and economic power as well as its moral and intellectual vitality.

Boccaccio spends his childhood in his father's Florentine residence and receives the first rudiments of schooling from Giovanni da Strada, a grammarian and father of the humanist Zanobi. When he was still a boy, perhaps in 1325 or shortly later, he was sent to Naples in order to engage in the merchandising practice with the Bardi establishment, the powerful bankers of the Angevin court. After six years, he abandons his commercial activity and begins unwillingly to study canon law, an endeavor that he will abandon after six more years. But he had already turned to deepen his literary preparation and had begun quite early to write in prose and poetry and mingle with the elegant and well educated society of the capital.

In a very famous passage of the *Genealogia deorum*, he himself stressed the power of his exclusive poetic vocation, contrasting it to the useless, tedious efforts he made for many years in his business apprenticeship and then in not disinterested studies: "My mind was so reluctant toward these things, that nothing could ever dispose it to either one of the two professions, entirely captivated as it was by a unique attraction for the studies of poetry. It was not a sudden fancy but a most ancient disposition that caused it to tend to poetry with all its strength ... Eventually, almost a grown up and independent man, without anyone prodding or teaching me, in fact, against my father's resistance who disapproved of my studies, I learned by myself whatever little I know of poetry and applied myself to it with very great eagerness and I saw, read and tried as much as I could to understand the poets' books."

One may think that these studies, undertaken with the passionate fervor of a self-taught person, as well as the devotion to courtly ways and refined habits that they seemed to harbor in themselves, opened for a very young Boccaccio not just the way to closeness with learned men and grammarians at court (such as the astronomer Andalò di Negro, the librarian Paolo di Perugia and even more the theologian Dionigi di Borgo San Sepolcro, the literary man and jurist Barbato da Sulmona and Giovanni Barrili who were already familiar with the curia of Avignon and corresponded with Petrarch), but also to the company of young people eager for amusement and luxury, not averse to refined conversations and storytelling, poetry and social games. At a later date, Boccaccio could boast that he, a commoner, had been able to live "in Naples ... among aristocratic young people," who were not ashamed to visit him and frequent his house where he lived "very discreetly."

If we do not consider the frequent interpolations that seem frankly autobiographical in his Florentine and Neapolitan writings, we should admit that the information at our disposal concerning young Boccaccio's life is scarce and spotty. Until a few years ago, scholarly criticism considered valid those autobiographical riddles and earnestly engaged itself to decipher them.

By interpreting cleverly the obscure chronological references, by opening the veil of his allegories, solving anagrams, replacing patiently together the scattered fragments of the difficult mosaic and especially by trying hard to reconcile somehow their internal discrepancies and contradictions, scholars, from Crescini to Torraca and Hauvette, were under the illusion of having defined with sufficient precision the episodes of a life that was not devoid of an adventurous and poetic fascination whose main episodes were constituted by the mysterious birth of the writer in Paris, the product of an illicit love affair between a Tuscan merchant and a French gentlewoman (or even a royal blooded princess), and of his relationship with Fiammetta in Naples, namely with a Mary, natural daughter of Robert of Anjou who was married into the house of the counts of Aquino.

Looking more closely in this reconstruction, there remained too many uncertainties while too many conjectures became necessary to put together, more or less precisely, the tiles of a mosaic that constantly changed shape and modified its details, attitudes and events of the primary characters of the legend. It will suffice to refer to the *Elegia di Madonna Fiammetta*, where the flattering, deceitful woman of the *Filostrato* suddenly becomes seduced and betrayed, forcing biographers to presume an absurd reversal in the narrative of the actual elements of the situation, and even more importantly, the task of reconciling the elements of the biographical tale with the scarce documents and the most reliable evidences of his contemporaries became more and more arduous. In these cases, the birth in Paris is contradicted by the unanimous evidence of the earliest biographers and of Boccaccio himself in his non-fictional writings, while the name of Maria d'Aquino is entirely unknown to the genealogists of that otherwise illustrious family. The new scholars were in a good position to demolish the weak castle built up laboriously by their predecessors and to select the little positive information, that is the same that we have explained above, out of abundant fiction that sprouted from an inventive and dreamy literature.

What's more, if criticism had no difficulties in proving the inconsistency of the lovely tale that Boccaccio used to embellish and adorn his humble origin and social position, it was not able, I do not say to destroy, but even to scratch the importance and significance, namely the authenticity, of his enthusiastic poetic and worldly apprenticeship that his literary works prove and documents do not contradict. Without doubt, the story of the author's indirectly aristocratic origins, vague and contradictory as it is, as well as that of his quasi-regal loves, are entirely fictional, the character of Maria d'Aquino is pure invention, and the name of Fiammetta that designates her in her literary transfiguration, is merely a *senhal* in the tradition of lyric genres.

But there is much truth, however, even from an autobiographical standpoint, in his familiarity with the elegant, courtly society and above all his vivid experience of love's joys and sorrows, anxiety and jealousy, seductions and betrayals, and the backgrounds of the merry groups, conversations and pastimes, of idyllic retreats in the country and the bathing recreation in Baia.

It would be pointless to reduce the apprenticeship of passions and worldly life to a web of dry, literary schematizations. The entire production of Boccaccio's youth proves what a varied and lively substance of non-bookish feelings, what a web of happy and painful sentiments governs from the beginning the imagination of the prose and poetry of the narrator, warmed by the nature of an experience that is only too close and, at times, intrusive, that determines not only the matter but the direction and expression of his art.

The person who, after opening the delicate veil of the pseudo-autobiographical allegories, thinks he may be able to reconnect inconsequentially the play of inventions to the precise and pedantic reflection of a set of consecrated models, deprives himself of every avenue to penetrate really Boccaccio's heart of poetry and his human essence.

Against such illusion and misunderstanding we should restate without fear the essential truth of the writer's confessions, their great autobiographical value, not external or anecdotal but intimate as much as authentic, as it is capable of offering us, together with some details of his real life also the dreams, hopes, apprehensions and delusions of a youth that seeks, even in books, the image of a shining, true adventure.

It is a fact that the known reality, and not the contrary, determines from the outset also the literary man's preferences, it limits the field of his readings within a scope that differs, for example, from the one where his contemporary Petrarch forces himself into, and gives a characteristic and unique imprint to his culture. A culture that is not the grammarian's and, strictly speaking, not even the humanist's, but that of a poet, a culture that is not fastidiously Latin and classical-like, but open to all the voices of the Romance world, from love poetry and Dante to the translations and rewritings of the French narration, the fabliaux, the ballads and the popular songs, eager, above all else, to capture the most passionate, imaginative, the most picturesque, dramatic or touching feelings: Ovid's *Metamorfosi* and *Eroidi,* Seneca's tragedies and Apuleius.

*

The evidence of this open and talented culture, at once excited and warm or stylized and dreamy, about that passionate biographical adventure, are the numerous writings composed by Boccaccio in vernacular or Latin, in prose or in verse, between the age of twenty and twenty-seven, before his Neapolitan stay ended a little abruptly in 1340.

The insufficient knowledge of the author's real life and the difficulty of interpreting persuasively the few internal evidences make useless all attempts to date those texts more accurately. They allow, at most, to establish an approximate chronological sequence of the most important among them, from the *Filocolo* to the *Filostrato* and the *Teseida*, that belong almost certainly to the last part (1336–1340) of the Neapolitan period (the latter may have been revised definitely in Florence), while the *Caccia di Diana*, must have preceded it shortly before, for it appears to be the work of a beginner. In that somewhat restricted period of time, there belong the earliest and most certain groups of the poems for Fiammetta as well as the first Latin exercises of the writer, that may be assigned, by the author's own admission, to the spring of 1339.

The most evident characteristic of this abundant and slightly jumbled activity is a literary tradition of a Tuscan nature, between "stil nuovo" and Dante, devoid, however, of its deepest ideological values and reduced to a mere series of rhetorical formulations. The Latin epistles follow closely the model of the most scholastic style of Dante's *ars dictandi*, not only in their obedience toward all the traditional stylistic and metric devices and in the choice of an extremely intricate and precious language, but even in the faithful following of its thematic inspiration and structural patterns.

The poems adopt formally the metaphoric and linguistic pattern of Cavalcanti, Cino and the early Dante: the "spiritelli," the "angiolette," the ecstatic tones of the "lode," the elegiac, cold and symbolic visions of the "pietrose" that form the background of cruel love's attacks:

> *Vetro son fatti i fiumi ed i ruscelli*
> *gli serra di fuor ora la freddura ...*
> *E l'umido vapor, che si raccoglie*
> *nell'aria, attrista il cielo.*
> *S'i' avessi in mano gli capegli avvolti*
> *di te, c'ha' lo mio cuor per mezzo aperto,*
> *prima ch'i' gli lasciassi i' vedria certo*
> *pianger quegli occhi che da amor son volti ...*

In the *Caccia*, the very choice of the meter, the terza rima, carries in itself parts of the language of the *Commedia* ("verde smalto," "calor diurno," "fiera snella," "mentre con gli occhi fra le verdi fronde," "chinaron gli occhi tacite aspettando"). Situations, patterns, and constructions clearly taken from the thirteenth century poetic collections and from the *Vita nuova*, appear frequently both in the details and in the very structure of the *Filocolo, Teseida* and the *Filostrato*, where, at a certain point, Cino's canzone *La dolce vita* is literally transcribed with slight variations.

In this thick web of citations, at times manifest, other times barely disguised, one notices, besides the already mentioned weakening of the intellectual and sentimental contents, also a decline in expression. On the one hand, the "stilnovo" patterns lose their intensity and become embellishing contrivances: the stylized situations of the *Vita nuova* are adopted in the *Caccia,* that consists, in fact, of a long list of Neapolitan ladies of rank, as a gallant and courtly pretext that is not much more than a society game. Dante's ideal and lyrical autobiographical narration becomes in Boccaccio's romance and short poems simple, trite autobiography, complicated by dim conundrums. On the other hand, an originally poetic expression becomes prosaic, humble and burdensome, thus causing, especially in the verses, frequent imbalance and dissonance and a constant debasing of the lexical, metaphorical and syntactical repertory. Really, rather than of debasing, one should speak of transition from the elevated and concentrated form of lyricism to the expanded and analytical style of narrative prose. The dissonance derives from the reason that Boccaccio's narrative vocation, in order to express and ennoble itself, adopts traditionally lyrical forms that sound odd and impermanent compared with the changed contents of inspiration. The newest parts of the rhymes, for example, originate from a descriptive source that is realistic, at least potentially, where images and constructions deriving from the models of the "stilnovo," such as "angioletta," "miracol nuovo," "spiritelli," are more than ever inappropriate:

> *Sulla poppa sedea d'una barchetta,*
> *che 'l mar segando presta era tirata,*
> *la donna mia con altre accompagnata,*
> *cantando or una or altra canzonetta.*
> *Or questo lito ed or quest'isoletta*
> *ed ora questa ed or quella brigata*
> *di donne visitando, era mirata*
> *qual discesa dal cielo una angioletta.*
> *Io, che, seguendo lei, vedeva farsi*
> *da tutte parti incontro a rimirarla*
> *gente, vedea come miracol nuovo.*
> *Ogni spirito mio in me destarsi*
> *sentiva e, con amor di commendarla,*
> *sazio non vedea mai il ben ch'io provo.*

Elsewhere one may notice the breaking of the poetic narration and the creation of a new, slower and more analytical syntax, rich with relative forms, subordinate and interpolated clauses and secondary genitive forms that halt the melodic flow as they create something different, a situation tinged with grace and roguishness. The reader senses a "prose" that tries, without succeeding completely, to shed a fictitious cover:

Intorn' ad una fonte, in un pratello
di verdi erbette pieno e di bei fiori,
sedean tre angiolette, i loro amori
forse narrando, ed a ciascuna 'l bello
viso adombrava un verde ramicello
ch'i capei d'or cingea, al qual di fuori
e dentro insieme i due vaghi colori
avvolgea un suave venticello.
E dopo alquanto l'una alle due disse,
com'io udi':- Deh se per avventura
di ciascuna l'amante or qui venisse,
fuggiremmo noi quinci per paura?-
A cui le due risposer:- Chi fuggisse
poco savia saria co' tal ventura!

Within the picture of Boccaccio's early production and generally of all his literary activity, even at a later time, his poetical works constitute no more than a marginal experience and reflect only one aspect, perhaps the most ambitious, of his prolonged rhetorical apprenticeship. His human, affectionate and lively disposition, at once sensual and imaginative, his education eminently manifold and eclectic, are much better reflected by his prose and the octaves of his romances.

Beginning from the *Filocolo*, which, by being the first definitively narrative labor in vernacular prose and the composition that includes with indiscriminate exuberance all the artistic motifs and devices that will be developed in the following works, is the text that appears more suitable to reveal the typical qualities of that disposition and education and to reconstruct its historical genesis. Its contents and forms, humanity and literature, are characterized by an identical fervor, and bear witness to the enthusiastic presence of a sensibility by then detached from the ideological and moralistic schemes of the preceding age, passionate and inquisitive, open to all expressions of life but equally reluctant to become locked within the limits of a rigorously classical rule. It is a confused and unique blend of medieval and humanistic, stately and mediocre, learned and popular elements.

The romance deals with the contrasted love of Florio and Biancofiore. The former is the son of the king of Spain, the latter, unbeknownst to her, is the descendant of a very noble Roman family. The two are brought up together and fall in love with each other from their childhood. But Florio's relatives try to hinder the development of this love and send Biancofiore away by selling her to some merchants who take her to the Orient and give her to the admiral of Alexandria. After encountering many adventures, she is found by Florio, who had left to look for her under the assumed name of Filocolo ("Love Labor," according to Boccaccio's exaggerated etymology). Hidden in a wicker trunk full of roses, he steals into the tower where the woman is kept but while he is with her he is discovered by the admiral's guards and both are condemned to die at the stake. But, at the last moment, the admiral finds out that Florio is his nephew and, at the same time, Biancofiore's noble origin is revealed. The two lovers marry and the book concludes with a general conversion of all pagan characters to the Christian faith.

This subject, that lends itself to different developments, at times in its psychological representation and, at other times, in its adventures as well as picturesque and exotic aspects, derives even in its details from a very widespread legend in medieval Europe whose most important late versions are two French poems of the twelth century and an Italian ballad of the early fourteenth century.

Boccaccio's indication in the preface of his book of having resumed the narration of Florio and Biancofiore's traditional story so that the "memory of the loving young people," and the "great constancy of their minds that were always steadfast in one will, owing to the power of their love, remaining faithful to each other," could be at last "exalted by the rhymes of a poet, while it had been until then "left only to the imaginary tales of the ignorant," clarifies appropriately the author's attitude toward his sources, because, while he shows us his vivid interest for that tradition of passionate, colorful fables, it reflects at the same time the awareness of a cultural superiority that was to find its demonstration in the artistic elaboration of that worn and debased material, that would raise, by virtue of knowledge and style, to the level of literature and true poetry.

Boccaccio could have easily repeated something similar for the material that flows into all his Neapolitan works and then into the Florentine ones till the *Decameron,* and, likewise, for the contributions of the medieval and classical rhetoric that contribute confusedly to the intention of giving a learned transcription to a shapeless and popular material: on the one hand the legends of the Trojan cycle (in the *Filostrato*) and of the Theban one (in the *Teseida*); the fabulous and sentimental world of courtly romances, the short stories, fabliaux and chronicles, the somewhat easy and prosaic narrative rhythm and naïve nature of the ballads, the taste for the adventurous, the astonishing and the exotic that holds a large part in the minor literatures of the Romance civilizations that bring ideas, impulse and thematic suggestions to his vivid imagination. On the other hand, there is the tradition of the *ars dictandi,* the literary prose, elevated language of poetry and the schemes of the treatise on love of Andreas Capellanus, the elegiac patterns of Arrigo da Settimello, and finally, the contributions of some of the most suitable elements of his pre-humanistic readings: Ovid, above all, with the fascination of his mythological inventions, his rich, shrewd, erotic repertory, penetrating psychology, fiery pathos of the *Eroidi,* and then Virgil, in his highest moments of noble and tender passion, Seneca's dramatic eloquence, the dark and precious creations of Apuleius and the anecdotic wisdom of Valerius Maximus.

Many, in fact almost all of the elements that we have listed here concerning an entirely literary and poetic culture where even the implicit ideological substance is expressed entirely in terms of sentiments and imagination, are met and teem in the pages of the *Filocolo* and, with their intrusive presence, they contribute to determine the plot's dispersive and episodic unfolding and, within each episode, the profuseness of developments and the decorative excess while accentuating, in short, the impression of a fundamental incoherence that can be attributed only in part to the sources of the structure.

The most glaring defect may be noticed here, but also the book's wealth and novelty that herald and summarize in embryonic form the writer's entire future experience. The main events of a long love adventure, in the story of the two protagonists—the early irresistible arising of a feeling that is one and the same with the anxiety and dreamy shocks of puberty, the pains of separation, the torments of nostalgia and jealousy, Filocolo's strenuous search, the lovers' encounter in the Arab's tower with that exploding of the senses where the full sentimental fervor is not dissolved but exalted, bring about the desire to study a subtle and penetrating investigation of the feelings and create pages rich in human sentiment and poetry that represent the eminent prototypes of psychological narrative that, precisely in this case, elaborates here for the first time its technique and its special rhythm and starts to become autonomous by freeing itself from every intellectual and moralistic scheme.

Elsewhere, in the episodes of Idalagos and Galeone, the same preference for an analyzed, non-schematic psychology, having a more immediate and cordial connection with the reality of intimate life, grows more complicated, with auto-biographical elements and it accentuates its lyrical resonance along the lines of a confession and elegiac sorrowing.

In other places, the lesser components of an exuberant and restless imagination become prominent, such as the idea of exoticism and wonder, of an atmosphere of wealth and luxury, in the self-satisfied description of Alexandria's tower, the attraction for fantastic and adventurous deeds in the long and varied narration of Florio's vicissitudes, the propensity for the sensual idyll, in the pauses and scenery of peaceful landscapes that determine, as musical intervals, the rhythm of the adventurous journey and, above all, in the vast episode of the sentimental court of young men and women who, under the rule of Fiammetta, gather not far from Naples to indulge in pleasant leisure protected by the lovely shade of a garden in bloom.

The latter episode, with its long digression on the thirteen questions on love that are modeled on the patterns of courtly treatises, always likely to reduce abstract situations in dramatic figures and actions and, at least in two cases, to the complete form of a true short story, constitutes almost a book in itself, that, with its structure and internal divisions, heralds in, from afar, the motif of the framework and outlines precise narrative lines that will flourish in the *Decameron*.

Ready to lend such a disparate and dispersive material a relative unity of form, one finds the constant disposition of the writer who connects all the individual motifs that come to his dynamic and restless imagination in the light of a personal experience whereby events and characters do not reach a degree of total objectivity anywhere as they live in an atmosphere of passionate eloquence, surrounded by an aura of clouded and frantic emotionality. From this emerges a kind of compromise, always renewed and precarious, between an attitude of virtual realism and the recurring intrusions of a pressing and superabundant lyricism as well as between the truth of feelings and the massive ornamental apparatus built on a repertory of bookish images that are, nevertheless, admired with a warm, youthful participation.

Instrument and indication of this compromise is the poetic prose of the *Filocolo*, the expression of a lyricism characterized by psychological truth, a psychology bathed in lyrical emotion, a prose that is still far from that of the masterpiece but that is a foreboding of some of its aspects where the latter indulges more in musical rhythms and agrees with the fascination for the elaborate and precious verbal and syntactical structures.

The stylistic novelty of this prose may be measured against its nearest predecessor, Dante's *Vita nuova*. Among the many pages that might be mentioned, one could observe the one where Boccaccio describes an attempt to seduce Florio by two maidens instigated by his masters who want to make him forget Biancofiore. Here the situation is somewhat similar to that of Dante's episode of the "merciful," and not so different are some formal processes, the reserve of the speech, the preciosity in the choice of some lexical preferences, the rhetorical embellishment and the forms borrowed from the lyrical language as well as the constant observance of the *cursus* in each major or minor clause. Thus, as in Boccaccio, the situation becomes more dynamic and vividly realistic, pervaded by a sensitive and sensual restlessness that in young Alighieri was entirely absent or unmentioned. Also the style begins to dissolve and the rhythm complies with the need of narration without losing that lyrical halo that is the evidence of the active presence of the writer:

"Assai graziosa era a Florio la compagnia di costoro, e molto gli dilettava di mirarle, notando nell'animo ciascuna loro bellezza, fra sè tal volta dicendo: "Beato colui a cui gli iddii tanta bellezza daranno a possedere!" Egli le metteva in diversi ragionamenti d'amore, ed esse lui. Egli aveva la testa dell'una in grembo, e dell'altra il dilicato braccio sopra il candido collo; e sovente con sottile sguardo metteva l'occhio tra 'l bianco vestimento e le colorite carni, per vedere più apertamente quel che i sottili drappi non perfettamente coprivano. Egli toccava loro alcuna volta la candida gola con la debile mano, e altra volta s'ingegnava di mettere le dita tra la scollatura del vestimento e le mammelle; e ciascuna parte del corpo con festevole atto andava tentando, nè niuna gliene era negata, di che egli spesse fiate in se medesimo di

tanta dimestichezza e di tale avvenimento si maravigliava. Ma non per tanto egli era in se stesso tanto contento, che niente gli pareva star male, e la misera Biancofiore del tutto gli era della mente uscita. E in questa maniera stando non picciolo spazio, questi loro e esse lui s'erano a tanto recato, che altro che vergogna non gli riteneva di pervenire a quell'effetto del quale più inanzi da femina non si può disiderare. Ma il leale amore, il quale tutte queste cose sentiva, sentendosi offendere, non sofferse che Biancofiore ricevesse questa ingiuria, la quale mai verso Florio non l'aveva simigliante pensata; ma tosto con le sue agute saette soccorse al core, che per oblio già in altra parte stoltamente si piegava. E dico che stando Florio con queste così intimamente ristretto, e già quasi avevano le due giovani il loro intendimento presso che a fine recato senza troppo affanno di parole, l'altra delle due donzelle chiamata Calmena, levata alta la bionda testa, riguardandolo nel viso disse: - "Deh, Florio, dimmi qual'è la cagione della tua pallidezza? Tu mi pari da poco tempo in qua tutto cambiato. Hai tu sentito alcuna cosa noiosa?- Allora Florio, volendo rispondere a costei, si ricordò della sua Biancofiore, la quale della dimandata pallidezza era cagione, e senza rispondere a quella, gittò un grandissimo sospiro, dicendo:- Ohimè, che ho io fatto? E quasi ripentuto di ciò che fatto aveva, alquanto da queste si tirò indietro, cominciando forte a pensare con gli occhi in terra a quello che fatto aveva ..."

With respect to the average level of the book, pages like this represent particularly high and exceptional cases; nevertheless, even in those the style seems to maintain everywhere a measure of appropriateness and efficacy of expression. At any rate, on the formal ground, the narrative and descriptive prose of the *Filocolo* represents even with its discontinuity and variations, Boccaccio's most important achievement of the Neapolitan period and the most fertile in the history of his artistic development.

From this standpoint, the other experience of the narration in verse, brought about in the *Filostrato* and *Teseida*, is much less significant and rather marginal. It is based on the popular ballads that had just started to circulate, and more indirectly, in the wake of the poetic-narrative genre that had been amply practiced in Romance literature, mainly in that in French. Even in this case the author does not reject his artistic intentions that are clearly identifiable in the attempt to reconcile an utterly modern, accessible and amiable matter with an ideal of a decorous and stylistic reserve. And while, on the one hand, he searches within the limits imposed by the tradition of the poetic language and poetry, a freer and plainer syntactic form and a more concrete and realistic expression, he tries, at the same time, to introduce a measure of decorum and order, albeit at the level of the "mediocre" style, in the loose and prosaic manner of the popular poets. The true interest and the significance of the two poems must be traced, however, beyond the stylistic results that are quite uneven and approximate, as seen in a widening of the psychological themes and progress in the narrative technique.

The *Filostrato* derives its subject matter from an episode of the *Roman de Troie* by Benoît de Saint-More, that he knew directly or through a vernacular version by Binduccio dello Scelto: Troilus, the son of King Priam, loves the beautiful widow Criseyde, daughter of Calchas, a Trojan soothsayer who had sided with the Greeks. With the help of Pandarus, his friend and her cousin, he easily succeeds in gaining her love. But in an exchange of prisoners, Criseyde is recalled by her father and leaves for the Greek camp, after swearing eternal faith to her lover. Shortly afterwards, however, she betrays him by yielding to Diomedes. When Troilus is informed of her betrayal, he desperately throws himself into the battle with the intention of killing his rival, but is killed instead by Achilles.

Compared with the *Filocolo,* the plot of the story appears much more compact and organic, the development of the events follows a direct, close line without digressions and frills. Equally noteworthy is the degree of ability reached in the characters' somewhat precise and coherent development: Troilus, passionate and tragic lover, Criseyde, shrewd, inconstant and experienced woman, Pandarus, subtly expert of women's mind and eloquent seducer, Diomedes, resolute suitor and totally unsentimental. Under the cloak of courtly romance it is not hard to recognize the already outlined draft of the modern novel, and behind the name of the epic tradition and the obvious pagan scenes one can easily perceive situations and aspects of the habits, cases and figures of contemporary Neapolitan society.

It is especially in the minor characters and in the clever and natural progress of the events that Boccaccio takes a long step ahead and reaches, at times, a degree of detachment and free creativity that is typical of a pure narrator even if, in the final analysis, this truth and, at times, roughness in details and terse analyses of psychological elements contribute mainly to emphasize the essentially lyrical situation of the protagonist whose internal sequence of tormenting desires, lost happiness, and cruel disappointment the writer partakes with a close autobiographical participation that reaches at times, with a genuine, moving warmth, the various keys of enthusiastic, sad, elegiac and tragic emotions.

The love topic as well as the sentimental and sensual notes constitute the keenest parts also of the *Teseida,* that seconds, in the writer's mind, a much more ambitious literary plan. As it appears in the very form of the title (patterned on the medieval examples *Eneida, Tebaida* and the like) and the breadth of the structure of the work divided into twelve books like the most famous Latin poems, Boccaccio intended to renew in vernacular poetry the epic genre. In the epilogue of his work as well as in the notes that accompany the original manuscript, resuming the three parts of poetic treatments, arms, love, and virtue, proposed in the *De vulgari eloquentia,* he boasts of being the first to sing in verse, "with a beautiful style … Mars' troubles … never seen in the vernacular language."

In reality, Virgil and Statius supply little more than the scene and decoration to a story that, in effect, follows once again the themes and tones of medieval courtly romance. The plot begins with the narration of the victorious wars of

Theseus, Lord of Athens, against the Amazons and Creon, King of Thebes. But it soon focuses on the love of two Theban princes, Arcites and Palaemon, for young Emilia, sister of the hero's wife, Hippolyta. From a window of a jail where the two youths are being kept prisoners together, one day they see the maiden in the garden below who is singing and intertwining garlands and both fall in love with her.

Arcites is then liberated through the intercession of Peirithous, on condition of staying forever away from the city. After a year, however, unable to stand the separation, he returns to the city in disguise under an assumed name and is hired at court as a valet. Emilia recognizes him but says nothing, yet, Palaemon learns of this fact and is consumed with jealousy. After his escape from prison, he comes upon his friend who is asleep in a forest, attacks and forces him to fight. But Theseus, with Emilia and their retinue arrive. The two enemies/friends are forced to desist from their furious duel and, by order of the Duke of Athens, they have to settle their differences in a regular tournament, each one flanked by one hundred knights with Emilia being given to the winner. Arcites wins but Venus, who protects Palaemon, arouses a fury against the hero and causes him to fall from his horse.

Although seriously wounded, Arcites is declared the groom of the marvelous woman but cannot enjoy his happiness for long so he himself, before dying, makes the woman promise to accept his more fortunate rival for a husband.

The connection between the epic material and the sentimental digressions, which in the Latin models are merely accessory and episodic, is, in the *Teseida*, more or less consciously overturned. The epic part, following the first two books dedicated to the wars of Theseus that function as an introduction, is included in the peripheral elements, such as duels, tournaments, lists of warriors, descriptions of celebratory rituals of the two champions in honor of Mars and Venus, Arcites' funeral pyre, the temple erected in his honor and the nuptials of Emilia. These episodes and ornamental setup have the function of broadening and strengthening the weak narrative plot, but in reality, they only render it heavier and stifle it. Compared to the results achieved in the *Filostrato*, there arises a lesser unity in the development of the story, an evident uncertainty in the definition of the main characters, a literary sense of tension and exasperation that often borders improbability just in the culminating moments of the story, in the insufficiently deep analyses and in the facile and superficial development of the sharp contrast of the two protagonists' minds concerning friendship and hatred, jealousy and generosity, instinctive passion and superior rational balance.

There remain some well defined pages: Emilia's first appearance and the early blossoming of love's fervor against the idyllic background of springtime, the other portrait of Emilia as a huntress and, above all, the final conversation between the woman and the dying Arcites. They are, once again, the most lyrical pages, the richest in autobiographical emotion where even the frequent literary memories adhere naturally to the idyllic or sentimental sensitivity of the young writer and the very rhythm of the octaves lightens, hinting like a song at the motifs of arising feelings: marvel, morbid sensuality and the regret for vanishing life and pleasure, outlining, in short, the early signs of an experience that will be lived by Poliziano a century and a half later.

*

The serious crisis of the Bardi's and Peruzzi's business, that caught in its ruinous course also the destiny of its agents and clients, among whom was Boccaccio's father, forced Boccaccio to return reluctantly to Florence. We know very little about his life in the following decade: a letter to Niccolò Acciaiuoli written in August, 1341, mentions the sadness of his new stay and the very strong desire to return to Naples through the help of a very powerful friend at that court. Among similar attempts at evading and settling down more conveniently is his stay in Ravenna between 1345 and 1346, at the court of Ostasio da Polenta (stated in a letter of Petrarch), and soon afterwards in 1347, at the service of Francesco Ordelaffi in Forlì from where he sent a letter to Zanobi da Strada and carried out a poetic correspondence in Latin with the grammarian Checco di Meletto Rossi. In 1348 he was again in Florence where he saw with his own eyes the terrible consequences of the plague and, to establish his permanence in that city, there came his father's death in the following year that put on him the obligation of administering the scanty family revenues due to the guardianship of his stepbrother Jacopo. It is clear that the external circumstances that forced Boccaccio to leave Naples in 1340 caused a sudden break in a life that had just settled into a precarious and unstable balance. They certainly marked the end of the most enchanted and dreamy phase of the writer's youth that, from then on, was to continue as a nostalgic thought, dream and substance of poetic creations. It is equally certain, however, that they do not represent a substantial break in the coherent development of his personality and literary activity.

The conditions of financial hardship that will remain with him till the end of his life, and the new concerns that bind him to his family and city, did not modify radically, at least in that period of time, the direction of his life, studies and tastes but they defined perhaps in a more precise fashion the feeling as well as the humanistic and realistic drive of his art, saving them from the danger of an elegant, refined amateurishness and placing them in a less stylized and chivalric atmosphere by directing them toward a more open, varied and unbiased world of passions and interests.

The books that he composed at that time, from the *Ameto* to the *Amorosa visione*, the *Fiammetta* and the *Ninfale fiesolano*, show the slow but organic progress of a poetic experience still connected to bookish models and ambitions. But it was also more and more prone to accept the reality of history, involved more and more in the minute representation of things and affections, free in its choices and bold in the development of its creations; the experience that between 1348 and 1351 will reach the peak of its perfect maturity in the *Decameron*.

In the *Ameto o Commedia delle ninfe fiorentine*, Boccaccio resumes with a more conscious commitment the structural problem that he had outlined previously in the episode on the questions of love in the *Filocolo* and conceives of seven stories enclosed in a single narrative frame which is already, in synthesis, the external scheme of his masterpiece, except that in this case the frame has still a major function, allowing the individual stories a minor autonomy so that the relationship between the two elements materializes in a sense that is precisely the opposite of the one that will be adopted in the *Decameron*. Furthermore, the converging and overlapping of various and confused cultural and fictional needs introduce between the frame and the stories a difference of tones and meanings, of substance and language, that, at times, reach the level of disharmony and contradiction. The knowledge of the Florentine literary culture, amplified and brought together in its ambiance, causes the writer to acquire and emphasize allegorical and moralistic motifs that had obtained great favor in that literature and various degrees and forms of elaboration not only in the "stilnovo" writers and in Dante but also in the minor followers and imitators of the *Roman de la Rose* and in Francesco da Barberino.

On the other hand, the natural disposition to enter the picture of a world of concrete social relationships implies a lively and precise curiosity, gossipy at times, carried out on the ground of the local society chronicle.

Finally, the attention paid to the numerous formal experiments of a more strictly rhetorical nature is reflected in the book's external structure and the search for a new kind of prose, within a largely classical-like concept of a typically medieval classicism replete with encyclopedic erudition intended to reproduce, or better to follow laboriously, the creative and stylistic patterns deriving from an ampler rather than rigorous repertory.

The complexity of the work arises from such an encounter of various and disparate themes, above all the complicated intellectualism of the structure. Ameto, an unrefined shepherd and hunter, one day comes upon a group of nymphs who are bathing in a river and falls in love with one of them, Lia. The new sensitivity that slowly blossoms in his heart forces him to neglect his favorite occupations and seek those places where he knows he can meet the loved person again. On the day dedicated to Venus he meets Lia, with six other nymphs and three shepherds, near the goddess's temple and hears from the seven women the detailed story of their loves while he becomes excited in gazing at them and is consumed by sensual desire. When the narrations are over, after Lia immerses him in a purifying spring, the light of Venus is revealed to him in all its splendor.

It is not difficult to grasp the symbolic meaning behind the letter of the fable. The nymphs—Mopsa, Emilia, Adiona, Acrimonia, Agapes, Fiammetta and Lia— represent respectively the four cardinal and the three theological virtues. The men loved by each one of them are the vices that oppose those virtues. Ameto represents the uncultured, wild humankind that is renewed and refined under the influence of love, and becomes pure and exalted in the practice of virtues and is finally capable of contemplating divinity in its secret essence. The goddess who presides over the rite is not, naturally, "that Venus whom foolish people in their disorderly lust call goddess, but the one from whom the true, just and holy loves descend upon the mortals," "the light of heaven, one and three, beginning and end of everything," under whose guidance humankind ascends to contemplate the "angelic rays" to enjoy the "eternal wealth."

The initial points of this general allegory, Love, source of all refinement, Love, substance and light of the world, are inferred from the still living patrimony of Tuscan culture that reaches its height with Alighieri's poem and remains alive, if not necessarily in the sentiment, certainly in Boccaccio's intellectual experience. He, however, is not in a position to fully adhere to that set of values and finding in his conscience that relationship which, to the men of the preceding generation, appeared so immediate and spontaneous between the two areas of reality, the historical and the metaphysical. Therefore, the realization never fully corresponds to the idea. It assumes strong realistic colors, sensual and even lascivious, that are not easily reconciled with the edifying concept that governs the structure of the book. It should be added that the nymphs and the erotic adventures that they retell correspond to persons and events of contemporary Florentine life and the writer designates those persons and portrays those events, not rarely spicy and scandalous, with allusions and enigmatic references of easy solution so that, from this standpoint, the *Ameto* contains a sort of roman à clef that the modern reader may still partially reconstruct but that had to seem very clear to contemporaries.

The structural allegory and social intentions that in themselves reflect varying and almost opposing interests, yet both of cerebral origin and equally dull poetically, are reflected in a not entirely negative function on the third element that is the only lively one in the feelings and imagination of the writer—the direct representation of a psychological situation—in that both the one and the other contribute to mitigate the warm lyricism and intrusive autobiographism that spread without restraint in the Neapolitan writings; they establish, in sum, a measure of detachment and relative objectivity between subject matter and author from which derives the possibility of a freer narrative experience in the dual direction of thematic choice and formal elaboration.

Toward an identical end converge also the overwhelming meticulousness of cultural citations, the echoing of the Latin and vernacular literary tradition, the alternate composition in prose and verse (along a traditional line that from Boethius leads to the *Vita nuova*) and, mainly in the rhymes, the direct but reduced imitation of Ovidian and bucolic patterns.

The most vivid elements from the reader's point of view should not be sought in the rhymed parts, that with their tortuous syntax, lexical untidiness, inaccuracy, and the rare adherence of the discursive rhythm to the three-syllable meter, which may help to emphasize by contrast Boccaccio's essential vocation for prose, but in the prose and particularly in parts that require a remarkable narrative movement both in the frame and in the stories.

The episode with the purest lyrical inspiration originates from the very core of the book's generating idea and is the description of the renewal that takes place in Ameto's mind on account of the sudden revelation of beauty and love. It is a description pervaded by sensitivity and developed with a careful concern for minute touches that forebodes not only the theme but also the analytical rhythm and psychological savvy of Cimone's short story in the fifth day of the *Decameron*. At first, the young shepherd is portrayed in his environment of natural and wild roughness, busy playing with his dogs but surprised almost in a moment by tiredness and physical relaxation that creates a state of suspense and wait, suddenly interrupted by a woman's voice that is singing from the close bank of the Mugnone. An attitude of confused amazement arises from it, "Deities have descended on earth," and, immediately after, an unusual sight that turns amazement into emotion and causes a new anxiety, a never experienced throb of the senses and the heart.

> "... verso quella parte dove udiva la dolce nota volse i passi suoi; e, colla testa alzata, non prima le chiare onde scoperse del fiumicello che egli all'ombra di piacevoli arbuscelli, fra' fiori e l'erba altissima, sopra la chiara riva vide più giovinette, delle quali alcuna mostrando nelle basse acque i bianchi piedi per quelle con lento passo vagando s'andavano; altre, posti giuso i boscherecci archi e gli strali, sopra quelle sospesi i caldi visi, sbracciate, colle candide mani rifaceano belli con le fresche onde; e alcune, data da'loro vestimenti da ogni parte dell'aure via, sedeano attente a ciò che una di loro più gioconda sedendo cantava; dalla quale conobbe la canzone prima alle sue orecchie esser venuta. Nè più tosto le vide che, lor dee stimando, indietro timido ritratto s'inginocchiò e, stupefatto, che dir si dovesse non conoscea."

Of a different nature are the pages that are inspired by the intention to present a careful and accurate description. They are many and characterize better than the others the fundamental attitude of the writer; they are no longer lyrically vibrant but lucid, detached and entirely experimental. They are mainly episodes, such as the description of the nymphs gazed upon admiringly in every detail of their physical beauty and Pomona's garden that he analyzes in every part of its orderly structure, with all its trees, saplings, flowers and fruits, leaving the impression of excessive care for details, profuseness and monotony.

But even here one should look for the seed of a new stylistic intonation, an even and calm attention for the various aspects of reality that results in a clarity of design, richness and verbal creativity, relationship and connection of syntactical parts, as in certain representations of scenes and landscapes, as in this portrayal of the wintry season:'

"Egli alcuna volta, uscendo delle sue case, il mondo biancheggiante riguarda; e vede li rivi, per addietro chiari e correnti con soave mormorio, ora turbidissimi, con ispumosi ravvolgimenti e con veloce corso tirandosi dietro grandissime pietre dagli alti monti, con romore spiacevole gli ascoltanti infestando, discendere; o quelli tutti in pietra per lo strignente freddo essere tornati pigri; e i prati, altra volta bellissimi, ora ignudi, dolenti aspetti mostranti, riguarda; e gli spaziosi campi, se alcuno senza neve ne truova, con vedovi solchi soli può rimirare. Nè le voci d'alcuno uccello sente che le sue orecchie con dolcezza solliciti, nè alcuna piaggia conosce che tenga pecora o pastore; e il cielo, già stato ridente e chiaro e promettente con la sua luce letizia, vede spesso chiudersi di nuvoli stigi, li quali con la terra congiunti hanno potenzia di fare profonda notte nel mezzo giorno, e da quelli crepitanti alcuna volta prima con subita luce, poi con terribile suono, è spaventato; e per le regnanti Pliade a' venti ogni legge essere tolta conosce, onde essi, discorrenti con soffiamento impetuoso, agli alberi e all'alte torri nonchè agli uomini minacciano ruina, sovente diradando gli robusti cerri del luogo loro; e la terra, guazzosa per le versate piove dal cielo, specevole si rende a' viandanti..." or in this description of Ameto's sensual excitement:

"Mentre che la giovane ninfa co' lunghi ragionamenti si tira il tempo indietro, Ameto con occhio ladro riguarda l'aperte bellezze di tutte quante. E mentre che egli fisamente rimira l'una, quella in sè più che l'altre giudica bella; poi, gli occhi rimossi da questa, mirandone un'altra, loda più l'altra e danna il parere primo, e quinci alla terza, tanto quanto la guarda, tanto tutte l'altre men belle consente. E così di ciascuna dice in se medesimo, e tutte insieme tenendole mente, non conosce a quale apponga alcuna cosa che guasti la sua bellezza e vie meno conosce da dire quale sia la più bella. Egli, mirandole affettuosamente con ardente disio, in se medesimo fa diverse immaginazioni concordevoli a' suoi disii. Egli alcuna volta immagina d'essere stretto dalle braccia dell'una e dell'altra strignere il candido collo, e quasi come se d'alcuna sentisse i dolci baci cotale gusta la saporita saliva e, tenente alquanto la bocca aperta, nulla altra cosa prende che le vane aure; poi più innanzi colla immaginazione procedendo, si pensa dovere ad alcuna scovrire i suoi disii e tremebundo diventa, e già nel pensiero non conosce come esser possa; ma pure parendogli quasi averne sopra la verde erba con parole convertita alcuna, d'allegrezza fatto caldissimo, sè tutto di sudore bagnato dimostra, e più una volta che un'altra divenuto vermiglio, dà nel viso segnali dell'ansia mente ... Egli non intende cosa che vi si dica, anzi tiene l'anima con tutte le forze legata nelle dilicate braccia e ne' candidi seni delle donne, e così dimora come se non vi fosse ...;" or also in this caricature/portrait, drawn with grudging and merciless touches of Agapes' husband:

"Egli ... avente forse veduti più secoli che il rinnovante cervio, dagli anni in poca forma era tirato, e la testa con pochi capelli e bianchi ne dà a noi certissimo indizio, e le sue guance per crespezza ruvide e la fronte rugosa e la barba grossa e prolissa, nè più nè meno

pugnente che le penne d'uno istrice, più certa me ne rendono assai. Egli ha ancora, che più mi spiace, gli occhi più rossi che bianchi. nascosi sotto le grottose ciglia folte di lunghi peli, e continuo sono lacrimosi; le labbra sue sono come quelle dell'orecchiuto asino pendule e senza alcuno colore palide, danti luogo alla vista de' mal composti e logori e gialli, anzi più tosto rugginosi e fracidi denti, dei quali il numero in molte parti si vede scemo; e il sottile collo nè vena nè osso nasconde, anzi tremante spesso con tutto il corpo muove le vizze parti, e così le braccia deboli e il secco petto e le callose mani e il già voto corpo, con quanto poi seguita, alle parti predette rispondono con proporzione più dannabile; e nel suo andare continuamente curvo la terra rimira, la quale credo contempli lui tosto dovere ricevere (e ora l'avesse ella già ricevuto, però che sua ragione egli ha di molti anni levato.)

Even from a few excerpts it is possible to notice the variety and progress of this prose from the *Filocolo*'s. As the lyrical and emotional aura that strengthened the prose of the adolescent writer ebbs, the awareness of a structural and rhythmic rigor grows as it aims at describing and defining objects and situations following the progress of narration. Even without renouncing entirely the effects of the *ars dictandi*, the cherished echoing of poetic patterns, the close use of the *cursus* and rhythmic frames, the syntactic structure becomes stronger by using the classical writers as models.

The search for a more complex and constant linkage, the abundant subordinate relative and participial constructions carried out in a deliberate contrast with the tendency of contemporary vernacular and the very spirit of the new language, the inversions, the function of clause given prevalently to the main verb, reveal the presence of a more learned style. One notices now the precise influence of the translators of classical texts that is doubtlessly a determining factor in the elaboration of artistic prose as far as style, grammar, syntax and vocabulary are concerned, an experience where the writer is authoritatively involved during those years by translating patiently the third and fourth decade of Livy. But behind the stylistic diligence that is renewed with a different attitude, one should note above all the mentioned ability to observe firmly and realistically that, at times, disappears in an excessive but never confused search for analytical details that sometimes defines things and actions and results in the use of adjectives no longer approximate and conventional but variedly rich and effective.

In the history of the artistic development that culminates with the *Decameron*, the prose of the *Ameto* represents a prominent episode.

In the time lapse between the first Florentine drafting and the *Decameron*, the *Elegia di madonna Fiammetta* takes its place as a landing point and supreme resolution of a human and literary experience, pursued tenaciously and coherently for more than ten years, "a page of intimate history of the human soul, expressed in a serious and forthright fashion," to repeat the lucid judgement of De Sanctis who was the first to recognize its importance and novelty in spite of the annoying "exaggerations and amplifications" of a naïve and intrusive rhetoric. The predominant love topic of the early writings is isolated here in its genuine nucleus and, at the same time, it exhausts its strength and weight of autobiographical lyricism. And in order to measure the degree of participation and detachment with which the writer alternately resumes and deepens it, it will be significant to consider both the evident need to erect an objective screen by transposing the event into a feminine character and the renewed intention to relate it in the first person under the aegis of that transparent and fragile screen.

The book consists only of the narration that Fiammetta, a Neapolitan gentlewoman, makes of her adulterous affairs with Panfilo, a Florentine, addressing it to the "ladies in love." [She tells how] she met him and lived with him for a brief period of boundless happiness and how he abandoned her afterwards to go to Florence at the insistence of his aging father, which gave rise to a troubled period of impatient waiting, nostalgia, intimate anguish and hope until the time when she learned that he had forgotten her and had met another love. She fell, then, in deep despair considering and then attempting suicide.

The scanty plot of events (which is the same, except for the inversion of the roles, of the *Filostrato*) is part of a long lamentation, according to the model of an "elegy," openly drawn from Ovid's *Eroidi*. Besides Ovid, and his *Metamorfosi*, Virgil, Lucan, Statius, Valerius Maximus and Seneca's tragedies, often literally imitated and translated, supply details to the painful and at times prolix oratorical practice.

In this work, however, the writer includes the process of a novel exclusively woven with intimate situations that are accurately analyzed on the line of a long medieval narrative tradition that is introduced and imitated in its most sensitive and passionate tones. Not by chance, in the eighth chapter, where the protagonist compares her destiny with that of the "ancient ladies" of classical literature and mythology, Fiammetta does not omit mentioning also the story of Tristan and Isolde and remembers her repeated readings of the "French romances." The scheme of the lamentation and the choice of the direct narration would seem to indicate an attitude of dominant lyricism but for the fact that it reflects itself and attenuates in a structure of eloquent erudition that is entirely ornamental and in the taste of a flowery, exuberant and showy Gothic form and, on the other hand, it opens the way to a detached vision and a lucid, minute analysis of the emotional elements.

The narrator's form, at least in the most successful pages, is that of a person who has overcome and eliminated in their acute humanity the experiences that he is going to portray, with a very attentive and sharp view, as objects of study and not of passion. The plot, concentrated around a single topic, gains in consistency and unity; it excludes every digression of adventurous, idyllic or descriptive nature, or better, it subordinates rigorously the elements of ambiance, landscape and history to the fundamental scheme in a strictly functional treatment and it isolates and confirms the intention of offering a strict psychological analysis that is brought gradually to a maximum of touching tension until it explodes in the final dramatic catharsis. The acumen, subtlety, reality and truth of this representation of the passions of the soul, when it is freed from erudite ornamentation and literary references, gains prominence and constitutes the book's uniting texture by becoming embodied both in the minor characters yet realistically represented by the shrewd and inconstant lover, by the gentle, solicitous husband, by the loving and anxious nurse, by the friends, and, above all, by the great character of Fiammetta, that already ushers in the touching and tragic heroines of some of the best short stories of the *Decameron*.

Realistic and in harmony in a more explicit fashion with the free and unbiased mentality that characterizes Boccaccio's humanism is the ideal motif that covers the entire invention: the irresistible power of love that does not tolerate obstacles and knows no moral or rational restraints which "being stronger, it annuls unconcerned all other laws and imposes its own."

Although it does not renounce completely rhetorical forms, modulations, rhythmic musical rules and classical orders, the *Fiammetta's* prose, more than the one of the *Filostrato* and the *Ameto*, complies with internal reasons and the natural course of the narration and finds greater freedom and variety of attitudes as well as a broader and smoother stylistic range. It is found not only in the episodes of keen and impassioned emotion, such as that of the two lovers' parting or the attempted suicide that are described with a dynamic and ardent consideration, with a tumultuous crescendo expressed with quick and intense forms ("It seems to me I had grown wings, and I was rushing to my death faster than any wind."), but also in the slower and more analytical parts, that are the most frequent and that better reflect the tone of the book:

Ma poi che le operazioni predette e altre me aveano per lungo spazio tenuta occupata, quasi a forza, assai bene conoscendo che invano, ancora me n'andava a dormire, anzi piuttosto a giacere per dormire. E nel mio letto dimorando sola, e da niuno romore impedita, quasi tutti i preteriti pensieri del dì mi venivano nella mente, e mal mio grado con molti più argomenti e pro e contra mi si faceano ripetere, e molte volte volli entrare in altri, e rade furono quelle che io il potessi ottenere, ma pure alcuna volta, loro a forza lasciati, giacendo in quella parte ove il mio Panfilo era giaciuto, quasi sentendo di lui alcuno odore, mi pareva essere contenta, e lui tra me medesima chiamava, e, quasi mi dovesse udire, il pregava che tosto tornasse. Poi lui immaginava tornato, e meco fingendolo, molte cose gli dicea, e di molte il dimandava, e io stessa in suo luogo mi rispondea; e alcuna volta mi avvenne che io in cotali pensieri m'addormentai. E certo il sonno m'era alcuna volta più grazioso che la vigilia, perciò che quello che io con meco falsamente vagheggiando fingeva, esso, se durato fosse, non altramente che vero mel concedeva. Egli mi pareva alcuna volta con lui tornato vagare in giardini bellissimi di frondi, di fiori e di frutti varii adorni, con lui insieme quasi d'ogni temenza rimoti, come già facemmo, e quivi lui per la mano tenendo, ed esso me, farmi ogni suo accidente contare; e molte volte avanti che 'l suo dire avesse fornito, mi parea baciandolo rompergli le parole, e quasi appena vero parendomi ciò che io vedea, diceva:—Deh, è egli vero che tu sii tornato? Certo si è, io ti pur tengo.—E quindi da capo il baciava. Altra volta mi parea essere con lui sopra i marini liti in lieta festa, e tal fu che io affermai meco medesima dicendo: "Ora pur non sogno io d'averlo nelle mie braccia." Oh quanto m'era discaro quando ciò m'avveniva che 'l sonno da me si partisse! Il quale partendosi, sempre seco se ne portava ciò che senza sua fatica m'avea prestato, e ancora ch'io ne rimanessi malinconosa assai, non per tanto tutto il dì seguente bene sperando contentissima dimorava, disiderando che tosto la notte tornasse, acciò ch'io, dormendo, quello avessi che vagheggiando avere non potea.

In them the narrator has completely found his style and rhythm, complicated at times, keen toward details, nuances and differences yet constant and flowing, adhering in every part to the immediate meaning of things and the reality of the psychological process. The rhythm of his prose is so strong and confident that it can absorb and utilize, with perfect correspondence to the gradual development of the situations, all the devices of a musical expression—symmetry, parallelisms, metric clauses, even the frequent endecasyllabic structures, without ever allowing anyone of them a separate prominence but rather disguising them in its constant flow which is specifically "prosaic."

But among Boccaccio's minor works, written when he was barely thirty, and not too far from the elaboration of his masterpiece, it is still, as in the *Filostrato* and *Teseida*, a small poem in octaves that marks the arrival point, as it were, of the narrator in verse, as the *Fiammetta* did for the prose writer. In this regard, the *Ninfale fiesolano* preserves, even formally, a significance of its own, coming at the apex of an experience that will not have a continuation in the writer's artistic development but will largely determine, already in the fourteenth century and even more in the following centuries, the genre of mythological, idyllic and rustic narrative, with a very broad spectrum of references that is centered in the *Ambra* and reaches its peak in the *Stanze* and the *Nencia*. Also in the *Ninfale*, the metric style remains somewhat superficial, hurried and approximate but it appears more complex and varied by including, besides the songs of popular form and the weakened echoes of the aulic lyrics, also the contributions of the minor poetry and perhaps the colorful lexical and metaphorical repertory of burlesque poets, on the plan of obscenity used in allusive and jesting tone, as it will occur in some stories of the *Decameron*, until it reaches, in the best cases, the type of "andante cantabile" that will appear in the improvised popular "respects" that contain fragments of an extensive learned tradition in Latin and in vernacular language:

E tu sola, fanciulla bionda e bella,
morbida bianca angelica e vezzosa
con leggiadro atto e benigna favella,
fresca e giuliva più che bianca rosa
e risplendente più ch'ogni altra stella,
se', che mi piaci sopra ogni altra cosa …
Tu se' viva fontana di bellezza
e d'ogni bel costume chiara luce;
tu se' colei 'n cui sola si riduce
ogni vertù ed ogni gentilezza,
e quella che la mia vita conduce …
Se tu pur fuggi, tu se' più crudele
che non è l'orsa quand'ha gli orsacchini,
e se' più amara che non è il fiele
e dura più che sassi marmorini;
se tu m'aspetti, più dolce che 'l mele
sei, o che l'uva ond'esce i dolci vini,
e più che 'l sol se' bella e avvenente,
morbida e bianca e umile e piacente …

At any rate, also in this, as in the other poems, the strongest interest lies, beyond and against the uncertain formal solutions, in the contents and forms of the "love story," that unfolds with a freshness of feeling and inventive freedom that are really new, lively and active in a world of full and fertile maturity. The framework is, as in Lorenzo's *Ambra*, an etiologic fable of Ovidian inspiration, the origin, through the overused pattern of the metamorphosis, of the two streams Africo and Mensola, against the background of the legends of Fiesole and Florence, the favorite of the local chroniclers. This framework remains a pretext and represents the dullest part, fortunately entirely marginal, of the book. The background is an idyllic, mythical ambiance that serves to contain and filter, in the shape of remote fable, the more genuine matter of warm and sincere passions. This background, however, contradicts, with the realism and humanity of the situations, the idyllic tone, and holds its most authentic parts of a naughty bourgeois account to the point that it was not hard for a few critics to perceive, behind the fiction of the nymphs, their chastity vows, their masked infractions soon found and rigorously punished, a fourteenth century episode of conventual scandals.

This is, then, the heart and also the most completely developed part of the tale: Africo, a shepherd, observing unseen a gathering of nymphs consecrated to Diana's laws, falls in love with one of them, fifteen year old Mensola. During the following days he wanders restlessly, looking for her, through woods and hills. When he finally finds her, he pursues her with amorous entreaties but she is frightened and shoots an arrow without hitting him. Then, immediately, without looking at her pursuer, repents for her action and lets pity get hold of her heart. This is already the subconscious prelude of a tender affection. Advised by Venus, Africo wears a dress and mingles with the nymphs who are bathing in a small lake. When he also undresses, they run away in fright but he succeeds in holding Mensola in his arms, overcomes her desperate resistance and possesses her who first resists and then accepts and seconds his actions with increasing abandon of her senses and her soul. Afterwards, the maiden repents of her error and, afraid of the goddess's wrath, decides not to be seen by her lover any more and he, desperate, kills himself and his body, having fallen into a torrent, coloring its waters with his blood. Mensola gives birth to a baby but is discovered and cursed by Diana and, trying to escape, falls into a stream and dissolves in its waters. Little Pruneo, tenderly raised by Africo's parents, becomes later a seneschal of Attalante, the founder of Fiesole and eradicator of the cruel customs imposed by Diana on the nymphs who are finally liberated from their vows and returned to the human law of love and nuptials.

Even from the plot one can easily notice the moments of most intense emotional participation of the writer: the early beginning and growing ardor of Africo's passion, tenderness and sexual throbs, a consuming desire that implies acts of violence and abduction climaxing in the manly exultation of possession and grows sharper in the torment of waiting until it precipitates in a suicide; Mensola's naïve grace expressed through the various phases of an experience that assails and overwhelms her in its whirl, unaware and unknowing and makes her a woman without marring the veil of an adolescent, timid and modest sensitivity.

Some of the most successful scenes concern precisely the character of Mensola, such as that where, after shooting the arrow at her lover, she is caught by pity and cries to the youth to beware, or the very beautiful octaves where Boccaccio portrays Mensola's clash of feelings after the forced embrace, a combination of sweetness and shame, tenderness and fear, unknowing sensuality and reluctance as well as the slow, sinuous process of love that asserts itself little by little, hindered, however, by childish modesty, or the episode of the conversation with the elderly nymph Sinedecchia who reveals to her her condition and inquires about her fault while she turns "red in her beautiful face" and "with eyes downcast, timidly, is lost in reverie" and cries silently, or even Mensola's last images while she plays "with her beautiful baby" and remains a young girl, even in that new condition, and is at once mother and woman, while she joyfully sees Africo's features revive in the child's face until, in that tenderness, she is caught and undone by Diana's ire and death.

Next to Mensola's character, described with an equally tender mind and no weaker intuition of psychological truth, also other minor figures act against that background of simple humanity and popular feelings, such as Africo's parents.

Whether we see them participate in their son's suffering that they sense without daring to investigate its causes, torn between the wish to comfort him and a kind of modest restraint or, at a later time, lamenting desperately his death, or receiving from Sinedecchia's hands their grandchild, mingling tears of tenderness, joy and grief, while the child, responding to his grandfather's affectionate playing, "smiles moved by a natural love for him." These are episodes and little vignettes, embellished by genuine poetry and remarkable above all because they reveal how varied and rich had become the writer's imagination just when his qualities of expression, freed from the most obvious superfluity of a long rhetorical apprenticeship, were gaining simplicity and spontaneity.

*

The elements that concern taste and culture and contribute to constitute the poetic world of the minor works that we have briefly described, mark from the beginning, and according to a line of coherent development and growing awareness, the art of young Boccaccio, when compared with Dante's and Petrarch's, both for what concerns the eclectic and curious sentimental disposition, at once restless and effusive, and for what lies within the province of the means of expression that were decidedly addressed to narration, the minute and warm analysis of events, places, and figures that in Alighieri is condensed in a dramatic synthesis, related to a doctrine and a powerful individuality and in Petrarch, instead, is turned inwardly and reveals itself in lyrical forms. One could say that while the other two great figures of the fourteenth century have a tendency to direct the poetic contents to their individual persons, Boccaccio instead tends to expand his autobiographic experience and forget it in the contemplation of an external reality, in the creation of events, views and characters. This means that the popular culture of the age of the communes (that was not generically "medieval," as it has been reiterated recently) works in Boccaccio with a more immediate and direct relationship, not as hampered by doctrinal concerns and cultural patterns.

In Boccaccio, more than in the others, that culture is expressed in all its wealth and the most varied and contrasting expressions, whose meanings and aspirations he synthesizes explicitly and clearly, discovering progressively the most appropriate forms suitable to correspond to his concrete and realistic needs together with his ideals of decorum and refinement: the novel and the short story.

If this order of things implies the presence of his optimistic acceptance of a reality of feelings and customs, we should also consider that he works within a regional civilization where the elements of communal pre-humanism are anything but exhausted and, rather than opposing him, they have the tendency to come together in the spirit of the rising humanism, to which they contributed, also in the early part of the following century, some important ideas of civil and moral polemic through the thoughts and actions of Salutati, Bruni and Bracciolini. Furthermore, it is exactly this attitude of cordial understanding that allows him to grasp transformations, discoveries and contrasts of a society on the ethnic ground and in the endless nuances of everyday reality, with an immediacy and a variety of plans and perspectives that would otherwise seem unthinkable.

And we should not forget that this attitude of Boccaccio toward popular life and culture, that matured in Florence toward the end of the thirteenth and the early decades of the fourteenth centuries, if it is always open and confident, it is never completely passive. Facing that matter where he feels and appreciates an uncommon freedom and lack of prejudice of feeling and ideas and an extraordinary abundance of crude poetic motifs, there is always the artist who reacts with his intention to rebuild in a superior dignity and in a more classical harmony those scattered and unsystematic experiences, and, with his rhetorical and lyrical preparation patterned on the examples of neo-Latin art prose and aulic poets, there is the man with his personal erotic and mundane experience, his courteous and refined aspirations, his confessions and ambitions.

From this derives the twofold tension that characterizes the development of Boccaccio's art until the appearance of the *Decameron,* in the attempt to reach and adapt the balance of affections with that of the form, spiritual serenity and the quiet rhythm of the narration. The entire history of his art may be summarized, in some measure, in the contrast between a sentimental, exuberant and tumultuous experience and the ambition of a culture rich but muddled and still unripe; between an intrusive autobiography and a still scholastic rhetoric and also in the contrast that, up to a certain point, coincides with the previous one, between the persistence of lyrical motives and the need of narrative rhythm, robust and agile at the same time, as well as sensitive and detached. From that there arise a number of incongruities, uncertainties and tonal decline that will be solved only in the human and stylistic maturity achieved in the masterpiece. Within the framework of these contrasts is found also, as a less evident but persistent problem, the need of an organism where one may find, in an orderly and harmonic composition, all those scattered and fragmentary experiences, the need, that is, of a structural norm, of that "frame" that, perceived and outlined in the episode of the questions on love in the *Ameto,* becomes the essential and necessary element in the unity of the *Decameron.* It was a necessity for the lyrical themes to shed their prevailing subjective and autobiographical character through a diligent exercise of literary transcription, so that the author could finally reduce them to the living and vibrant matter of an objective psychological reconstruction and put them together with the other themes that surface persistently and a bit harshly in the early Neapolitan writings with a realism that is both agreeable and biting. The satisfied admiration of an idealized world of refined customs and courtly elegance had to dissolve progressively in the set patterns of a conventional literature and become an ideal norm, a measure of decorum and virtue, capable of suiting the endless variety of real situations in the various levels and distinct variations of social life. Literary culture and technique had to cease slowly to become ornamental and stylizing instruments and acquire freedom and flexibility of movement so as to adapt from time to time to the mutable situations of the mind. Finally, to organize this multiform material it was necessary that a resolute and strong criterion of evaluation and interpretation appeared and got the upper hand so that the complex reality experienced in the totality of its expressions could become organic material in a broad and orderly inspiration, governed by a firm and lucid principle and strengthened by a deep and vital polemic impulse.

This is the meaning and the importance of the prolonged spiritual and stylistic experience that involves the entire youth of the writer and unfolds in his minor works, movements and evidences of a maturing and broadening process of poetic scopes that will find its completion in the serene and powerful human comedy of the *Decameron*. They are the totally temporary stages and experiments of an intricate, linguistic and formal apprenticeship in which the syntax of the dialogue develops itself and progressively spreads while the vocabulary gets free from literary models and grows rich by being in touch with a lively and sensuous matter.

In the minor works, therefore, one can find in synthesis all the premises of the masterpiece. But the latter takes shape in the mind of its author only when a broad vision capable of lending it unity comes to organize such a vast and detailed material, in other words, when Boccaccio's cultural consciousness, that is aware of a higher, more refined and more unbiased culture, rises beyond and above the matter, to observe and judge it. An assumption of such an attitude is the liberation from every residue of autobiographic lyricism and constitutes the artist's perfect objectivity.

When Boccaccio sets about writing the *Decameron* (whose drawing up will be accomplished entirely in the span of a few years), he has reached that supreme point of his life, between the difficult experiences of young age and the stern and somewhat narrow consideration in imminent early old age. Free at last from the urging of passion, he may allow himself to reconsider it in himself and other people with that understanding that is typical of persons who have experienced a great deal and also with that detachment that allows him to feel it no longer as a torment and a present happiness but like a pleasure and final comfort of the soul that is close to withdrawing in itself. In this frame of mind, described in the preamble of the book and created in the atmosphere of freedom and decorous lack of bias of the "frame," the contrast between autobiographism and culture in the writer is solved and his poetic world, becoming independent from an oppressing and exclusive interest, opens gradually to the understanding of a number of different feelings.

The opportunity, necessary for the definition and organization of this attitude in a guiding principle, namely an organic concept of the world, is offered to the writer by his approach, after his return to Florence, and adherence, with increasing awareness, to the spirit of the popular civilization of the commune, from the complete assimilation that occurs in him at a certain time, of the tendencies and norms of a society that has completed its development and is already on its way to decline, to the tendencies and norms that find in him for the first time their full formulation in terms of poetry. They may be synthesized in a freer, bolder and cordial consideration of human feelings accepted in their concrete and solid validity, redeemed from any law of ascetic or transcendental morality and in the cult of human intelligence, working itself on the ground of reality, often victorious and always combative against the obstacles created by nature and fortune, proud of its own power that becomes mature in a series of concrete experiences and not of sterile doctrine and abstract speculations.

All popular culture (the written part to be found in treatises and chronicles, and the gnomic, political, satirical and love poems, as well as the other one contained in the works of merchants, jurists, magistrates and technicians of subtle or satirical minds, with its endless curiosity of human events and passions, with its worldly sense of life and its needs of dignity and decorum, modeled without servility along the lines of the splendid chivalric and feudal society, with its realistic skepticism and courtly ideals, its indulgent consideration of vices and values and polemic attitude against all forms of hypocrisy and corruption) may now be accepted by the writer's free and impartial mind and arranged in a structure that in its broadness and complexity can be compared only with Dante's *Commedia*. It does not side with it, however, as a complementary work but it contrasts it, and while Alighieri's book concludes an epoch of human spirit and sums it up, the *Decameron* is rather the presage of a new age and the beginning of modern literature.

This work, that entered the minds of the majority as a series of comic or licentious situations, opens with some pages of gloomy and tragic solemnity: the description of the plague in Florence in 1348, portrayed with the stern, detached style of an historian who blends in the rigorous, almost scientific objectivity of narration, represents the reactions of a wounded and offended sensitivity, and imparts a moral lesson that emanates spontaneously from the events and affects the reader, without the author's feeling the necessity to emphasize or even declare the fact explicitly. It is not only the description of a physical undoing and disintegration, but also of the ruin of the ethical and social organism, of a progressive break-up of instincts, norms, customs and conventions that rule the usual rapport of coexistence among the various social levels, to the point that one witnesses the destruction, in the triumph of the most elementary and brutal selfishness, of even the closest friendship and family ties and, among the survivors, there arise "almost out of necessity, things that are contrary to the primary customs of the citizenry."

Against this background of death, moral disorder and almost renewed primitive condition, there takes shape, by contrast, the condition voluntarily brought about and artificially built, in a certain sense, of some young people—seven maidens and three men—who, having met by chance in the church of Santa Maria Novella, decide to seclude themselves and live together for some time in a villa on a hill. Here they will try to escape from that mournful and nightmarish atmosphere of the city with alternating pastimes, dances, playing and pleasant conversation, banquets and excursions, and with the telling of amusing and interesting stories, the same ones that constitute the substance of the book—one hundred in all—narrated in ten days by the ten storytellers on the theme proposed from time to time by the person who is entrusted with ruling the group for that day.

This intention to evade determines a precise antithesis whereby, against the medieval triumph of death, there sets in resolutely, stripped of every ascetic or edifying influence, the triumph of life with the glorification of earthly values, of natural instincts and reason; the robust, optimistic concept of Boccaccio becomes embodied, almost emblematically, in the very skillful image of the ten young persons "wearing oak leaf garlands, their hands full of fragrant herbs and flowers," so that one who "would have met them would have said only 'Either they are not going to be overcome by death or he will kill them in their delight.'" It is an image and emblem of a purely humanistic, even renaissance, taste whose significance is fully measured only when we keep in mind that the writer's ideas and art are above the two terms of the afore mentioned antithesis, holding the sense of life and joy in all its complexity together with its counterparts of pain and death, comedy and tragedy of events, lights and shadows, man's virtue and wisdom and the blind power of chance.

Although the frame, as a background, supplies a decorative function, with its elaborate situations, terse episodic motifs, reflections and tenuous poetic inventions, it reflects an initial idea, an organic and deeply unifying concept. While it gives prominence from the beginning to the sense of seriousness that rules the book, with the marvelous description of the contagious disease, it justifies, on the moral level, the openness and freedom of some stories by setting them in an exceptional atmosphere, through the picture of the happy villa and the joyful ambient where the lively conversations take place. It embodies and portrays the suspense and detachment, the fine and serene emotion in which each story must be envisioned and understood. In that picture the nostalgia for the emotional and literary world of the writer's youth is revived as well as that of an entire civilization that is not resigned to die.

The storytellers' characters recall, and not only in their names, the passionate figures of youthful romances, in an air of distant, attenuated, almost evanescent fervor. Thus Panfilo, the lucky lover, Filostrato, the betrayed, desperate lover and Dioneo, the hedonistic, unscrupulous man, represent three aspects, three idealized moments of Boccaccio the man, only transposed in a motionless diaphanous light, beyond the limits of time, as it were.

No different is the task and the character of the women: Pampinea, in the full bloom of her youth, a wise, serene and reciprocated lover; Filomena, wise and discreet yet full of "fiery desire;" Elissa, young adolescent, enslaved by a violent and painful love; Neifile, also extremely young but happy and ready to sing, naïvely lascivious; Emilia, in love with herself like Narcissus; Lauretta, a jealous lover; Fiammetta, happy in a reciprocated love yet always concerned that it may be taken away from her; they are exemplary and typical projections of that world of affections that had built up, until the coming of this work, the canvas of Boccaccio's work.

Against this background where also literature has a large role in its twofold aspects of imaginary contemplation and refined rhetoric, there pour in and take shape the powerful humanity, vigorous realism, vastness and complexity of the new narrative topics matured through experience that is rich and conscious yet still suffused and warmed by an original ferment of remaining poetry.

It would be difficult to indicate a fundamental theme that may include the entire sense of the hundred stories: love, pleasure, the exaltation of intelligence and courteousness, the celebration of the conscious and generous will, and so on. Any attempt to focus on an exclusive formulation is soon proved inadequate. It may be appropriate perhaps to recall that the subject matter is arranged according to a masterly design: from the harsh polemic of the first day against the vices and corruption of people of authority to the last day, with the praise of the sublime example of magnanimity and courteousness through the description of "various events" of fortune and the expressions of "human ingenuity" that contrast blind fortune and holds it at bay and, at times, may even overcome it. Within this picture, defined with amplitude and flexibility that allows the maximum freedom in the choice of themes, the whole comedy of human life unfolds, with its greatness and cowardice in an immense gamut from the sublime to the comic.

As in Dante, imagination ranges in an extraordinarily ample world of experience and the tone of inspiration varies from the tragic patterns to the pathetic ones, and as far as mediocrity and humility, the stylistic degree and quality, the linguistic structure, the rhetorical diligence and lexical repertory all conform from case to case with the diversity of inspiration.

In order to weigh the potential of Boccaccio's genius on the grounds of his creativity and the realm of tragedy that he keeps entirely at a very high level of tension, that then leads it to its catastrophe with a rigorous coherence of feelings and language, a few great stories will suffice. One is that of Guiglielmo Rossiglione's wife, who, forced by her jealous husband to eat her lover's heart, commits suicide by throwing herself "without hesitation" from the window of the castle; or the other tale of Ghismonda da Salerno who takes poison and dies with stoic decisiveness after her father ordered the murder of the valet with whom she had fallen in love "not by chance … as many women do, but after a deliberate decision." Both women are examples of one of the ways in which "spiritual greatness" can be revealed, where the intensity of feeling is united with a reasoned awareness and the pride of social and intellectual dignity.

The same greatness or virtue, transposed on a ground of more common experiences, is everywhere the mark that characterizes the positive personages of the writer. It turns into loftiness and nobility of thought, composure of actions, harmony of behavior, refinement of sentiments that reject every vulgar, petty or narrow-minded impulse: it will be the heroic nobility of Federico degli Alberighi, the magnanimous refinement of Natan, the sad wisdom of Carlo d'Angiò, and the splendid regalness of Pietro d'Aragona but it can blossom also in less visible forms, in the characters of poets and artists like Giotto and Guido Cavalcanti, in the reserved decorum of a courtier like Bergamino, in the mute, ardent passion of a simple girl like Isabetta from Messina, in the quick subtlety of Melchisedech the Jew, in the instinctive refinement of Cisti the baker, or even tinged with eccentricity and whimsical keenness in Ghino di Tacco, the gentlemanly brigand.

In these and similar stories where the ideal of grandeur and refinement of a very civilized bourgeoisie sides with the cult of a superior literary and rhetorical tradition, Boccaccio's concept of virtue finds its paradigmatic expressions, barely nearing, at times, the risk of stylization, emphasis and artifice, as, for example, in the stories of Griselda or Tito and Gisippo. It more frequently, however, brightens in the writer an availability of creations and expressive resources that go well beyond the limit of his well known skill in the area of comicality.

Although in a very different manner, we are still in the midst of a positive attitude, or at the limit of the writer's fundamental optimism in some stories where the natural resources of human intelligence or even of a truthful instinct are contrasted by the whimsical power of chance or fortune against which sometimes it is useless to foresee, behave cautiously and prepare the appropriate remedies, because fortune takes pleasure in destroying and rendering all measures of the most attentive intelligence useless, while it helps meekly those who give in to it, always ready, however, to grasp the favorable opportunity and disposed to turn misfortunes into instruments of increased wisdom and experience. In these stories, the concept of fortune, that is already entirely human and free from theological assumptions (a forerunner in imaginary form of a humanistic concept, that will be developed by Alberti and then Machiavelli), sides with an inspirational motif that was already vigorous in the writings of his youth, such as the taste for adventure, romance ideals and a well constructed network of vicissitudes.

An eminent example of this kind is the story of Andreuccio da Perugia where, more than in other cases, the taste for adventure is enclosed in a realistic representation of the ambient, events and the varied psychology of the characters. Closer to a narrative of adventures, in fact, almost like short schemes and outlines of novels, are the other stories of Landolfo Ruffolo, or Alatiel, the former more dynamic and persuasive on account of the constant presence of a human will that does not surrender against the whim of chance and tries to oppose it to the last. And also the latter that, in its development, might appear at first sight mechanical and complicated, yet is lively and amusing for the reader who can let himself go along with the rhythm of narration and grasp in that motif of furious passions that multiply inescapably around the impassive idol of feminine beauty, the sympathy, wonderment and superior irony of Boccaccio.

Elsewhere this adventurous vein becomes a taste for surprise that takes shape in a variety of events and places with a very effective rhythm of suspense and détente, as in the most beautiful story of Pietro Boccamazza and of the Agnolella, or when it borders amusement and jest as in the tale of Rinaldo d'Esti, in whose favor the mutable turns of chance destiny, as a reward for the dreadful misfortunes he has suffered, a marvelous night of love, or in the story of Salabaetto and the Sicilian woman that turns into a situation of mockery and comedy.

With these later examples, we are already bordering comicality, that comic sense which, in the *Decameron*, enjoys such a large part, perhaps the largest in quantity and is not secondary even from a qualitative standpoint, if we recall that some of the best and certainly the most famous and popular stories go back to it. But this comic material has been considered too often and for too long (even in the protracted short story tradition that initiates from the *Decameron*) in an excessively external and superficial manner, as a mere play of practical jokes, lascivious behavior and equivocations, whereas it almost always unfolds in complicated relationships with the other motifs of the writer's intelligence and art and is interwoven with his deepest poetic inspiration. This occurs not only in those characters and stories where the erotic theme is an evident pretext for the open statement of an anti-ascetic attitude, as in the case of Madonna Filippa, or of the wife of Ricciardo da Chinzica and Alibech, but also in every other one where the rouguish or frankly obscene is used to extoll the fundamental theme of human intelligence and foolishness. This is the case in the following stories: in the merry adventures of Pinuccio and Adriano in the three-bed inn where the writer's attention is absorbed on the one hand by the pleasure of the comic adventure and on the other it turns understandingly to underscore the hostess's presence of mind in such an unforeseeable predicament, in the tale of the nun and the abbess, where the emphasis will be directed to the subtle, biting portrayal of the conventual environment with its hypocrisy and envious gossips, in the story of Masetto da Lamporecchio, introducing the penetrating psychology that defines with equal firmness the repressed longing of the young nuns and the shrewd brutishness of the protagonist, and finally in the tale of Ferondo where the admiration that cherishes the elaborate and refined astuteness of the abbot triumphs not only over the foolish antagonist and all the crude people of the countryside but also over all the cleverness of the monks.

Nor should one neglect the fact that this very theme of intelligence, seen in its most immediate meaning of shrewdness and practical wisdom in the erotic or simply comical stories, is far from condensing into a constant and abstract pattern because, from the one hand, it often becomes more complex in a further polemic motive, at least in those cases where the character personifies it and belongs to a fundamentally alien world toward the writer's bourgeois ideals (shrewd and hypocritical monks and clerics, like brother Cipolla or the priest of Varlungo, but also swindlers and rascals like Ciappelletto), but then it is at once idolized in the infinite resourcefulness of its capacity and portrayed in the true nature and moral degradation of its condition and environment.

Furthermore, the irony that attacks the world of the simpletons does not exclude at any time the awareness of their humanity and a consideration, at once detached and compassionate, of their destiny whereby the narration develops in a complicated situation, in a dramatic solution that derives from a not simplistic plot of psychological relationships, as in the most evident cases of the stories based on the ridiculous and at the same time pathetic and very human character of Calandrino. It is perhaps in this complexity, in this intertwining of ideal and imaginary inducements that one can find the relative superiority of the reason for the popular acclaim of some comic stories when compared with the "serious" ones that originate from a more linear and less rich inspiration.

The broadness of the thematic choice, the limitless inventive wisdom (that is revealed also in the various sources, both popular and learned, classical and romance, all treated as raw material, a mere inspiration for a story—consider, for example, what happens to the plot in the story about Nastagio degli Onesti that is an *exemplum* of preachers, already treated, but in its strict religious sense by Passavanti, the extraordinary variety of aspects, feelings and narrative styles that we have indicated briefly, acquire then their entity in the deep seriousness of a single inspiring concept, in the light of a superior intelligence that considers human faults and virtues, and takes and studies them thoroughly in their secret causes, never in abstraction but always incorporated in a discussion of concrete passions and probable occurrences. Thus, by avoiding to describe any further, and by exemplifying the various manners of Boccaccio's imagination and renouncing the abstract pretence to reduce all of them to an ideal common denominator, one will have to admit the sole constant element is offered by the writer's realistic disposition.

Also the most tragic, sad or mournful representations are observed in their sensual and earthly roots and the most sublime glorification of moral liberty and intelligence are reduced to a strict coherence and an inflexible logic. The taste for the adventurous and the wonderful is contained and mitigated by the alert presence of an ironic and light-hearted bourgeois spirit; the contempt for vulgar minds and situations does not exclude the admiration for the examples of intelligence that blossom unexpectedly even in the least educated minds and in the humblest environments, while the comedic spirit is softened by human compassion and stern wisdom, and the polemic inspiration does not preclude the spontaneous impulse of empathy and fascinated amazement.

Each character is set in a clearly defined social and historical situation; every event is rigorously determined in a clear concatenation of actions, so that even the most fantastic situations, suggested by written or oral sources, acquire a perfect illusion of truth. The lively polemic activity and robust optimism of Florentine popular culture, still rich with strong temperament and vitality and aware of its strength and prestige, is transposed in those forms of generous objectivity that characterize the greatest epochs of the arts.

To the large abundance of the matter and the balance that is reached by the ideal concept of the writer there adheres in every part his stylistic maturity while he takes advantage of his long, experimental work and his style is exceeded and consumed in the fire of the renewed creativity. Syntax and language operate in the most different directions with an unusual freedom of movement. The high and harmonious manner or the robust structures blended with the psychological knowledge of "love," descriptive or dramatic prose of the *Filocolo, Ameto* and *Fiammetta,* are joined or alternated by new formal inventions, drawn, when necessary, from the elliptical liveliness of popular speech and do not reject, in some cases, even the expressionist resources of the dialect or, as in the story of Monna Belcore, the strong colors of country satire, and by daring, as in the portrayals and language of Brother Cipolla and Guccio Porco, to introduce an ironic, almost parodistic inflection of the use of pauses, harmony and rhymes of the *ars dictandi.* Thus originates the marvelous prose of the *Decameron,* that prose that is, at once, relaxed and flowing, held back but without useless slowness, strong and agile, artistically elaborate but nowhere scholastic, flexible, varied and ready to second the various comic or dramatic, elegiac or pathetic, humble or solemn harmony of the narration.

No other book like this gives us, at the verge of modern civilization, such a vast documentation of facts, figures and customs, a view so picturesque and varied, dynamic and profound of the society and history of an age. But since this realistic disposition and rigorous documentation appear at the apex of a tormented personal experience, they imply at all times an intense human participation and transform themselves without any rejection, into poetry. So rich and intense had been in the author of the *Decameron* the poetic recreation of a civilization, which contains *in nuce* the entire development of modern history, that the whole of Europe could recognize itself in it for a long time and move at ease within that scope of ideas and feelings and draw from it endless ideas for new fictional creations, determining the fortune that has lasted for centuries in the most vital book of our literature.

*

After 1351, Boccaccio's artistic bent may be considered expended. The first meeting with the highly admired Petrarch that occurred in the fall of the preceding year and the devout friendship that tied him, from then on, with the poet from Arezzo, the weariness and scruples of an early old age, the ever increasing urgency of an economic settlement that might have freed him, at least in part, from his family situation, all combine to cause in him a profound spiritual upheaval, a new serious and severe spiritual disposition whereby he progressively withdraws from his youthful experiences and passions and is led to even repudiate, in part, his fictional work.

The newly gained solemnity of this illustrious citizen is accompanied by the honorary assignments given to him, with increasing trust by the commune, by sending him in an ambassadorial capacity to the lords of Romagna (1350), to the Marquis of Brandenburg in Tyrol (1351) and to Popes Innocent VI (1354) and Urban V in Avignon and Rome (1365, 1367). In the meantime, he receives Holy Orders and in 1360 the authorization to receive benefits for spiritual assistance. Literature, as invention and analysis of human experiences, seems to be far from his interests and, under the influence of Petrarch, he turns toward the humanistic cult of the wisdom and morality of the ancients, and around him arises and grows the most active group of early Florentine humanists, such as Filippo Villani, Luigi Marsili and Coluccio Salutati.

One has the impression of witnessing a kind of old-age regression or, at least, a radical transformation of the writer's personality. Already in *Corbaccio*, that is the last work of a content and rhythm of fictional and narrative gender, the ideal positions of Boccaccio appear quite changed, if not entirely overturned. The unprejudiced exaltation of love and woman is replaced by a sour, misogynic attitude and a resolute condemnation of passion. If we have to believe a most recent fascinating hypothesis, the very title of the book would allude to his attitude with the implicit reference to bestiaries, where the raven that removes first the eyes and then the brains of the carrions it feeds on is compared to the symbol of love that blinds man and makes him go insane.

At any rate, the meaning of the little work may be summarized in the intention of detachment from the troubled sentimental experience in favor of a life dedicated entirely to solitude and the cult of studies that make man perfect. All of Boccaccio's subsequent writings will find their place within the framework of an activity that is no longer poetic but erudite and moral.

However, even in this new attitude, something belonging to the old spirit survives; the man's humanism more curious to know facts and ideas than precepts, his education that is a bit adventurous and always open to the most varied and discordant ideas and his moralism more restless, polemic and intimately tormented are quite different from Petrarch's. Even if, with the passing of time, there was a decline in the passionate and free pleasure for adventures and passions, his ability to participate that inspired his creative fervor, his love of poetry where that world of passions is reflected serenely in classically harmonious forms, did not die away. There remains his enthusiasm for poetry, while even his interest for artistic experience and pure and technical research do not disappear.

It is precisely the *Corbaccio*, composed shortly after the masterpiece, that even under its harshly polemic disguise and the sincere desire of a more solid and strict morality, is still influenced by the realistic torment of its style and the way to look with detachment but also with lucid perception, by the dark, sensual matter of those experiences that had dominated the writer's entire preceding activity.

As for the Latin and vernacular writings conceived and completed in his later years, they may all be viewed as emanating from the same intention: find the value and the moral and educative function of culture and poetry. But, in the generic concept derived from Petrarch, there creeps in an enthusiasm that is entirely proper of Boccaccio concerning poetry considered in its human substance and in its imaginative forms. It is this enthusiasm that inspires in him the courage and pride to approach, first among humanists, the Greek world, inviting to Florence at his own expense the Calabrian Leonzio Pilato. It is the same enthusiasm that inspires the sensitive defenses of poetry in the *Trattatello in laude di Dante* and in the last two books of the *Genealogie*, where the topics of the dispute against theologians and jurists, disparagers of poetry, are drawn from the preceding polemics of Mussato and Petrarch, while the novelty resides in the vastness of their development and entirely personal is the spirit of his reasoning in alternate moments of irony and satire.

We are certainly far from the self-confident combativeness expressed in some places of the *Decameron*, entirely lay and worldly, directed to unmask hypocrisy and deride the moralists' scruples. Yet, an instinctive sense of greatness and of the necessity of poets, as well as classic and modern works, persists. And so does the taste for imaginary literature, independently from every secret sense, of which consists above all the substance and influence of that poetry that is the "soul of the world," because it arms kings and peoples, it describes earth, sky and seas, it adorns the virgins with flowers, awakens those who are asleep, it heartens the weary, it restrains the daring, it pursues the wicked and exalts the virtuous.

Furthermore, also in these later writings we notice a lingering sense of reality, a vein or at least a nostalgia for ancient narratives and descriptions, not only in those interwoven with anecdotes, such as the *De claris mulieribus* and the *De casibus virorum illustrium*, but also in the great erudite repertories written for the readers of poetic texts, the *Genealogie deorum gentilium* and the *De montibus*, in the weak *Commento* of Dante's *Inferno* and the *Trattatello*.

Everywhere, in the midst of the erudite matter, the psychological taste, the narrative ability, above all the taste for details and concreteness of Boccaccio poet and narrator, come to the fore. While Petrarch's literature tends toward the general, the expression in clear symbols and firm manifestations of emotional experiences, Boccaccio's, even in his old age, stays close to the fact, the individual image, gathering and analyzing them. The *studium poesis*, that is characteristic of poetry as narration of human incidents, portrait of characters, representation of things and psychological description, remains to the end at the center of his personality and culture. When death came to him, in his home in Certaldo, on December 21, 1375, his contemporaries realized through Franco Sacchetti's words that, with his departure, the last, most pure and warm voice of the great "Trecento" had passed away: "Now all poetry has gone away, and empty are all abodes in Parnassus."

CHAPTER SIX

The Literature of the Minor Writers

The problem of a deep crisis and radical transformation of culture, customs and institutions whose main phases are noticeable in the superior art of Dante, Petrarch and Boccaccio, may be seen also, at a much lower level, but endured rather than dominated, in the pleiad of minor and lowest poets through whom are expressed in an immediate, almost documentary form, contrasting sentiments as well as the various ambitions and simpler tastes of the century.

In the great writers' works the cultural experience draws inspiration from that supreme rigor that characterizes the most noticeable and sensitive peaks of a civilization, it refines the instruments of intellectual understanding, it invents its typical forms and it creates stylistic and linguistic models that are destined to prevail and bear fruit.

The other writers, however, are quite far from such rigor and it would not be easy to group them scholastically, as it happens for the literature of the thirteenth century, according to essential frameworks reduced to a common direction in a kind of homogeneous and collective research. One is struck, instead, by the number and variety of expressions that arise in a very broad area of mediocre cultural experiences that are, within their limitations, still genuine and lively, and by the unusual importance of a subdued, popular literature behind which one may perceive the needs of a large, less educated public or even uneducated but not dull and passive readership.

Considered in their totality, these minor writers never assume an image of imitators or repeaters of the great ones nor do they allow us to identify the most external and mechanical moments of a thematic or technical experimentation destined to flow into the structural and stylistic frameworks of the masterpieces, rather, they shed light on a background of feelings and ideas, anxieties and hopes that, although based on different levels and not conventionally spread in width and depth, help to explain, at least in part, the intensity, richness, powerful vitality and immediate resonance of those supreme contributions.

If it is almost fruitless to attempt to reach or descend from the spiritual or formal patterns of the minor writers to the level of the stylistic novelty of Petrarch and vice versa, from the various activity of the narrators to that of the *Decameron,* between the two cultural and artistic levels there remains always an overwhelming distance that worsens and borders incomprehension concerning a work that seems to be entirely directed toward the past, as is Dante's poem. It is possible, instead, to find within the areas of an essentially documentary scrutiny, some indications of spiritual themes and directions that, by appearing in the minor writers in a harsh and shapeless stage, are present in Boccaccio, Petrarch and even Dante as the material of a total and profoundly elaborated vision of reality.

In the meantime, the world of heated political clashes, the harsh developments of the communal fights, with their painful aftermath of destruction, death and exile and, after that, the deep crisis of institutions and moral values—the complicated web of civil sentiment and human mercy, that is found at the basis of Dante's structural creation, and, indirectly of Petrarch's anguish—are all reflected with major or minor awareness in the pages of the chroniclers, especially the Florentine, such as Compagni and Villani, and on a more subdued tone, in Marchionne (1336–1385), down to the memoirs of Naddo da Montecatini and Gino Capponi (d. 1421); and in the anonymous *Storie pistoresi,* in the Sienese annals by Andrea Dei and Angelo di Tura, not to mention the contemporary chronicles in Latin, that reflect in the different areas of northern Italy the quicker transition from the commune to the seigniory, such as the Milanese work of Giovanni da Cermenate, or the other work from Faenza by Pietro Cantinelli, from Ferrara by Riccobaldo as well as the more ambitious historical reconstructions by Mussato and Ferreto, the Venetian annals by Andrea Dandolo, Benintendi de' Ravagnani, Raffaino Caresini and so on.

Quite appropriately, the work of one of these chroniclers, the Florentine Dino Compagni (approx. 1255–1324), deserved to be chosen by De Sanctis as an example to test the importance of some elements of experienced events, for the purpose of reconstructing the structural genesis of the *Commedia*. Indeed, the events of the chronicler's life, an active and thoroughly involved citizen, yet not factious, in the commune's politics in the years between Giano della Bella's reform and Charles

Valois' enterprise, twice prior and the last time in that seigniory that was eliminated by the violence of the Black party and saved from exile only by virtue of the law that safeguarded the priors who had completed their term for less than a year, is quite similar to Dante's experience until 1302. Also the writer's moral reaction and his appeal to divine justice with which he comforts and strengthens his honest contempt are not unfamiliar motifs in Alighieri's conscience, although in the latter writer they converge in an infinitely ampler and unlimited vision of history and human destiny.

Without doubt, Compagni's knowledge is much more limited and, in a certain sense, more medieval, his religiosity is more popular, and naïve is also his nostalgia for the solemn moral values that, in the rapid dwindling process of institutions and laws, were slowly becoming corrupt and stripped of their power.

In order to spread light on the limits of this mentality, it is interesting to consider the "laud" canzone where the ideals of a fading society are exalted within a precise hierarchical order, from the emperor to the city rulers, from the merchant to the artesan, while the deep cracks that threaten to destroy that order are indirectly felt and pointed out in the crises of the highest authorities, the magistrates' greed, the misdeeds of the knights, jurists, notaries and the merchants' avarice and usury. But it is precisely this sincere religious feeling and attachment for the ways of a more orderly and stern civilization that cause the noble expressions and the vigorous personal statements of the chronicle and increase the intelligence lending quickness and effectiveness to the narrator's style.

Noteworthy also is the discernment that he shows in finding and identifying the reasons and connections among contrasting political forces. Equally powerful is the outlining of the portraits of the personalities that arouse his polemic nature (Corso Donati, Charles of Valois, Pecora the Butcher), warm and proud in his eloquence, without emphasis in passages that deal with reflection and invective while the rhythm of the narration remains rapid and incisive.

The spirit is different and much weaker in the personal mark left in the twelve-book chronicle authored by Giovanni Villani who died in 1348, that was continued in ten more books by his brother Matteo (d. 1363) and in one more book written by the latter's son, the humanist Filippo, whose life continued beyond the first decade of the following century.

The plan of the work is archaic (as it happens in Marchionne's much later writing) and in the entire first part (biblical and Roman topics and myths about the origin of Fiesole and Florence) it seems a rough compilation. Interest grows naturally as one nears the author's times and the internal and external activity of the Florentine commune. Villani supplies historians with precious information on administrative measures and on the commune's revenues and expenses, financial transactions of the great merchants and bankers. Generally his attitude is that of a person who looks with satisfaction at the growth and progress of his land and with trust in the near future. It is an optimistic attitude consistent with the spirit of the Florentine bourgeoisie at the moment of its greatest prosperity, similar to Boccaccio's, but mitigated by a firmer and simpler religiosity and sustained by a naïve municipal pride.

Among the book's purposes is exactly the glorification of Florence, "daughter and creation of Rome," that, differently from Rome, entered into a phase of decadence at the height of its destiny, completely involved in "building and pursuing great things."

Another of its purposes is the moral teaching that may be deduced from the narration of the "changes and things of the past" and their "causes and reasons." It ends with an exhortation to placate dissensions, accept the existing conditions and avoid being "too presumptuous," remain within the limits of the "common citizenry," and support the current "rule of the rich and powerful members of the people," avoiding the two contrasting but not seldom converging obstacles of demagogy and tyranny. This absence of polemic spirit, this tone of acquiescing optimism sets Villani in a considerable place among the sources of local historiography, but it also explains in a literary manner, the lesser importance of his style that is lucid and clear but faint and weak.

The fine chronicle in Roman vernacular of the events that occurred from 1327 to 1354, referring particularly to Cola di Rienzo, should be mentioned separately, also because it is among the rare documents concerning an area of peripheral culture, along with the *Cronaca di Partenope* and the Sicilian texts on the Vespers. It constitutes, in fact, one of the most sensitive texts of the minor literature of the fourteenth century. In this book the tendency to dramatize and use a fluid and colorful narrative style is carried to an extreme degree, as it was already evident in the chroniclers of Florence and Siena, more than in those of Pistoia. The recourse to the vernacular language and the clause construction contribute to emphasize the stylistic expressionism and mark the polemic and scornful mind of the anonymous writer with respect to his hero, especially in the excellent pages on the tribune's flight and dismal death. It is not easy to forget the image of that mutilated, tortured body dragged by a ferocious mob, "horribly bloated, as white as milk and bloody," resembling an "enormous buffalo or a cow in a slaughter house."

In order to complete this brief survey of historiographical literature, we should mention again Donato Velluti (1313–1370), who offers the first example of a genre destined to have a great success in Florence in the following century, the "domestic chronicle," written for private use in a naturally quick and bright style as well as the travel reports, that take advantage of a no less frank and natural form of expression owing to a curious and colorful subject matter, such as the very appealing ones of the pilgrimages to the Holy Land of the Friar Minor Niccolò da

Poggibonsi and the three Florentine companions Leonardo Frescobaldi, Simone Sigoli and Giorgio Gucci.

*

The practical purpose—of private or public remembrance, admonishment or polemic judgment—that is manifest in large or small measure but a bit everywhere in chronicle prose (whence the impression of close adherence to facts and absolute expressive spontaneity that derives from the absence or scanty presence of a conscious literary mediation) can be found, albeit in a different form, in the other devotional and edification prose works that make up one of the richest parts of this minor literature and the most fruitful breeding ground of exquisite linguistic experiences but not in the courtly or pseudo-popular direction of the academicians, purists and lovers of the golden "Trecento."

In our times, it may be more appropriate to underscore in these texts the fervent, leavening, energetic and intact substance of a religiosity that still seemed a vital and predominant component of culture, that even in the mediocre and the humble was vitalized through a full participation, not only in liturgy and rites, but in the essence of memories, sentiments and ideas of the Christian tradition. In general, it concerns versions into vernacular or rewritings and compilations from old Latin or even recent sources. What is noteworthy is the presence of the vastness and variety of the original repertory, from the Bible and agiographical legends, the collections of "examples" and "miracles," to the theological and mystical treatises, the polemic documents of the para-heterodox or decidedly heretical circles of the spiritual Franciscans, "fraticelli" and Beghards. No less relevant is the expansion, geographically speaking, of this activity that is centralized in Tuscany and neighboring regions, but flourishes a little everywhere and finds in every place wide and prompt circulation, such as the *De miseria humanae conditionis* by Lotario Diacono (Pope Innocent III), after the arrangement by Bono Giamboni and the thirteenth century copies of the Lombard and Venetian poets that is translated into Tuscan twice by an anonymous writer and in the third decade of the century by Agnolo Torini and translated again two more times from Tuscan into Ligurian vernacular; the *Dialogus* by St. Gregory the Great, available in three Tuscan versions among which the famous one by Cavalca, but also the translation into Sicilian vernacular by Joanni Campulu from Messina; of the *Miracoli della Vergine* there remains the anonymous collection in Venetian vernacular beside the vulgate edition as a "language text" and the large collection by Duccio di Gano from Pisa; and also in Venetian language there are, along those composed in central Italy, several collections of *exempla* while similar to the best known *Meditazioni della vita di Gesù* (based on a successful Latin text of Franciscan background) is the Sicilian *Sposizione* of the Gospel of St. Matthew's Passion that originated in 1373.

Finally, we should point out the promptness of translators, compilers and adapters into vernacular whose work develops both by starting from the most used hagiographic texts, the letters of the Fathers of the Church (St. John Chrysostom, Jerome, Augustine), medieval mystics and dialectitians (Anselm, Bernard, John from Fécamp, William from Saint Thierry), and by making immediately available to non literary people the documents of recent and immediate experiences still present in the spiritual tradition, such as the *Vitae patrum* and the *Dialogus* by St. Gregory, the *Legenda aurea* by Jacopo da Varazze, the legends of the great saints of the last evangelical rebirth, St. Dominic and St. Francis, and the memoirs of the early followers of the latter, Sylvester, Aegidius, Brother Ginepro and the beautiful life of Blessed Umiliana dei Cerchi. Together with the medieval mystics, there are the representatives of the new meditation that developed within the recent Franciscan experience: the minor writings of St. Bonaventura, the *Mistica teologia* by Ugo di Balma, the *Stimulus amoris* by Jacopo da Milano and the *Viridarium consolationis* by the Dominican Jacopo da Benevento, the *doctrine* by Blessed Angela da Foligno who died in the early years of the fourteenth century, and the revelations and treatises attributed to St. Elizabeth of Hungary.

There occurred also the rapid circulation of the polemic texts of the "spirituals" supporting the rigorous interpretation of the rule of the Friars Minor, with the various versions of the *Cronaca delle tribolazioni* by Angelo Clareno (d. 1337) and several other pamphlets, documents and letters divulged in the same area of Joachim's prophetic principles as well as versions and reductions that border heresy, which were composed by the quietists and sectarians of the "spirit of liberty," as the one of French or middle Latin origin entitled *Mirouer des simples ames* by Margherita Porete. Quite varied is the tone of these vernacular versions and distinct in the degree of knowledge of the anonymous writers who attempt from time to time, and with major or minor success, to reproduce the easier narrative texts, the mystics' difficult language, the scholastics' dry terminology or the passionate dialectics of the polemists. Equal in all is the humble attitude of the translator who attempts to remain in the shade while stressing the edifying material that is offered to the public's meditation. Nevertheless, in that humbleness there remains some room for art, the choice of the detail to be emphasized, and the syntactical and lexical inventions.

Without doubt we must become used to evaluating with a more suitable criterion some writings that the academic and purist tradition introduced to a century old admiration, such as the *Vite dei santi padri* and the *Dialogo* by Domenico Cavalca (d. 1342), or the *Fioretti di San Francesco*, and to learn how to read them in a constant comparison with their Latin sources in order to distinguish better their relative originality that consists of the reading and acquisition of a style in the process of taking shape, almost without any artistic intention, in search of a rhythm and syntax created by a long, tried tradition and, in the cases of the "little flowers" and the "maxims," from Franciscan material.

Precisely in Cavalca, if we go from the actual version in the vernacular (*Vite, Dialogo, Atti degli Apostoli, Epistola ad Eustachio* by St. Jerome) to the rewritings and compilations, such as the *Trattato della pazienza*, the *Pungilingua*, the *Specchio di Croce*, the *Specchio dei peccati*, the *Disciplina degli spirituali*, the *Frutti della lingua*, the *Espozizione del Simbolo degli Apostoli*, we will be able to catch in its progress the transition from the ways of the translator who is never unoriginal and passive, to the presence of a style that unfolds with new freshness and persuasive power, rapt in an aura of collected wonderment and candid imagination. Thus, we will be on our way to recognize and circumscribe the spiritual and stylistic ground where the highest and newest expressions of this religious literature come to maturity, with its rich human substance, narrative repertory, psychological refinement and its didactical and oratorical effectiveness.

In the limited and schematic précis of the Dominican Giordano da Pisa's sermons (d. 1311), we will value above all the ease with which he is able to fit in tidy forms the concepts, the distinctions, the very dialectical method of the theological schools. But in the other Dominican, Jacopo Passavanti (d. 1357), who is decidedly the most scholarly person among these religious writers for his totally original and synthetic structure of a long practice as a preacher, confessor and teacher, we will admire in his *Specchio di vera penitenza* not only its "orderly and humble doctrine," the lucid and clear exposition of a theological and sapiential subject, but also his accomplished knowledge of the writer, the acquisition of a terse and severe style, with a firm syntactical structure and power of expression that originates from a profound humanity, a deep knowledge of passions that reaches its apex in the very lively and dramatic "examples" that never become mere transcriptions but re-elaborations composed with a most subtle artistic sense in a worn out narrative substance. Passavanti is perhaps the only one, among these treatise writers, who reaches in his own way a measure of classic quality. When compared with his work, how archaic and naïvely common appear the *Assempri* of the Sienese Filippo degli Agazzori (d. 1422), and minor importance is achieved by the documents of a mystic and pietistic theorization that abound in our century and take an important place in the still unexplored history of his religiosity, from the treatises of the Franciscan Ugo Panziera da Prato to the pamphlets of Simone da Cascia (d. 1348), of Giovanni da Salerno (1317–1388), of the Florentine Agnolo Torini and Girolamo da Siena.

Perhaps Friar Giovanni dalle Celle (d. 1396) is artistically close to Passavanti for his stylistic vigor and cohesion, derived from the traits of a culture that is already pre-humanistic. He was a prominent writer in that religious history, familiar with the experiences of Colombini and St. Catherine and involved in a lively confrontation with the "fraticelli" and the spirituals but also a friend of Marsili and not unaware of the new classicism established by Petrarch.

Separately, but within the same background, one should recall the letters of a good secular apostle, the notary Lapo Mazzei (1350–1412) from Prato, addressed to the well-known merchant Francesco Datini. We are led into a personally experienced and contrasted religious world by the most dramatic, if not the boldest, heretical text of the century, the *Storia di Fra Michele minorita*, the account of the capture, trial, conviction and fearless death of "fraticello" Michele da Calci that occurred in 1389. His text is anything but naïve, rather it is composed with refined art on the model of the ancient "passions" and martirologies, with a rapid and pressing sense of rhythm, intense and objective narrative style, devoid of frills and comments that echoes the style of the secular chronicles.

The writings of two Sienese saints introduce us more intensely into the heart of personal experiences. They summarize, albeit with different emphasis, the religious spirit of their time: Giovanni Colombini (1304–1367) and Caterina Benincasa (1347–1380). Both are more and less than a writer. The significance not only of their practical lives but also of their words closely connected as they are with the needs and purposes of their lives, transcends literary history, or better, it touches it but only marginally. Which is true, against the general opinion, more for St. Catherine than for the founder of the Gesuati. In Colombini's letters, not only the intensity of a personal mystic experience, but the memories of the difficulties that were met, of a long, distressing battle, anxiety, hopes, firm intentions finally crowned by victory are represented by a colorful language, rich in spontaneity, enthusiasm and kindness, where the more or less direct resonance of the medieval mystic tradition springs out in more accessible, popular form.

Quite differently, but similar to those models and much more complicated, is the stylistic experience of St. Catherine, entirely constructed in a thick network of analogical, metaphoric and emblematic expressions that originate from a profound and personal feeling experienced in traditional schemes, transposed from a literary ground to that of a concrete, intimate suffering. For this reason, they tend to elude the limits of expression in order to flow into the forms of a strenuous, turbid and torrential eloquence.

Behind the brightness of a tumultuous and mutable style there remains, among quick transitions from polemic and harsh to gentle and ecstatic expressions, the essence of a strong personality, overflowing with authority and fascination, almost the mark of an exemplary existence spent in a strong power of action and sacrifice. More than in her *Dialogo della divina provvidenza* and in the letters of patently mystical contents, with their flashing and vigorous images, that may even be tangled and almost never artistically controlled, the power of her personality impresses the reader with a sharper and more persuasive stress in some texts of a more concrete and humble humanity, or of a more concerned functional virtue, as in the recounting of the death and conversion of a man sentenced to die on the gallows, or in the letters of reprimand and exhortation directed to popes, prelates and rulers.

*

To the practical purpose, in the present case, which is that of meeting the growing cultural curiosity or need of pastime of the bourgeois society that the new wealth has polished and refined in its tastes and ambitions, one should add also an evident, conscious artistic intention in the translation of secular material, if for no other reason than that of reproducing with the greatest possible effectiveness the logical, oratorical or even poetic progress of the models. If in the vernacular translations of religious texts the intention of edifying prevails over the artistic style, in this case, instead, the moral and didascalic purposes are essentially subordinated to the formal ones. Naturally, even in this area, the value, the cultural significance and the degree of awareness of the individual works are quite varied.

The elaboration that had already begun the previous century continues on a more unpretentious, popular level in French narrative texts, epic or romance material and in the analogous renditions of classical works, from the *Fatti di Cesare* to the versions of the *Roman de Troie*, summarized and rewritten by the Sienese Binduccio dello Scelto and, through the mediation of the *Historia* by Guido delle Colonne, reproduced two more times by the Florentine Filippo Ceffi and Mazzeo Bellebuoni from Pistoia. One notices the continuation of collections of varied and easy erudition, both historical and proverbial, between the recording for private use and the liking of easy circulation, as in the various *Fiorite* (by Armannino da Bologna, and the other, significantly flavorless that goes by the conventional title of *Avventuroso Ciciliano*) that may be considered in one with the so called notebook or *Libro di varie storie* by Pucci, a typical example of the repertory of a culture already built, through the more common vernacular versions, at a popular level.

But the main fact, in this area, is the growing importance of the translations from Latin, and of the classic authors in particular, which is, besides everything else, a way to bring to the level of custom and a field of culture on a rapid process of expansion, a larger public for the benefit of the "many who would like to know and were prevented from studying," as Guido da Pisa said, echoing a point of Dante's *Convivio*. It is certain that the translator's activity, at least in its most advanced levels, represents the closest literary experience to the great examples of the art of prose, as it developed from Dante to Boccaccio; and even if it does not determine it, as it was indicated with a certain amount of exaggeration, it certainly accompanies and supports the fundamental line of the stylistic progress of that prose that will be our classicizing tradition.

Yet it seems, at first, to affect it, a bit deliberatedly and a bit because of lack of experience and uneasiness toward the chosen models, an attitude that appears in lexical and syntactical examples that are roughly modeled on the peculiar patterns of the learned language (a tendency that often enough pleases also Boccaccio in the *Decameron* and in hid minor works.) The person who, on the one hand, analyzes the complicated structures and elaborate rhythms of the time in the romances of young Boccaccio and, on the other hand, examines the fourteenth century translations of the great ancient prose writers suh as the one attempted twice by an anonymous of Valerius Maximus, or the other one carried out in two phases and by two different persons, of Livy's third and fourth decade, of even the *boezio*, rendered with a most appropriate sense of class gravity, of the Florentine notary Alberto della Piagentina or other texts by Cicero and Seneca that one could mention at this point and that run together on the way traveled in the preceding century by Brunetto Latini and Bono Giamboni with their translations of the *Retorica* by Orosius and Vegetius, or some passages of the *Filocolo*, of the *Ameto* and *Fiammetta* where the author brings often images and constructions of Virgil, Ovid and Seneca that may be compared with the versions of the *Ars amandi* and *Remedia amoris* attributed to Andrea Lancia, with the *Eroidi* by Filippo Ceffi, with the *Metamorfosi* by Arrigo Simintendi from Prato, or with the *Eneide,* transcribed into vernacular Sienese by Ciampolo degli Ugurgieri and summarized by the afore-mentioned Andrea Lancia and, later, by Guido da Pisa, and finally with the anonymous version in verse of the *Arrighetto* (namely of Arrigo da Settimello's elegy) has the impression of being in an area of similar experiences, an impression that is destined to receive an authoritative confirmation, if one will consider as admissible Boccaccio's authorship of Livy's third and fourth decades. Forthermore, one may find similarities from both sides in some daring lexical borrowings, syntactical inversions and forms that are patterned on the ancient rather than on the spirit of the new language, such as the case of the present participle in function of gerund or of the past participle and of the ablative absolute. In both one may find also the same faithfulness that stimulates the freedom of verbal and structural innovations and reveals a decided preference for decorum and stylistic nobility. Naturally, the artistic result does not always correspond in equal measure to that intention; rather, in the major part of the cases the translator's labor is evident as in the lack of skill of the hack writers. Rarely one is struck, as in the case of the *Boezio,* by the presence of a high literary dignity or is one moved, as in the *Arrighetto*, by the fresh resonance of an effusive and pathetic eloquence, or in the cases of Simintendi or Ugurgieri by a candid indulgence for the fascination and rhythm of classical fables.

Two writers, among the others, going in almost opposite directions, may be selected to represent the most successful accomplishments of an experience that, in its totality, covers a great part of the literature of the time. Both were clerics and teachers of uncommon knowledge, authors of writings in Latin, in possession of a solid ecclesiastical, secular, theological and grammatical education, for whom the work of translating develops at the peak of a long mental and stylistic practice aimed at acquiring a mode of expression that is original in its own way. In the former, the Dominican Bartolomeo da San Concordio (d. 1347), both in his *Ammaestramenti degli antichi*, a vernacular version of an ample collection drawn from biblical maxims that he had compiled and arranged, and also from the classics and the Fathers of the Church, and in the translation of the *Catilina* and the *Giugurta*, by Sallust, it is valuable above all the intention of following a close, yet not mechanic adherence to the text, the awareness of the project's difficulty and, mainly in the vernacular versions of Sallust's works, the twofold tension that originates from the intention of rendering fully the *brevitas*, energy and dramatic movement of the original without crossing the limits of the modern language, "because the vernacular words and forms do not correspond fully to the letter … In fact, it is often appropriate to say several words in the vernacular for a single one of the original (although they will not be equally fitting), and other times it will be appropriate to go beyond the words in order to expound the phrase and to express ourselves more clearly and openly." Out of it there arises a steady, robust, lean, elegant and concise prose that ranges along the best examples of the art of prose in this century.

The other writer is the Carmelite Guido da Pisa (who lived in the first half of the fourteenth century) who was already mentioned among the early commentators of the *Commedia*. He belongs, rather, to the current of translators of poetic texts, like Simintendi and Ugurgieri, whose prose is leavened by a secret yearning for music and imaginative abandon. In fact, he is not a pure translator in the strict sense of the word because in his *Fiore d'Italia* he collects and elaborates again a narrative subject that derives, now by echoing it and then by summarizing or amplifying it, from various sources, especially in the first book that includes the fantastic origins of humankind and the Greek legends up to the Trojan war, while in the second he follows more closely the development and often the very words of the *Eneide*. In his attitude there is an implicit freedom that distinguished him sharply from Bartolomeo's dedication to accuracy, a freedom that involves both the choice of themes and the stylistic set up, that is more agile and free, achieving results that, in comparison, appear certainly more naïve and almost casual but that originate, after a closer look, from a different yet equally conscious artistic intention as in the frequent preference of translating Virgil with Dante's words.

In Guido da Pisa's peculiar manner of reproducing the solemn material of the ancient poets into the medieval romances, with strokes and colors of everyday life and homely language, the experience of the translators, or at least of some among them, whose interest focuses on a wealth of legends and images, prevails over the laborious resolution of a scrupulously formal result and achieves an inventive freshness and easy narrative ability that brings it close to the affective and stylistic canons of contemporary fiction.

*

A large amount of this narrative prose continues in the fourteenth century a tradition of basic and semi-popular art that was already established in its fundamental characteristics mainly in Tuscany in the preceding century. It includes reductions and adaptations of the Breton literature (such as the *Storia di Merlino,* by Paolino Pieri, or the *Tavola ritonda*) or the Carolingian material (such as the *Libro di Fioravante,* the *Rinaldino da Montalbano,* the *Viaggio di Carlomagno,* and so on).

A later reduction of this epic and legendary material, already adapted to a popular taste and a need of pleasant entertainment, with modest ambitions of order and completeness as well as of historic and psychological truth, is represented by the *Reali di Francia,* the *Storie nerbonesi,* the *Guerrin meschino* and *Aspromonte,* in addition to the other romances destined to a popular success that lasted almost to our days. The ballad singer Andrea de' Mengabotti da Barberino in Val d'Elsa, who lived beyond the third decade of the fifteenth century, is a slow, verbose writer who lists facts without any prominence and in whose works only some flashes of natural wit and lively representation emerge with difficulty from a sea of generic monotony. Yet his documentary importance is great for the scholar who studies from its origins the formation of a secondary cultural tradition that will decline little by little from the level of a bourgeois group of merchants and artisans to the taste of the populace and the rural people.

The end of the century storywriters have to confront other and more difficult problems. They must consider somehow the great model of Boccaccio, in fact they try to imitate it, especially its structure that they use in their books by arranging the stories in a semi-autobiographical framework. The author of the *Pecorone,* a ser Giovanni Fiorentino, who reduced himself to live, around 1378, in Dovadola, near Forlì, "hit and chased by fortune," fancies that his fifty short stories are narrated in turns, two every day, in the parlor of a nunnery by Sister Saturnina and Chaplain Auretto, to soothe their love. The stories are interspersed with the singing of love ballads, as it happens in the *Decameron.*

Giovanni Sercambi (1347–1424) from Lucca, who was one of the main champions of that seigneurial government, praised adviser and collaborator of Lazzaro and then Paolo Guinigi, author of a valuable chronicle of the events in which he had taken a great part, pretends to tell himself his hundred stories (but another manuscript, without the frame, contained one hundred fifty-five) to console and entertain a group that escaped from Lucca during the plague of 1374 and was wandering through different lands. Fortunately, the author of the *Pecorone* keeps himself out essentially pretending to write before Boccaccio and is more connected with the tradition of the short story writing of the thirteenth century, eager for strange events and fine witticism, without any pretense of stylistic reconstruction or psychological characterization, indifferent to the choice of the themes to the point of plagiarism (thirty-two stories derive from Villani's chronicle), but with a certain measure of whim and grace, which is fresh and sensitive if not profound.

Sercambi, instead, is a much less effective, unpolished and quite awkward narrator in whose works there occurs for the first time that reduction of Boccaccio's world to its most external and topical aspects, with a taste that sometimes is heavy and never redeemed poetically from lewdness and obscenity. Rather, his book constitutes an important document for the student of comparative short story writing, to whom it supplies a large amount of narrative material in sometimes rare or even unpublished versions drawn in part from the oral repertory of tales.

A much richer and livelier personality, also from the literary point of view, is evidenced by Franco Sacchetti who is the main representative of the attitudes and feelings as well as of the limited artistic ambitions of the various technical experimentations that grew out of a "mediocre" ground, substantially unrelated to the great humanistic vein, yet quite lively and spread out with subtle ramifications especially in Tuscany.

Born into an ancient Florentine Guelph family of merchant tradition, probably in Ragusa, around 1330, he had spent his youth practicing a trade, traveling a lot and acquiring a large experience of people and things. He then participated actively in communal politics, holding even important posts (he was one of the Eight of Authority in 1383, and prior in 1384) in difficult years, troubled by severe external wars and serious civil strife, adhering mostly to the ideal of the rule by the "middle people," and being equally opposed to the attempts of oligarchic tyranny and to the movements of popular anarchy. As an old man, he accepted for his livelihood the charges of "podestà" and rector in Bibbiena, San Miniato, Faenza and Portico di Romagna until his death that occurred around 1400.

In his *Libro delle rime,* that reached us in its autograph form, are reflected the successive phases of his human and literary experiences. After a final period that ends between the age of 30 and 40, dedicated to elegant and free stylistic exercises in the field of poetry for music, there is a second period, that starts in his early fifties, dedicated to sonnets and moral songs, with touches of satire and polemics, strongly involved in the problems of civic affairs, politics and customs. Between these two periods, in the pause of poetic silence that separates them with a clean break, there come the *Sposizioni di Vangeli,* notes and outlines of intimate meditations, discussions on questions and issues of conscience, not abstract but connected with the themes of everyday life and personal experience, where the writer studies the motives and forms of his moralism, of his rich and varied human observation, trying at times some narrative parts.

At the peak of this literary career, around the last decade of the writer's life, there are the composition and arrangement of his main work, the *Trecentonovelle,* whose original manuscripts were lost or ruined already before the sixteenth century and whose later copies that remain comprise only two hundred twenty three, of which some are fragmentary or miss some parts. Their development, that is briefly indicated here, circumscribes and defines in a sufficiently clear manner the essential components of the artistic inspiration that appear in the short story writer. On the one hand he is inspired by a sincere moralism that generates from a serious religious spirit and from the long experience of a varied and broad observation, even though it is a relatively profound one; on the other hand we notice an agile and colorful technique of representation, that matured through the practice of verses for music and satirical "nonsense" rhymes and the early octaves of the *Battaglia delle belle donne di Firenze con le vecchie.* One should add a store of knowledge, as he says, of a "madcap, crude man," an extempore, self-taught knowledge that does not ignore, but is far from investigating, the new experiences of Petrarch's and Boccaccio's humanism, and draws its strength mainly from marginal texts, compilations and vernacular versions.

From this standpoint it is easy to explain the qualities and limitations of this narrative experience. And the author himself is quite aware of his limitations since he makes a point of distinguishing from the start his attempts at the great work of the *Decameron* and to establish the limitations of the mediocre public that he addresses and the intentions behind the writing of the book that aspires only to comply with the mood of the people "eager to hear new things" and anxious to have "readings that are easy to understand, especially when they bring some comfort so that among so many woes there may be some laughter."

It is, therefore, an intention to offer consolation among life's miseries, to give a pleasant pastime, without any ambition of solemn art, yet not deprived of art, on the basis of an agreeable, witty and at times even thoughtful conversation. The variety of cases, ambients and situations stimulates the most frequent motives of a cutting and bitter moralism that, at times, borders with sarcasm and scorn against the clergymen's corruption, the decadence of the mores, the venality of justice, and the abuses of the rich and powerful who easily overwhelm "the poor and powerless," the cruelty and greed of the tyrants, "rapacious wolves, enemies of justice and friends of force," the increasing decline of civic order and institutions, whereby all of Italy "goes from bad to worse in great troubles, upset by the despots' whims, torn by cruel wars, ravaged by plunder and the savagery of mercenary troops."

Against this dim picture stands the surviving remedy of a religion expressed through deeds and not superstitions, the recourse to a "natural philosophy" built on practice and common sense that may reach the "pleasurable," sharp and sententious "logics" of the innkeeper Basso della Penna.

This moral ground lends the book its unfettered framework, its signification and justification, a basis of wisdom and usefulness in the variety of inventions and tones of a material that is mostly comical and always blithe. But within the scope of this material, and in the closed and limited field of that culture and morality, the terms of a narrative technique come about and they are defined in the picturesque nature of the ideas, in the rhythm of the representations of tumults and brawls, in the representative ability of cameo images, the smiling grace of the maxims, but it never rises from the limits of the sketch and the anecdote to a deep psychological scheme or a true definition of the background, stories and characters. Only the reader who does not expect to search in it a richer material and a greater art will be able to appreciate its pleasure and recognize in its good qualities the artistic wisdom of these stories that "created by a smile, cause a smile, and in this lives often their humble poetry." (Croce)

*

Sacchetti's autograph manuscripts of the *Rime,* offers us, through the same abundance and great variety of the texts that it handed down to us, a valuable mirror of the main aspects of the minor literature in verse of the "Trecento", from the various patterns of poetry for music to the sonnets, political, moral and didactical songs as well as the nonsense rhymes and the three-syllable lines. It did that with the attention to the suggestions of autobiography, chronicle and customs, that constant, fortuitous theme, that easy and eclectic empirism of technical forms and patterns that characterize precisely such literature and place between it and the absolute rigor of Petrarchan diligence a pronounced detachment similar to that which separates the attempts in a lower key of the minor prose from Boccaccio's masterpiece.

As we attempt to study the poets, it is necessary to bear in mind, first of all, this fundamental difference of values and change, according to this factor, the spiritual disposition and the requirements of judgment on the basis of an interest that is much more historic and documentary than poetic.

The earliest part of Sacchetti's poems and also the poetic parts of the *Pecorone* belong to that style of literature for music that enjoyed great popularity at that time among the bourgeois and courtly circles reflecting their demands for elegance and refinement. In fact, in some cases, especially in some of Sacchetti's ballads (such as *O vaghe montanine* or *Innamorato pruno*), or in some refined hunts

(*Passando con pensier per un boschetto*), those compositions offer us the most perfect examples of that kind, the richest in grace, charm and imagination.

We come across others, of a rare technical nature, of weak but sincere inventiveness and a remarkable charge of figurative and narrative images, in the song books of the Florentine exile Niccolò Soldanieri (where they are grouped, as in Sacchetti's works, with sonnets and "canzoni" of moral topics), or in those by another Florentine, Alessio Donati, and on the level of a more modest and faint art, in the works by the Bolognese Matteo Grifoni, besides the least engaged parts of the rhyme collections of Boccaccio himself and Petrarch. But most of them are preserved without any authors' names, in the great music codices of the fourteenth and fifteenth centuries that include not only Tuscan texts, but those from central Italy and other regions, particularly Veneto, emphasizing, naturally, the names of the "composers", that are the most famous experts of the *ars nova:* Giovanni da Cascia and Jacopo da Bologna, Vincenzo da Rimini, the Florentine Gherardello, Lorenzo Masini, Niccolò da Perugia, Andrea de' Servi, down to the most celebrated organist Francesco Landini (d. 1397) who, it seems, dictated himself the words of the texts to be put in music.

Connected with the success of this important development of the polyphonic uses in an essentially profane sphere, the literary texts that are of particular interest here must be evaluated above all as one of the most pleasant entertainments of a society that is eager to transform its prestige and wealth into terms of elegance and exquisite behavior. Within this frame of preciosity, where the novelties of the Italian masters are conjoined with the more and more frequent contributions of French and Flemish art, poetry for music adapts its metric structures and its thematic and stylistic functionality to the requirements of musical technique, from the most frequent types of madrigals and ballads for multiple parts to the rarer and complicated one of the hunt that derives its name from the structure of the canon composition, where the successive turns of the two higher voices that repeat the same melodic phrase gives the impression that the second pursues the first and puts it to flight.

The more or less constant characteristics of these compositions are a graceful albeit superficial sensitivity, that is gratified by its own bland, idyllic or elegiac modulations, a conventional psychology that develops in carefully stylized situations, an imagination ready to grasp and emphasize the pictorial or fantastic moments. Particular importance is gained in them by a major or minor technical dexterity in the quick narrative points, in the aspects of the scenes, in the illusion of a busy movement, in the intense hues of the verbal expressions. They will have to be considered not so much as pure lyrical expressions but as tasteful society games.

A richly detailed picture of that society that abounds in details and valuable documentation is presented by some pages of the *Decameron* and the *Paradiso degli*

Alberti, especially the late *Saporetto* and the *Sollazzo* of Simone Prudenzani, a citizen of Orvieto (who lived beyond the fourth decade of the fifteenth century). In those works, perhaps with an art that is a bit awkward but lively and colorful, there come in succession descriptions of a happy group's pastimes, such as hunts with hounds and falcons, rides, tournaments, card and chess games, ball playing, dances and singing with a very vast repertory that includes, with the typical models of the *ars nova*, also French rondeaux and Sicilian satirical poems, the various dance figures for halls and squares, accompanied by different string or wind instruments. But the newest and strangest part of Prudenzani's book consists in a series of narrative ballads that draw their material from the prose short story tradition (including Boccaccio's) and foreshadow, also in their conventional pace and agile and colloquial rhythm, the kind of popular Tuscan ballad of the late fifteenth century.

*

Linked with the forms of poetry for music are also some anonymous texts of probable popular propagation included in manuscripts, mostly of the fifteenth century, that appear, at least in part, to belong to the chronological limits of our study. They are lyrical or descriptive ballads with erotic or roguish hints and rustic parodies (as the one that begins *Fatevi all'uscio, madonna dolciata,* or the other one *Io innamorai d'una fanciulla all'onda*), and the early examples of Sicilian and Tuscan satirical poems that appear in the manuscripts under the titles *ciciliane* and *napolitane*, a probable reference to models of musical compositions that were still in existence in the following century. Certainly, dating them is always difficult and uncertain, especially if one takes into account the possibility of various and successive versions within a very free tradition not quite observant of formal details. Yet, some allusions in their context as well as linguistic and stylistic formulations have a fourteenth century–like flavor, and at least the "nicchio" and the "grasta di basilico" ballads have the advantage of being explicitly mentioned in the *Decameron*.

Anonymous or partly anonymous is also a large part of the production more closely connected with the lyrical genre as it was conceived at that time, I mean in the established patterns of the song and the sonnet. They are compositions of gnomic and reflective subjects that regard the most pressing themes of feelings and morality of a difficult and troubled time, as the various versions of the very widespread ballad on Fortune, attributed to a friar, Stoppa de' Bostichi, or a song of similar topic by Gano da Colle, and also the two sonnets that attracted Croce's attention on the way to behave in calamitous times by complying meekly with the varying movements of the winds, bending when necessary but always keeping in one's heart the intention of revenge and vengeance as soon as a favorable opportunity arises.

To be considered are also the numerous texts on poverty, that is viewed sympathetically, at times, as an ideal of evangelical life along the line of heretical or orthodox movements, or exalted and idealized, at other times, in function of a conservative mentality that was meant to insure among the humblest social classes an attitude of resignation and submission, composed, in some occasions, with a polemic spirit (as in the case of a beautiful song attributed to Giotto) and conceived as cause of corruption and social disorder and, in those who exalted it, exposed as hypocrisy that masked ambitions and greedy intentions.

Other texts develop ideas of anticlerical satire or varied political propaganda, serving the expansionist trends of northern Italy's rulers (especially during the years that witnessed the strong hegemonic drive of Giangaleazzo Visconti, portrayed as the restorer of order and healer of the plagues of Italy) or, on the contrary, in defense of the anti-tyrannical action of the communes in central Italy, particularly in Florence. In this literature about public affairs in verse, there participate in behalf of different factions also the best known poets, such as Sacchetti, who fights against the greed of the Visconti's viper, and Bruscaccio da Rovezzano, who writes a song against Ladislaus of Anjou, as well as Saviozzo, who authored another song in praise of Giangaleazzo, and Vannozzo, who composed a *Cantilena pro Comite virtutum*. Other compositions contain more lyrical inspirational motifs, both in character and imagination, and will have to be included in the area of popular literature, as in the case of the Aesopian fables in verse, that recall Pucci's characteristics, or in the case of the transcriptions of historical material of romance and chivalric character (such as the sonnet-portraits of famous ancient men in the hall of Castelnuovo in Naples), or of the other sonnets that continue the aulic tradition of *plazer*, adapted to a humble taste. They foreshadow closely, both in subject matter and in language, the "rispetti" that were used widely in the traditional repertory (*Io vorria in mezzo al mare una montagna, S'io il potessi far, madonna bella*), or recalled the art poetry, as the witty portrayal of the arrogant and spiteful maiden who throws a snowball at her lover (*Passa per via la bella giovinetta*), and the other sonnet sketched with grace where the author pretends to be unseen and observes his woman praying in church and becomes oblivious as he contemplates that sweet and pious image (*Ad uno altar dinanzi ginocchione*).

*

It is difficult to present a homogeneous picture of the true art lyrics and of the writers who represent them, as it is also hard to portray a solid and organic development process. Compared with the adherence of the Sicilian school to the "stil nuovo", what mainly stands out is the extremely empirical and eclectic character of the attempts that emerge from the various poets, their reluctance to accept a precise system of contents and language, the promptness with which they comply with the most different backgrounds and the group of humble masters of whom it is always hard to portray an image and a stylistic impression, whose importance perhaps consists only in the immediacy with which they reflect the features of a disconnected and hybrid culture, adapting them to the mediocre demands of their uncertain and often shady lives.

It is possible to record in the first half of the century a wealth of poets who echo, in an entirely external and superficial way, the teaching of the "stilnovisti", showing often the influence of the Tuscan style and the acknowledged hegemony of that type of literary language in peripheral areas, as Guido Novello da Polenta from Emilia, who was the last person to offer hospitality to Dante, the Venetians Giovanni and Niccolò Quirini and Niccolò del Rosso from Treviso. Florentines are, instead, the notary and chancellor of the commune Ventura Monachi and Matteo Frescobaldi as well as other Florentines that reside in the Avignon curia and are in close connection and friendship with Petrarch.

They partake of the early establishment, albeit with an awkward and scholastic manner, of that great tradition of vernacular poetry, such as Franceschino degli Albizzi and particularly Sennuccio del Bene who is decidedly the most prominent figure among these followers of the thirteenth century school of poetry. Dead in 1349, he had probably been in contact with Dante and had shared at least in part his political passion and ideas, by participating with other exiles in Harry VII's expeditions to the city walls of Florence and by composing one of the most solemn songs on the occasion of the emperor's death. Furthermore, he had also been able to become one of the early confidants and correspondents in verse with the great poet from Arezzo. His sonnets, entirely interspersed with elements from the two Guidos, Cino and the young Alighieri, develop, not without artistic ability and elegance, a worn out form of expression almost devoid of substance. More original is the song where he expresses his anxiety and hesitation of a mature age love with trepidation and disconsolate adoration. A friend, who perhaps was Dante, answered him with a sonnet personifying Love, making fun affectionately of the elderly poet in love, if we can believe an explicit statement of the only codex that brought the text to us.

Along this current of a late and weak "stilnovo" literature that will continue for the entire fourteenth century and will mark a strong renewal at the end of the century, runs the anti-stilnovo current whose writers follow the pattern of Rustico, Angiolieri and Folgore. Also this was a "style" with an established tradition of themes, images, constructions and language but more willing to accept the suggestions of a personal experience and ready to comply with the variety and liveliness of characters and attitudes.

It is possible, for example, to discover the line and the rich series of anecdotes of an autobiographical current developed in very genuine and kind ways, with its moments of internal reflection, nostalgia and repentance from the many sonnets by the Florentine Pieraccio Tedaldi (dead shortly after mid-century) that supply us one of the most complete repertories of the situation and gnomic motifs favored by this "bourgeois" literature.

In the little collection of Pietro dei Faitinelli (d. 1349) from Lucca, there emerge the vigorous political sonnets where the Guelphs exile vents his anger against the tyrannical rule of Uguccione della Faggiuola and even more against the cowardliness and worthlessness of the Florentines and Robert of Anjou who should act resolutely against him while they, instead, were busy "enjoying and collecting florins." No less sincere and heartfelt appear in another sonnet his homesickness for the "fair" fatherland and the bitterness of the exiles' wandering existence. But, in general, all his poems always referred to precise events, and exhibit a sincere and determined attitude that isolates the figure of this poet, a passionate and vexed political advocate, within the generic realm of the poetic "style".

Even in this area the growing power of the Tuscan models in the provincial cultures will have to be emphasized. Niccolò del Rosso from Treviso, who roughly imitates in many poems, as we said, Dante's and Cavalcanti's forms, in other no less numerous compositions resumes, with equal awkwardness, the themes and patterns of the "bourgeois"; he collects and orders carefully prepared transcriptions of their texts in that codex Barberiniano 3953 that is one of the most valuable documents of our ancient lyrical poetry.

More noteworthy is the "colony" of the writers from Perugia who also reflect the Tuscan examples with an equally eclectic taste and confirm its success well beyond the middle of the century within the limits of an exclusive academy, almost a society game. But at least the best of them, from Nerio Moscolo to Cecco Nuccoli and Marino Ceccoli, compose with a fresher and bolder attitude and with a certain novelty and sharpness of color and images.

Apart from them (also because he reflects a more archaic phase, still connected by way of Rustico, with the early attempts of the "genre" with the Guittone's school), one should mention Bindo Bonichi from Siena who died in old age in 1338, a person among the most notable, a representative of that rich merchant class, who was awarded the highest legal authority and was very active in charities. Also his abundant poetic activity complies with an essentially practical function of teaching, guiding and exercising criticism for his fellow citizens within the framework of a traditional and conservative morality. He never composed in abstraction but was always connected with concrete problems of behavior and judgement and in some sonnets, more than in the songs, his gnomic vein is able to find from time to time a good measure of gentle and fluid wit.

*

The activity of some poets who were writing around the middle of the century or later until the early decades of the fifteenth century, proceeds against the background of a more varied and complex culture that is not as closely connected with a precise school tradition. One may notice in these poets the power and weight of that tradition in some thematic choices and stylistic conventions and in the common acceptance of a vernacular practice, and of the linguistic institution of learned Tuscan. Yet, just within the very limits of tradition, they enjoy a wider range of experiences that include the "post-stilnovo" phases, or in any case, outside "stilnovo", Dante the poem writer and author of the *Commedia*. Furthermore, they, and those of Tuscan origin, spend their wandering lives mostly at the courts of northern Italy and the moods and vicissitudes of such existence are reflected in their art and culture, broadening their picture within ampler and more eclectic limits of interest and curiosity, forcing a stricter adherence to current events and autobiography and even the simplest demands of their clients. Finally, they have to consider, in a major or minor measure, the examples that were spread around of Petrarch's new poetry and generally the contributions of humanism and the changed intellectual and spiritual conditions that are visible in Petrarch's literary activity as well as in Boccaccio's mythological and narrative works.

Among these writers the most noticeable personality is Fazio degli Uberti (d. 1367), whom we mentioned already in connection with his major labor, the *Dittamondo*. Born in the first decade of the century, probably in Pisa, from the illustrious Ghibelline family of Farinata, he worked for the Scaligeri family, then the Visconti and later for Giovanni d'Oleggio, Lord of Bologna. As it seems certain, he met in Verona the woman for whom almost all his love poems were composed, a Malaspina, perhaps Ghidola, who later married Feltrino of Montefeltro. The indigence and humiliations of a courtier's wandering life, the desire of death invoked as a "devoted, sweet dear friend," the frequently surging temptation of committing suicide appear with sincere expressions in a song on fortune, that initiates the genre that will be followed frequently among those persons of the "desperate" compositions.

The Ghibelline's genuine passion demonstrated abundantly also by the digressions and invectives of the didactic poem, the experienced suffering of the exile, the contemplation of the sorry destiny that affects so many innocent victims of factions, strife, "widows and children, who roam for bread in foreign lands/with great shame and mortal anguish," are common in his political poems, particularly the sorrowing lament by the personification of Florence. Other poems have moral topics, as the series of sonnets on the capital sins that echo Dantesque concepts and images. Also in the love lyrics, the most evident and overwhelming presence is represented by Dante's "stony" rhymes. One notices in them a desire of lofty language, an ample structure, and an intense, active technique to the point of showing artificiality.

But in every situation that seems prone to laxity and decline there prevails an abundance of sensitivity, the urgency of an immediate venting that allows the artist to remain detached and perform a textual refinement.

It is precisely this weakness of stylistic elaboration, too often satisfied with only worn out patterns, that relegates Fazio's voice in the field of a minor poetry that is not profound and of an uneven intensity, limited within its own world of warm images and tender confessions. Yet his capacity for immediacy, his sentimental and sensual fervor, the warmth of human expressions are sufficient to break the conventions of a stagnant set of clichés and distinguish and raise him well above the anonymous jargon of too many mediocre writers, and his love songs remain some of the most cherished, sensitive and moving voices of the fourteenth century minor lyrical poems.

Antonio da Ferrara leads us deeply into the dark, troubled world of courtly literary men. He was not bad but extravagant, *non mali vir ingenii, sed vagi*, as Petrarch defined him, with whom he exchanged sonnets and had friendly relations. Born in 1315, he wandered through several parts of Italy driven by indigence and natural restlessness, at the service of several lords: in Bologna at the Pepoli's and then Giovanni d'Oleggio, in Ravenna at the Da Polenta, in Forlì with the Ordelaffi, and then in Venice, Padua and Siena, to mention only some of the many stops of his wandering. He was constantly pursued by his unrestrainable passions and above all by the demon of gambling, with sporadic lapses of repentance and weak conversions until his death that occurred probably around 1370. His large group of compositions that include three syllable lines, songs, sonnets, ballads and popular rhymes, partly of autobiographical or gnomic topics, partly of political or occasional nature, is one of the most conspicuous documents of that cultural circle that is still in want of a scholar that may restore it to its authentic form, separating attributed compositions and establishing the text with its dialect tints against the neutral background of aulic language. In the large thematic variety and cultural components that draw from the style of high lyricism and bourgeois poetry and include Dantesque and Petrarchan influences, a spontaneous and sharp attitude emerges that has its roots in a turbid and torn way of life, rich in moods, oddities, as well as polemic and rebellious impulses. At times, as in the song *Le stelle universali e' ciel rotanti*, that is one among the most typical and sincere among the genre of the "disperate", in some sonnets and in the chapters, there echoes a more intense and sorrowful voice, the sign of a genuine and vigorous albeit fragmentary and unruly lyrical personality.

Similar in many respects to the experience of the writer from Ferrara is the life of Francesco di Vannozzo. Born in Padua, in a family from Arezzo, between 1330 and 1340, in 1363 he was in Verona at the court of Cansignorio della Scala. Then we find him in Venice, Bologna and Padua, again in Verona and finally in

Milan where he composes, in honor of Giangaleazzo, the *Cantilena pro Comite Virtutum*. He died almost certainly at the beginning of the century's last decade. In his personality, the common image of the courtier acquires more distinct attitudes, professional, as it were, to the limit of a properly troubadour-like activity. It is probable, among other things, that he combined his literary activity with the practice of an expert musician of various instruments and perhaps of an organizer of simple shows for entertainment in behalf of his occasional protectors.

Also in his poetic collection the autobiographical poems that reflect an agitated and always uncertain life alternate with the conventional political poems, the moral compositions, the artificial practices and the attempts of aulic imitation as far as the delightful transcriptions in a bourgeois character and mediocre style of Petrarchan ideas and situations.

More interesting is his bent for popular patterns and expressions, in the lively "maritazo" and in the "nonsense" rhymes in Venetian dialect where, along a line of objective literary tradition and verbal expression of a typically northern nature, he lets his uncommon descriptive and mimic qualities run free.

In one he portrays himself and the humiliating indigence in which he lives because of his gambling obsession. Once he had nurtured great hopes with an "uncommon and brave heart," now he has fallen down and is held in no account like an "oven broom," compelled to wander "scratching" the lute and the guitar or "singing stories/at other people's tables/with this or that person for a glass of wine." It is not easy to say how true this painful confession is or if it is a literary motif common in the troubadour circles, of which the fourteenth century left us other examples as in the compositions of the Florentine Zaffarino and Niccolò Povero.

Quite different is the environment that constitutes the background of Giannozzo Sacchetti's life but somewhat similar are the vicissitudes and apprehensions that form the essence of a dissipated and troubled existence. Born around 1340 in Florence, he was at variance with his relatives, mainly with his older brother Franco, to whom had been trusted his property after he had been interdicted as a gambler and squanderer. His marriage in 1366 to Margherita Peruzzi and his adherence to the political convictions of his wife's relatives who were aristocratic Guelphs, worsened later on his break with Franco who sided with the moderates. Sent as an ambassador to Milan in 1369, he established relations with northern Italy's court poets. In 1377 his financial situation caused him to get away to the countryside in order to escape from his creditors' instances. From April to May 1379, he was imprisoned at the Stinche because of debts. Meanwhile, he established connections with St. Catherine, attended Catherine's groups in Florence, composed "laude" and performed devotional practices "in order to extort peoples' money," if we want to believe a chronicler of his time, but more probably he sought some form of reward and amelioration of his adventurous and hopeless life. When he was released from prison, he joined the side of Carlo di Durazzo where he met Benedetto Peruzzi and other political exiles and established agreements with them. Shortly afterwards, he reentered the city with letters from Carlo with the charge of organizing a conspiracy against the popular government but he was arrested and sentenced to death. The execution was carried out in October 1379.

His poems do not possess any professional elements. Probably rare and awkwardly developed, they were all inspired by precise conditions of sadness, scorn, enthusiasm or despair, and are always marked by a vigorous and intense expression. Besides the "laude" that originate from a sincere religious fervor, his moral compositions and a "hunt" for music, one will have to notice a "desperate" song against Fortune, another political one on the occasion of the persecutions inflicted on the heirs of the seneschal Niccolò Acciaiuoli by Queen Giovanna of Naples, and a lament-song in the person of the Church inspired by the ideas of St. Catherine's companions. But more unique and new are the stanzas of a macabre taste of an ascetic and perverse inspiration where he describes his woman's dead body, the beautiful sonnet where he exhorts his companions in debauchery to withdraw in time with their fragile bark from the cruel storms of the world and turn their minds to God.

Besides the writers that have been mentioned, several other poets deserve at least a brief mention, such as Braccio Bracci from Arezzo, who was among the men of letters paid by the Visconti's court, Matteo degli Albizzi, Lorenzo Moschi, Count Ricciardo (probably of the Battifolle, Lords of Casentino). The latter ones have connections with Petrarch and echo with major or minor earnestness his themes and language, sometimes with remarkable stylistic ability as in Ricciardo's case.

Some names live on because of a single composition. By Riccardo degli Albizzi, son of Franceschino, there is a passionate *canzone* dealing with separation and jealousy; by Jacopo Cecchi the well structured and dignified *canzone* to Death, based on Dantesque motifs and attributed to Dante for a long time; by Bruzio Visconti, the ballad based on ideas of stoic pride against Fortune; under the name of Matteo Correggiaio from Padua there is a "canzone" *Gentil Madonna, mia speranza cara,* that reveals an abundant and festive inspiration, inclined to the warm abandonment of imagination and expansive confessions, not too different from the forms of Fazio's love poems.

Toward the end of the century, a tendency that might be defined "of manner" reveals itself in different ways. On the one hand, there continue the expressions of court poets but with an increased artificiality and an ever-increasing persistence of decorative elements reflecting a current humanistic and mythological repertory. Thus, there is the case of Bartolomeo della Pieve and the abundant collection of

Simone Serdini, called Saviozzo, from Siena, who committed suicide around 1420. "Desperate" songs, political and propaganda poems, plaintive autobiographical sonnets are composed along with the new genre of the recent writings modeled on the *Eroidi*, with historic, poetic and even imaginary figures, such as Bartolomeo's story of betrayed Dido and the "canzone" of the young maiden abandoned by her lover, or Saviozzo's similar lament of a seduced girl as well as the jealous young woman who entertains and reasons about the idea of committing suicide.

On the other hand, there is a flowering of the literary men's illusion that attempts to bring back the fascination of the lyrical, illustrious tradition on the purely verbal ground of a more or less dignified academy.

A subtle polemic spirit, contrary to the bold exclusivism of the new humanists, and a tired loyalty for the Tuscan vernacular tradition inspire the late resumption of schemes and constructions drawn from Cavalcanti and Dante and, in a lesser measure, from Petrarch, along the line of a refined and elegant taste where the fashion of the difficult sextet flourishes again. In this area one may point out Antonio degli Alberti (c. 1360–1415) and Cino Rinuccini (c. 1350–1417). Both currents arise in an atmosphere of decline and will converge in the minor forms of the vernacular literature of the fifteenth century. We cite, in particular, Rinuccini's style that will acquire a certain posthumous success among the late admirers and restorers of Italian poetry toward the end of the fifteenth century, such as Mario Equicola and Lorenzo de' Medici, that will reconstruct lovingly the *corpus* of poems in order to include them in the *Raccolta aragonese*.

*

The various aspects of the fourteenth century minor literature that were mentioned above indicate the crumbling and weakening development of a cultural process that goes back largely to the thirteenth century, or that, to say it better, had reached its maturity in the century as well as its most evident settlement. Considered in their totality, they constitute the more or less partial and often contradictory document of a profound crisis of its ideal, religious, moral and political values. The impression that we have from reading these texts is an impression of decadence that assails and overwhelms every form of a civilization. While a system of human and civic relationships breaks up and is replaced by another, where the space allowed for the development for individual life is more limited, the hearts of men seem to be clutched by a feeling of fear and discouragement. The great institutions, on which rested the order of medieval Christianity, entered a phase of serious decline and became empty names or, at least in part, they became deprived of their power. The Church, humiliated by the Avignon captivity, torn by schisms and internal corruption, seems to have lost the sense of its function as well as its ability to be an example and a guide. Among the high ranks are lustful and simoniac prelates. In the lower ranks, priests and monks are thirsting for gain and power. The tasks assigned to the vicars of Christ "are all transmuted in order to spill blood and sell benefits/in infamous vices," states Antonio da Ferrara. And Pietro Alighieri portrays the principles of the Church as "driven to lust and enrich relatives." Giannozzo Sacchetti confirms that "hypocrisy ... opens all favors in behalf of priests," and Braccio Bracci is astounded that the spiritual power and a doctrine of peace are made to serve worldly interests and reduced to war instruments ("In vain you read God's gospel, that preached peace everywhere, but you urge war and lead us to heresy.") "Under the cloak of religion," adds further Franco Sacchetti, clergymen "commit abusive actions all day long against other people's property," and "under a veil of honesty ... [they indulge in] every vice of gluttony, lust and others, as their desires demand," and "they get involved in any deal for money regardless of whether it is honest or dishonest."

The invocation for a justice of God that may come to prostrate the "greedy Babylon," is so frequent to become commonplace while from all sides, from the words both of heretics and saints, as well as in Clareno's, St. Catherine's, and Colombini's statements, arises the request of a deep reform of the entire religious life and every level of the ecclesiastical establishment.

In addition, the shame and even the more ridiculous impotence of the Empire aren't any lesser, because the vain hopes placed in its intervention to restore order and justice in the peninsula become more and more evident.

Italy's situation, in its relationship with the imperial authority, is effectively summarized in the words of a writer of Ghibelline tradition, Pietro di Dante: "King without power and useless laws," a sovereign who "is more prone to empty words/than ever was the frogs' croak," on whose account "almost every land is under tyranny," words that seem to epitomize through his son's words the well recognized failure of Alighieri's great utopia.

Such utopia, however, reappears from time to time in people's minds and resounds in some of Petrarch's letters or Fazio's poems as well as in a famous "canzone" by Bindo di Cione del Frate; but it is no longer inspired by an unshakeable certainty. It expresses, instead, a state of weariness and hopeless anxiety rather than firm hope.

Yet, more serious than the decline of the medieval institutions is the deep crisis of the communal rules. Already in the more ancient texts, even in those where the new concept of bourgeois customs are expressed in more proudly polemic terms, as in the *Fiore,* or in those who naïvely theorize the ideals of the ruling class, such as the treatises by Francesco da Barberino or the song of "esteem" by Dino Compagni, the reader perceives the real back side of an apparently vivacious, thriving and proud condition, namely the honesty in merchant relationship failed, the magistracies corrupt, justice made venal and the hypocrisy of the knightly oaths unmasked.

And the complaint grows in the following years, not only from the adversaries but from the Florentine writers more faithful to their tradition of a moderate freedom (Sacchetti, Pucci and Adriano de' Rossi), as the threat of violent solutions of the lower classes revolt, or of the arrogance of unscrupulous and lucky adventurers becomes serious internally and externally. The commune was not able to create a solid system of order and justice, civil strife caused long lasting grudges and desperate homesickness among the exiles, the exclusive oligarchies took the upper hand, stifling the drive of the ephemeral democratic reforms and the rural areas remained detached and extraneous, if not outright hostile, while the subject cities or those threatened with subjection were always ready to take any opportunity to rebel or attack.

The history of the last great Italian commune, the only one to reveal an extraordinary vitality and a quick ability to recover from every crisis, I mean the history of Florence between the tyranny of the Duke of Athens and the Ciampi uprising, is almost symbolic of the internal weakness and impossibility of real development and progress of the communal rules.

Even the achievement of wealth and power that had constituted one of the proud affirmations of a new, worldly and material way to conceive life, slowly reveals itself in its narrow-mindedness, it becomes the norm and assumption of a deeper form of injustice: "The base world had been reaching the point/where neither wisdom nor refinement count/unless they are mingled with wealth/which seasons and salts every good food," Pieraccio Tedaldi states. And Niccolò Soldanieri adds: "Common people consider favorably/even peasants as long as they have money ... in the world ... those who have more money are most important." The appeal against such an overturning of values broadens and underscores the injustice of social interactions. Even a moderate character like Sacchetti observes that everything is denied to a poor person; even the injustice committed against him goes unpunished. A harsh and narrow-minded society condemns him to a condition of servitude without any hope of redemption.

The theme of poverty, transposed into the form of a widespread religious ideology, becomes the symbol of protest or instrument of resignation. This feeling of deep imbalance in the social order remains the sign of an impending danger, the remorse of a shattered ideal law, the desire of an elusive justice, and is echoed in different manners and statements in the poetical and prose writings of the time, in the lyrics of the courtly men of letters and in the pages of chroniclers and short story writers as well.

Even in the religious "laude" (and in the "prophecies," nonsense rhymes and moral songs) slips in the utopia of a world where human beings are finally equal:

"If all of us have a Father/then we are brothers/why are we not equal/all enjoying the same wealth?/One is rich, the other is not./He who can get the most, is the one who owns the most." These are the words of a "lauda" from Perugia on the theme of the parable of Lazarus and the rich man. And against the background of the daring polemics of the *Fiore*, suddenly flashes with an extraordinarily vigorous representation, the image of the starving and forsaken throngs: "And when I see those wretches go bare/trembling among piles of dung/broken by cold and hunger/so that they may not praise either God or saints/I run away from them as fast as I can ..."

In a world so troubled by the awareness of anarchy and the injustice that pervades it, also the threat of tyranny may put on the mask of a hope for order and social peace. The lordship of a single person may seem to insure, within some limits, a semblance of equality and, for the most oppressed and persecuted, of greater freedom. The skillfully funded propaganda of the court writers stresses precisely this point and utilizes this widespread desire of justice. It happens, however, that experience disperses very quickly the most promising illusions: "In the tyrant's land/fools are those who remain," Francesco da Barberino admonishes; and the short story writers like Sacchetti portray in lively colors the whimsical and cruel mentality of the lords. And Saviozzo, or someone in his behalf, confirms: "The tyrant gets for himself all that he wants/he deprives this man of his property and that one of his life/from one he takes his daughter, and the wife from another," while Pietro Alighieri warns against the "new publicans" who "constantly gnaw at people with bigger bites."

In any case, above all disappointments there remains the steady, anxious, insisting and painful invocation for a new order that may offer everybody peace and safety, namely, peace whatever it may be, ordained by an emperor or promoted by a pope who should be more aware of their function or perhaps imposed by a tyrant upon seditious and quarrelsome communities. The image of "sweet peace" is present as a supreme good and always elusive for all people; it sustains the exiles' hopes, it inspires the thinking and admonishments of the most thoughtful citizens, it warms the eloquence of preachers and mystics, it echoes in the speech of rhetoricians and it is usurped in order to serve the most disparate forms of propaganda.

Meantime, in the absence of a lasting and regular order of civic and moral economical relationships, the individual feels like a straw at the mercy of adverse forces that tend to harm and oppress him. Fortune rules the world whether it is viewed as blind and shapeless power of chance or like the expression of God's inscrutable will or even as a kind of material power against which, as in Bruzio Visconti's song, the brave man stands not as a winner yet tenacious in claiming his remaining human dignity. But this important claim for dignity escapes a large part of people: "One cannot go against Fortune ..." Vannozzo says, "nor can the course of a star be stopped/by preaching or sermonizing." One can only adapt oneself to the anonymous's cynical advise: "As a piece of advise I give you the following/turn your cloak as the wind blows," or to the even more humiliating suggestions that one may read in Bindo Bonichi's writings: "There is one way you may live amidst people ... stay away from the poor and get closer to the rich."

One should stress in this literature the recurrance of some persistent themes, undoubtedly present and lively in the mind of the composers as well as of the teachers, songsters and "laude" writers, chroniclers, storytellers, moralists and religious treatise-writers: the issue of fortune, namely of man's behavior against the overpowering forces of surrounding reality, the problem of poverty, or of the unbalance, injustice and social disorder, the issue of freedom, "sweet and longed for good," and the corresponding one of tyranny, impending threat upon the remaining communities and, at the same time, frequent promise of a less unstable order and a less unequal justice where the troubled destiny of every individual may find some calm in any way and at any cost.

From too many pages of these minor writers one derives the impression of a civilization that is dying out, together with its political and moral orders and even with its wisdom and poetry. The lamentation of Giovanni Quirini for Dante's death (*Or son le Muse tornate a dichino/or son le rime in basso decadute*) is answered at the end of the century by Franco Sacchetti's for Boccaccio's demise. It is not by chance that such lamentations keep recurring persistently in the words of minor writers by whom the crisis of values and ideologies of that century-old tradition that is synthesized in the concept of the Middle Ages is suffered and openly expressed without rewards.

They are the unwitting victims and testimonies of the crisis whereas the great poets, Dante, Petrarch and Boccaccio represent its lucid awareness and, at the same time, they forebode its overcoming. In the decadence of traditional values that is reflected on the ideological ground by the disintegration of scholastic synthesis, of a learned and encyclopedic culture, of a refined but schematic rhetorical doctrine, they see the loss of an irretrievable good and they, the best of them, react by desperately clinging to the norms of a morality and religiosity detached from any pretense of rational justification while the others allow themselves to be carried away by a whirlwind of anguish, intemperance and bewilderment.

Meantime, on that basis of decadence whose deep anxiety he feels in his own being, Petrarch builds the foundation and prepares the instruments for the dawning of humanism and rediscovers in literature the beginning of a new, albeit unstable, harmony and Boccaccio gathers and selects the most independent, manifest, bold and polemic ideas of the recent tradition and hands them down as a precious legacy to the civilization of the Renaissance.

*

It would not be right to consider all of this fourteenth century minor literature under an exclusively negative light. If it is appropriate to underscore the difference that always recurs between literature and poetry, between the immediate document and the conscious, originally elaborated transcription into a real experience, it is also necessary not to lose sight of the fundamental relationship in contents that connects, in countless linguistic and stylistic forms, literature and poetry and makes the former an essential instrument for the understanding of the latter not only from the standpoint of admiration but also from a critical angle.

This is even more important because we intend to represent the features of an epoch that is, in one, a conclusion and a beginning, an epoch that is a crisis of the values inherited from a century old tradition and, in another, an opening toward a new, radically transformed civilization. Only in this manner, without confusing aspects and moments that must be kept separated, will we become aware of the continuity of the historical process. For example, in our case, we will evaluate better which medieval character continues not only in Dante, but also in Boccaccio and in Petrarch and, more generally, we will learn how to appreciate with a finer mind the importance and the weight of the traditional forces that contribute, not only negatively but as antithetical elements to history's progress.

It is precisely among these latest representatives of a dying civilization, the fourteenth century minor writers, that we will have to search the last documents, already confused chronologically, but precisely because of this fact more sad, of an epoch that had been able to build an individual organic synthesis of reflection and work, of culture and life, characterized by a still intact and fervent understanding without any conformity, inspired by a strong civic spirit, a resolute faith in the norms of a strict attitude of relationship and hierarchy. They consist of those values of pure faith, intense political passion, of deeply ethical minds that will be partially lost with the triumph of humanism but that will be re-evaluated after a long oblivion by the romantic and Risorgimento historians who will rediscover the premise of an autonomous civic order and, above all, will recognize its characteristics of strong and wide popularity against the closed and aristocratic attitude of Renaissance culture.

One of the most unique and positive aspects of this minor literature is represented precisely by the presence of a strong element of popular origin that will no longer be visible or will appear greatly diminished in the following ages. Almost none of these minor texts—chronicles, short stories, sermons and treatises, "laude" and sirventes, vernacular versions and poetic confessions—escapes completely from this common characteristic that includes, at least in part, also the success of the greater works, from the *Commedia* to Petrarch's lyrics and the *Decameron*.

What is important, at this point, is to stress the humblest areas, which are often the most original and inventive, of this literary culture of a closer origin and popular propagation. A poet whose life spans over most of the century, the Florentine Antonio Pucci, seems to personify and summarize it in all its aspects and forms. Born around 1310, from a bronze smith or bell foundry man, he practiced for a certain time his father's art until, around 1334, he obtained the position of commune bell-ringer, and later, in 1349, that of comptroller and town-crier. A petition of his written in 1369 and addressed to the Signiory is still extant. In this petition, referring to his good service to the commune for more than thirty years of service, and in consideration of his declining health, he asks to be exonerated from the exhausting task of town crier and kept in that of comptroller. A large part of his literary activity is connected with his task as an intermediary and interpreter among the highest magistracies of the commune and the people, even of the lower level. He composed serventes that describe the various events of city life as well as the struggles and victories of Florence against its enemies, the seven ballads of the *Guerra di Pisa* and the poetic version of Villani's chronicle in the *Centiloquio*. Also another part of his abundant production is connected with his main tasks, such as the poems of moral and satirical nature about the commune, the "laude," the chapter on the beautiful ladies of Florence, the three-syllabic composition of the *Proprietà di Mercato Vecchio* and even the ballads of legendary and romance character because of their entertaining and popular aim that originally inspired them.

Even after the time that he relinquished his public posts, which he outlived for about twenty years, he continued to follow with professional attention the main events of city life and commented on them in his sirventes; he completed the *Centiloquio*, drew up a list of Florence's *podestà*, while the song *Canzone della vecchiezza* was composed shortly before his death that occurred in October 1388. This very abundant production may be considered in its entirety like a bit of a gossipy mirror of daily events and public opinion, which it reflects in itself and determines in part in its most elementary reactions in the political and in the moral, religious and cultural fields as well.

Pucci, a self-taught man of humble extraction but tied as a minor official to the commune's ruling class, a friend of Sacchetti, on good terms with Antonio da Ferrara, carried out his task of unofficial informer as a chronicler and educator with considerable liveliness and skill and a spontaneous adherence to popular sensitivity as well as his slightly concise and schematic way to see and judge contemporary things and personalities. His poems have all the characteristics of that improvisation that in our days would be defined journalistic, an easy and flowing talent that shows too often a tendency to become verbose and sloppy. But he has also a good amount of immediacy and candor of feelings that in the compositions of a narrative nature may rise to a fresh recreation of historical epic or imaginative material, as in the *Proprietà di Mercato Vecchio,* with a warm and dynamic representation of days and seasons, events and characters of a little world of female greengrocers and peddlers, artisans and barterers, country squires and swindlers. For his part, the good town crier contributes his witty and sometimes odd humor but essentially full of common sense and a certain quickness in observing and portraying the motions and customs of the people around him. It is this humor that we grasp better in the rich collection of sonnets jotted down day by day as different events occurred (autobiographical, jesting, gnomic). But it resounds a bit everywhere in his rhymes and also in his didactic material (as in the one that develops the old theme of the *Noie*), in the "crowns" of sonnets on women's good qualities, on the "message of love," on poetic art, in the story/song on the motif of Galvano or the odd guest. And it represents the sign of the fragile and unwitting grace that brightens his long, somewhat bungled and a little anonymous poetic labor.

In this production there emerge conspicuously the two sections of sirventes (on the flood, the famine, the plague, the wars of Padua and Lucca and the expulsion of the Duke of Athens), and of the historical ballads (as the already mentioned *Guerra di Pisa*) or of legendary topics (*Brito di Brettagna, Apollonio di Tiro, Gismirante, Madonna Lionessa, Reina d'Oriente*). Up to a certain point, they are distinguished by the subject matter that in the sirventes is mostly historical (but it may occur also in his epic ballads,) and more distinctly the metric structure that in the sirventes is the tercet (with the variations of the tercet followed by a five-syllable group, AAAb, BBBc, etc., and the quatrain ABbC, CDdE, etc.), while in the ballads the narrative octave is used. They are similar, instead, because of the linguistic and stylistic characteristics and the common attitude of the epic inspiration adapted to the taste and the moods of a humble public, yet somewhat light-hearted and discerning because of a long experience. Concerning this point, Pucci's activity gets into the broad picture of popular literature and contributes to characterize it in its two most conspicuous currents of the narrative genre. The third most important current of lyrical origin is that of religious poetry, such as lauds and sacred plays of Umbria and Abruzzo that resume and prolong the ways of an already established tradition of the preceding century and prepare the success of the Tuscan sacred representations of the fifteenth century. But not a few texts reflect a subjective inspiration and are composed by writers who were not lacking education among whom stand out in the first decades of the century the Franciscan Ugo Panziera, and, at its end, the rather colorless figure of Bianco da Siena who, at times, echoes weakly Jacopone's mystic eloquence.

The ballads in "ottava rima" have a considerable place in fourteenth century minor literature and represent one of its newest and most fertile inventions. We know the authors' names only in a few cases but it is probable that they go back to a degree and type of culture not different from those that we can identify in a better known personality, such as Pucci: a semi-popular culture with a precise function of connection between the ideological contents and the tastes of the highest social and refined groups and the dawning cultural and artistic interests of the humblest social levels.

The texts, or at least the shortest ones, were brought to the city squares and recited with musical accompaniment by the authors who, at times, were ballad singers themselves, and more often perhaps by professional singers and minstrels, while the more broadly developed compositions, such as the *Spagna* or the *Orlando,* were probably reserved for reading (for a public, however, that was not too different from that of the streets). Their contents might have varied within very broad limits, from contemporary events, the same that supply the material of the sirventes (ballads on the death of Bernabò Visconti, Giangaleazzo and the "condottiere" Giovanni Aguto) to religious stories (*Passione di Gesù,* by Niccolò Cicerchia from Siena, *Fanciullezza di Gesù,* by Brother Felice da Massa, *Resurrezione di Cristo,* apart from the long *Pianto de la Verzene,* in tercets, by Enselmino da Montebelluna that stands out because of its metric structure and its strongly vernacular color), from the Breton romances (*Sala di Malagigi, Carduino, Febusso e Breusso, Lancillotto, Tristano,* etc.) to the Carolingian legends (*Fierabraccia, Carlo Mainetto, Rinaldo, Spagna, Orlando,* etc.); from the romance adaptations of classical history (*Guerra di Troia, Fatti di Cesare*) to mythology (*Piramo e Tisbe, Progne e Filomena*); from the "lais" (*Florio e Biancifiore, Donna del Vergiù, Polcella Gaia, Bel Gherardino, Gibello, Liombruno*) to the "fabliaux" and short story writing (*Novella dell'Indovinello, Lusignacca*), and so on.

Dating is very uncertain in most cases. (Within the limits of the fourteenth century we are absolutely certain only when we know the author's name—Pucci, Pietro da Siena—or where it is possible to ascertain the ancient date of the manuscript that brought us the text. It is less probable in the rare cases where we are helped by internal indications or external evidences, as for the *Florio,* the *Donna del Vergiù,* cited by Boccaccio, and the *Gibello,* already known by Andrea da Barberino; but they might be late compilations and certainly the major part of the transcriptions that reached us cannot go back to the early decades of the fifteenth century.)

In the large variety of the material, the genre's unity is represented by the common narrative purpose that distinguishes all this literature in the predominantly lyrical picture of contemporary poetry and it implies the invention of a new technique to suit the purpose, of an open and fluid meter and a language detached from formality and entirely directed to a rapid and dynamic representation: an extreme simplification, or even elementariness, of the instruments of expression in function of the pre-eminent values attributed to the contents, the plot and the various unforeseeable events, the popular aims and the light literature, almost like serial stories, within the field of the publications of the time. Utmost importance was attributed to fantastic or supernatural elements portraying strength, courage, and adventures mitigated, however, by the frequent emergence of an ironic, common-people spirit that leads the narration to a situation of an immediate and not too demanding entertainment that does not exclude a fanciful evasion, without implying a full participation in the eroic ideal of life.

Literary historiography, after a long period of scorn, stressed too often also in recent times, the extreme deficiency of this literature from a formal point of view. It emphasized its uncertain, disconnected syntax, a heavy, prosaic, approximate language worsened by the requirements of rhyming that the singer overcomes in the hurried casualness of a hack writer, and by the mechanic forms of some fixed patterns of a representative, decorative or structural nature.

But even if one does not take into account the characteristics of authentic and naïve poetry of at least some of these small poems (and often of the oldest ones, such as the romance-like *Florio* and the moving *Donna del Vergiù*, as well as the fantastic *Liombruno*), and apart from the fact that the formal flaws always appear accentuated, in the texts that reached us, by the bad conditions of the process of transmission that was entrusted to extremely uneducated scribes and later to disgraceful printers, it seems appropriate to underscore the precise historical significance of an experience whose novelty and importance of creativity could be hardly exaggerated.

Already in the fourteenth century, the direct connections of contents and form between the ballad literature and Boccaccio's minor works, romances and small poems, and in the following century those of Pulci and Boiardo (not to mention Ariosto that comes at the end of this cultural literary event), reveal conspicuous moments in history (that are always difficult to explain and insufficiently explored) concerning the connection between popular poetry and art poetry that draws from the former the life of a new material, namely a wealth of inventions as well as of technical and communicative procedures that seem more dynamic, free, original and daring.

Similar observations could be repeated about the versifications of historical topics that have many linguistic and stylistic characteristics in common with the ballads that depend on the type of narrative approach and by the fact that these and others are directed to a largely common public with informative and communicative purposes (that in the historical compositions have a truly propagandistic function). Sometimes this literature borrows from the ballads even the metric structure, as we have said already, but it adopts more frequently the narrative forms created in the thirteenth century, that continued until the sixteenth century, such as the sirvente and, more rarely, the ballad.

The quality of these texts is very different but it always shows an intense participation of the writer in the human substance of the theme and its changing attitude, that may be either heroic or dramatic and sad; in one with the tendency to transfer the chronicle material to a level that is much more poetic than closely realistic. Thus, even in this sense, there occurs an encounter and conforming of all narrative literature in verse because, as the authors of the ballads tend to lower the tone and simplify the topics of their epic and fabular compositions, the authors of the sirventes are inclined to embellish the present events elevating them, almost without realizing it, to an aura of epic and fabular splendor.

This epic inclination appears stronger in the older compositions, such as the ballad on the defeat of Montecatini (1315), written by a Tuscan to encourage the Guelph party to secure a prompt revenge. It is developed dramatically mainly in its sorrowful yet proud lament of Queen Mary of Hungary on the death of her son Peter and her nephew Carlotto, or the other lament on the death of Charles of Calabria, son of King Robert (1328) as well as the sirvente, composed with a strong and effective narrative rhythm on the deeds of Cangrande della Scala (1329).

Similar in its inspiration but quite different in its stylistic characterization is the beautiful Aquila chronicle by Buccio di Ranallo (d. 1363), which should be considered separately as the product of a provincial and peripheral culture. The archaic origin of its development is clearly visible even in his other work that is still extant, a life of St. Catherine of Alexandria in seven-syllable couplets that is very close to the troubadour-like texts of the preceding century in the way of treating the topic, in its language and metric form. In the single rhyme quatrains of the chronicle that recounts the fights, sufferings, sorrows and glories of a country commune, there comes the pure sense of a chanson de geste that was drawn perhaps directly from the French models that could not have been unknown in the south, in the Angevin period.

In later compositions, the tone resembles that of the chronicles with an added dramatic emphasis as, for instance, in the lament on the death of Pietro Gambacorti, Lord of Pisa, written by Giovanni Guazzalotri (1392) from Prato, or it even adapts to the style of a lively and witty reportage as in some sirventes by Pucci on the city's misfortunes.

In general, one should point out the importance and novelty of this historical literature. With its epic ballads and prose romances, its popular rhymes, prophecies, short stories and poems it always contributes to establish that popular component that acquires, in the fourteenth century, an unusual importance due to its quantity and quality. This implies, then, still within the picture of a declining medieval culture, the sense of a broader opening, of a more varied wealth, namely the appearing, at least potentially, of more supple and modern literary themes that, in the triumph of humanism, was going to be almost entirely lost, but that constitutes nevertheless the not negligible sign of a great blossoming of our communal culture's vitality.

Bibliography

Introduction

For a detailed bibliography of the themes discussed in this volume, see, besides the main literary histories and the special lists, N. Sapegno, *Il Trecento* ("Storia Letteraria d'Italia"), Milano, F. Vallardi, 1960.

On the problems regarding the concepts of Middle Ages, Humanism and Renaissance, see the eccellent critical overview by E. Garin's essay *Umanesimo e Rinascimento*, in the third volume of *Problemi ed orientamenti critici di lingua e letteratura italiana*, by A. Momigliano, Milano, Marzorati, 1949. Other books by the same author are *L'umanesimo italiano*, Bari. Laterza, 1958, *Medioevo e Rinascimento, Studi e ricerche*, Bari, Laterza, 1954. See also, D. Cantimori, *Sulla storia del concetto di Rinascimento* in "Annali della Scuola Normale di Pisa", serie II, I (1932), and F. Chabod *Il Rinascimento* in *Questioni di storia moderna, Milano, Marzorati, 1948; Il Rinascimento nelle sue recenti interpretazioni, in "Bulletin of the International Committee of Historical Sciences,"* xix (1933), p. 215–29. For the various interpretations offered by the critics we consider J. Huizinga, *Das Problem der Renaissance*, in *Wege der Kulturgeschichte*, München, Drei Masken Verlag, 1930; E. Walser, *Gesammelte Studien zur Geistesgeschichte der Renaissance*, Basel, Schwabe, 1932; K. Burdach, *Reformation, Renaissance, Humanismus*, Berlin, Gebr. Paetel, 1926; F. Simone, *Le Moyen Age, la Renaissance et la critique moderne*, in "Revue de literature comparée." xviii (1938); W. R Ferguson, *The Renaissance in Historical Thought.* Cambridge, Mass., Harvard University Press, 1948; P.O. Kristeller, *Studies in Renaissance Thought and Letters,* Roma, Edizioni di Storia e Letteratura, 1956 as well as *Survey of recent Scholarship in the period of Renaissance* compiled for the Committee on Renaissance Studies of the American Council of Learned Societies, series I, 1945; *Il Rinascimento, Significato e Limiti,* Atti del III Convegno Internazionale sul Rinascimento, Firenze, Sansoni, 1953.

The following works are of interest in various ways concerning the relationship and continuity between the medieval and the humanistic culture: J. Huizinga, *L'autunno del medioevo,* Firenze, Sansoni, 1940; G. de Lagarde, *La naisance de l'esprit laïque au déclin du Moyen Age,* Paris, Les presses universitaires de France, 1934–1946; É. Gilson, *Héloise et Abélard,* Vrin, 1950; R. Weiss, *The Dawn of Humanism in Italy,* London, Lewis, 1947, e *Il primo secolo dell'umanesimo,* Roma, Edizioni di Storia e Letteratura, 1949; C.H. Haskins, *The Renaissance of the Twelfth Century,* Cambridge, Mass. Harvard University Press, 1927, and *Studies in Medieval Culture,* Oxford, Clarendon Press, 1929; G. Paré, A. Brunet, P. Tremblay, *La renaissance du XII siècle et l'enseignement, Paris, Vrin, 1933.* M. Apollonio, *Uomini e forme nella cultura italiana delle origini,* Firenze, Sansoni, 1933. G Weise, *Die geistige Welt der Gothik und ihre Bedeutung für Italien,* Halle, Niemayer, *1939,* E.R. Curtius, *Europäische Literatur und lateinisches Mittelalter,* Bern, Francke, 1948. Concerning religious values of fourteenth century humanism see K. Burdach, *Vom Mittelalter zur Reformation. Forschungen zur Geschichte der deutschen Bildung,* Berlin, Weidmann, 1912–1939.

For the development of the juridical and political thought one may, at present, consult R.W. Carlyle and A.F. Carlyle, *A History of Medieval Political Theory in the West,* vols. v and vi, London-Edinburgh, Blackwood, 1928 and 1936 as well as G. Galasso, *Medio Evo del diritto,* Milano Giuffrè, 1954.

Chapter One

A great part of the material mentioned in this chapter lies outside our chronological range and will be amply developed in the volume of this series devoted to the origins and the thirteenth century. This exempts us from the obligation of indicating minutely the sources of our discussion. It will suffice to mention, among the most recent and useful works, the chapters *Il problema del Duecento* and *Poesia politica e poesia amorosa nel Duecento* in A. Monteverdi's *Studi e saggi sulla letteratura italiana dei primi secoli,* Milano-Napoli, Ricciardi, 1954 and the up-to-date (also bibliographically) studies on *La prima elaborazione della forma poetica italiana* and the *Avviamenti della prosa del secolo XIII,* in A. Schiaffini's *Momenti di storia della lingua italiana,* Roma, Edizioni di storia e letteratura, 1950. Furthermore, concerning the origins of a poetic literary tradition, see V. De Bartholomaeis, *Primordi della lirica d'arte in Italia.* Torino, Società Editrice Internazionale, 1943. On the developments from the Sicilian to the Stil Nuovo poetry, see the introduction by, *La poesia lirica del Duecento,* Torino, UTET, 1951; on the history of prose, C. Segre, *La sintassi del periodo nei primi prosatori italiani,* in "Memorie dell'Accademia dei Lincei," Serie VIII, IX 1952), pp. 39–193, and the penetrating introductory essay on the *Volgarizzamenti del Due e Trecento,* Torino, UTET, 1953 and *La Prosa del Duecento,* Milano-Napoli, Ricciardi, 1959. For a quick but clear and precise synthesis of the development process of the literary language, see the first chapters of G. Devoto's *Profilo di storia linguistica italiana,* Firenze, Le Monnier, 1953, and, in addition, B. Migliorini, *Storia della lingua italiana,* Firenze, Sansoni, 1960.

Important and rich in essential methodological suggestions is C. Dionisotti's *Geografia e storia della letteratura italiana,* in "Italian Studies," VI (1951), pp. 70–93.

Concerning the Stil Nuovo, the conclusions of my studies in the revised volume *Il Trecento,* seem still valid to me; but in order to assay the tendencies of the most recent criticism, see D. De Robertis, *Definizione dello Stil Nuovo,* in "Approdo," III (1954), pp. 59–64, and for a retrospective view, E. Bigi, *Genesi di un concetto storiografico: "dolce stil nuovo,"* in "Giornale storico della letteratura italiana," CXXXXII (1956), pp. 337–71. Concerning the realist poets, the theory that I advanced concerning their "conscious" literature was resumed and abundantly documented recently by M. Marti, *Cultura e stile nei poeti giocosi del tempo di Dante,* Pisa, Nistri-Lischi, 1953 (but for another differentiation, see also G. Caravacci, *Folgore da San Gimignano,* Milano, Ceschina, 1960.) The bibliography for the other aspects of the literary culture between the end of the thirteenth and the early fourteenth century will appear in the ensuing chapters. At this point, for a more precise chronology of the Franco-Venetian texts and their Tuscan derivations, mention is made here of a fundamental study by C. Dionisotti, *Entrée d'Espagne, Spagna, Rotta di Roncisvalle,* in *Studi in onore di A. Monteversi,* Modena, Società tipografico-editrice modenese, 1959, I, pp. 207–41.

Chapter Two

For the general bibliography on Dante (lists, dictionaries, concordances, bibliographical manuals, reference books, biography and historical background, cultural development, philosophical and political thought) and the specific bibliography on the *Commedia,* I refer the reader to the abundant information that I have collected and arranged in the Bibliography of my commentary of the poem (Vol. 4, XXIII–XXXVI.) I shall mention, at this point, the most useful "guides" for a first guidance in the immense literature on Dante: N. Zingarelli. *La vita, i tempi e le opere di Dante,* Milano. F. Vallardi, 1931; M. Barbi, *Dante: vita, opere e fortuna,* Firenze, Sansoni, 1933; U. Cosmo, *Vita di Dante,* Bari, Laterza, 1930 and *Guida a Dante,* Torino, De Silva, 1947; F Maggini, *Introduzione allo studio di Dante,* Bari, Laterza, 1942; M. Apollonio, *Dante, Storia della Commedia,* Milano, F. Vallardi, 1951; S.A. Chimenz, *Dante,* Milano, Marzorati, 1956; as well as the cross reference to special journals: "Bullettino della *Società dantesca italiana* (1890–1921), *Studi danteschi,* (1920 and ff), as well as, from 1960 "L'Alighieri," directed by B. Nardi and A Vallone.

Except for the *Vita Nuova,* there is not a really critical edition of Dante's works. The most reliable texts are the following. both lacking justification and apparatus: *Le opere di Dante,* Testo critico della Società dantesca italiana, ed. M. Barbi, E.G. Parodi, F. Pellegrini, R. Rajna, E. Rostagno, G. Vandelli, Firenze, F. Bemporad, 1921 (reprinted by *Società dantesca italiana,* 1960); *Tutte le opere di Dante,* E Moore, fourth edition by P. Toynbee, Oxford, Clarendon Press, 1924.)

For the text of the *Rime,* a fundamental work is M. Barbi, *Studi sul Canzoniere di Dante, con nuove indagini sulle raccolte manoscritte e a stampa d'antiche rime italiane,* Firenze, Sansoni, 1915 (For partial corrections of the conclusions reached in this work, see B. Panvini, *Studio sui manoscritti dell'antica lirica italiana,* in "Studi di filologia italiana," XI, 1951, pp. 5–135; D. De Robertis, *Il Canzoniere Escurialense e la tradizione "veneziana" delle rime dello Stil Nuovo,* supplemento 27, 1954 of the *Giornale Storico della Letteratura Italiana; Censimento dei manoscritti di rime di Dante,* in "Studi danteschi," XXXVII, 1960, pp. 141–273. Also by Barbi there are important essays on the interpretation of some groups of compositions in *Problemi di critica dantesca,* Seconda Serie, Firenze, Sansoni, 1941, pp. 87–304. Some of the most noteworthy commentaries are, *Rime,* by G. Contini, Torino, Einaudi, 1946; *Rime,* with notes by D. Mattalia, Torino, Paravia, 1943; *"Rime della Vita Nuova e della Giovinezza,* by M. Barbi, and F. Maggini, Firenze, Le Monnier, 1956. Concerning the aesthetic value of Dante's poetry, besides Contini's introduction of the mentioned commentary, see E.G. Parodi, *Le Rime,* in the volume *Dante, la vita, le opere, le grandi città dantesche, Dante e l'Impero, Dante e l'Europa,* Milano, Treves, 1921, pp. 53–67; N. Sapegno, *Le Rime di Dante,* in "La Cultura," IX (1930), pp. 721–37; F. Maggini, *Dalle Rime alla lirica del Paradiso dantesco, Firenze, Le Monnier, 1938.* On the issues concerning order related to contents and themes, D. Mattalia, *La critica dantesca, Questioni e correnti,* Firenze, La Nuova Italia, 1950.

La Vita Nuova. Edizione critica by M. Barbi, Firenze, Bemporad, 1932: the ample work on the manuscript tradition, the apparatus and the notes on the text, make the edition one of the monuments of modern philological technique; but on the text of the "libello" see also the important remarks by E.G. Parodi, in *Bullettino della società dantesca*, N.S. XIV (1907), pp. 81–97; N. Zingarelli, in "Giorn. stor. d. lett. ital. LII (1908), pp. 201–211 and F. Beck, in "Zeitschrift für romanische Philologie," XXXII (1907), pp. 371–384; XL (1915), pp. 257–85. Noteworthy are the commented editions by A. D'Ancona (Pisa Lib. Galileo, 1884), T. Casini, Firenze, Sansoni, 1885), G. Melodia (Milano, F. Vallardi, 1905), G.A. Cesareo, Messina, Principato, 1914, D. Guerri (Firenze, Perrella, 1922), K. Makenzie (Boston, Heath, 1922), N. Sapegno, (Firenze, Vallecchi, 1929), D. Mattalia, (Torino, Paravia, 1936:) these editions are often preceded by ample essays that represent the most important bibliography on the subject. For a linguistic and stylistic analysis of the composition, see G. Lisio, *L'arte del periodo nelle opere volgari di Dante Alighieri e del sec. XIII*, Bologna, Zingarelli, 1902; A. Schiaffini, *Tradizione e poesia nella prosa d'arte italiana dalla latinità medievale al Boccaccio*, Roma, Edizioni di Storia e Letteratura, 1943; C. Segre, *La sintassi del periodo nei primi prosatori italiani, in* "Atti dell'Acc. Naz. dei Lincei," Memorie, S. VIII, IV (1952), fasc. 2, pp. 39–193; B. Terracini, *Pagine e appunti di linguistica storica*, Firenze, Le Monnier, 1957.

Correctly limiting but a bit concise is the opinion of B. Croce, *La poesia di Dante*, Bari, Laterza, 1921, but see also *Conversazioni critiche, III*, Bari, Laterza, 1933, pp. 187–190. On the cultural elements of the book see A. Marigo, *Mistica e scienza nella Vita Nuova*, Padova, Drucker, 1914; J.E. Shaw, *Essays on the Vita Nuova*, Princeton Univ. Press, 1929; C.S. Singleton, *Essay on the Vita Nuova*, Cambridge, Mass., Harvard. Univ. Press, 1948; D. De Robertis, *Il libro della Vita Nuova*, Firenze, Sansoni, 1961. For the chronology see M. Barbi, *Problemi di critica dantesca*, Prima Serie, Firenze, Sansoni, 1934, pp. 99–139. Totally groundless in the opinion of those who ascribe, completely or in part, to a time after the exile, the composition of the "libello" (see, for example, L. Pietrobono, *Saggi danteschi*, Roma, Signorelli, *1936*, pp. 1–137; B. Nardi, *Nel mondo di Dante*, Roma, Edizioni di Storia e Letteratura, *1944, pp. 1–20* and *Dal Convivio alla Commedia*, Roma, Istituto Storico Italiano, 1960, pp. 127–31.

Il Convivio, ed. by G. Busnelli and G. Vandelli, introd. by M. Barbi, Firenze, Le Monnier, 1934–37. Concerning textual issues, see E. Moore, *Textual Criticism of the Convivio, in Studies on Dante*, Oxford, Clarendon Press, 1917; A Pézard, *Le Convivio de Dante, in* "Annales de l'Université de Lyon, III Série, *IX (1940)*; M. Casella, *Per il testo critico del Convivio, in* "Studi di filologia italiana," VII (1944), pp. 29–77; V. Pernicone, *Per il testo critico del Convivio, in* "Studi danteschi," XXVIII (1949), pp. 145–82; M. Sampoli Simonelli, *Contributi al testo critico del Convivio, in* "Studi danteschi," XXX (1952), pp. 26–46, and XXXI (1953), pp. 56–161. For the interpretation see B. Nardi, *Note al Convivio* and *Dante e la filosofia*, in the mentioned book *Nel mondo di Dante;* see furthermore, some chapters in the other books on Dante's thoughts by Nardi, *Saggi di filosofia dantesca,* M. Perrella, 1930; *Dante e la cultura medievale, Bari, Laterza, 1942; La filosofia di Dante*. Milano, Marzorati, *1954;* as well as the fundamental work by E. Gilson, *Dante et la philosophie,* Paris, Vrin, 1939. We shall indicate further on additional bibliography on the specific issue of the vulgar language and the Empire. For the prose style of the *Convivio,* see above all the already mentioned studies of Lisio, Schiaffini, Segre and Terracini.

De Vulgari Eloquentia. Improved edition and commentary by A. Marigo, Firenze, Le Monnier, 1938; revised edition by P.G. Ricci, ibid., 1957. For the text one may still consult the critical editions by P. Rajna, before the discovery of the basic Berlin MS (*editio maior,* 1896; *editio minor, 1897);* the reproduction of the above MS by L. Bertalot (Frankfurt, 1917); the observations by A. Marigo, *Per il testo critico del De vulgari eloquentia,* in "Giorn. stor. d. lett. ital.," LXXXVI (1925), pp. 289–339, and XCIX (1932.) pp. 1–54; and finally the latest conclusions by P. Rajna, *Per un'edizione del De Vulgari Eloquentia,* in "Studi danteschi." XIV (1930), p. 1 and ff. Besides Marigo's ample introduction, see, in general, the previous studies by F. D'Ovidio, *Sul trattato De Vulgari Eloquentia* (1873), republished in *Versificazione romanza: Poetica e Poesia Medievale, II,* Napoli, Guida, 1832, p. 217, and by P. Rajna, *Il trattato De Vulgari eloquentia,* Firenze, Sansoni, 1906, and *Il primo capitolo del trattato De Vulgari Eloquentia* in "Studi danteschi." xiv (1830) and ff. Besides Marigo's ample introduction, see, in general, the previous studies by F. D'Ovidio, *Sul trattato De Vulgari Eloquentia* (1873) republished in *Versificazione Romanza: Poetica e Poesia Medievale, II,* Napoli, Guida, 1932, p. 217, and by P. Rajna, *Il Trattato De Vulgari Eloquentia,* Firenze, Sansoni, 1906, and *Il primo capitolo del trattato De Vulgari Eloquentia Tradotto e Commentato,* in *Miscellanea Hortis,* Trieste, Caprin, 1910. For the theory of language in Dante, see M. Casella, *Il volgare illustre di Dante,* in *"Giornale della cultura italiana," I, 3, (1925), pp. 33–40; B. Nardi,* Dante e la cultura medievale, op. cit., pp. 148–175; A Pagliaro, *Nuovi saggi di critica semantica,* Messina, D'Anna, 1956, pp. 215–246; B. Terracini, *Pagine e appunti di linguistica storica, op. cit.,* pp. 237 and ff. On Dante's rhetoric, see E.R. Curtius, *Europäische Literatur und lateinisches Mittelalter,* Bern, Francke, 1948; A. Schiaffini, *Poesis e poeta in Dante,* in *Studia philologica et litteraria in honorem L. Spitzer,* Bern, Francke, 1958; F. Di Capua, *Insegnamenti retorici medievali e dottrine estetiche moderne nel De Vulgari Eloquentia di Dante,* in *Scritti minori,* Roma, Desclée, 1959, II, pp. 252–355; G. Vinay, *Ricerche sul De Vulgari Eloquentia,* in "Giorn. stor. d. lett. ital." CXXXVI (1959), pp. 236–74, 367–89; S. Pellegrini, *De Vulgari Eloquentia,* I, 10–19, in "Studi mediolatini e volgari," VIII, (1960), pp. 155–63.

Monarchia. Text, translation and commentary by G. Vinay, Firenze, San-soni, 1950, and another edition with translation by C.A. Volpe, Modena, Società tipografica-editrice modenese, 1946. On the textual issue, besides the edition of the Vatican Codex (Roma, 1930) and the Berlin codex (Weimar, Böhlan, 1930), both provided by F. Schneider, see N. Vianello *Il testo critico della "Monarchia" di Dante,* in "Rassegna," XXXIX, 1931), pp. 89–111; P.G. Ricci, *Primi approcci per l'edizione nazionale della "Monarchia",* in "Studi danteschi," 1953, pp. 31–58 and *Un codice della "Monarchia" mai utilizzato,* ibid., 163–72. On Dante's political doctrine: E. Jordan, *Dante et la théorie romaine de l'Empire,* in "Nouvelle revue historique du droit," 1921–1922; G. Solari, *Il pensiero politico di Dante,* in "Rivista storica italiana," N.S. I (1923), pp. 273–455; F. Ercole, *Il pensiero politico di Dante,* Milano, Alpes, 1827–1928; F. Battaglia, *Impero, Chiesa e stati particolari nel pensiero di Dante,* Bologna, Zanichelli, 1944; A. Passerini d'Entrève, *Dante politico e altri saggi,* Torino, Einaudi, 1955, (cf. G. Vinay, in "Gior. stor. d. letter. ital." LXXIII, 1956, pp. 149–55); U. Mariani, *La posizione di Dante fra i teorici dell'imperialismo ghibellino,* in "Giornale dantesco"; XXX (1927), pp. 111–117; M. Barbi, *Problemi fondamentali per un nuovo commento alla Divina Commedia,* Firenze, Sansoni, 1956, pp. 49–114; L. Minio-Paluello, Tre note alla *Monarchia,* in *Medioevo e Rinascimento, Scritti in onore di B. Nardi,* Firenze, Sansoni, 1955, p. 51 and ff. Not to be forgotten are the two clear syntheses by E.G. Parodi, *La Monarchia,* in the mentioned volume *Dante, la Vita, le Opere,* etc. pp. 87–100, and *L'ideale politico di Dante,* in *Dante e l'Italia,* Roma, Fondaz. Basso, 1921, pp. 75–131. Of importance is the discussion between M Marcassone's *Il terzo libro della Monarchia,* in "Studi danteschi", XXXIII (1955), pp. 5–142 and B. Nardi, *Dal "Convivio" alla "Commedia,"* pp. 151–313 and G. Vinay, *Interpretazione della Monarchia di Dante,* Firenze, Le Monnier, 1962.

Dantis Alagherii Epistolae. Emended text with *Introduction, Translation, Notes, Indices and Appendix on the Cursus* by P. Toynbee, Oxford University Press, 1920; another edition with Italian translation and commentary by A. Monti, Milano, Hoepli, 1921. cf. *Lingua e letteratura* by G. Folena, Venezia, Neri Pozza, 1957, II, pp. 399–442. Among the most recent studies concerning the epistles (textual and authenticity issues) one should remember: R. Morghen, *La lettera di Dante ai car-dinali italiani,* in *"Bullettino dell'Istituto storico italiano per il medioevo", n. 68 (1956),* pp. 1–31; G. Vinay, *A proposito della lettera di Dante ai cardinali,* in "Giornale, stor. d. letter. ital., CXXXV, (1958), pp. 71–80; A. Mancini, *Nuovi dubbi e ipotesi sull'epistola a Cangrande,* in" Rendiconti della Classe di scienze culturali e storiche dell'Accademia d'Italia, VII, IV (1943, pp. 227–42; F. Mazzoni, *L'epistola a Can-grande,* in "Studi dedicati a A. Monteverdi", Modena, Società tipografico-editrice modenese, 1958, pp. 498–516; B. Nardi, *Il punto sull'Epistola a Cangrande,* Firenze, Le Monnier, 1960.

Dantis Eclogae, Johannis de Virgilio Carmen et Ecloga responsiva, by G. Albini, Firenze, Sansoni, 1903; also P.H. Wicksteed—E.G. Gardner, *Dante e Giovanni del Virgilio, including a critical edition of the text of Dante's "Eclogae Latine"* and of the poetic Remains of Giovanni del Virgilio, Westminster, Constable, 1902. See important observations on the text by E.G. Parodi, in "Giornale dantesco", (1902), pp. 205–43; XXVII (1924)), pp. 79–90; XXVIII (1925), pp. 266–73, 324–35; XXIX (1026), pp. 141–50.

Quaestio de aqua et terra, probable text, newly translated and commented by F. Angelitti, Palermo, 1915 (1832); another commented edition is the one by V. Biagi, Modena, Società tipografico-editrice modenese, 1907. The authenticity of the book is supported with valid reasoning by F. Mazzoni, La *"Questio de aqua et terra"*, "Studi danteschi", XXXIV (1957), pp. 163–204.

The most reliable edition of the *Commedia* is, for the time being, the last issued by G. Vandelli (in the most recent revision of Scartazzini's commentary, Milano, Hoepli, 1929); but one should keep in mind also the preceding ones by Vandelli (Firenze, Bemporad, 1929; Firenze, Le Monnier, 1927) and those by E. Moore-P. Toynbee (Oxford, clarendon Press, 1924), M. Casella, Bologna, Zanichelli, 1923, N. Zingarelli, (Bergamo, Istituto di Arti Grafiche, 1934), D. Guerri, Bari, Laterza, 1933), as well as mine (Milano-Napoli, Ricciardi, 1957). In the latter one, on pp. 1199–1209, there is a brief précis of the history of the textual question, still far from an organic and persuasive solution, and a list of the most important commentaries from the fourteenth century to the present. Among the most recent studies, that deal with general or particular questions concerning the text, we mention E.G. Parodi's *Il testo critico delle opere di Dante,* in "Bullettino, società dantesca," XXVIII, (1921), pp. 7–46; M. Casella, *Sul testo della Divina Commedia,* in "Studi danteschi, VIII (1924), pp. 5–85; M. Barbi, *Ancora sul testo della Divina Commedia,* in "Studi danteschi", XVIII (1934), pp. 5–57; S. Debenedetti, *Intorno ad alcuni versi di Dante, in* "Giorn. Stor, d. lett. ital." LXXXVII (1926), pp. 74–99; S.A. Chimenz, *Per il testo e la chiosa della Divina Commedia, ibid.,* CXXXIII (1956), pp. 161–87; G. Petrocchi, *Proposte per un testo base della Divina Commedia,* in *Filologia romanza,* II (1955), pp. 337–65; *L'antica tradizione manoscritta della Commedia,* in "Studi danteschi", XXXIV, (1957), pp. 7–126 and *Radiografia del Landiano,* ibid., XXXV (1958), pp. 5–27. The Question concerning the chronology of the composition is summarized in A. Vallone, *Per la datazione della Divina Commedia, in "Studi sulla Divina Commedia",* Firenze, Olschki, 1955; of a later time is the important essay by G. Petrocchi, *Intorno alla pubblicazione dell'Inferno e del Purgatorio,* in "Convivium", N.S., VI (1957), pp. 652–9. G. Ferretti defended with insight and erudition the reliability of Boccaccio's statement that places the beginning of its writing to the last years of his stay in Florence. G.

Il *due tempi della composizione della Divina Commedia,* Bari, Laterza, 1935; and *La data dei primi sette canti dell'Inferno,* in *Saggi danteschi,* Firenze, Le Monnier, 1950.

For the history of criticism, besides my above mentioned bibliographical note, the following may be helpful, D. Mattalia, in *I classici italiani nella storia della critica,* directed by W. Binni, Firenze, La Nuova Italia, 1954, I, pp. 3–93; L Caretti, *Guida a Dante,* in "Studi urbinati", XXVI (1952), pp. 181–95; A. Vallone, *La critica dantesca nell'Ottocento,* Firenze, Olschki, 1958; *Gli studi danteschi dal 1940 al 1949,* ibid. 1951, and *La critica dantesca,* Pisa, Nistri-Lischi, 1953; and, finally, the ample listing by R. Frattarolo, *Dalle origini a Dante,* (Bibliografia della critica), Roma, Gismondi, 1957. Among the many works on this topic, the related contributions of the historical school masters, are particularly significant such as: M. Barbi, *Problemi* and (*I Problemi fondamentali per un nuovo commento della Divina Commedia, Con Dante e coi suoi interpreti,* Firenze, Le Monnier, 1941 and G. Parodi, *Poesia e storia nella Divina Commedia,* Napoli, Perrella, 1935; *Lingua e letteratura,* II, cit.). For the approach to criticism issues, the are the fundamental studies by F. De Sanctis, *Lezioni e saggi su Dante,* S. Romagnoli, Torino, Einaudi, 1955; for its influence on the latest criticism, B. Croce's *La poesia di Dante,* Bari, Laterza, 1921. On the issue of the poem's structure see, L. Russo, *Problemi di metodo critico,* Bari, Laterza, 1929; M. Sandone, *Studi di storia letteraria,* Bari, Adriatica, 1950; C. Garboli, in "Società", VIII, (1952), pp. 20–44. Worthy of consultation are, Vossler, *La Divina Commedia studiata nella sua genesi e interpretata,* Bari, Laterza, 1927 as well as E Auerbach, *Dante als Dichter der irdischen Welt,* Berlin-Leipzig, Teubner, 1929, and the eighth chapter of *Mimesis,* traduzione italiana, Torino, Einaudi, 1956. From the most recent bibliography, we shall mention in a bit helter-skelter list Th. Spoerri, *Einführung in die Göttliche Komödie,* Zurich, Speer, 1946; G. Getto, *Aspetti della poesia di Dante,* Firenze, Sansoni, 1947; M. Malagoli, *Linguaggio e poesia nella Divina Commedia,* Genova, Briano, 1949, and *Storia della poesia nella Divina Commedia,* ibid. 1850; C.S. Singleton *Dante Studies, I Commedia; Elements of structure,* Cambridge, Mass., Harvard U.P., 1954; II, *Journey to Beatrice,* ibid., 1958, D.L. Sayers, *Introductory Papers on Dante,* London, Methuen, 1954; G. Contini, *Dante come personaggio-poeta della Commedia* in l' "L'Approdo letterario," IV (1958), pp. 19–46; F. Montanari, *L'Esperienza poetica di Dante,* Firenze, Le Monnier, 1959; G. Fallani, *Poesia e teologia nella D.C.,* Milano, Marzorati, 1959; S.A. Chimenz, *Classicità e medioevo nello spirito e nell'arte di Dante,* in "Nuova Antologia", issue 1902 (1959), pp. 205–22; N. Sapegno, *Introduzione alla "Commedia",* in "Pagine di Storia Letteraria'" Palermo, Manfredi, 1960, pp. 31–49; E Sanguineti, *Interpretazione di Malebolge,* Firenze, Olschki, 1962, and *Tre studi danteschi,* ibid. Le Monnier, 1961. On Dante's success in western criticism and literature, a large body of information is given by W.P. Friedrich, *Dante's Fame Abroad:* 1350–1850, Roma, Edizioni di Storia e Letteratura, 1956.

Chapter Three

For the didactical texts in verse closely connected with the *Roman de la Rose,* the fundamental edition is *Il Fiore e il Detto d'amore,* by E.G. Parodi, Firenze, Bamporad, 1921; for the other Tuscan poems: *l'Intelligenza,* ed. by V. Mistruzzi, Bologna, Commissione per i Testi di lingua, 1928 (cf. S. Debenedetti, in "Giorn. stor. d.lett. ital.", XCIV, 1929, pp. 141 ff.) and, by Francesco da Barberino, *I Documenti d'Amore secondo i manoscritti originali,* by F. Egidi, Roma, Società filologica romana, 1905–1927; *Del reggimento e costumi di donna,* ed. by C. Baudi di Vesme, Bologna, Romagnoli, 1875, then by G.E. Sansone, Torino, Loescher-Chiantore, 1957 (on the limitations of this critical edition, cf. L. Caretti, *Interrogativi filologici,* in *"Letterature moderne"* IX, 1958, pp. 93–9 and C. Battisti, *Osservazioni e correzioni ad una recente edizione del "Reggimento" di Francesco da Barberino,* Modena, Società tipografico-editrice modenese, 1959). Consider also the *Poemetti allegorico-didattici del secolo XIII,* ed. by L. Di Benedetto, Bari, Laterza, 1941 and the *Poemetti del Duecento,* ed. by G. Petronio, Torino, UTET, 1951. A limited selection of all the works that are considered here is included in my *Poemetti minori del Trecento,* Milano-Napoli, Ricciardi 1952 (further bibliographical information can be found in my *Trecento* published by Vallardi). The book by A. Thomas *Francesco da Barberino et la littérature provençale en Italie au moyen âge,* Paris, Thorin, 1883 is still an important study.

A modern, reliable edition of the writer in question is still not available; but one may mention, because of the usefulness of its critical contents, *L'Acerba,* with an improved text and interpreted for the first time with the aid of all the author's works and their sources by A. Crespi, Ascoli Piceno, Cesari, 1927.

For the other texts see: *Il Dottrinale,* by Jacopo Alighieri, ed. by G. Crocioni, Città di Castello, Lapi, 1895; *Il Ristorato,* ed. by L. Razzolini, Firenze, Tipografia galileiana, 1847; *Il Dittamondo e le Rime,* by Fazio degli Uberti, ed. by G. Corsi, Bari, Laterza, 1952; *La Pietosa Fonte,* ed. by E. Zambrini, Bologna, Romagnoli, 1874; *Il Quadriregio* by F. Frezzi, ed. by E. Filippini, Bari, Laterza, 1914; the *Fimerodia* and the *Leandreide* in the imposing collection by C. Del Balzo, *Poesie di mille autori intorno a Dante Alighieri raccolte e ordinate cronologicamente,* Roma, Forzani, 1889–1891. Concerning the anon. *Virtù e vizio,* cf. M. Cornacchia and F. Pellegrini, *Di un ignoto poema d'imitazione dantesca,* in "Propugnatore", N.S., I (1888) pp. 185–225; II (1889) pp. 335–86. Fundamental is the ample and scholarly study by L.F. Benedetto *Il Roman de la Rose e la letteratura italiana,* Halle, Niemeyer, 1910.

A scarcely organized but abundant material concerning Dante's fourteenth century is collected in the volume by E. Cavallari, *La fortuna di Dante nel Trecento,* Firenze, Perrella, 1921; a synthetic view is in V. Rossi's *Scritti di critica letteraria,* Firenze, Sansoni, 1930, I, pp. 293–332. On the debate concerning Dante's orthodoxy see N. Matteini, *Il più antico oppositore politico di Dante; Guido Vernani da Rimini,* Padova, Cedam, 1958. The essential bibliography of the editions of the oldest commentaries can be found in my annotated edition of the *Commedia,* Milano-Napoli, Ricciardi, 1957, pp. 1206 and ff. On this topic consult also: K Hegel, *Ueber den historischen Werth der älteren Dante-Commentare,* Leipzig, 1878, and L. Rocca, *Di alcuni commenti della Divina Commedia composti nei primi vent'anni dopo la morte di Dante,* Firenze, Sansoni, 1891. Among the most recent studies, one should remember: M. Barbi, *Problemi della critica dantesca,* I, Firenze, Sansoni, 1934, pp. 359–93, 492–553; II, ibid. 1941, pp. 435–70; F Schmidt-Knatz, *Jacopo della Lana und sein Commedia-Kommentar,* in "Deutsches Dante-Jahrbuch", XII (1930), pp. 1–40; J.P. Bowden, *An Analysis of Pietro Alighieri's Commentary on the Divine Comedy,* New York, 1951; L.R. Rossi, *Dante and the poetic tradition in the commentary of Benvenuto da Imola,* in "Italica", XXXII (1955), pp. 215–23; D. Minuto, *Note sul valore letterario del Commentum di Benvenuto da Imola,* in "Aevum", XXXI (1957), pp. 449–64; and, above all, F. Mazzoni, *Iacopo Alighieri e Graziolo Bambagliuoli,* in "Studi danteschi", XXIX (1951), pp. 157–202; *Guido da Pisa interprete di Dante e la sua fortuna presso il Boccaccio,* ibid. XXXV (1958), pp. 29–128.

Concerning the early prehumanistic groups in Veneto and Aemilia see: L. Padrin, *Lupati de Lupatis, Bovetini de Bovetinis, Albertini Mussati necnon Iamboni Andreae de Favafuschis Carmina,* Padova, 1887; C. Foligno and R. Sabbadini, *Epistole inedite di Lovato de' Lovati e d'altri a lui,* in "Studi medievali", II (1906–1907), pp. 37 and ff.; F. Novati, *Nuovi aneddoti sul cenacolo letterario padovano del primissimo Trecento,* in *Scritti storici in memoria di Giovanni Monticolo,* Padova, Editrice universitaria, 1922, pp. 169–92; *Nuovi studi su A. Mussato,* in "Giorn. stor. d. lett. ital.", VI (1885), pp. 177–200; VII (1886), pp. 1–47; M. Minoia, *Della vita e delle opere di A. Mussato,* Roma, Forzani, 1884; A. Zardo, *A. Mussato, Studio storico e letterario,* Padova, Draghi, 1884; M.T. Dazzi, *L'"Ecerinide," di A. Mussato,* in "Giorn. stor. d. lett. ital." LXXVIII (1921), pp. 241–89; *Il Mussato storico,* in "Archivio veneto", LIX (1929), serie V, nn. 11–12, pp. 357–471; G Girardi, *Rolando da Piazzola,* Padova, 1909; G. Billanovich, *"Veterum vestigia vatum" nei carmi dei preumanisti padovani,* in "Italia medievale e umanistica", (1958), pp. 155–243; B.L. Ullmann, *Hieremias de Montagnone and his Citations from Catullus,* in "Classical Philology", V (1910); A Avena, *Guglielmo da Pastrengo e gli inizi dell'umanesimo in Verona,* Verona, Franchini, 1907; C. Marchesi, *Le allegorie ovidiane di Giovanni del Virgilio,* in "Studi romanzi", VI (1909), pp. 85 and ff.; E. Carrara, *Il "Diaffonus" di Giovanni del Virgilio",* *in* "Atti e memorie soc. storia patria Romagne", IV, XV series (1925), pp. 1 ff.; F. Ghisalberti, *Giovanni del Virgilio espositore delle Metamorfosi"*, in "Giornale dantesco", Annuario, IV (1933); M. Laue, *Ferreto von Vicenza, seine Dichtungen und sein Geschichtwerk*, Halle, Niemeyer, 1884; C. Cipolla, *Studi su Ferreto dei Ferreti*, in "Giorn. stor. d. letter. ital.", VI, (1885), pp. 53–112. Concerning the *Ecerinide* we have the edition of L. Padrin, with an introductory study by G. Carducci, Bologna, Zanichelli, 1900 (see also the translation by M.T. Dazzi, Città di Castello, Lapi, 1914; Ferreti's work were published and edited by C. Cipolla, Roma, Istituto storico italiano, 1908–1920, in "Fonti per la storia d'Italia". On Mussato's discussion in defense of poetry consult: A. Galletti, *La "ragione poetica" di A. Mussato, ed i poeti-teologi*, in *Scritti varii in onore di R. Reiner*, Torino, Bocca, 1912, pp. 331–59; E.R. Curtius, *Europäische Literatur und lateinisches Mittelalter*, Bern, Francke, 1948; G. Vinay, *Studi sul Mussato, I: Il Mussato e l'estetica medievale*, in "Giorn. stor. d. letter. ital.", CXXVI (1949), pp. 113–59; A. Buck, *Italienische Dichtungslehren vom Mittelalter bis zum Ausgang der Renaissance*, Tübingen, 1952; and on the entire development of the discussion on the Trecento and Quattrocento see: E. Garin, *Le favole antiche*, now in *"Medioevo e Rinascimento*, Bari, Adriatica editrice, 1954, pp. 67–9; and also: F. Tateo, *"Retorica" e "poesia" fra Medioevo e Rinascimento*, Bari, Adriatica editrice, 1960. Finally, consider also the study, still important from several standpoints, by K. Vossler, *Poetische Theorien in der italienischen Frührenaissance*, Berlin, Felber, 1900.

For the meaning of the Trecento's humanism, one should consult, above all, G. Billanovich, *I primi umanisti e le tradizioni dei classici latini*, Friburgo, Edizioni Universitarie, 1953. See also: M. Vattasso, *Del Petrarca e di alcuni suoi amici*, Roma, Tipografia Vaticana, 1904; P. Guidotti, *Un amico del Petrarca e del Boccaccio: Zanobi da Strada, poeta laureato*, in "Arch. stor. ital., LXXXVIII (1930), vol. XIII, 1, pp. 249–93; E.G Léonard, *Un ami de Pétrarque, sénéchal de Provence: Giovanni Barrili*, in the volume *Pétrarque. Mélanges de littérature et d'histoire*, Paris, Leroux, 1928, pp. 109–42; R. Sabbadini, *Giovanni da Ravenna*, Como, Ostinelli, 1924; P. Zambeccari, *Epistolario*, ed. by L. Frati, Roma, Istituto storico italiano, 1929; L. Lazzarini, *Paolo de Bernardo e i primordi dell'umanesimo in Venezia*, Genève, Olschki, 1930. For other bibliographical information consult my book, *Trecento*, cit. pp. 164–6.

Chapter Four

Besides the old bibliographies (G.J. Ferrazzi, *Bibliografia petrarchesca*, Bassano, Pozzato, 1887; E. Calvi, *Bibliografia analitica petrarchesca, 1877–1904 in continuazione a quella del Ferrazzi*, Roma, Loescher, 1904) and the catalogues of important collections (A. Hortis, *Catalogo delle opere di F. Petrarca esistenti nella Petrarchesca*

Rossettiana, Trieste, Apollonio e Caprin, 1874; L. Suttina, *Bibliografia delle opere a stampa intorno a F. Petrarca, esistenti nella Biblioteca Petrarchesca Rossettiana,* Trieste, issued by the Comune, 1908; L. Olschki, *Collection pétrarquesque formée, possédée et décrite à l'occasion du sixième centenaire de Pétrarque,* in "Bibliofilia", VI, 1904–1905, pp. 19 and ff. 67 and ff., 155 and ff., 331 and ff.; M. Fowler, *Catalogue of the Petrarch Collection bequeathed by W. Fiske,* Cornell University Library, Oxford University Press, 1916) as well as the general lists of the history of the Italian literature. It is useful, above all, to refer to the special bibliographies of A. Della Torre, (1904) in "Archivio storico italiano"; E. Carrara, (1906), C. Calcaterra (1928–1929) and, at present, of E. Bonora in the "Giorn. stor. d. lett. ital." and to the diligent bulletin of "Studi petrarcheschi" (Bologna, from 1948 on). An annotated bibliographical selection may be found in my book *Trecento,* pp. 267–79; at the bottom of the entries *Petrarca* by E. Carrara, in *Enciclopedia italiana, XXVII, pp. 8–23* (printed later in a more ample form, Roma, Istituto della Enciclopedia italiana, 1937), and by P.G. Ricci, in *Enciclopedia cattolica,* IX, coll. 1288–99, and in E.H. Wilkins, *An introductory Petrarch Bibliography,* In "Philological Quarterly", XXVII (1948), pp. 27–36; C. Calcaterra, *Il Petrarca e il petrarchismo,* in the volume *Questioni e correnti di storia letteraria,* Milano, Marzorati, 1949. Of importance is the survey of the history of criticism by E. Bonora, *Lineamenti di storia della critica petrarchesca,* for *I classici italiani nella storia della critica,* by W. Binni, I, Firenze, La Nuova Italia, 1954, pp. 95–166; see also H. Baron, *The Evolution of Petrarch's Thought; Reflections on the State of Petrarch's Studies,* in "Bibliothèque d'Humanisme et Renaissance". XXIV (1962), pp. 7–41.

The most up-to-date comprehensive monograph on the man and the writer is by U. Bosco, *Francesco Petrarca,* Bari, Laterza, 1961, along which we mention the fundamental collection of studies arranged by C. Calcaterra, *Nella selva del Petrarca.* Bologna, Cappelli, 1942, as well as E. Carrara, *Studi petrarcheschi.* Torino, Bottega d'Erasmo, 1959.

For the biographical reconstruction, one should begin, at present, from the very reliable studies of E.H. Wilkins, *Studies in the Life and Works of Petrarch,* Cambridge, Mass., The Medieval Academy of America, 1955; *Petrarch's eight years in Milan,* ibid. 1958; *Petrarch's Later Years, ibid. 1959;* Life of Petrarch, Chicago, The University of Chicago Press, 1961. Still extremely useful is the analytical research of A. Foresti, *Aneddoti della vita di Francesco Petrarca,* Brescia, Vannini, 1928. One should not neglect the data offered by the ancient biographers (*Le vite di Dante, Petrarca e Boccaccio scritte fino al secolo XVI,* collected by A. Solerti, Milano, Vallardi, 1904), the fundamental texts of the erudition in the eighteenth century (J.F.de Sade, *Mémoires pour la vie de F. Pétrarque tiré de ses oeuvres et des auteurs contempo-rains,* Amsterdam, Arskée et Mercus, 1764–1767; G.B. Baldelli-Boni, *Del Petrarca e delle sue opere,* Firenze, Poligrafica Fiesolana, 1837) and of the nineteenth century

G. Koerting, *Petrarca's Leben und Werke*, Leipzig, Reisland, 1878; A Bartoli, *Storia della letteratura italiana*, VII, Firenze, Sansoni, 1884).

A critical edition of all the works of the writer from Arezzo is not yet available at present, (the national edition has published, thus far, only six volumes, four with the *Familiari*, one with the *Rerum memorandarum libri*, and one with the *Africa*—that will be indicated at their place). The most useful and practical collections are those of the *Poesie*, by F. Neri, N. Sapegno, E. Bianchi and G. Martellotti, Milano-Napoli, Ricciardi, 1951, and the other one with the *Prose*, ed. by G. Martellotti, E. Carrara, P.G. Ricci, ibid. 1955 (vols 6 and 7 of this collection). However, for some writings it will be necessary to rely on the incorrect printings of the sixteenth century (Venezia 1501 and 1503; Basel 1554 and 1581).

Concerning the main epistolary collection one could use an excellent edition which sheds abundant light on the process of stratification of the ensuing editions: *Le Familiari*, by V. Rossi (for the first three volumes) and by U. Bosco (for the fourth), Firenze, Sansoni, 1933–1942. Of the *Senili*, only a few are found in sufficiently correct texts in the modern anthologies (besides the mentioned *Prose* of the Ricciardi collection, we shall remember the *Lettere autobiografiche* by E. Carrara, Milano, Signorelli, 1928; the *Epistolae selectae*, by A.F. Johnson, Oxford, Clarendon Press, 1923, and *Briefe des F. Petrarca*, by H. Nachold and P. Stern, Berlin, Die Runde, 1931). An incomplete collection can be found in *F. Petrarcae Epistolae de rebus familiaribus et variae* by G. Fracassetti, Firenze, Le Monnier, 1859 (and by the same Fracassetti see the annotated translation of the *Familiari*, Firenze, Le Monnier, 1863–1867 and of the *Senili*, ibid., 1869–1870). An excellent edition of the *Sine nomine* provided by P. Piur, *Petrarcas "Buch ohne Namen" und die päpstliche Kurie. Ein Beitrag zur Geistesgeschichte der Frührenaissance*, Halle, Niemeyer, 1925. For the *Posteritati* we have the accurate reconstruction by E. Carrara, *L'espistola "Posteritati" e la leggenda petrarchesca*, in "Annali dell'Istituto di Magistero del Piemonte", III (1929), pp. 273 ff., reprinted in *Studi petrarcheschi*, cit., p. 3 ff., and the rearranged edition with new criteria by P.G. Ricci in the mentioned *Prose* (cf. "Studi petrarcheschi", VI, 1956, pp. 5–21). In order to loosen the tangle of the chronological issues the very accurate list by E.H. Wilkins, *Petrarch's Correspondence*, Padova, Editrice Antenore, 1960 is useful (in this work the previous contributions of the same author are enclosed: *Modern Discussions of the Dates of Petrarch's Prose Letters*, Chicago, The University of Chicago Press, 1929; *A Tentative Chronological List of Petrarch's Prose Letters*, ibid., 1929; *The Prose Letters of Petrarch; a Manual*, New York, Vanni, 1951). On the literary value of the epistolary collections, cf. M. Marcazzan, *Le "Familiari" del Petrarca*, in "Civiltà moderna", VI (1934), pp. 267–95; N. Sapegno, *Le lettere del Petrarca*, in *Pagine di storia letteraria*, Palermo, Manfredi, 1960, pp. 65–114; G. Pasquali, *Pagine meno stravaganti*,

Firenze, Sansoni, 1935, pp. 177–201; E. Raimondi, *Una pagina satirica delle "Sine nomine"*, in "Studi petrarcheschi", VI (1956), pp. 55–61.

Of the Africa we have the critical text by N. Festa, in the first volume of the national edition, Firenze, Sansoni, 1926 (concerning which see R. Sabbadini, in "Giorn. stor. d. lett. ital.", LXXXIX, 1927, pp. 354–6; A. Gandiglio, ibid., XC, 1927, pp. 289 ff., and XCII, 1928, pp. 203 ff.; E. Carrara, in "Rassegna", XXXVI, 1928, pp. 113–37). Important is the study by G. Martellotti, *Sulla composizione del "De viris" e dell'"Africa"*, in "Annali della Scuola Normale di Pisa", series II, X (1941), pp. 247–62; Furthermore, see also: N. Festa, *Saggio sull' "Africa" del Petrarca*, Palermo-Roma, Sandron, 1926; P.P. Trompeo and G. Martellotti, *Cartaginesi a Roma*, in Trompeo's volume, *La scala del sole*, Roma 1945, pp. 35 ff.

Besides the few texts included in the modern anthologies, for the *Espitolae metricae* and the "extravaganti" poems, we must still use the old collection of the *Poemata minora*, by D. Rossetti, II and III, Milano, Società tipografica dei Classici italiani, 1829–1834. Cf. E. Bianchi, *Le Epistole Metriche del Petrarca*, in "Annali della Scuola Normale di Pisa", series II, IX (1940), pp. 251–66; R. Di Sabatino, *Le epistole metriche a Benedetto XII e Clemente VI*, in "Studi petrarcheschi", VI (1956), pp. 43–54; R. Argenio, *Per un'edizione critica delle Epistole Metriche*, in "Convivium", XXIX (1961), pp. 482–9. For chronology the listing by E.H. Wilkins, The *"Epistolae metricae" of Petrarch; a Manual*, Roma, Edizioni di Storia e Letteratura, 1956; G. Ponte, *Datazione e significato dell'epistola "ad seipsum"*, in "Rassegna", LXV (1961), pp. 453–63.

A. Avena has reprinted the text of the eclogues in its final form from the MS. Vaticano 3358, *Il "Bucolicum carmen" e i suoi commenti inediti*, Padova, Società Cooperativa Tipografica, 1906. Cf. E. Carrara, *I commenti antichi e la cronologia delle Ecloghe petrarchesche*, in "Gior. Stor. d. lett. ital.", XXVIII (1896), pp. 123–53; G. Albini, *La prima Egloga del Petrarca*, in "Atti e Memorie dell'Accademia virgiliana di Mantova", N.S., XIX–XX (1926–1927), pp. 111–24.

G. Billanovich prepared an eccellent critical edition of the *Rerum memorandarum*, Firenze, Sansoni, 1943; we are waiting for the edition of the *De viris* that is being prepared by G. Martellotti (besides the study we mentioned about the *Africa* see also the other important contributions, in "Orientamenti culturali", 1946, pp. 205–15; in "Annali della Scuola Normale di Pisa", 1947, pp. 149 ff.; in "Studi petrarcheschi", II, 1949, pp. 51–99; in "Convivium, 1947, pp. 739 ff.). Meantime one may consult the very defective edition by L. Razzolini, *Le vite degli uomini illustri di F. Petrarca, volgarizzate da Donato degli Albanzani*, Bologna, Romagnoli, 1874–1879; a partial reproduction of the text of the Parisian code 6069, in P. De Nolhac, *Le "De viris illustribus" de Pétrarque*, Paris. Imprimerie nationale. 1890; the three draftings of the *Vita di Scipione*, edited critically by G. Martellotti,

Milano-Napoli, Ricciardi, 1954; as for the *De gestis Caesaris*, the photographic reproduction of the Parisian autograph was prepared by L. Dorez, Paris, Berthaud, 1906; W. Simpson, *A New Codex of Petrarch's De Viris illustribus*, in "Italia medievale e umanistica", III (1960), pp. 267–70).

For the time being, the best text of the *Secretum* is that edited by E. Carrara, in the mentioned *Prose* by Ricciardi. Cf. C Segrè, *Il "Secretum" del Petrarca e le "Confessioni" di S. Agostino*, in *Studi petrarcheschi*, Firenze, Le Monnier, 1911; R. Sabbadini, *Note filologiche sul "Secretum" del Petrarca*, in "Rivista di filologia e d'istruzione classica", XLV (1917; pp. 24–37; G.A. Levi, *Pensiero classico e pensiero cristiano nel "Secretum" e nelle "Familiari" del Petrarca*, in 'Atene e Roma", XXXV (1933), pp. 63–82.

For the *De vita solitaria* the most reliable edition, based on the valuable apograph Vaticano 3357, is the one by G. Martellotti, in the mentioned *Prose*. Cf. B.L. Ullman, *The composition of Petrarch's "De vita solitaria" and the History of the Vatican Manuscript*, in *Miscellanea G. Mercati*, IV, Città del Vaticano, Biblioteca apostolica vaticana, pp. 117–31.

De otio religioso, ed. by G. Rotondi, Città del Vaticano, Biblioteca apostolica vaticana, 1958. Cf. H. Cochin, *Le frère de Pétrarque et le livre "Du repos des religieux"*, Paris, Bouillon, 1903; G. Rotondi, *Le due redazioni del "De otio"*, in "Aevum", IX (1935), pp. 17–77.

An even temporary modern edition of the *De remediis* is not available; the fifteenth century translation by Giovanni da San Miniato, was published with editorial work by C. Stolfi, Bologna, Romagnoli, 1867. Cf. K. Heitmann, *La genesi del "De remediis"*, in "Convivium", N.S., I (1957), pp. 9–30, and *Fortuna und Virtus. Eine Studie zu Petrarcas Lebensweisheit*, Köln-Graz, Böhlau, 1957.

There is a good edition of the *Salmi penitenziali*, ed. by H. Cochin, (*Les psaumes pénitentiaux publiés d'après le manuscrit de la bibliothèque de Lucerne*, Paris, Rouart, 1929). Cf. M. Casali, *Per una più precisa datazione dei "Salmi penitenziali"*, in "Humanitas", X (1955), pp. 697–704; *Imitazione e ispirazione nei "Salmi penitenziali"* in "Studi petrarcheschi", VII (1961), pp. 151–70.

Awaiting the next critical edition by G. Billanovich, one may read the *Itinerarium* in G. Lumbroso's *Memorie italiane del buon tempo antico*, Torino, Loescher, 1889.

Polemic writings: *De sui ipsius et multorum ignorantia*, an edition based on the Vatican autograph 3359, by L.M. Cappelli, Paris, Champion, 1906; *Invectivarum contra medicum libri IV*, published by P.G. Ricci (with Domenico Silvestri's fourteenth century translation into the vernacular), Roma, Edizioni di Storia e Letteratura, 1950; *Invectiva contra quendam magni status hominem sed nullius scientiae aut virtutis*, a cura di P.G. Ricci, Firenze, Le Monnier 1949; *Contra eum qui maledixit Italiae,* by the same critic, in the mentioned *Prose* (and, together with Jean de Hesdin text, by E. Cocchia, in "Atti della R. Accademia di archeologia, lettere e belle arti di Napoli", VII, 1920, pp. 93–201). Cf. P.G. Ricci, *Per il testo e l'interpretazione del "de ignorantia" petrarchesco,* in "Rendiconti dell'Accademia dei Lincei", s. VII, vol. III (1943), pp. 401–8; *Per il testo dell'invettiva petrarchesca "contra quendam innominatum",* in "Studi petrarcheschi:, III, 1950, pp. 37–46; *per il testo della petrarchesca "Apologia contra Gallum",* ibid., IV (1951), pp. 23–35; *La cronologia dell'ultimo certamen petrarchesco,* ibid. IV(1951), pp. 47–57; U. Bosco, *Precisazioni sulle "Invective contra medicum",* ibid., I (1948)), pp. 97–109.

As for the autograph codex of the poems, we have the diplomatic reproduction (*Il Canzoniere di F. Petrarca riprodotto letteralmente dal cod. Vaticano Lat. 3195,* ed. by E. Modigliani, Roma, Società filologica romana, 1904) and the phototype copy ed. by M. Vattasso, Milano, Hoepli, 1906). All the modern printings follow it more or less rigorously up to the most recent and close ones by E. Chiorboli (*Le Rime sparse e i Trionfi,* Bari, Laterza, 1930), and by G. Contini (*Rerum vulgarium fragmenta,* Parigi, Tallone, 1949.) The two most important complete commentaries on the poems collect and discuss the imposing critical production, from the fifteenth century to our days concerning the *Rime:* they are by G. Carducci and S. Ferrari (Firenze, Sansoni, 1899; reprinted in 1957 with a foreword by G. Contini) and by E. Chiorboli (Milano, Trevisini, 1924); with these one may also consult the complete commentaries of G. Rigutini, with additions by M. Scherillo (Milano, Hoepli, 1925), by A. Moschetti (Milano, F. Vallardi, 1912), F. Neri (Torino, UTET, 1952, by C. Muscetta (Torino, Einaudi, 1960) and the other partial ones by N. Scarano, (Livorno, Giusti, 1909), N. Vaccalluzzo (Messina 1950), N. Zingarelli (Firenze, Sansoni, 1927), N. Sapegno (Firenze, La Nuova Italia, 1936), R. Ramat (Milano, Rizzoli, 1957), D. Mattalia (Milano, Hoepli, 1944), etc. The most persuasive research on the various phases of the composition and the internal order of the collection is by E.H. Wilkins, *The Making of the Canzoniere and other Petrarchan Studies,* Roma, Edizioni di Storia e Letteratura, 1951; but it will be useful not to neglect completely the earlier bibliography on the topic: A. Pakscher, *Die Chronologie der Gedischte Petrarcas,* Berlin, Weidmann, 1887; C. Appel, *Zur Entwickelung italienischer Dichtungen Petrarcas,* Halle, Niemeyer, 1891; G.A. Cesareo, *Sulle poesie volgari del Petrarca, nuove ricerche,* Rocca San Casciano, Cappelli, 1898; H. Cochin, *La chronologie du Canzoniere de Pétrarque,* Paris, Bouillon, 1898; E.N. Chiaradia, *La storia del Canzoniere di F. Petrarca,* Bologna, Zanichelli, 1908; G. Melodia, *Studi sulle rime del Petrarca,* Catania, Giannotta, 1909; R.S. Phelps, *The Earlier and Later Forms of Petrarch's "Canzoniere",* Chicago, The University of Chicago Press, 1925; H. Hauvette, *Les poésies lyriques de Pétrarque,* Paris, Editions Littéraires et techniques, 1931.

The most recent phototype reproduction of the ms. Vaticano 3196, an important collection of remaining autographic copies and workbooks containing rhymes that were not included completely in the final edition, was edited by M. Porena (Roma, Bardi, 1941); the best critical edition, with a precise commentary of the variations, is the one by A. Romanò, *Il codice degli abbozzi di F. Petrarca*, Roma, Bardi, 1955 (cf. F. Figurelli, in "Filologia romanza", IV, 1957, pp. 88–109).

Still to be explored almost completely is the area of the "extravagant" rhymes that present very difficult problems of text and authorship: practically useless is the collection by A. Solerti, *Rime disperse di F. Petrarca o a lui attribuite*, Firenze, Sansoni, 1909) concerning which one should see an important essay by E.G. Parodi, now included in the volume *Poeti antichi e moderni*, Firenze, Sansoni, 1923, pp. 143–53); the choices included within very prudent limits mentioned in the edition from Bari were done by E. Chiorboli and by N. Sapegno in the *Poesie* of the Ricciardi collection. Cf. the studies by S. Debenedetti, in "Giorn. stor. d. lett. ital.", LVI (1910), pp. 98–106, and by D. Bianchi, in the miscellany *Studi petrarcheschi*, Arezzo, by the Accademia Petrarca, 1928, pp. 79–86; in "Bibliofilia", XLVII (1945), pp. 60–160; in "Studi petrarcheschi", II (1949), pp. 107–35; V (1952), pp. 13–84; VI (1956), pp. 81–121; and in "Bollettino storico pavese", III (1940), II, pp. 25–72.

Concerning the technique and the language of the rhymes, the fundamental studies are by G. Contini, *Saggio di un commento alle correzioni del Petrarca volgare*, Firenze, Sansoni, 1943, and *La lingua del Petrarca*, in the miscellany *Il Trecento*, ibid. 1953. See fourthermore G. De Robertis, *Valore del Petrarca*, in *Studi*, Firenze, Le Monnier, 1944, pp. 32–47; M. Fubini, *Il Petrarca artefice*, in *Studi sulla letteratura del Rinascimento*, Firenze, Sansoni, 1947, pp. 1–12; *La rima del Petrarca*, in "Studi petrarcheschi", VII (1961), pp. 135–45; A. Noferi, *L'esperienza poetica del Petrarca*, Firenze, Sansoni, 1942; and D. Alonzo, *La poesia del Petrarca e il petrarchismo*, in "Studi petrarcheschi", VII (1961), pp. 73–120.

Valuable documents for the historical and literary criticism are essentially: U. Foscolo, *Saggi sul Petrarca* (1823), now in *Saggi e discorsi critici*, by C. Foligno, Firenze, Le Monnier, 1953; F. De Sanctis, *Saggio critico sul Petrarca* (1869), by N. Gallo and N. Sapegno, Torino, Einaudi, 1952, or by E. Bonora, Bari, Laterza, 1955; B. Croce, *La poesia del Petrarca*, in *Poesia popolare e poesia d'arte*, Bari, Laterza, 1933 (and by the same the essays included in *Poesia antica e moderna*, ibid. 1943 and in *Conversazioni critiche, Series III*, Bari, Laterza, 1832), A. Momigliano, *L'elegia politica del Petrarca* in *Introduzione ai poeti*, Roma, Tumminelli, 1946; N. Sapegno, *Prefazione al Petrarca*, in the mentioned *Pagine di storia letteraria*, *pp. 53–62*; R. Bacchelli, *Chiose petrarchesche*, in *Saggi critici*, Milano, Mondadori, 1962, pp. 739–841. besides the already mentioned studies by Bosco and Contini,

De Robertis, Noferi, and Bigi. Among the recent studies, we shall mention F. Montanari, *Studi sul Canzoniere del Petrarca,* Roma, Studium, 1958; F. Figurelli, in "Studi petrarcheschi", VI (1956), pp. 201–20, and in "Annali dell'Istituto Santa Chiara di Napoli, 1957, pp. 502–607.

An important edition of the Trionfi is that by C. Appel, *Die Triumphe F. Petrarcas in kritischem Texte herausgegeben,* Halle, Niemeyer, 1901, followed by the already mentioned ones by Chiorboli, Neri and Moscetta as well as the commented one by C. Calcaterra, Torino, Utet, 1923. In addition, see R. Weiss, *Un inedito petrarchesco. La redazione sconosciuta di un capitolo del Trionfo della Fama,* Roma, Edizioni di Storia e Letteratura, 1950. Cf. V. Branca, *Per la genesi dei Trionfi,* in "Rinascita", I, (1941), pp. 681–708; G. Billanovich, *Dalla Commedia e dall'Amorosa Visione ai Trionfi,* in "Gior. Stor. d. lett. ital.", CXXIII (1945–46), pp. 1–52; C.F. Goffis, *Originalità dei Trionfi,* Firenze, La Nuova Italia, 1951, and *L'ordinamento del Triumphus Famae,* in "Rassegna", LIX (1955) pp. 446–59. Important for its literary analysis is R. Serra, *Dei "Trionfi" di F. Petrarca,* Bologna. Zanichelli, 1929 (now in *Scritti, Firenze, Le Monnier, 1938, II, pp. 31–146*).

On Petrarch's contribution to the beginning of humanistic philology: P. De Nolhac, *Pétrarque et l'humanisme,* Paris, Champion, 1907; R. Dabbadini, *La scoperta dei codici latini e greci nei secoli XIV e XV,* I, Firenze, Sansoni, 1905; U Bosco, *Il Petrarca e l'umanesimo filologico,* in "Gior. stor. d. lett. ital." CXX, (1943), pp. 65–119, and, above all, G. Billanovich, *Petrarca letterato, I, Lo scrittoio del Petrarca,* Roma, Linee di sviluppo dell'umanesimo petrarchesco Edizioni di Storia e Letteratura, 1947; *Petrarca e Cicerone,* in *Miscellanea G. Mercati,* Città del Vaticano, Biblioteca apostolica vaticana, 1946; *Petrarch and the Textual Tradition of Livy,* in "Journal of Warburg and Courtauld Institutes", XIV (1951), pp. 137–208; *Un nuovo codice della biblioteca di Petrarca: Il San Paolo,* in "Rendiconti dell'Accademia di Napoli", XXVI, (1951), pp. 253–56; *Uno Svetonio della biblioteca del Petrarca,* in "Studi petrarcheschi", VI (1956), pp. 23–33; E. Pellegrini, *Nouveaux manuscrits annotés par Pétrarque à la Bibliothèque Nationale de Paris,* in "Scriptorium". V (1951), pp. 265–78; and again the summary report with other bibliographical data by G. Billanovich, *Petrarca e i classici,* in "Atti del III Congresso dell'Associazione per gli studi di letteratura italiana", Bologna, Edizioni della Commissione per i testi di lingua, 1961, pp. 21–33. Noteworthy are the essays by G. Martellotti, *Linee di sviluppo dell'umanesimo petrarchesco,* in "Studi petrarcheschi", II (1949), pp. 51–80; P.O. Kristeller, *Il Petrarca, l'umanesimo e la scolastica,* in "Lettere italiane", VII (1955), pp. 367–88; Th. Mommsen, *Petrarch's concept of the Dark Ages,* in the volume *Medieval and Renaissance Studies,* Ithaca, Cornell Univ. Press, 1959. On the style of Petrarch's Latin writings see G. Martellotti, *Clausole e ritmi della prosa narrativa del Petrarca,* in "Studi petrarcheschi", IV (1951), pp. 35–46; *Latinità del*

Petrarca, in the "Atti del III Congresso dell'Associazione per gli studi di letteratura italiana", op. cit., pp. 219–30; E. Raimondi, *Ritrattistica petrarchesca*, in the miscellany volume *Dai Dettatori al Novecento*, Torino, S.E.I., 1953, pp. 74–86.

On Petrarch and politics, cf. R. De Mattei, *Il sentimento politico del Petrarca*, Firenze, Sansoni, 1944; as for the ideologies of his time see H. Helbling, *Saeculum Humanum. Ansätze zu einem Versuch über spätmittelalterliches Geschichtsdenken*, Napoli, Istituto italiano per gli studi storici, 1958; G. Pirchan, *Italien und Kaiser Karl IV in der Zeit der zweiten kaiserlichen Romfahrt*, Prag, Deutsche Gesellschaft der Wissenschaften, 1929. See furthermore G. Brizzolara, *Il Petrarca e Cola di Rienzo*, in "Studi storici", VIII (1899), pp. 239–51, 423–63; *Ancora Cola di Rienzo e F. Petrarca, ibid. XII (1903), pp. 353–411*; M.E. Cosenza, *F. Petrarca and the Revolution of Cola di Rienzo*, Chicago, The Univ. of Chicago Press, 1913; F. Novati, *Il Petrarca ed i Visconti*, in the volume *F. Petrarca e la Lombardia*, Milano, Hoepli, 1904; G. Petronio, *Storicità della lirica politica del Petrarca*, in "Studi petrarcheschi", VII (1961), pp. 247–64.

On Petrarch's religion see: G. Gerosa, *L'umanesimo agostiniano del Petrarca*, Torino, S.E.I., 1927; C. Calcaterra, *S. Agostino nelle opere di Dante e del Petrarca*, in *Nella selva del Petrarca*, cit, pp. 247–360; U. Mariani, *Il Petrarca e gli agostiniani*, Roma, Edizioni di Storia e Letteratura, 1946; E. van Moé, *Les Ermites de Saint-Augustin amis de Pétrarque*, in "Mélanges d'archéologie et d'histoire" of the French School of Rome, XLVI (1929), pp. 258–80; K. Heitmann, *Augustins lehre in Petrarcas "Secretum"*, in "Bibliothèque d'Humanisme et Renaissance", XXII (1960), pp. 34–53; P. Courcelle, *Pétrarque entre Saint-Augustin et les Augustins du XIV siècle*, in "Atti del III Congresso dell'Associazione per gli studi di letteratura italiana', cit., pp. 51–71.

Chapter Five

For detailed information it will be necessary to consult the lists of F. Zambrini and A. Bacchi della Lega, *Bibliografia boccaccesca; serie delle edizioni delle opere di Giovanni Boccaccio latine, volgari, tradotte e trasformate*, Bologna, Romagnoli, 1875, and of G. Traversari, *Bibliografia boccaccesca. Scritti intorno al Boccaccio e alla fortuna delle sue opere*, Città di Castello, Lapi, 1907. A commented selection can be found in the bibliography of my *Trecento*, cit., pp. 395–405; and also in L. Caretti, *Guida al Boccaccio*, in "Studi urbinati", XXVI, 1952, n. 2, p. 87 ff., as well as in V. Branca's *Boccaccio*, in the miscellany *I maggiori*, Milano, Marzorati, 1956, pp. 185–244. For the most recent studies the reviews by F. Ageno, in the "Giorn. stor. d. letter. ital.", CXXX (1954), pp. 227–38; CXXXV (1958), pp. 116–26 are useful. Concerning the aspects of the critical opinions, one may consult: V. Branca, *Linee di una storia della critica al "Decameron", con bibliografia boccaccesca*, Milano=Roma, Società editrice Dante Alighieri, 1939, and the survey by G. Petronio, in the *Classici italiani nella storia della critica*, ed. by W. Binni, I, Firenze, La Nuova Italia, 1954, pp. 167–228.

The reconstruction of the biography, after the old monographs by G.B. Baldelli-Boni, Firenze, Ciardetti, 1906; by M. Landau, Stuttgart 1877; by G. Körting, Leipzig, Reisland, 1880; by A. Wesselofsky, Pietroburgo 1893–1894, was developed essentially through the analysis and the interpretation of the ideas of concealed confessions contained in the minor works. Noticeable contributions were given in this direction by V. Crescini, *Contributo agli studi sul Boccaccio*, Torino, Loescher, 1887; A. della Torre, *La giovinezza di Giovanni Boccaccio*, Città di Castello, Lapi, 1905; F. Torraca, *Per la biografia di Giovanni Boccaccio*, Milano-Roma-Napoli, Albrighi e Segati, 1912 at the end of this find a limpid and lively monographic work by G. Hauvette, *Boccace, Étude biographique et littéraire*, Paris, Colin, 1914. The criticism of this method of reconstruction, that is too trustingly conjectural, was begun by S. Battaglia, *Elementi autobiografici nell'arte del Boccaccio*, in "La Cultura", IX (1930), pp. 241 ff. and developed by G. Billanovich, *Restauri boccacceschi*, Roma, Edizioni di Storia e Letteratura, 1945.

Editions with an ample critical apparatus are available at present only for some of the minor works: *Rime*, by A.F. Massera, Bologna, Romagnoli-Dell'Acqua, 1914; *Teseida*, by S. Battaglia, Firenze, Sansoni, 1938; *Amorosa Visione*, by V. Branca, Firenze, Sansoni, 1945. A comprehensive edition of all the vernacular texts and of some in Latin, reconstructed on a somewhat partial comparison of the manuscripts, is to be found in "Scrittori d'Italia" by Laterza (*Filocolo*, by S. Battaglia, Bari, 1938; *Filostrato* and *Ninfale fiesolano*, by V. Pernicone, 1937; *Teseida*, by G. Roncaglia, 1941; *Fiammetta*, by V. Pernicone, 1939; *Ameto, Corbaccio e Lettere*, by N. Bruscoli, 1940; *Rime, Amorosa Visione* e *Caccia di Diana*, by V. Branca, 1939; *Commento alla Commedia e altri scritti intorno a Dante*, by D. Guerri, 1918; *Opere latine minori*, by A.F. Massera, 1928; *Genealogie deorum gentilium*, by V. Romano, 1951; *Decameron*, by A.F. Massera, 1927, then in C.S. Singleton, 1955.) Another edition of all the works is being prepared under the direction of V. Branca in the "Classici Mondadori". For the time being, the most reliable edition of the definitive text of the masterpiece is the *Decameron* by V. Branca, Firenze, Le Monnier, 1960, with an ample commentary. One should not disregard, however, the other commented editions, by G. Petronio, (Torino, Einaudi, 1950), and by E. Bianchi (with the addition of the *Filocolo, Ameto,* and *Fiammetta*, Salinari, Milano-Napoli, Ricciardi, 1952), by N. Sapegno (Torino, Utet, 1956), by M. Marti (Milano, Rizzoli, 1958). An annotated reprint of the *Rime* and the *Caccia di Diana*, was done by V. Branca (Padova, Liviana editrice, 1958). A more accurate edition of the *Elegia di Madonna Fiammetta* was prepared by F. Ageno and A. Schiaffini (Parigi, Tallone, 1955). For the major part of the works in Latin one must still go to the prints of the fifteenth and sixteenth century; but some works are reproduced in the volume of O. Hecker, *Boccaccio-Funde,* Braunschweig, Westermann, 1902. The most important preparatory philological writings will be mentioned at the proper place, together with the bibliography of the individual works; but let us remember, at this time, V. Branca, *Tradizione delle opere giovanili del Boccaccio,* Roma, Edizioni di Storia e Letteratura, 1958.

For the *Filocolo* it will be useful to read: B. Zumbini, *Il "Filocopo" del Boccaccio,* Firenze, Le Monnier, 1879; P. Rajna, *L'Episodio delle questioni d'amore nel Filocolo del Boccaccio,* in "Romania", (1902), pp. 28 ff; and above all (but the reference concerns the understanding of the entire period of the writer's creative activity) S. Battaglia, *Schemi lirici nell'arte del Boccaccio,* in "Archivum romanicum", XIX (1935), pp. 61–78. The question of the sources, besides its connection with the legend of Florio and Biancofiore in the romance literatures (one will have to consult the editions of the French poem by Reinhold and Lorenz, and that of the Italian ballad edited by Crescini), must be examined also in reference with the other areas of the medieval culture, among which the fortune of Ovid's myths. Cf. now A.E. Quaglio, *Tra fonti e testo del "Filocolo",* in "Giorn. stor. d. lett. ital.", CXXXIX (1962), pp. 321–69, 513–40.

Concerning the *Filostrato*: P. Savj-Lopez, *Il "Filostrato" di Giovanni Boccaccio,* in "Romania", XXVII (1898), pp. 442 ff.; V. Pernicone, *Il "Filostrato" di G. Boccaccio,* in "Studi di filologia italiana", II (1929), pp. 77–128; *I manoscritti del "Filostrato" di G. Boccaccio,* ibid. V (1938), pp. 41–82; V. Branca, *Il cantare trecentesco e il Boccaccio del "Filostrato" e del "Teseida",* Firenze, Sansoni, 1936.

On the *Teseida:* P. Savj-Lopez, *Sulle fonti della "Teseida",* in "Giorn. stor. d. lett. ital.", XXXVI (1900), pp. 57 ff., and *Storie tebane in Italia,* Bergamo, Istituto italiano d'arti grafiche, 1905; J.W. Whitfield, *Boccaccio and Fiammetta in the Teseide,* in "Modern Language Review, XXXIII (1938); G. Vandelli, *Un autografo della "Teseide",* in "Studi di filologia italiana", II (1929), pp. 5–76; E. Follieri, *I commenti al Teseida del Boccaccio e un codice corsiniano,* in "Atti dell'Accademia dei Lincei", series VIII, vol. XI (1956), pp. 351–7; A. Limentani, *Tendenze della prosa del Boccaccio ai margini del Teseida,* in "Gior. stor. d. lett. ital.", CXXXV (1958), pp. 524–51.

On the *Rime*: H. Hauvette, *Les poésies lyriques de Boccace,* in "Bulletin italien", XVI (1916), pp. 10–26, 57–70; G. Silber, *The influence of Dante and Petrarch on certain of Boccaccio's Lyrics,* Menasha, Wisc., 1940; and in particular the introduction and the notes of Branca in the mentioned Paduan edition of the poems.

On the writings of the Florentine period see: G. De Robertis, *L'Ameto e La Fiammetta,* in *Studi,* Firenze, Le Monnier, 1944; V. Branca L'*"Amorosa Visione",* in "Annali della Scuola Normale di Pisa", XI (1942), pp. 20–47; D. Rastelli, L'*Elegia di Fiammetta,* in "Studia Ghisleriana", I (1950), pp. 151–74, and in "Lettere italiane", III (1951), pp. 85–98; A.E. Quaglio, *Per il testo della Fiammetta,* in "Studi di filologia italiana", XV (1957) pp. 5–206, and *Le chiose all'Elegia di Madonna Fiammetta*, Padova, Cedam, 1957; F. Ageno, *Per il testo della Fiammetta*, in "Lettere italiane", IV (1954), pp. 152–64; D. Rastelli, *Pagine sul Ninfale fiesolano*, in "Saggi di umanismo cristiano", Pavia, Collegio Borromeo, n. 2, 1951, and *"Notizie storiche e bibliografiche sulla composizione e sulla fortuna dell'"Elegia di Fiammetta" e del "Ninfale fiesolano" di G. Boccaccio*, in "Annali della Biblioteca di Cremona", vol. iv (1951), fasc. 2 (Cremona, Biblioteca civica, 1952); H. Hauvette, *Une confession de Boccace, "Il Corbaccio*, in "Bulletin italien" I (1901), pp. 3–21; T. Nurmela, *Manuscrits et édition du Corbaccio*, in "Neuphilologische Mitteilungen" of Helsinki, LIV (1953); G.J. Lopriore, *Il Corbaccio.* in "Rassegna della letteratura italiana", VI (1956), pp. 483–9; A. Rossi, *Proposta per un titolo del Boccaccio: il Corbaccio*, in "Studi di filologia italiana, XX (1962), pp. 383–90.

On the Dante studies: O. Zenatti, *Dante e Firenze. Prose antiche*, Firenze, Sansoni, 1903; M. Barbi, *Qual'è la seconda redazione del "Trattatello in laude di Dante"?*, in "Miscellanea storica della Valdelsa", XXI (1913), pp. 101–41; G. Vandelli, *Giovanni Boccaccio editore di Dante*, in "Atti della R. Accademia della Crusca", 1921–1922, pp. 19 ff.; D. Guerri, *Il commento del Boccaccio a Dante*, Bari, Laterza, 1926; G.J. Lopriore, *Le due redazioni del Trattatello*, in "Studi mediolatini e volgari", III (1955), pp. 35–60; G. Padoan, *Per una nuova edizione del Commento*, in "Studi danteschi", XXXV (1958), pp. 129–249, and *L'ultima opera di G. Boccaccio: le Esposizioni sopra il Dante*, Padova, Cedam, 1959.

For Boccaccio's Latin writings, besides the mentioned work by O. Hecker, A. Hortis, *Studi sulle opere latine di Giovanni Boccaccio*, Trieste, Libreria Dase, 1879; H. Hauvette, *Recherches sur le "De casibus" de Boccace*, Paris, Allan, 1901 (taken from the miscellany *Entre camarades*, pp. 271 ff; L. Torretta, see *Il Liber de claris mulieribus*, in "Gior. stor. d. lett. ital." XXXIX (1902), pp. 252 ff.; XI (1903), pp. 35 ff; G. Traversari, *Appunti sulle redazioni del "De claris mulieribus di Giovanni Boccaccio*, in *Miscellanea di studi critici in onore di Guido Mazzoni*, Firenze, Tipografia Galileiana, 1907, I, pp. 225 ff; G. Martellotti, *Le due redazioni delle "Genealogie" del Boccaccio*, Roma, Edizioni di Storia e Letteratura", 1951; E. Garin, *Le favole antiche*, in *Medioevo e Rinascimento*, Bari, Laterza, 1954; F. Tateo, *"Retorica" e "poetica" fra Medioevo e Rinascimento*, Bari, Adriatica editrice, 1960.

Concerning the issue of the text of the *Decameron:* M. Barbi, *Sul testo del Decameron* (1927), in *La nuova filologia e l'edizione dei nostri scrittori*, Firenze, Sansoni, 1938; M. Sampoli Simonelli, *Il Decameron. Problemi e discussioni di critica testuale*, in "Annali della Scuola Normale di Pisa, XVIII (1949), pp. 129–72); V. Branca, *Per il testo del Decameron*, in "Studi di filologia italiana", VIII (1950), pp. 29–143, and XI (1953), pp. 163–243; also F. Ageno, in "Giorn. stor. d. lett. ital.", CXXXI (1954), pp. 227–48; N. Sapegno, ibid., CXXXIII (1956), pp. 48–66; A.E. Quaglio, in "Paideia'", X (1955), pp. 449–72; N. Vianello, in "Convivium", VI

(1956), pp. 735–42, and VII (1957), pp. 738–42; V. Romano, in "Belfagor"", XII (1957), pp. 303–12; P.G. Ricci, in "Rinascimento", VIII (1957), pp. 159–76).

For the interpretation and critical evaluation of Boccaccio's masterpiece besides the numerous total or partial commentaries, and the studies on its sources, (M. Landau, *Die Quellen des Dekameron*, Stuttgart, Scheible, 1884; A. Collingwood Lee, *The Decameron; its Sources and Analogues*, London, Dutt, 1909; L. Di Francia, *Alcune novelle del Decameron illustrate nelle fonti*, in "Giorn. stor. d. lett. ital.", XLIV, 1904, pp. 1 ff., and XLIX, 1907, pp. 201 ff; G. Gröber, *Ueber die Quellen von Boccaccios Dekameron*, Strassburg, Heitz, 1913), and besides the classical writings by Foscolo, De Sanctis, Settembrini, Carducci, consult also: C Trabalza, *Studi sul Boccaccio*, Città di Castello, Lapi, 1906; E.G. Parodi, *Osservazioni sul "cursus" nelle opere latine e volgari del Boccaccio*, in *Lingua e letteratura*, ed. by G. Folena, Venezia, Neri-Pozza, 1957, II, pp. 480–92 (ibid. also the study on La cultura e lo stile del Boccaccio, pp. 470–9); U. Bosco, *Il Decameron*, Rieti, Bibliotheca Editrice, 1929; M. Bonfantini, *Boccaccio e il "Decamerone"*, in "Pegaso", II (1930), Part II, pp. 13–28; B. Croce, *Poesia popolare e poesia d'arte*, Bari, Laterza, 1933; G. Petronio, Il Decameron, *Bari, Laterza, 1935; F. Neri*, Storia e poesia, *Torino, Gambino, 1936; L. Russo*, Ritratti e disegni storici, III, Bari, Laterza, 1951, and *Letture critiche del Decameron*, ibid. 1956; E. De' Negri, *The Legendary Style of the "Decameron"*, The Romanic Review", XLIII (1952), pp. 166–89; G. Di Pino, *La polemica del Boccaccio*, Firenze, Vallecchi, 1953; F. Tateo, *Il realismo del Decameron nella storia della critica*, in "Dialoghi", X (1957), pp. 18–36; V. Branca, *Boccaccio medievale*, Firenze, Sansoni, 1956; G. Getto, *Vita di forme e forme di vita nel Decameron*, Torino, Petrini, 1958; G. Petronio, *La posizione del Decameron*, in "Rassegna della letteratura italiana", VII (1957), pp. 189–207; N. Sapegno, *Prefazione al Boccaccio*, in *Pagine di storia letteraria*, Palermo, Manfredi, 1960, pp. 117–32; L. Malagoli, *Decameron e primo Boccaccio*, Pisa, Nistri-Lischi, 1961.

Chapter Six

For an ample choice of texts and for the essential information on chroniclers, treatise writers, narrators, and translators into the vernacular, we refer the reader to the two volumes of the *Prosatori minori del Trecento*, that form the twelfth book of this collection (the first volume concerning the *Scrittori di religione*, by G. De Luca was published in 1954; the second volume, that will include chroniclers, moralists, etc., by G. Aquilecchia and A. Canova, is being printed.

For the chroniclers, furthermore, see I. Del Lungo, *Dino Compagni e la sua Cronica* Firenze, Le Monnier, 1879–1887, 3 volumes in 4 tomes (in the second volume, third tome, find the text of the *Cronica*, republished by Del Lungo himself in *Rerum italicarum scriptores,* Città di Castello, Lapi, 1913–1916, and, in a minor edition, Firenze, Le Monnier, 1889); *Storia esterna, vicende, avventure d'un piccol libro de' tempi di Dante,* Milano-Roma, Società editrice "Dante Alighieri, 1917–1918- *Cronache di Giovanni, Matteo e Filippo Villani,* Firenze, Magheri, 1823, and 1825–1826 (other editions: ibid. Coen, 1844, and 1846; Trieste, Lloyd, 1857–1858)- *Storie pistoiesi,* ed. by S.A. Barbi, Città di Castello, Lapi, 1914 (nei *Rerum italicarum scriptores*).—*Cronica fiorentina di Marchionne di Coppo Stefani,* ed. by N. Rodolico, ibid. 1903- *La vita di Cola di Rienzo,* by A.M. Ghisalberti, Firenze, Olschki, 1028, by A. Frugoni, Firenze, Le Monnier, 1957; F.A. Ugolini, *La prosa degli "Historiae romanae fragmenta" e della cosiddetta "Vita di Cola di Rienzo",* in "Archivio della R. Deputazione romana di storia patria', LVIII (1935), pp. 1–68; G. Contini, *Invito a un capolavoro,* in "Letteratura", IV (1940), pp. 3–6—*La Cronica domestica di messer Donato Velluti,* by I. Del Lungo and G. Volpi, Firenze, Sansoni, 1914.—*Libro d'oltremare di fra Niccolò da Poggibonsi,* by A. Bacchi della Lega, Bologna, Romagnoli, 1881, *Viaggi in Terra Santa di L. Frescobaldi e d'altri del secolo XIV,* by C. Garciolli, Firenze, Barbera, 1862 (reprinted by C. Angelini, Firenze, Le Monnier, 1944). It is appropriate to mention at least here, the interesting *Libro di buoni costumi,* that is partly e domestic diary and a collection of sayings and proverbs by Paolo da Certaldo (ed. by S. Morpurgo, Firenze, Le Monnier, 1921, and reproduced by A. Schiaffini, ibid. 1945).—*Cronisti del Trecento,* by R. Palmarocchi, Milano, Rizzoli, 1935.

Concerning religious literature, refering the reader to the information supplied by De Luca in the mentioned anthological collection, one should at least remember that the book by G. Petrocchi, *Ascesi e mistica trecentesca,* Firenze, Le Monnier, 1957, considers almost all the most important representatives of this section of our survey. See also V. Branca, *Note sulla letteratura religiosa del trecento,* in "La Nuova Italia", X (1939) pp. 198–212; N. Sapegno, *La letteratura religiosa del Due e del Trecento e la critica moderna,* in "Studi cateriniani. XIV, (1937), pp. 63–80.—Concerning the editions of the sermons of Fra Giordano see the useful work by S. Pasquali, *Giordano da Pisa, Tradizione manoscritta e cronologica delle prediche,* Roma, Gismondi, 1955, to which one may add M. Pecoraro, *Giordano da Pisa e altri testi religiosi del cod. 1381 dell'Università di Padova,* in "Lettere italiane", VII (1955), pp. 209–10. There is no critical edition of the *Specchio* by Passavanti. The most recent reprint is that by M. Lenardon, Firenze, Libreria editrice fiorentina, 1925. See A. Monteverdi, *Gli "esempi" di Iacopo Passavanti,* in *Studi e saggi sulla letteratura italiana dei primi secoli,* Milano-Napoli, Ricciardi, 1954; G. Getto, *Umanità e stile in Iacopo Passavanti,* Milano, Leonardo, 1943; M. Aurigemma, *Saggio sul Passavanti,* Firenze, Le Monnier, 1957, and, *La fortuna critica dello Specchio di vera penitenza, in Studi in onore di A. Monteverdi,* Modena, Società tipografico-editrice modenese, 1959, I, pp. 48–75. One may consult the edition of the *Vite dei Santi Padri* ed. by B. Sorio and A. Racheli, Trieste, LLoyd, 1858; for the other works by Cavalca one may consult the prints of the 18th and 19th century; for all the abundant hagiographic literature, see *Collezione di leggende inedite scritte nel buon secolo della lingua toscana,* by F. Zambrini, Bologna, Sassi, 1855; *Leggende del secolo XIV,* by I. Del Lungo, Firenze, Barbera, 1863; *Le più belle leggende cristiane tratte da codici e da antiche stampe,* by G. Battelli, Milano, Hoepli, 1924. For the collections of "examples" and "miracles" see *Il libro dei cinquanta miracoli della Vergine,* ed. by E. Levi, Bologna, Romagnoli, 1917; E. Cerulli, *Il libro etiopico dei miracoli di Maria e le sue fonti nelle letterature del Medio Evo latino,* Roma, Bardi, 1943. The ample collection by Duccio di Gano da Pisa included in Florentine and Vatican manuscripts is being prepared by Giuliana Cavalloni.—*Gli Assempri di fra Filippo da Siena,* ed. by A. Marenduzzo, Siena, Nava, 1899 and by P. Misciattelli, ibid. Giuntini e Bentivoglio, 1922—*Storia di fra Michele minorita,* ed by F. Zambrini, Bologna, Romagnoli, 1864; reprinted by F. Flora, Firenze, Le Monnier, 1942.- *Lettere del beato Giovanni Colombini,* ed by A. Bartoli, Lucca, Balatresi, 1856 (reprinted by P. Misciattelli, Firenze, Libreria editrice fiorentina, 1923, and by D. Fantozzi, Lanciano, Carabba, 1925); G. Pardi, *Della vita e degli scritti di G. Colombini,* Siena, Tip. Lazzeri, 1895, and *Il beato G. Colombini,* in "Nuova rivista storica", XI (1927), pp. 286–336.— P. Brocardo, *Gerolamo da Siena,* Torino, S.E.I., 1952.—J. Hijmans-Tromp, *Vita e opere di Agnolo Torini,* Leiden, Universitaire Pers, 1957. Only the first volume was published of the *Epistolario di S. Caterina da Siena, a* critical edition by E. Dupré-Theseider (Roma, Istituto storico italiano, 1940); for the remainder one should consult the *Lettere,* ed. by L. Ferretti, Siena, 1918–1930; as for the *Libro della Divina Dottrina,* see the edition by M. Fiorilli and S. Caramella, Bari, Laterza, 1928. For an initial direction in the consultations, see L. Zanini, *Bibliografia analitica di S. Caterina,* in "Miscellanea del centro di studi medievali", series I (1955), pp. 325–74; on the saint's life, R. Fawtier, *S. te Catherine de Sienne. Essai de critique des sources,* Paris, De Boccard, 1821–1930; on culture, A. Grion, *S. Caterina da Siena, Dottrina e fonti,* Brescia, Morcelliana, 1953; G. D'Urso, *Il pensiero di S. Caterina e le sue fonti,* in "Sapienza", VII (1954), pp. 335–88; on language and style, G. Getto, *Saggio letterario su S. Caterina da Siena,* Firenze, Sansoni, 1939. A good anthology of translated and original texts can be found in *Mistici del Duecento e del Trecento,* ed. by A. Levasti, Milano, Rizzoli, 1935. For the *Fioretti di S. Francesco,* the best recent editions are those by B. Bughetti, Firenze, Salani, 1925, and by M. Casella, ibid. Sansoni, 1926. From the ample bibliography we indicate: B. Bughetti, *Alcune idee fondamentali sui "Fioretti di S. Francesco",* in "Archivum franciscanum historicum", XIX (1926), pp. 321–33; G. Tosi, *La lingua dei Fioretti,* Milano, Messina, Principato, 1938; L. Pellegrini, *I Fioretti del glorioso Messere Santo Francesco e de' suoi frati,* in 'Annali della Scuola

Normale di Pisa", XXI (1952), pp. 131–57, in addition to the important study by G. Petrocchi, in the mentiond book.

For the historical and cultural significance of the translators one should consult, above all, the rich anthology of *Volgarizzamenti del Due e del Trecento,* by C. Segre, Torino, Utet, 1953, with an excellent introduction and ample bibliographical references from which one may refer to the other anthology, edited also by C. Segre and M. Marti, *La prosa del Duecento* (Vol. 3 of the present collection). Important are the studies of F. Maggini, *I primi volgarizzamenti dei classici latini,* Firenze, Le Monnier, 1951; by A. Schiaffini, *Tradizione e poesia nella prosa d'arte italiana dalla latinità medievale a G. Boccaccio,* Roma, Edizioni di Storia e Letteratura, 1943; E.G. Parodi, *I rifacimenti e le traduzioni italiane dell' "Eneide" di Virgilio prima del Rinascimento,* in *"Studi di filologia romanza",* II (1887), pp. 97–358; C. Marchesi, in *Miscellanea di studi critici in onore di G. Mazzoni,* I, Firenze, Tip. Galileiana, 1907, pp. 279–303; in "Memorie dell'Istituto Lombardo", XXIII (1917), pp. 313–42; in "Atene e Roma", XI, (1908), pp. 275–85, etc. Concerning the Sicilian translations into vernacular language of the *Storia di Enea* and of the *Sposizione del Vangelo di San Matteo,* see the editions, respectively, by G. Folena (Palermo, Stab. tip. G. Mori, 1956) and by P. Palumbo (ibid, 1954); on another translation into the vernacular from Valerius Maximus, cf. F.A. Uglini, in "Bollettino del Centro di studi siciliani", I (1953).—*Le Metamorfodi di Ovidio volgarizzate da Arrigo Simintendi,* by C. Basi and C. Guasti, Prato, Guasti, 1846–1850).—*L'Eneide volgarizzata da Ciampolo degli Ugurgieri,* a cura di A. Gotti, Firenze, Le Monnier, 1858.—*Il Boezio e l'Arrighetto,* a cura di C. Milanesi, ibid. 1864; and with an introduction and notes by S. Battaglia, Torino, Utet, 1929.—*Gli Ammaestramenti degli antichi di Bartolomeo da San Concordio,* ed. by V. Nannucci, Firenze, Ricordi, 1840; *Della congiura catilinaria e Della guerra giugurtina,* ed. by G. Cioni, ibid. Grazioli, (1790)—*Fiore d'Italia di Guido da Pisa,* ed by L. Muzzi, Bologna, Turchi, 1824; *Fatti d'Enea,* ed. by D. Carbone, Firenze, Barbera, 1967; by F. Foffano, ibid. Sansoni, 1900; ed. by A. Marenduzzo, Milano, F. Vallardi, 1906.

Concerning Andrea da Barberino see the editions of the *Reali di Francia,* ed. by G. Vandelli e G. Gambarin, Bari, Laterza, 1947, and of the *Aspromonte,* ed. by M. Boni, Bologna, Palmaverse, 1951; and G. Osella, *Il Guerrin Meschino,* Torino, Chiantore, 1932.

Of Franco Sacchetti's minor works, the following were published ed. by A. Chiari: *Il libro delle rime,* Bari, Laterza, 1936; *La battaglia delle belle donne, le Lettere, le Sposizioni di Vangeli,* ibid. 1938; of the *Trecentonovelle,* we have the modern annotated editions by V. Pernicone, Firenze, Sansoni, 1946; by E. Li Gotti, Milano, Bompiani, 1946; by A. Borlenghi, (with a selection of the other works), Milano, Rizzoli, 1957; on the text cf. F. Ageno, in "Giorn. stor. d. lett. ital.", CXXXIV (1957), pp. 638–40. For Sacchetti one should consult: L. Di Francia, *F. Sacchetti novelliere,* Pisa, Nistri, 1902; G. Gotti and N. Pirrotta, *Il Sacchetti e la tecnica musicale del Trecento italiano,* Firenze, Sansoni, 1935, E. Li Gotti, *F. Sacchetti: uomo "discolo" e grosso,* ibid. 1940; V. Pernicone, *Fra rime e novelle del Sacchetti,* ibid., 1941; R. Ramat, *F. Sacchetti: le Rime,* Bari, Macrì, 1947; L Caretti, *Saggio sul Sacchetti,* Bari, Laterza, 1951; A. Borlenghi, *La questione delle morali nel Trecentonovelle,* in: Studi urbinati", XXVIII (1953), pp. 73–111; F. Ageno, *Ispirazione proverbiale delle Trecentonovelle,* in "Lettere italiane", X (1956) pp. 288–305.

There is no good modern edition of the *Pecorone,* therefore the reader should consult the prints of the last century, (Milano. Silvestri, 1815–1816; Torino, Pomba, 1853); the partial reprint has a good introduction; *Il Pecorone e due racconti anonimi del Trecento,* ed. by S. Battaglia, Milano, Bompiani, 1944 (to be consulted also for the preceding bibliography).

By Sercambi: *Novelle,* ed by A. D'Ancona, Bologna, Romagnoli, 1897; *Novelle inedite,* edited by the same, Firenze, Libreria Dante, 1886; *Novelle inedite tratte dal codice Trivulziano CXCIII,* edited by R Reiner, Torino, Loescher, 1889; *Croniche,* published by S. Bongi, Roma, Istituto storico italiano, 1892, Cf. G. Petrocchi, *Il novelliere medievale del Sercambi,* in "Convivium", V (1949), pp. 74–89 (that we mention also for the preceding bibliography).

A large anthology of the poetic texts (with essential bibiography) may be found in the *Poeti minori del Trecento,* ed by N. Sapegno, Milano, Napoli, Ricciardi, 1952 (the tenth volume of the present collection); this book integrates and amply substitutes, the preceding collections by G. Carducci (*Rime di Cino da Pistoia e d'altri del secolo XIV,* Firenze, Barbera, 1862; *Cantilene, e ballate. strambotti e madrigali dei secoli XIII e XIV,* Pisa, Nistri, 1871; *Antica lirica italiana,* Firenze, Sansoni, 1907). Another useful anthology is C. Muscetta and P. Rivalta's, *Poesia del Duecento e del Trecento,* Torino, Einaudi, 1956.

For Fazio degli Uberti's poems, one should consult the already mentioned edition by G. Corsi, Bari, Laterza, 1951. Dr. A. Tartaro has already proved the groundlessness of the heterogeneous collection of poems attributed to Matteo Correggiaio in a soon to be publishes thesis of specialization at the Scuola di filologia moderna of the Università di Roma. At the university of Bologna is in preparation the critical edition of the poems by Antonio da Ferrara and Saviozzo. My writings on Pucci, Soldanieri and other minor poets may be read now in *Pagine di storia letteraria,* Palermo, Manfredi, 1960, pp. 133–209. On the chronology of the narrative poems, consult the observations, mainly acceptable but perhaps too rigid, of D. De Robertis, *Problemi di metodo nell'edizione dei cantari,* in *Studi e problemi di critica testuale,* Bologna, Commissione per i Testi di lingua, 1961, pp. 119–38. Buccio di Ranallo chronicle may be found in the good edition by V. De Bartholomaeis, Roma, Istituto storico italiano, 1907.

Currents in Comparative Romance Languages and Literatures

This series was founded in 1987, and actively solicits book-length manuscripts (approximately 200–400 pages) that treat aspects of Romance languages and literatures. Originally established for works dealing with two or more Romance literatures, the series has broadened its horizons and now includes studies on themes within a single literature or between different literatures, civilizations, art, music, film and social movements, as well as comparative linguistics. Studies on individual writers with an influence on other literatures/civilizations are also welcome. We entertain a variety of approaches and formats, provided the scholarship and methodology are appropriate.

For additional information about the series or for the submission of manuscripts, please contact:

Acquisitions Department
c/o Peter Lang Publishing, Inc.
29 Broadway, 18th floor
New York, NY 10006

To order other books in this series, please contact our Customer Service Department:

800-770-LANG (within the U.S.)
212-647-7706 (outside the U.S.)
212-647-7707 FAX

or browse online by series at:

www.peterlang.com

Printed in the USA
CPSIA information can be obtained
at www.ICGtesting.com
LVHW022204101123
763606LV00005B/374